Learning
Leadership

Learning
Leadership

Cases and commentaries on abuses of power in organizations

Abraham Zaleznik

Konosuke Matsushita
Professor of Leadership (Emeritus)

HARVARD BUSINESS SCHOOL

Bonus Books, Inc., Chicago

97 96 95 94 93   5 4 3 2 1

Library of Congress Catalog Card Number: 91-77019

International Standard Book Number: 0-929387-71-6

Bonus Books, Inc.
160 East Illinois Street
Chicago, Illinois 60611

Printed in the United States of America

To Danny, Eli, and Aaron

CONTENTS

ACKNOWLEDGMENTS

I want to extend my sincere thanks and appreciation to all the people who helped in the preparation of this book. I thank all of my research assistants who wrote the case studies that appear in this book. They are too numerous to list here, but each person is named in the footnote that appears with each case study.

Among all of my research assistants, I owe special thanks to Dr. Elizabeth Altman, with whom I worked very closely in writing some of the cases, in revising others, and in thinking about the intellectual foundation necessary for the interpretation of the narratives. In the same vein, I want to thank Dr. Sharon Kleefield, whose help I appreciate.

In the actual preparation of the manuscript, Eileen Hankins was extraordinary in her careful work and dedication. The book would not have been completed without her help. While not as directly involved in the manuscript as Eileen, Jane Barrett proved extremely helpful in overseeing many of the routines of my office at Harvard while I worked on the chapters. Both Eileen and Jane are in charge of the Senior Faculty Center at the Harvard Business School, a marvelous office for the now growing number of Professors Emeriti, who while relinquishing the normal duties of a Harvard professor, continue to pursue actively their many academic interests.

You will notice that the case studies bear the copyright of the President and Fellows of Harvard College. I am grateful to this august body for permission to use the case studies appearing in this book.

All of the work in *Learning Leadership* depended upon the support of four deans of the Harvard Business School: the late Stanley F. Teele, George P. Baker, Lawrence E. Fouraker, and John H. McArthur. I appreciate all their practical as well as moral support over the years for the new venture in education for leadership at the Harvard Business School that ultimately led to the writing of this book. In memory of Konosuke Matsushita, the founder of the Matsushita Electric Company, I gratefully acknowledge his support of my program at the Harvard Business School, as well as the support of the late Sidney Rabb and Norman Cahners, may they both rest in peace. It was my privilege to inaugurate two chairs at the Harvard Business School, the first in honor of Sidney Rabb and Norman Cahners and the second in honor of Konosuke Matsushita.

If I have omitted anyone in this acknowledgment, I apologize. I have left more than a few names unspoken, knowing that I have been the beneficiary of the enthusiasm and support of fine people, including especially the many MBA students at the Harvard Business School who worked over these cases with me in our mutual quest for insights into the human dilemmas of leadership.

To all of the staff at Bonus Books goes my appreciation for a job well done. Special thanks go to Traci Taghon and to Aaron Cohodes.

Finally, my heartfelt thanks to my family: to Bibs, Dori, Ira, Janet, Daniel, Eli, and Aaron, who all love me, understand me, and who are often bemused by my ideas. In dedicating this book to the last three named, my grandsons, I cast my lot with the future, hoping they will learn from the past and thereby free themselves, along with their generation, from its chains.

Abraham Zaleznik
May 1992

INTRODUCTION

The best way to learn the art of leadership is to learn by doing. Discover for yourself who you are and how to position yourself in a situation to consolidate and use power in an effective and ethically sound way.

The second best way to learn the arts of leadership is to learn from other people's mistakes. I can't do much for you in learning by doing. But I can do a lot for you by helping you to learn from other people's mistakes. That's what this book is about!

The book is a collection of case studies on leadership. I collected these cases over many years just as I taught them for many years at the Harvard Business School. There isn't a single colleague at the Harvard Business School who does not lay claim to teaching leadership. The students in their classrooms are all potential leaders and whatever my colleagues do to enhance their capacities surely embraces the problem of making leaders.

If I am not mistaken, I believe I am the first to lay claim explicitly to designing a course on leadership at the Harvard Business School and to teaching it for many years, first under the title of

"Social Psychology of Management," and then the title, "The Psychodynamics of Leadership." I changed the title because I discovered that management and leadership are different, and I spelled out the differences in a *Harvard Business Review* article entitled "Managers and Leaders: Are They Different," (published in 1977, see Appendix) and later in a book entitled *The Managerial Mystique*, (Harper and Row, 1989).

Obviously, I do not lay claim to being the first academic to research and teach leadership. But the unique quality of the approach reflected in this book is the idea of learning leadership by observing the mistakes of others. This book is to leadership what pathology is to medicine; hence it relies on case studies, typically of individuals in situations in which power comes into play and all sorts of things go wrong. The question we have to ask ourselves is: why did they go wrong?

Why things go wrong in power relations is a complicated question. It is different than laying blame at someone's feet. To continue with my analogy, no one particularly blames a patient for becoming ill, even though we may identify things the patient did that were bad for him or her or things the patient should have done to prevent bad things from happening. We don't even blame a heavy cigarette smoker for becoming ill with lung cancer. In the same vein, we put people and situations under the glare of the "post mortem" and ask, "What went wrong?" in the expectation that we shall learn much from the travails of other people, mostly good-hearted people, who dreamed dreams of mastery, control, and even greatness, only to find life fell short of their expectations.

Not content like the ancient Greeks to blame misfortune on the gods, exacting their punishment in revenge for man's hubris, we want a detailed understanding of the motives and delusions, the expectations and the misrepresentations, that led power figures to find themselves in a blind alley with no way out. While I don't necessarily represent this work as science, it bears a resemblance to clinical science, where investigators try to learn from cases, leading to avenues of further thought, observation, and possibly even experimentation.

This book of case studies, or narratives if you prefer, has another feature that makes it different from the ordinary casebooks that academics produce. I make available to the reader my interpretations of the cases under examination. So each chapter opens with the frame that will contain the narrative. The purpose of the frame is to position the narrative and the audience so that the picture appears in a specific perspective. This does not prevent you, the reader, from altering this perspective.

Following this framing, the narrative appears as pure as is humanly possible, given all the limitations of bias and subjective response, without explicit interpretations. You can ask yourself the questions that grow out of the framing of the case, as well as ask yourself questions that only you can ask given the specific experience you bring to the reading.

Following the narrative, my interpretations and commentaries appear. I ask you to consider my interpretations, but not necessarily to agree with them. Make up your own mind as to what went awry in the situation and compare your conclusions with mine.

I am a psychoanalyst and a clinician. The psychoanalyst part of my identity leads me to view situations from the particular frame of reference that Sigmund Freud discovered and developed in the course of his research on mental illness and his attempts at finding a cure. There is nothing doctrinaire in my attitudes as a Freudian, but there is also little taste in my intellectual appetites for being an entrepreneur. I am not dying to make original discoveries and, therefore, will not quickly cast aside ideas not my own.

For six years, I taught a course on psychoanalytic theory at the Boston Psychoanalytic Institute. The students were doctors as well as psychiatrists, who were studying to become psychoanalysts. The basic theory course at the Institute had a bad name, largely because the students were distressed over the reading of Freud. They often wondered why the basic theory of psychoanalysis was not taught as a body of contemporary knowledge, including the latest information, findings, and questions as these had evolved over the many years of inquiry from Freud to the present day. The journals are packed with articles published over the years, scores of books have been written; the controversies in psychoanalysis as science and as therapy have been fully represented in the literature. It is easy to conceive a textbook, an up-to-date compendium of this knowledge, available for teaching the basic concepts of psychoanalysis (and indeed many textbooks on psychoanalysis are already available).

The narrowest and most uncharitable explanation of why students were asked to read Freud (as he wrote and not as others interpreted him) was to indoctrinate the new generations of psychoanalysts into the Freudian orthodoxy. I never believed that interpretation for a minute. Furthermore, even if it were true, it had little to do with my intentions and concerns. What intrigued me about reading Freud directly was the possibility of entering his head and struggling with the problems of the neuroses as he had. It seemed possible to me to teach theory by the case method.

Here is how it worked. In reading Freud, clarify the problem that was bugging him and that led him to write the particular piece in the way that he had. Examine the problem carefully and decide what would be a satisfactory, if not perfect, resolution. Then, in reading the work, ask yourself how well Freud did in solving the problem. I get as excited writing about this venture in teaching theory as I did years ago actually doing it.

My point is this: one can be doctrinaire about almost anything. It is a state of mind. One can also be flexible, playful, adept at conducting thought experiments on most any subject, but *especially* when it comes to understanding and using psychoanalysis. As I say, it's all a state of mind! The only thing I don't care for is being promiscuous, what I have called entrepreneurial, or rushing to get into business on one's own, when it comes to ideas. Hence my predilection for working with Freud's ideas and asking my students to try it out while engaged in learning from other people's mistakes.

Thanks to Aaron Cohodes, the owner and publisher of Bonus Books, the theory book is available for your use as you work over the case studies and commentaries on leadership presented in this book. The theory book is entitled *Executives' Guide to Motivating People*, published by Bonus Books in 1990.

I have divided the book into five parts. The first part begins with a fundamental question: What do people want from authority figures? A question that follows is this: What are people's conscious and unconscious fantasies about power?

The answers to these questions establish the conditions for the misuse and abuse of power and for disappointment. Since every would-be leader experiences dependency in his or her development, many lessons are learned about the nature of power. All too frequently these lessons distort reality and set the stage for trouble during the years when positions are reversed—when instead of being dependent, one is being depended upon. And the erroneous lessons about power take charge, affecting images of self and others in organizations. The title of part one is "Power and Dependency."

Part two takes us beyond dependency into the experience with rivalry. There is a law of nature that says no two objects can occupy the same space at the same time. We all know that two or more contradictory feelings can occupy the same space in the human psyche alongside the conviction that in order to get what one wants, somebody else has to be pushed aside. For Macbeth to be king, he had to get rid of Duncan. While ambition seldom makes its presence felt in its purest form, as in Shakespeare's plays, you can nevertheless count on its appearance in organizations, where power is the currency of the realm.

Part three is called, "The Psychodynamics of Leadership." The biographies that appear in part three trace the development of gifted individuals who were indisputably leaders in their own fields. You can figure out what makes talented people tick, and how they came to embrace and exemplify what President George Bush plaintively calls "the vision thing." The leaders described had visions of their life and work. All of them, in one way or another, derived their vision from a drive, desperate at times, to rewrite their personal history. The case studies are an invitation to clarify Lord Acton's formula, "power tends to corrupt; absolute power corrupts absolutely."

The fourth and final part of this book presents case studies of "Organizations in Crisis." We took special care in writing these cases to preserve the richness of the situation so that you can do much more than pay lip service to the idea that leadership is the fateful encounter between person and situation.

POWER AND
DEPENDENCY

PART

I

JOSHUA BITTNER'S DREAM

This case study is a fragment from a complicated life. Joshua Bittner, age 28, entered psychoanalytic treatment for depressive reactions. These reactions included low self-esteem, an unsatisfactory marriage, and low motivation to work and advance in his career. He was a well-educated man, who had elected to specialize in computer sciences.

Early in his psychoanalytic treatment, he had a dream, which forms the basis for this case study. If you are new to case studies, you may wonder why this book starts with this fragment from a complicated life, garnered as it was in the flow of a psychoanalysis. You may also wonder why a casebook on leadership should begin with a specimen from a man who feels himself, and actually is, anything but a leader.

Please keep in mind that this first part of the book is entitled "Power and Dependency." This subject offers many rich clues on the profound question, "What do people expect from their leaders, and what do they expect from themselves when they gain power and have to direct, guide, inspire, and generally lead other people?"

CHAPTER

1

What people expect of their leaders and of themselves when wielding power is often unrealistic, and these expectations can lead to the kind of depressive reactions that Joshua Bittner had experienced in his life to date.

You are probably asking yourself another question: What do dreams have to do with expectations, real or fantastic? Sigmund Freud, who discovered the dynamic unconscious and pioneered psychoanalysis, both as therapy and as a new field of knowledge and investigation, detailed his views of dreams in his book, *The Interpretation of Dreams*. He hypothesized that underlying the complicated imagery and mental process that leads to dreaming and, perhaps more importantly for our purposes, that causes us to remember our dreams, is the urgent need to fulfill wishes. Wishes have both a present and a past, as you will see in the elaborations of Joshua Bittner's dream. There is a contemporary version of the wish for a leader, and also a version that bears the burden of a continuous, historically relevant, thematically consistent, and narratively true wish that can exert enormous influence on an individual's life. (Incidentally, for those who are skeptical about the ubiquity of dreaming, a number of studies of dreaming conducted in sleep laboratories, in correlation with electroencephalographic studies, indicate that dreaming occupies about 25 per cent of our sleep time.)

Interpreting a dream is difficult. No code book permits the deciphering of symbols in the dream. It really depends upon free associations, some of which you will have available in helping you figure out what Joshua Bittner's dream meant. This material will appear in three parts. Let us start with the first part, which is the dream itself as Joshua Bittner presented it to his psychoanalyst.

A DREAM SPECIMEN

A 28-year-old man who worked in computers and data processing reported the following dream during one of his psychoanalytic hours.

"I was a young person maybe 16, 17, or 18 years old. The dream had to do with work, industry, and technology. It was an office or a laboratory. I was working at the computer company, in their Township Laboratory. The people I saw there were working for the computer company, but the place didn't look like the company or the Township Laboratory.

"There was an assembly line and a row of desks and benches. The room had a low ceiling. I could see the slant of the roof. Above the benches there were large wooden boxes with electronic equipment. I could see the titles, but I was curious and I wanted to know exactly how to use the equipment. I wanted to impress the people that I could use this equipment. I was a newcomer to the plant or lab. I wanted to convince them that even though I was young and inexperienced, I could do it."

COMMENTARY

Part of what makes a dream rich and compelling is its structure of implied opposites, or pairings of ideas, feelings, locales, and situations appearing in the dream content. Here are some of the pairings that appear to me in this dream. The locale of the dream is the *company*, the *Township Laboratory*. Its opposite could be *home*. According to Joshua Bittner, the theme of the dream is *work*. The opposites might be *play*, *love*, and all the other activities and states of mind that appear to oppose the reality-driven notions of *industry* and *technology*.

You have probably noticed two anomalies in the reported dream. One is the absence of specific people, or even people in some specific relationship to Joshua. The people in the dream were just that, people who worked for the laboratory, except the place itself didn't look like the laboratory. The second, and perhaps even more important anomaly is Joshua's appearance in the dream as an adolescent, a good ten years younger than his actual age.

Another striking feature of the dream is the absence of affect, except in the notion of striving: he is a newcomer who wants to prove himself, "that I could do it." The physical features of the room in the dream suggest a constricted atmosphere: boxes lined neatly in a row, a low ceiling. Curiously, he refers to the notations on the boxes as "titles," a term, I presume, ordinarily reserved for books and not labels on boxes. If we wanted to be a bit rash, we could note with some interest that what he wants to prove is that he can use this equipment. I hope you won't consider it outrageous if I wonder whether part of an adolescent's anxiety has to do with his use of his "sexual equipment"; and the ability to perform need not be restricted to work, but to love as well.

If you suspect I am taking some license in the use of the dream, you are correct. A dream, appears in highly diverse, yet concrete symbols that make little sense on the surface. One of the most important handles on a dream comes from hearing how a person introduces it to himself or herself and anyone else who happens to be listening, which is what a psychoanalyst gets paid to do.

Joshua reported this dream on Monday, following a weekend interruption in the analysis. He said, when he first lay down on the couch that Monday morning, "I had a dream Saturday night." He then described what had occurred that weekend night.

ELABORATION OF THE DREAM SPECIMEN

Joshua, who reported the dream described earlier, said that he had had the dream on a Saturday night. He presented the dream during his analytic hour on the following Monday. Before he reported the dream, he described what he had been doing that Saturday night. There was a party at his house. He had busied himself in the kitchen instead of joining the folk singing. His wife sent a woman with a message for him instead of coming herself. He wanted the woman to take him into a room, put her arms around him, tell him everything was fine and then to come with him and join the folk singing. But she didn't do that. He left the party early and went to bed. He felt pangs of guilt that as host, he had left the party. But then he thought, "Fuck it and fuck them. It's my house and I'll do just as I please."

COMMENTARY

What Joshua Bittner details in his description of Saturday night at his house is a man in a state of deprivation. It may strike you as very odd that he should feel deprived in the midst of a party that, presumably, he had something to do with arranging. Another way of looking at this state of deprivation, self-inflicted though it may appear, is that he is angry. Certainly he appears to be angry at his wife, who did not come herself to get him to join the party. But it appears to go beyond his wife's presence or absence, or her efforts, or lack of them, to overcome his passivity. But do not dismiss too quickly the passivity as absurd, childish, or even perverse. It may be all of those things, but also a lot more. He is in a state of waiting for someone to appear, to take over, to reassure him, and assuage the anger and loneliness that threaten to swamp him. The question to consider is: For whom is he waiting? Who is the missing person in this narrative of loneliness in the midst of an assembly of people; of sadness, in the midst of a joyous gathering of young people engaged in folk singing; and of anger (toward whom?) that, to make matters worse, is diffuse. He could express his feelings in the generalized, "Fuck it and fuck them!" as he went off to sleep, abandoning his guests as he feels abandoned by some mysterious figure in his life.

The real test of our understanding of a dream such as Joshua Bittner's is the meaning that emerges from the dreamer's associations, including the thoughts that served as a preamble to the dream. You will notice that in the course of hearing Joshua's thoughts about the dream, the psychoanalyst offered his interpretations of the dream, almost as though he and Joshua were in a verbal ballet, with both approaches and avoidances on Joshua's part. Their dialogue led inexorably to discovering for whom Joshua was waiting and who was frustrating him, engendering his anger, and stimulating the longing he could only experience as depression. Here is that verbal ballet.

ASSOCIATION TO THE DREAM

After reporting the dream, the patient had associations which he reported to his psychoanalyst. The following material presents the patient's associations and the comments of the psychoanalyst.

> Patient: When I was at [college], I would get confused about how old I was. When I was 20 years old and people would ask me how old I was, I would get confused and tell them I was 17. In fact I was 20. I guess I had a lot of growing up to do. Thinking of age reminds me of [name of older man]. I used to work with him at [name of company] in the lab.

> Psychoanalyst: Perhaps the sense of insecurity you feel and the idea of starting a new job has to do with your wanting to do well in analysis.

Patient: I don't think that's right. (Silence) I'm thinking of the discussions I had with one of our customers over at the [plant]. The work isn't going well over there. (Silence) I don't want to make you into my father. Even if I did, you wouldn't respond to me as a father.

Psychoanalyst: It seems as though there are two sides. One side of you wants to avoid making me into a father and the other side of you is unhappy because you believe that I won't respond to you as a father.

Patient: (Silence) I'm trying to detach myself here by staring out into the window. (Pause) That reminds me of going to Sunday school and to church. I would stare into the light for a long time until I desensitized my retina. And then I would have an after shadow.

Psychoanalyst: [After reminding the patient that his father was an eye surgeon] Do you think these thoughts have something to do with your father?

Patient: I would play at injuring my eyes and even thought that I would go blind. Then my father would have to help me. While I was at Sunday school and in church, my father would be out playing golf. When I was in college I tried so hard to go out of my way to establish contact with my professors. But if I was successful, I would knock them down and discredit them in my eyes. There was Professor [Name]. I would call him by his first name and we would go on outings together. I tried to see him as perfect, but then I found fault in him, and I would knock him down because he didn't meet my standards.

COMMENTARY

Ask yourself some questions. Do you know who was missing in Joshua's life? Was it his professors? His father? Was it his analyst? If you said to yourself that Joshua needs a leader to put some structure and direction into his life, would you consider this a legitimate need, one capable of fulfillment? Something about him distrusts a leader, a father figure if you will. The distrust seems to circle around the idea: "You can't get what you want from a leader, so don't invest your confidence in someone who appears to represent that figure missing from the past." Yet the need is persistent, urgent, and compelling. It just will not go away. Imagine the consternation and confusion in the minds of Joshua's authority figures, who might sense his efforts to engage them in a verbal ballet of approach and avoidance. They might end up feeling put off by this interesting man and prove to him again and again there will always be someone missing in his life. With a handle on his need, and instead of looking for something he can't get, he could alter the need. In changing the need, he will change himself.

Here is another interesting question to contemplate as you think about Joshua Bittner and his dream: If a man wants a leader and looks for a man to fulfill that position in his life, why does he flee into intimacy with a woman? And given that flight, why can't he satisfy that need, or resolve it, in his relationship with a woman?

WILLIAM GARFIELD'S
DISAPPOINTMENT

In reading the story of William Garfield's disappointment at Christmastime you may be struck, as I was, with the impression that William was carrying a time bomb, waiting for the right moment to explode. Neither you nor I could have predicted the exact event or its timing that would set off a turbulent period in his life, and cause William, his wife, and his boss to scrutinize carefully their relationship to him.

As with Joshua Bittner, who provided us with an intriguing dream of power and dependency, you may find yourself wondering what William is waiting for, or perhaps more precisely, whom he is waiting for. His life is on the verge of being undermined by his passivity. While he seems habituated to waiting, his wife is tired of waiting. Sooner, if not later, William's boss will get tired of waiting and will fire him.

Unlike Joshua Bittner, William has little time to expend in waiting. The question he faces, and you and I face in unraveling his story, is this: Why can he not get a grip on life, assert himself, and seek and use power in a legitimate way? Here is the story.

WILLIAM GARFIELD

William Garfield arrived home from work to begin his Christmas holiday. He felt weary and depressed. Earlier in the day he had talked with his superior, the general manager of the Midwest Division of the Steelcraft Corporation. Garfield had expected the meeting, since at the end of the year a performance review for bonus award consideration was customary.

Nineteen seventy-four had been a difficult year; business conditions were unsettled, and there were stresses in the firm arising from the higher interest rates and from the sharp drop in construction industry activity. But the corporation employing Garfield, and the division in which he worked, had managed to weather the turbulent business climate to the point where it could approximate its budgeted sales and profits. With these results in mind, Garfield expected to receive a full bonus award of $5,000. That day his superior had informed him that he would receive only $4,000. In the context of this firm, the lower amount reflected a penalty. According to his superior, Garfield had not been careful in managing certain customer contracts, and therefore accounts receivable losses for the year had been higher than anticipated.

Ruth Garfield sensed immediately that her husband felt "down"; she assumed that some difficult problems at work were burdening him. When he told her about his performance review and the reduced bonus, she was surprised and angry. She had counted on that extra thousand dollars for a much needed vacation; besides, she thought her husband was being held responsible for problems over which he had had no control. Almost without realizing the intensity of her feelings, Ruth Garfield began to criticize the Midwest Division's general manager, the Steelcraft Corporation, and the town in which the Garfields lived and worked. She said her husband was continually being underrated, and that she hoped he would leave the company and move the family back to the South, where they both had been raised. She asked William what he had said to his superior; when William indicated there was very little he could have said under the circumstances, Ruth became openly enraged. She berated her husband for acting helplessly while he was being unjustifiably criticized and penalized.

This case was prepared by Professor Abraham Zaleznik. Copyright © 1975 by the president and fellows of Harvard College.

At age 37, William Garfield sometimes wished he could turn back the clock to begin his career and life all over again. He was not sure what he would do differently, but somehow his present life and achievements fell short of what he wanted. Garfield had joined Steelcraft after finishing law school. Hoping to work in Atlanta, Georgia, his hometown and the company's headquarters, Garfield had had to decide whether to move to the Midwest as counsel for the Midwest Division or whether to look elsewhere for work. He decided to go to the Midwest. Joining a large and expanding company should provide him with opportunity, he felt, including an eventual chance to become a member of the headquarters office of the corporate counsel. After ten years in the Midwest, Garfield still hoped to move back to Atlanta, but he was uncertain whether this would, in fact, materialize. In addition, he no longer considered it essential that he continue his career as a corporate attorney. His exposure to executive committee meetings had stimulated his interest in business decisions, and he thought he would like to try general management instead of legal staff work.

His desire to return to his hometown was as strong as ever, but he was uncertain of his goals and of how to pursue them. Garfield felt uneasy about himself. The events of the past year and the disappointment over his bonus award had precipitated in him an urgent need to get "on track" in his career. Garfield also recognized that his wife's sudden and unusual outburst at him reflected dissatisfaction with him. While that dissatisfaction had previously been submerged beneath their mutual, cooperative efforts to foster his career, it appeared now as a major issue in their marriage. Ruth Garfield had strong ambitions for her husband and strong opinions as to where and how they should live and raise their family. Until now she had been prepared to bide her time, knowing that a career in a large corporation required patience and the ability to go along with decisions from the top. But she was now 35 years old, with three children ranging in age from six to two years; she was beginning to wonder anxiously whether William would ever provide her with the security and status (and vicarious achievement) she had always wanted in her life.

William Garfield was born in Atlanta, Georgia, in 1938. His father was then employed by the State of Georgia as supervisor of state construction. In this job, the elder Garfield oversaw performance on contracts to builders for roads, offices, and other public buildings. While the magnitude of the job appeared significant in regard to the value of the contracts let, Mr. Garfield actually did little more than accumulate cost records and prepare reports on contract performance for review by his superiors.

William's father had originally started work in a family business along with his father and an older brother. William's father had never had a good relationship with his brother, and decided to leave the business because the tension proved too much for the grandfather to tolerate. It was not easy to relocate, particularly with the depression and the scarcity of jobs. But because the Garfield family was well known in Georgia, William's father was able to land the state job with the help of family friends. Mr. Garfield settled into the job and married; almost immediately his wife became pregnant with William. Two other children followed—a daughter after two years and a son four years later. As far as William could recall, his early life was uneventful. The family was reasonably well-off financially; it appeared settled in its style of life.

The situation changed, however, with William's father's decision in 1944 to enlist in the service. The country was at war, and Mr. Garfield grew restless watching the young men leave for the military. He wanted to be a part of the war effort. Although his work with the state was justified in terms of its value to the economy of Georgia, he still felt that a great adventure was underway and was, perhaps, about to pass him by.

William's father enlisted when his wife was pregnant with her third child, shortly before she delivered the baby. After the delivery, Mrs. Garfield became depressed; upon her doctor's recommendation, she went to live with her sister. William had only vague memories of his father's departure and of his mother's illness. He had the impression she may have been hospitalized, but he could not recall with any certainty. He did remember, however, that he and his two siblings moved in with his father's mother "for the duration."

The family reunited after the war, when William's father returned from the service. The State of Georgia offered Mr. Garfield his old job; however, at the same time, his father urged him to return to the family business. Mr. Garfield learned that his father had developed advanced, terminal emphysema. Despite misgivings about working once again with his brother, Mr. Garfield felt he could not disappoint his dying father, so he rejoined the business.

The Garfield family business had been started by William's great-grandfather. It supplied stone, sand, and gravel for road building and other construction. The family owned property suitable for quarrying, and the business prospered. By the end of the war, with the advent of new kinds of construction materials and the substitution of cement for stone, the family business ceased to grow. William's grandfather did not want to diversify to cement processing; when William's father rejoined the family business he had the opportunity to move the firm into precast concrete but he hesitated. This would have involved technology with which he was unfamiliar and a considerable financial investment. The idea of seeking bank loans and risking equity in new ventures and diversification seemed hazardous. The decision fell to William's father, who did not want to be responsible for the livelihood and security of his elder brother and his immediate family. He also did not want to jeopardize his own retirement by risking existing assets for the chance of business growth and considerable wealth.

Mr. Garfield continued to run the business, and before he retired, he decided to liquidate the assets and close the operation. He eventually carried out the liquidation, and with the proceeds and personal savings, he and his wife were able to enjoy a comfortable retirement.

Reflecting on his father's business career, William Garfield thought his father had followed a reasonable course of action. He felt no personal criticism of his father's conservative thinking, nor did he regret losing the opportunity to carry on the family business. He was not sure that the chances for diversification and business growth were promising anyway.

Given the family's financial security, there was little doubt in William's mind during his school years that he would go to college. In high school and the first two years of college, William felt as though he were floating. He had no defined career goals nor did he have strong interests to guide his activity. He was an indifferent student, although he managed to pass his courses with little work or difficulty.

A change occurred during William's junior year in college. He had applied for and been accepted to the school's ROTC unit, and this experience with military training aroused his interest. He worked his way up the ranks to unit commander; the exercise of leadership excited his imagination. William thought he should make a career in the military, and his ROTC instructors encouraged his interest in securing a permanent commission. He applied for a commission. He hoped for an assignment to the infantry, but when he learned that he was to be assigned to ordnance, he changed his mind about the regular Army and completed his ROTC obligation in the reserves. After two years of service, he was discharged honorably, and he returned to civilian life.

In reflecting upon his Army experience, Garfield considered the highlight of his two years to have been the assignment to teach recruits the rudiments of map reading and enemy surveillance. At first, he felt uneasy standing in front of a group and speaking, but as he overcame his nervousness, he found he enjoyed the experience. Most of the two years, however, involved staff work; on the whole he also found that satisfactory. The assignment he disliked most was the brief time he spent as the executive officer of a unit. As second in command he was expected to maintain discipline, to establish work assignments, and to oversee performance. Garfield found that job lacking in stimulation and challenge.

After his release from the service, Garfield began to look for work. Armed with his bachelor's degree and his military experience, he took a job with an insurance agency. After some initial training, he moved to a branch office; eventually he became the manager of this small unit. During his stay with the insurance company, he met Ruth; they decided to get married. With her encouragement and support, he attended an evening law school, eventually becoming a full-time law student. Ultimately, he completed his degree.

During his last year at law school, encouraged by a fellow student with whom he'd struck up a friendship, Garfield applied to the Steelcraft Corporation for a job in its legal office. The company's business required a substantial legal staff to write and supervise contracts with customers and suppliers. The wording of contracts and the schedules of payments contained in their provisions were critical in determining whether the company would win sales over its competitors.

Garfield had hoped to be assigned at once to the headquarters' legal department in Atlanta. Instead he was offered a position in the Midwest Division, which he accepted. The Garfields settled in a suburb of Chicago and began their family there. Ruth Garfield gave birth to a son and two daughters, each two years apart. While Garfield's progression in the Midwest Division over a period of seven years had been slow, it was nevertheless steady. Eventually, he came to head the division's legal department. In this capacity, he attended executive committee meetings when legal issues were on the agenda. Garfield's exposure to executive committee meetings had stimulated his interest in moving ahead in the organization to a general management position.

Garfield's disappointment at receiving a reduced bonus, compounded by his wife's enraged outburst at him over the slow pace of his advancement led him to arrange an appointment with the Steelcraft Corporation's consultant. The purpose of this meeting was to discuss his career and to elicit suggestions on steps he might take to prepare himself for, and secure, a general management position. William Garfield met with the consultant; during the course of the meeting, when asked what he would like to do eventually, he said:

Answer: I can run the division or anything I put my mind to. I told _____ (my boss), "As far as I am concerned, I want your job." I want to get away from staff work and into an operating position.

Question: What kind of operating job would you like?

Answer: You mean specifically in the Midwest Division?

Question: Whatever.

Answer: I feel I can run the Midwest Division. I can do a good job in running the Midwest or whatever else.

Question: But there is a progression from where you are now to running the Midwest Division. What line of progression would please you?

Answer: _____ (my boss) is not clear in his mind what this progression would be. I would want to get out of the day-to-day legal work. I could, of course, still oversee it, but I would want to be out of the day-to-day responsibility. I would like to get some sort of a title and become a member of the executive committee. I guess maybe that's still staff, but I would like to get on to some special assignments as assistant to _____ [sales manager for the division] or _____ [general manager of the division]. This way I could get an overall view. I know _____ [general manager of the division] believes in coming up the ranks to get the nuts and bolts side of this business and he doesn't like to stick people in where other people are not familiar with them. But I believe people ought to have a chance to move to another area, even if they don't know the nuts and bolts of the business. If you are a manager, you ought to be able to manage. The principles are all the same. So my idea of a spot to go into is different from _____'s [general manager of the division]. Maybe I could go into a special assignment like doing research work plus responsibility for an operating department.

During this same meeting with the consultant, Garfield reviewed his administration of the contract for one of the company's large accounts. This account had fallen into grave financial difficulties; it could no longer meet the terms of the contract. It was specifically the experience with this account that led the general manager to cut Garfield's bonus. The significance of the contract difficulties with this large account went beyond Garfield's department, occupying considerable time and attention during executive committee meetings.

This larger customer, the Superior Construction Company, builders of large office buildings, shopping centers, and warehouses, used a considerable tonnage of preformed steel fabricated parts. The Superior Company also built prefabricated low-cost housing; its volume of business made it one of the Midwest Division's largest customers. The Superior Company had built up a large account with the Midwest Division; however, it became apparent that it would not be able to meet its payments to that division. To discuss what action should be taken on this problem, the executive committee of Steelcraft/Midwest held a series of meetings that Garfield attended, since they involved contract administration. Two opposing points of view were expressed during the meetings. While he offered no opinion himself, he realized that the opposing points of view had to be reconciled.

On one side, the sales manager of the Midwest Division favored revising the contract and continuing to extend credit to the Superior Company. He reasoned that the only way to salvage the account and retrieve the money owed by the Superior Company was to continue to supply Superior with materials enabling it to complete its own contracts, obtain cash, and pay back the money it owed to Steelcraft. On the other side, the assistant general manager of the Midwest Division took the position that the company should act quickly to foreclose and to retrieve whatever cash it could from the Superior account. He argued that supplying Superior with more materials and building up the account would not salvage the company; in fact, it would worsen the position of Steelcraft with respect to Superior.

The debate in the executive committee continued throughout the series of meetings. The general manager of the division inclined towards the view of the sales manager, favoring a continuation of credit. Garfield reported that he felt, as he listened to both points of view being argued, that he was sitting on the fence, waiting for the decision to be made.

At the suggestion of the general manager, the chief legal officer of Steelcraft Corporation visited the offices of the Midwest Division and reviewed the Superior account. He recommended that the Steelcraft Corporation rewrite the contract, taking a second mortgage on certain properties owned by the Superior Company. In this way, the chief counsel argued, Steelcraft would have security to cover some of the outstanding money in this account. The executive committee accepted the recommendation; in accepting it, they agreed to continue selling to Superior on open credit, with the past debt covered by the second mortgage.

Reflecting on this decision, Garfield believed the Midwest Division had made an error, although he had not voiced his opinion during the discussions. He indicated to the consultant that by taking a second mortgage, the Midwest Division had inadvertently placed itself in a subordinate position to the banks that had made the construction loans. It had failed to take advantage of an Illinois law giving tradesmen and construction industry material suppliers a special priority in loan repayments. Had the Midwest Division taken advantage of this special Illinois law, it would have been in a preferred position to the banks. It was not long after the second mortgage and the continued selling to the Superior account that Superior declared itself in bankruptcy. The Midwest Division's financial exposure in the Superior bankruptcy exceeded a million dollars.

At the time that Garfield met with the consultant, he knew he was at a crossroads in his career and that the general manager of the division was giving serious thought to his future in the company.

COMMENTARY

I would like you to consider what kinds of reactions William Garfield's story evoked in you. Over the years in which I discussed William Garfield's story with my students at the Harvard Business School, I was constantly impressed with their difficulties in grasping his story, let alone experiencing even a modicum of empathy for him. He is nobody's role model. Seeing his story in cold print does him an injustice. His bewilderment, naivete, and sense of wonder about the world seem incongruous in a man in sight of age 40. I say an injustice, because if you were to meet him in person, it might be difficult for you to grasp and hold on to the notion that you are seeing a man in the grip of passivity, which is the essence of his character. Garfield is waiting. Such people, and there are many, are not without charm. They are eager to please, want to be liked, and have developed a repertoire to assure they will please others and in turn be liked by others. William's boss knew about his egregious failure in taking responsibility (his failure to act will end up costing his company a million dollars!). But his boss's reaction hints that he has been charmed to the point that even he does not understand what is going on in William's performance as the division's attorney. If he understood, I suspect he would fire him rather than simply reduce his bonus from $5,000 to $4,000.

To empathize with William's story is not to be taken in by his charm, forthrightness, and boyish naivete. He would like his boss's job, or so he tells the consultant. He wants to be in a line job, and advance in general management, instead of staff and the law. When the consultant inquires into the progression William visualizes will get him to where he ostensibly wants to go, William responds that his boss is not clear on what this line of progression should be. It probably did not register in his awareness that the issue is what William thinks the line should be; when he had an open invitation to assert himself, to expose himself to desire and will as integral to his personality, William Garfield bares his weakness, his vulnerability. Implicitly, he communicates that he means no harm and in turn should be done no harm, much as in ethologists' accounts of how a wolf on the verge of defeat in a fight will expose its neck as a sign of surrender to its antagonist.

William uses various ploys, not consciously but nevertheless purposefully, to distract him from two kinds of reality. The first is the reality of the world (and the people important to him) as it is. It is a world that waits for no one. The second reality has to do with William as he is now, and as a carrier of a unique history. While it may be difficult to see past Garfield's compliant behavior, we have to account for the possibility that beneath his surface passivity exists a very angry man. To experience anger is to confront one's sense that an injustice has been committed. It is easy to see the injustice in Garfield's life. He was literally abandoned by his father, who was drawn to the war; he was abandoned by his mother, who fell into a deep depression following her husband's departure from home.

There is a difference between feeling angry over a felt injustice in one's present life, and a felt injustice that occurred in the past, particularly during the formative years of childhood. Present anger is often a route for taking action, to right wrongs and to bring about a better world. Anger from past felt injustices goes underground, subject to massive repressions that accentuate the appearance of a person waiting for something to happen. But anger, repressed or not, will have its way. Unless Garfield is lacking in intelligence (and I don't believe this for a minute) his failure to act in the case of the credit problem, his willingness to let a mistake ride at considerable expense to the company, is venting his anger at others in a form that allows him to bypass responsibility. He does not know he is angry, nor does he recognize he is "getting even" with authority by his failure to perform.

Garfield may have made a crucial error in his response to the childhood abandonment. He identified with his father, who seemed expert at bypassing responsibility. Going to war seems patriotic, but for the elder Garfield it was an escape, a chance to get away from the day-in-day-out burdens of responsibility without having to acknowledge to himself that he was running away. Who would fault him for meeting his patriotic duty? Certainly not himself; he bought off his conscience by wrapping himself in the flag. Evidently, the senior Garfield came out of the service with an aversion to risk. His conduct in the family business suggests that he could not extend himself to try to build the business. Instead, he played it safe.

A case can be made that William's attachment to this missing father had a deep hold on his personality. He showed the most enthusiasm for work in describing his military experience. Was this part of the search for his father? But even here, when it came to making a choice, he could not tolerate the responsibility that comes with command.

If these comments appear as a stern judgment of a man's life, take a second look. Self-delusion takes many forms and seldom spares us in times of stress and disappointment. Frequently, we take collusion for kindness in elaborating the many forms of self-delusion. It is intriguing to speculate on what Garfield's boss might have accomplished if he had been able to address his subordinate's self-delusion, instead of colluding with it in his token discipline by awarding less than full bonus. We can ask ourselves what a subordinate owes his or her boss. And in the same breath, what does a boss owe subordinates in perceptivity and honesty?

ROBERT GRAHAM'S ACCIDENT

Robert Graham was a successful air traffic controller until he fell and sustained a back injury. Instead of attention and concern for his injury, Graham received indifferent treatment and bureaucratic neutrality. The accident set in motion a chain of reactions that severely altered Graham's life. Instead of success on the job, he experienced failure. Where he was once confident, he became fearful. Formerly able to take care of himself and feel he was looking out for others, he became dependent, sorely lacking in self-esteem, and deeply depressed.

To add insult to injury, Graham had to deal with expressed and implied charges that he was malingering, using the accident to feather his nest with compensation payments. As you read Graham's story, ask yourself first whether Graham was malingering. Many other questions will occur to you.

CHAPTER

3

ROBERT GRAHAM

On February 24, 1967, Robert Graham, age 53, an air traffic controller in Vancouver, British Columbia, slipped on an iced-over outside stairway en route from the control tower cab to the restroom. As Graham described it, "I was on duty. I came out of the control cab. There was ice on the upper level step. My heel hit the ice. As I fell, I tried to stop myself by throwing my arm through the open iron stairsteps. I fell about eight feet, and stopped with a vicious stop. My back was bruised. My right shoulder was dislocated. I had hit the step with my neck. I was in a state of shock. I nearly fainted. I broke out in heavy perspiration, and asked a man to yank my arm. When he did that, the pain eased up a little. I had told them about those steps before and they got them fixed after I got hurt."

Immediately following the accident, Graham returned to the cab, and rested for an hour or two. Not unconscious, but in considerable pain, Graham returned home shortly before the end of his shift. The pain in his neck and shoulder persisted; the following day Graham went to a chiropractor who reported that he had "a strained lower back, right shoulder, and right arm." After resting at home for the weekend, Graham returned to work. He was very uncomfortable, tense, and had only limited use of his right arm. Feeling unsure of himself, he worked in one of the secondary, supporting jobs in the cab. When he had not improved appreciably by the end of the week, his supervisor insisted that he see a physician who observed that he did have "some swelling and limitation of motion in the right shoulder region and a limitation of flexion in the lumbar area of the spine." The physician also noted symptoms of a "cerebral depression with an anxiety reaction." At the insistence of the physician and his supervisor, Graham was placed on sick leave and treated with physiotherapy to the back, shoulder, and arm. Medications were prescribed for pain and tranquilization.

The pain and weakness persisted in Graham's arm and shoulder. He developed a tremor when attempting to use his right hand, tired easily, complained of dizziness, and became more anxious and unsure of himself. He was depressed and irritable around his home, flying into temper tantrums on minimal provocations. He got so angry he rammed his fist through door panels on a few occa-

This case was prepared by Professor Abraham Zaleznik. Copyright © 1970 by the president and fellows of Harvard College.

sions. Graham was seen in consultation by a neurosurgeon who was unable to find any physical explanation for these symptoms which the neurosurgeon described as "conversionary" with a considerable degree of "compensationitis."

Graham was hospitalized briefly in June 1968 under a psychiatrist's care. The psychiatrist noted that Graham was quite depressed, as well as anxious, and treated him with antidepressants and tranquilizers. Graham improved considerably, but not enough for him to feel he was able to go back to work. After being discharged from the hospital, Graham did not continue the suggested outpatient visits with his psychiatrist.

In October 1968 he attempted, for a month, to resume his duties, but he felt anxious, unsure of himself, and incapable of making decisions. Inwardly, he intensely resented that he had to come back to work on a provisional status, under the supervision of a man many years his junior. He wanted to continue on the job but was persuaded by his friends and supervisors to accept a medical retirement. He was told that accepting the medical retirement would not prejudice his claim for compensation due to injury. It was pointed out that if he did come back to the job, which his supervisor was reluctant to permit, he would then be fully responsible for any error he might make. This condition, in addition to the fact he might have difficulty passing the next annual physical examination, placed him in imminent danger of discharge and loss of all retirement rights. Graham reluctantly accepted the medical discharge after having been reexamined by other physicians who stated, "patient is unable, psychologically, at this time, to maintain stability enough to be left alone as a control tower operator."

Graham had been aware retirement was not far off. He was in the second of his "high five years" that would have been used in the calculation of his retirement income if he had retired at the end of 25 years of service in 1970. He had also begun to realize that the pressures on him were greater; there were more planes in the air, moving at faster speeds; the government was coming under increasing public pressure regarding its mission to prevent accidents. A belief, partly substantiated, was developing among air traffic controllers that if a man made one mistake, he was likely to be terminated immediately, losing all his retirement benefits and without hope of any alternative reemployment.

In November 1968, another psychiatric evaluation was requested by the Provincial Workman's Compensation Board (hereafter referred to as PWCB). This examination was carried out in February and March 1969, at which time psychotherapy was advised. The PWCB accepted the responsibility for the cost of this psychotherapy.

The PWCB had been attempting to determine Graham's future earning capacity in order to calculate the difference between it and his earning capacity before the injury. The PWCB was responsible for 75 per cent of this difference. In June 1969, the PWCB wrote Graham, stating that in its judgment, he could earn $56.12/week as a motel clerk, so that $97/week would represent 75 per cent of the difference between this first figure and that of his previous earning capacity. Graham was greatly disturbed and offended by this suggestion. He felt that he could not function at this time in any type of regular employment. His psychotherapist agreed; letters to this effect were sent to the PWCB.

Graham admitted intense resentment towards the government agency to which he gave the best years of his life, his devotion, and unquestioning loyalty. But he felt the agency had rejected him with no indication of any personal interest. He resented the "faceless bureaucracy" with which he had to deal, the investigators who were sent to check up on what he was doing, the long delays in answering his letters, and their attempts, in his mind, to evade their clear-cut responsibility to honor his legitimate claim. Above all, he resented the fact that he could not, at any time, reveal this resentment, since he felt totally dependent on the administrative whims of the "faceless officers" with whom he had to deal. He had marked periods of depression. He considered suicide very carefully but had not carried it out, only because he felt that his family was not adequately protected by his insurance.

Graham was born in 1914 in a small town in southern Alberta, Canada. He was the second of four children; two sisters were two years older and younger, and a brother was ten years younger. Graham's father had been born on a farm, attended school through the ninth grade, and then worked for the railroad for 46 years. The father, although vigorous, healthy, and active when he retired in 1960, died in 1963 of cancer.

Graham described his father as a forceful, dependable, highly respected man in his community and on the job, physically strong, never in debt, and a good provider. The father put all his children through college (except Graham, who quit after studying engineering for two and a half years to join the Royal Canadian Air Force);

he provided so methodically and carefully for his widow that there was no need for financial support from any of the children.

Graham described his mother as very affectionate, and had no recollection of marital problems between his parents. At age 78, the mother lived in the same small town where she had raised her family. She regularly visited Graham and the other children, travelling alone several hundred miles by train to do so. Her children were reportedly happily married without any divorces in the family. Graham's brother was a highly placed engineer with a petroleum company.

Graham had always been in excellent physical health and was very proud of this fact. He was strong physically, played hockey in high school, and worked out regularly lifting weights until the day of his injury. He had some dental difficulty, especially with teeth that were broken while playing hockey. He received artificial dentures in 1962, at about the same time that he had an operation for hemorrhoids, following four or five years of debate as to whether he should have the operation.

Graham left home in 1935, at age 21, to enlist in the Royal Canadian Air Force. He was accepted for pilot training four years later, but washed out; he left the Air Force in 1940. In 1942, at age 28, Graham married a young woman he had dated for the previous four and a half years. Neither had been married before. Graham denied any marital problems prior to the injury, but reported a great deal of difficulty afterward, due to his poor disposition. The couple's only child, a daughter born in 1948, was reported to be a good student, and a satisfactory child in all respects. She had completed two and a half years of college before quitting as a regular student to marry in December 1967, after which she continued her education as a part-time student.

In 1945, Graham entered government service as an air traffic controller; he served in this capacity at a variety of stations across Canada with stays of from two to five years at each. Investigations were unable to uncover any uncomplimentary reports of his 22-year work record, except that in 1963, he turned down a promotion from controller to supervisor. Graham explained by saying he loved the job he was doing, and could not bear to give it up in order to become the kind of "s.o.b." that a supervisor was apparently expected to be.

Graham described his work as requiring continuous attention to a great amount of detail. He had to maintain instant access to large amounts of precise information, and be able to keep as many as five conversations going simultaneously without making mistakes in any of them. He knew that all of those conversations were being recorded on tape and preserved for the determination of blame in case of an accident. On the basis of all this information, he continuously had to make decisions which directly affected the lives of the aircraft occupants and others who might be in their path. "I had adjusted to it being a business and had done it well. I was rendering service to the public. It made me feel worthwhile. I was doing something that made a difference. A man would come up and shake my hand or he might call me a month later and say, 'Thanks for saving my life.' I ate it up. They recognized me. The old pilots would remember me getting them out of a spot. Before the accident, I had something to live for. After that, I lost out on the job that was my life. Work was my hobby, my social outlet and my recreational outlet. It was all my contacts, all the people I knew. Pilots, managers, students, everything I had was right there. I could go anywhere in Canada, to any airport and see someone I knew and had worked with."

Graham stated, and his wife confirmed, that nothing had counted much with him except his home, his job and his physical well-being. His weightlifting and physical culture were the nearest he had to a hobby. He spent all his spare time working around the house and yard, and once commented, "We had the prettiest yard in town." Over the years, he had qualified by examination as an electrician and plumber; in addition, he was apparently quite competent in carpentry and cement work.

After the accident Graham tired easily, and could work in his yard for only 30 to 45 minutes at a time before he had to lie down for an hour or two. His wife attempted to interest him in some less strenuous activity, but nothing interested him. Although persuaded to make a minimal investment in rock-polishing and gem-cutting equipment, he was unable to develop any sustained interest in these activities.

Graham progressively withdrew from his previous active social contacts. He and his wife had had a modest social life, and within the social group, Graham apparently had been regarded as an outgoing, lively, and friendly person. After the accident, he found it difficult to join his few friends around the neighborhood and church. He was afraid that they would ask how he was and what he was doing. He accepted invitations from a few choice friends to go fishing or hunting, and would plan to go with some anticipation; but when the time for the trip arrived, feeling unable to go, he would offer some excuse and stay at home.

Graham left his house occasionally to do household shopping. On one such outing, as he was going into the back part of a lumberyard, he heard a clerk make a comment to "keep an eye on that fellow." This remark made him intensely angry. However, he said nothing because he did not feel capable of defending himself if the other person were to challenge him. He noted an immediate exacerbation of all his painful muscular symptoms, which persisted for several days thereafter.

He no longer continued his active correspondence with former associates; yet he desperately wanted to be back on the job and a part of the group that existed among the work staff. Graham occasionally visited the airport, but these visits so intensified his feelings of apartness and loss that he would become disturbed for days. Therefore, he rarely returned.

Graham's role in the family was radically altered by the accident. No longer the leader in the family, he depended on his wife for emotional support, direction, and guidance. She did all of the letter writing to the various agencies because it upset him too much to do it himself. The family felt it necessary to protect Graham from any upsetting news due to the disturbing effect such news had on him. He appreciated this, but also felt a growing resentment at having things kept from him. Although Graham believed his daughter's marriage was completely happy and successful, one day in October 1969, with no advance warning, the daughter and her 14-month-old child moved back into her parents' house. She announced she was divorcing her husband with no hope of reconciliation. She wanted to go back to college and asked her parents to care for the child while she attended school. Graham had withdrawn from contact with most family members, but he found great joy in contact with his grandson, even though he was able to tolerate him for only 30 minutes at a time.

As of July 1969, Graham had completed 25 hours of the psychiatric treatment suggested in November 1968, and paid for by the PWCB. Graham had received no response from the PWCB to his and his psychotherapist's letters stating that Graham was unable at this time to function in any type of regular employment.

COMMENTARY

According to Webster's *New Twentieth Century Dictionary*, malingering is "feigning illness in order to avoid duty." To malinger is to employ one's conscious intent to avoid responsibility and the performance of one's work. Did Graham consciously intend to shirk his duty as an air traffic controller? The evidence suggests the contrary. He consciously loved his work, took pride in its performance, and especially valued the idea that many people depended upon him for the safe landing of their aircraft. At least one physician, a neurosurgeon who examined him, reported that Graham suffered from a case of "compensationitis." In this same report, the neurosurgeon expressed the opinion that the case was "conversionary," meaning he could not find a physical cause for the symptoms. He said that by some unexplained activity of Graham's mind, psychic conflict managed to shift the locus of distress from the mind to the body. The notion of "compensationitis" implies something else again: that Graham was after a money settlement to take him into early retirement, presumably richer than he would have been, or no worse off, than if he had worked to his normal retirement age. A true conversion illness is a function of the dynamic unconscious, for which an individual cannot be blamed. He or she is not intending consciously to seek an outcome in which a certain amount of pain is endured for monetary and psychic gain.

It is unlikely that Graham consciously contrived the accident, feigned symptoms of physical distress, and fell into a depression, which appeared real enough, all in order to retire early with a compensation settlement. However, the accident very likely had a profound effect on the balance between active and passive motives, between his conscious need for independence and an unconscious desire for a dependency relationship.

The balance I am considering here is not the appearance of new forces or motives, but rather the realignment of forces and motives that had been quantitatively arrayed in a long-standing arrangement that formed the character and personality of Robert Graham. As we met him in his fifties, he was contemplating his future, the satisfactions he had derived from his work, and the prospect of technological and social change in his job.

The balance that existed before the accident permitted Graham's self-esteem to grow in the idea (illusion?) that others needed him, while he needed no one. Others were in danger; he was safe. Others were at risk of inclement weather and aircraft mechanical flaws; he was the ameliorator of risk, the conduit to safety for those endangered. In this context of a highly organized and easily sustained self-esteem without close relationships at work or at home, the threat of change surely entered his mind. With the upcoming technology, would he be able to perform? Was he too old to learn new skills? What would he be like as he grew older? What would retirement mean to him? These and undoubtedly other questions entered his mental preoccupations, probably making it more stressful to perform on the job, and causing added concerns to fuel his doubts and anxieties.

Graham's ambitions were limited in scope. He did not want to be a supervisor. Flunking flight school raises questions about just how much aggression, assertiveness, and activity his psyche could tolerate. Clearly, he was disinterested in the symbols of achievement and command that being an officer or a supervisor would have conferred upon him.

So it would not be beyond conjecture that the accident, perhaps only fleetingly, raised a possibility that now, perhaps, he had found a graceful way out. This was not to be!

His identifications took over. The primary identification was with his father, who stressed and enacted the life theme of independence. A man must take care of himself and look after those who are dependent upon him. Backing into passivity, gracefully or otherwise, would not stand up against such a powerful imago, an ego ideal that now played a prominent part in his suffering. He could not be what was expected of him in the independent man image which he had thoroughly internalized. His conscience would read his passive wishes and condemn him for them. He needed no physician to be his accuser. His conscience was accuser enough.

Left to its own devices, a large organization (a bureaucracy if that term suits our interests best) has a fatal incapacity. It does not understand a Robert Graham. It does not understand him at his best, let alone at his worst. Therefore, he is left to founder. Even the most basic concepts of supervision, such as the need for some personal attention from an authority figure in a moment of crisis, never came alive for Graham. This absence fed his conflict; as he grew more depressed, it also entered the trace elements of paranoid fantasies that began to appear as he became increasingly withdrawn. The more dependent he felt, the more deeply depressed he became. Eventually he no longer understood that he had certain abilities, using his hands and mechanical talents; he could not see that these existed, independent of organizations, bureaucracies, supervisors, doctors, lawyers, and other experts he came to see as part of "the faceless bureaucracy."

Putting the issue another way, perhaps what Graham needed, and needed most in times of distress, was a good father. We mostly believe this need, or wish, is unattainable, particularly as adults in the organized work world of today. Yet what leadership is often asked to do, microscopically in the case of Graham and his supervisor, or on a larger stage in the case of business and political leaders, is to provide this paternal or parental image to bring about genuine independence and minds freed from infantile longings.

To know and understand something about the underpinnings of leadership, particularly the relationship between the leader and the led, pay attention to the Robert Grahams of the world as they struggle to learn how to master life's demands. We have much to learn from his case history.

BILL RILEY'S DELUSION

Commonplace experiences are often the richest but they risk losing their dramatic import when no one is attending. What is missing is an observer, someone who is acutely aware of the irony imbedded in the ordinary. A fine line distinguishes the truly dramatic from the hopelessly banal. Attention to detail helps us see what is universal in the particular; what links kings and commoners and how, amidst the fatally deterministic, small elements of choice appear, providing a measure of hope to offset impending tragedy.

You already have some familiarity with depression—an emotional state characterized by a loss of interest in the world, feelings of deep sadness, low self-esteem, and hopelessness. Robert Graham's accident triggered a depressive reaction deep enough to prevent him from reestablishing control of his life.

Without clear-cut provocation, such as the physical accident in Graham's case or the unexpected bonus cut in Garfield's case, Deltronics Corporation provided the stage for the enactment of depression in a highly regarded senior executive. He was Bill Riley, corporate comptroller. The executives who worked most

CHAPTER

4

closely with Riley witnessed the changes in his behavior. Considering the circumstances, the executives waited a long time before recognizing that one of their number was in serious trouble. Try as they might, they could no longer avoid recognizing what was happening to Riley when his depressive reactions included a disturbance in his thought patterns. I suspect at some level of awareness they knew what was happening; but at another level, they needed to ignore or deny what was in front of their eyes, to avoid implicating themselves in some way with Riley's fate. In reading this case study, you will become witness to Riley's encounter with a strange process affecting his mood and thinking. As with the executives who work with Riley, you, too, may implement certain avoidance mechanisms—partially out of fright and partially out of the desire to avoid getting involved in somebody else's trouble. On the other hand, as a new witness to this drama, you will find yourself drawn to unravel the puzzle of what caused Bill Riley's depression, complicated as it was by an idea that seemed out of touch with reality. What caused Bill Riley's depression? What part, if any, did Bill's delusional idea play in this depression? These questions are good openers for learning to observe a human error and discerning from the details of the story the total picture. Your job for now is to make some sense of a confusing set of facts about an executive who, seemingly without warning, lost his capacity to function. Of crucial importance to your understanding is the way shifts in power and dependency altered Riley's state of mind.

DELTRONICS

Bill Riley, age 36, entered a psychiatric hospital, suffering from depression. The president of his company had recommended he see a psychiatrist, because of marked changes in Bill's behavior over the preceding six months.

Bill was the youngest and only unmarried member of an Irish Catholic family of four brothers and one sister. The oldest brother was 46, and the sister 41 years old. Most of the family had left

This case was prepared by John H. Howard, research associate, under the supervision of Professor Abraham Zaleznik. Copyright © 1969 by the president and fellows of Harvard College.

the city, except for Bill who lived with his mother in the family's large red brick house. Mrs. Riley was a 75-year-old widow.

After graduation from high school, Bill served four years in the Air Force, including a tour of duty overseas. He was honorably discharged; soon after leaving the service, Bill entered a local college to earn a bachelor's degree in business administration. Before coming to Deltronics Bill held two jobs as a junior accountant. He left the first job after little more than a year because of family reasons; he left the second job after a year because of lack of opportunity. Bill then joined Deltronics; five years later, at the time of his illness, he was the company's comptroller.

Many of Bill's associates considered him a quiet, withdrawn individual who limited his conversation, apart from specific work problems, to trivial matters such as the weather and the local baseball team. He almost always avoided the banter and good natured kidding which went on continuously between engineers and women who worked in the office.

Deltronics was a small electronics engineering company with 60 employees. Bill worked most closely with the president even though he reported directly to the administrative vice president. Normally his responsibilities included accounting, payment of vendors, and the preparation of financial statements and payroll. Once or twice a year Bill worked closely with the company's outside auditing firm.

During the early months of the year in which Bill became depressed, he was responsible for cash management. The company was on the verge of bankruptcy; Bill spent most of his time juggling the company's cash balances to meet vendor invoices and satisfy creditors. Company executives believed that Bill's work had been outstanding during this crisis.

Around the middle of the year, the company arranged refinancing so its cash problem eased. At the same time, Bill's assistant left the company. She was a young bookkeeper who moved when her husband was transferred to a distant city. Bill hired another bookkeeper to help him. She was younger than her predecessor, also married and very outgoing. Unlike Bill, she enjoyed bantering and often joked with others using seductive language.

About this time many of the company officials began to notice a change in Bill's behavior. Besides neglecting his work, Bill would sit in his office for one or two hours staring into space. He became even more withdrawn; at times he would not hear or understand conversations directed toward him. It also became obvious that Bill was losing weight.

Noticing these changes in Bill, the administrative vice president suggested he take a vacation. During his five years with the company Bill had hardly missed a day of work and except for one or two occasions he ignored vacations. Bill at first refused to accept the administrative vice president's suggestion, but later gave in and allowed the vice president to plan a two week vacation in Mexico. After spending only a few days in Mexico, Bill returned to his home in Los Angeles; however, he did not come to work.

When Bill returned to work, he continued to act peculiarly. He would stare into space for long periods of time and talk very little to others; he continued to lose weight.

Early in the second week after his vacation, Bill Riley entered the president's office to review routine financial matters. Bill and the president usually met once a week to review cash balances and other figures. During this routine meeting, Bill surprised the president by asking for permission to court and marry his daughter. The president had not been aware Bill had been seeing his daughter.

The president of Deltronics had two daughters, one of whom had worked in the office during the summer months. It had been more than one and a half years, however, since the daughter whom Bill Riley named had been in the offices. This young woman was living in another city enrolled as a graduate student.

Suddenly faced with the comptroller asking for permission to court and marry his daughter, the president was caught completely unaware. The comptroller seemed particularly concerned that the president would object on grounds of religious difference between the two families. The president said that while he was Jewish and Bill Catholic, in this day and age religious differences were unimportant. Later in the evening, the president mentioned the incident to his wife; but since his daughter was away at school, he made no effort to talk to her. The president remained somewhat uncertain about the whole matter.

Approximately one to two weeks later the comptroller returned to the president's office and said he wanted to discuss the problems he might face in courting and marrying the president's daughter. While curious about whether the comptroller had been seeing his daughter, the president still had not discussed it with her. The president talked again about religious differences and avoided direct questions about the comptroller's relationship with his daughter. Before leaving the president's office that morning the comptroller asked the president to lunch with him and the purchasing agent. Bill gave no indication of the purpose of the meeting, but since the purchasing agent had been with the company for only a little more than a month, a chance to discuss company purchasing problems at lunch seemed appropriate to the president.

Almost immediately after arriving at a nearby inn, the comptroller again said he wanted to marry the president's daughter. Expecting a business lunch, the purchasing agent was surprised by the conversation. The president tried to turn the talk to purchasing problems, but Bill persisted in talking about the president's daughter.

After returning from lunch, the president became deeply concerned; he called in the vice president for administration. Both men agreed that something needed to be done. The vice president called an acquaintance who was a psychoanalyst and asked his advice. The analyst suggested that the president first question his daughter: Had she and the comptroller been dating? Had there been any thought of marriage? The daughter said she had not seen the comptroller for more than a year, which was the last time she had been in the Deltronics offices; they had never dated. The analyst said Bill needed help; he recommended they refer him immediately for psychiatric consultation.

The president then called the comptroller's mother and told her he was worried about Bill. Mrs. Riley said Bill had been acting strangely at home. Bill would often sit for hours in one position, in the dark, and seemed uninterested in the surroundings. Agreeing that he needed medical help, they decided to refer him to the physician who consulted with the company. That same afternoon the president spoke to the comptroller and suggested he see the physician. The comptroller kept his appointment with the doctor and a psychiatric consultant and he also agreed to enter a hospital. During his hospitalization the company retained the comptroller on a leave of absence and continued his salary.

After about six months of treatment, Bill Riley returned to work. He continued psychotherapy as an outpatient. The psychiatrist treating Bill discussed his return with the president and saw no reason why Bill could not gradually resume his normal work responsibilities. Bill continued to improve and the president gave him authority once again to sign checks and make disbursements for the company.

COMMENTARY

If you consider depression from a layman's perspective, you will not wander too far from professional descriptions of depressive reactions. You have already considered the elements of this description (some loss of interest in reality, low self-esteem, etc.) in the comments preceding this case study. Thus, the phenomenology of mental illness displayed in this case permits the layman and the professional to observe together and to communicate with each other. Where the two part company is in trying to explain the illness. Nowadays, psychiatry is hard at work to discover the biological underpinnings of severe depressions and other mental illnesses. In an earlier day, when psychoanalysis was the dominant theory in psychiatry, psychiatrists examined life histories to discover the unconscious elements of inner conflict, which was the engine driving the various mental illnesses.

Typically, the kind of treatment Bill Riley would undergo whether in a hospital or as an outpatient includes a regimen of drugs along with psychotherapy, which is the famous "talking cure" that Sigmund Freud invented. This is practiced in its pure form in psychoanalysis and in an adaptive form in psychotherapy. Being what they are, human beings may never be satisfied to experience an illness and then be cured without making some sense of it to themselves. In the long run, as biological investigations uncover the organic side of mental illness and provide increasingly efficacious medications, the patient will still want (and need) to participate in the curative program with the curiosity that is so characteristic of the human mind.

This brings us back to Bill Riley. He suffered from a severe depression. Without being able to assess the relative influence of organic and psychological factors that came into play, we can do a lot to comprehend what propelled him in and out of his normal state of mind. We can try to understand what pushed him out of his characteristic capacities into a withdrawn, unhappy man. During his illness, he came alive, so it seemed, only when he was engaged with the president of the company in the expression of his delusional idea: "I want to marry your daughter, but I am afraid religious differences will stand in the way."

You may ask yourself, "What is so delusional about wanting to marry the boss's daughter?" Riley was single and so was the president's daughter. He saw her in the office on occasion, fell in love with her and decided he wanted to marry her. Isn't that normal enough? Furthermore, the president's initial reaction that religious differences did not matter anymore surely did not discourage Bill, let alone tell him that he was entertaining a crazy idea.

The president's behavior when presented with Riley's claim was itself bizarre. Why didn't he find out from Riley how long he had been courting his daughter? How had their interest in each other grown to the point of contemplating marriage?

Alas, the answer is painful. The president did not want to know. Probably he was characteristically unable to enter into another person's life. When he had warnings such a demand was being placed upon him he used his well-established mental mechanisms for avoiding the implication. Telling Riley religious differences did not matter anymore was a way of sloughing off the possibility that the president might have to *listen* to Riley and discover what was going on in this valued executive's life.

As the president discovered, Riley would not take the hint that he should stick to business and keep personal matters to himself (or bury them as necessary, given Riley's proficiency for sweeping dust under the carpet). Let us leave the marriage idea (delusional or not) for a moment to take a new tack in unraveling this mystery.

There is a tendency, both for the professional and layman, to ask what were the antecedents that possibly led to the situation we are trying to explain: to seek a cause that will explain an effect. While cause and effect have seemingly gone out of fashion, we need them in narrative discourse as well as scientific investigation; with one caveat, though—look for multiple causes that produce a single effect such as depression.

The idea here is that an event is *overdetermined*—many forces preexisting in personal history come together, become amplified in their intensity, and produce a massive, sometimes calamitous event. Such is probably the case with Bill Riley.

What were the circumstances in the company prior to the appearance of Riley's depression? Deltronics was in trouble. Its cash flow was inadequate to run the business. The company needed a cash infusion or it had to scale back operations, liquidate, and run a smaller business growing at a slower rate. The liquidity crisis was made to order for Riley. His boss and his peers turned to him to solve the problem and save the company.

Bill responded brilliantly. He negotiated with creditors

and lenders and solved the liquidity problem. After the cash crisis, life at Deltronics returned to its normal pace. Bill no longer occupied center stage. The dependence on him diminished.

Perhaps one of the consequences of this diminished dependency upon Bill was an experience of loss. This loss must be considered in the light of this possibility: one of the internal struggles Bill fought was over his own dependency needs. We saw in our previous case study (Robert Graham, the air traffic controller) the effects of the deprivation caused by a reversal of the balance between being depended upon and wanting to depend upon others.

You will recall Graham took pride in the fact that the pilots and passengers depended upon him to bring planes in safely. I interpreted this satisfaction as a method of warding off the effects of his own dependency needs, that is to say his latent or underlying desire to have someone look after him. Latent dependency needs are characteristically experienced as a longing, sometimes sadness verging on depression; when individuals safely repress these needs through structures such as their work activity, the longing comes and goes. It is seldom a serious problem until a major disruption occurs that shifts the balance between being depended upon and needing to depend on someone else.

The balance clearly shifted for Riley when the cash crisis ended. He was no longer the object upon whom others, especially the president, depended; therefore, he had to recede from center stage. This by itself may not have been decisive had there been heightened activities in other areas. But with the liquidity crisis ending there was a period of quiescence in the corporation causing Bill to turn into himself; at that point he probably reexperienced this deep longing.

At this juncture we should ask the question, longing for what or longing for whom? It was a constant source of interest and a mild source of amusement for me to watch my students at the Harvard Business School wrestle with this problem of longing in a dependency relationship. They managed to understand the notion that feeling dependent upon others often causes trouble, particularly in violation of an individual's self-image as an independent, resourceful person fully capable of taking care of himself or herself. Once the notion of longing enters into consideration and one begins to cast about for an object who may be the target of this feeling or longing, the problem begins anew. You will recall that just before Bill became depressed, his assistant, a bookkeeper, left the company. My students delighted in latching on to this departure to identify the person missing in Bill's life. They conjectured that he was attached to her, and his longing was toward her as the missing object in his life. For others, an equally plausible explanation, not necessarily contradicting the absence of the bookkeeper as explanation for object loss, was to identify the replacement bookkeeper as the source of Bill's problem. Bill was single; she evidently was sexually provocative; this set up a longing in Bill which he found intolerable. It caused him to shift the balance away from interest in the outside world to his inner conflict, another way of saying he turned in toward himself. Both the loss of the bookkeeper and the possible provocations of the replacement stand on their own. Regrettably, there is no way to prove or disprove the validity of each of these explanations. It is important to realize, however, that the two are not contradictory. Go back to what I said earlier: multiple causes can lead to a single effect, in this case Bill Riley's depression.

More difficult to accept is an explanation that caused a great deal of concern if not anxiety on the part of the students: the object missing in Bill's life was the president and his need for reversing dependency was in relation to the president. He could not tolerate being dependent upon the president, yet he wanted a close relationship with him. He found this close relationship when he worked closely with the president to overcome the liquidity crisis. This close relationship, however, was embedded in a structure in which Bill could feel quite content in the idea that the president was dependent upon him. Here was a means of disguising an underlying dependency on Bill's part.

What evidence is there to show this third possible conflict produced deep longing in Bill? The evidence is contained in the content of Bill's delusional idea. If it were possible for him to marry the boss's daughter, he once again could have a close relationship with his boss; however, it would be thoroughly disguised by his marriage to the daughter. What is so difficult to contemplate in the area of dependency upon authority is the possibility that the longing includes an erotic component. This is not to say the whole relationship, both conscious and unconscious, is colored by eroticism, but merely to suggest that this may be, and in fact often is, present in a relationship between senior and junior in an organization. The erotic component is so thoroughly disguised in the various structures used to repress these ideas that it scarcely comes to one's attention until an individual runs into some difficulty.

I am sure you have encountered instances in which subordinates have a great deal of difficulty working with their bosses. They report endless conflict, repetitive crises, battles with the superior officer, and a relationship often colored by hostile feelings. This hostility needs to be understood not necessarily for what it appears to be. In my experience (and I ask you to think about this) hostile relations are really a cover-up of something more dynamic and also more important: a deep longing for a close relationship with a strong male figure (in the case of male subordinates) colored by an erotic component which makes the entire sense of longing personally intolerable. The net result is the individual, the subordinate in this case, seeks to fight rather than to acknowledge his desires. This is not to say that an individual should act on his or her longings, but merely to say that in recognizing them for what they are, they become manageable. The conscious mind or the ego remains in control of an individual's behavior.

Saying to himself and to his listeners, "I want to marry your daughter," is in a more primitive language a statement that says, in effect, "I want to be close to you."

Bill Riley returned to work after a brief hospitalization with continuing therapy as an outpatient. We have no record of what occurred during the hospitalization and during the work as an outpatient in psychotherapy; however, it is reasonable to conclude that the treatment helped him restore the balance between his own longing and dependency and his need to see himself as an independent, self-sufficient individual. In the long term, the resolution of his deep longing, particularly the unacceptable erotic components, would depend upon establishing a solid alliance with his therapist and being able to tolerate the conflicting emotions in his attachment to the therapist. His underlying longing for a dependency relationship with a male would soon be revealed in his feelings toward the therapist. If the bedrock of his relationship to the therapist were positive and trusting, Bill then would successfully bring to light the wishes that he formerly found unacceptable and stressful.

Contrast the work that goes on in psychotherapy for an individual under stress with the notion that it would be a good idea for the individual to take a vacation to remove himself from the scene that was causing him this trouble. In fact, one of the executives in Deltronics had suggested to Bill that he take a vacation; you will notice Bill could not tolerate the absence from his familiar surroundings. However well intentioned, the advice to take it easy or take a vacation is ill-founded, because it ignores the fact that conflictual emotions push toward the surface with the change of scene and the passivity of leisure time. In a therapeutic relationship, the pacing of the removal of stress and the work entailed in revealing latent wishes make it possible to hold the world constant, as it were, while the psychological uncovering proceeds.

The chances are very good that through the course of this illness Bill learned a great deal about himself and would be capable of continuing to function as a responsible, highly regarded executive.

Arno Kasper Haupt's Demise

Arnold K. Haupt stood trial in 1978 in a federal district court on multiple charges of conspiracy to commit fraud, using the mails to defraud the federal government, committing perjury before a grand jury, and engaging in patterns of racketeering in the conduct of his businesses. The indictments leveled the same charges against Arnold Kasper Haupt's father, whom we shall refer to as Senior, along with two key employees in the Haupts' enterprises, which supplied furniture and equipment to hospitals. Subsequent to the indictments, the two employees plea bargained with the prosecution: they agreed to plead guilty and testify for the government. In return they received lighter sentences than they could have reasonably expected if they had gone to trial and had been found guilty of the charges against them.

Junior's trial was severed from his father's. Because of severe illnesses, Senior was judged incapable of defending himself. This severance also suited the attorneys for the defense. In the face of the employees' guilty pleas, the defense could not claim there had been no conspiracy with fraudulent activity and that even perjury had not taken place. Instead, the defense intended to show and convince the jury that because of Junior's state of mind, he did not have the requisite intent necessary to be deemed a participant in a criminal conspiracy. The defense attorneys intended to show the defendant was incapable of intent to conspire simply because he was totally dependent on his father. In other words, whatever Junior did was the result of blind obedience to a father whom he worshipped. The defense attorneys planned to make Senior the villain, with Junior as his helpless tool and ultimately the victim in this complicated case.

Whether Junior's psychological structure and accompanying state of mind was of such a character as to render him innocent of the charges was a matter for the jury to decide. If you wish to place yourself in the position of the juror, you may also reach your own conclusion on this question. The legal questions involved in the concept of *mens rea* (or requisite intent) were at the center of the major legal arguments in this case. Besides questions of definitions of legal requisites of state of mind, this case raises questions about the definitions of individual responsibility. This is far from a vacant or academic question. It touches on many problems in the relationship of individuals, organizations, and society.

The dependency issue in this case is familiar also as "brainwashing." The term brainwashing became popular following the Korean War when it was alleged that American servicemen taken prisoner by the Chinese had been subjected to systematic influence so they confessed crimes and took unpatriotic positions one would not expect from military personnel operating on their own volition. Earlier the concerns about brainwashing (although it had not been called that) arose when the civilized world fully realized the horrors perpetrated under the Nazis: their policy and practices of genocide. Albert Speer's autobiography, written while he was a convicted war criminal in Spandau Prison, explained his attraction to Adolf Hitler as a lack of individual will or ability to adhere to a set of commonly accepted moral standards. Instead Speer subordinated himself to the wishes of his Führer. Speer's account of his hypnotic-like attachment to Hitler deserves careful study to illuminate how otherwise highly educated and seemingly moral people can act without a sense of will and individual volition. To emphasize further the importance of these questions, we should remind ourselves of the mass suicides committed in Guyana when the members of the Jones' cult took poison at the urging of their leader. This behavior suggests the instinct for self-preservation may not be all that powerful in determining human behavior under circumstances where a hypnotic dependency relationship exists in the attachment of followers to their leaders.

If the examples of the Jones' cult in Guyana and of the Nazis appear too bizarre, we should remind ourselves of the case of Patty Hearst, whose defense was built on the concept that she had been brainwashed. The defense attorneys in that case ran the risk of appearing inconsistent, because they also attempted to defend her on the grounds that she had been coerced into criminal conduct. Brainwashing would appear to exist when individuals willingly act in accordance with directives, in ways they otherwise would find abhorrent in normal states of mind and circumstances. Coercion in the usual meaning of the term refers to force being exerted such as threat to one's life if the individual does not obey commands.

These examples suggest the possibility that powerful individuals and forces within group movements can control the behavior of individuals, to the point where individual conscience no longer acts as an operative force to allow a person to judge his own conduct before he acts. This question deserves special attention because of the existence of large-scale organizations as the dominant form of social structure. What is the relation of moral codes imbedded in the culture of the organization and the codes of conduct dominant in law and the larger society? What influences do organizations exert in affecting individual conscience?

These and related questions entered into the deliberations in the celebrated case of price-fixing and the electrical generating equipment industry. A group of executives employed in the sales departments of large electric equipment companies was accused and found guilty of conspiring to fix prices in contract bids for generating equipment sold to public utilities. From more than one pulpit on a Sunday morning rang impassioned defenses of these executives, who were facing jail sentences. Ministers defended their moral integrity, their exemplary conduct in family, community, and church. Yet these same individuals jeopardized their career, their families, and their personal standing in the community by acting in ways they claimed were in furtherance of the interests of their employers and of industry.

Finally, we should recall the circumstances surrounding the Watergate scandal and the crimes committed by figures as high in government as the attorney general and the president of the United States, let alone their lesser minions in the executive branch of the government.

A number of years ago a book appeared by Jeb Stuart Magruder, one of the individuals convicted of Watergate crimes. Psychologically astute readers found much to ponder in this book, including the effects of a diffuse sense of identity on the formation of compensatory goals and ambitions. Shortly after the book was published, I asked my students to prepare a psychological interpretation of Magruder's actions in the Watergate conspiracy, particularly referring to his own understanding of what had happened and his part in the events that led ultimately to serving a jail sentence. One intriguing feature of this case was Magruder's struggle with dual-identity elements. One element derived from his mother, the southern aristocrat; another derived from his background as an upwardly-mobile ambitious seeker of fame and fortune, first through business success and second through political power. This case lends support to certain propositions about how power can act as a compensatory motive—a motive to replace feelings of inferiority by seeking power and status. Magruder's case also lends support to propositions about how power acts as a motive to redeem the fate of love objects who live with a sense of failure. Through the internalization of the values of these love objects and identification with their goals, individuals seek to redeem the promises implicit in this adopted world view and way of life.

These problems of identity and the ways in which objects cast shadows on the egos of dependent individuals serve as my connecting link to the case of Arnold Kasper Haupt. These links serve, as well, to identify crucial problems in the relationship of individuals to the groups to which they belong. In the case of Arnold Kasper Haupt the link is in his membership and participation in a family with a pathological structure. To understand this case without some conception of how pathological patterns and families come to dominate individual struggles for identity is to conceive of an opera without music or a dance without choreography. To exist in a meaningful, psychological sense, a group requires some conception in the minds of its members as to the group's structure and their position in the structure, along with conceptions about the various purposes of this group. A commonsense conception of a group starts with its purposes and the definition of roles assigned to members. In most groups, more lies beneath the surface than common sense would indicate. Purposes can be latent (to be understood as unconscious). Individuals need to defend themselves against anxiety. Group structure consists of the various alliances individuals form to further personal as well as collective aims. Personal aims need not be conscious. In this connection the formation of alliances to defend against anxiety becomes an outstanding characteristic of group formations.

The family is the prototype of all groups. Parents are primary power figures and become central to the forces that determine the group's structure. In his book *Group Psychology in the Analysis of the Ego*, Freud offered the conceptual bridges that bring the psychology of the individual, the family, and larger aggregates into some relationship. The key element in this theory is identification and its precursors in earlier stages of development, specifically intrajection and internalization. The basis of group cohesion is the common identification members make with their leader. When individuals internalize the ideals of a leader and make him an object of idealization, the members are bound together in function as a cohesive unit. In this sense a leader exerts considerable influence over the members just as long as the members maintain the common identification with their leader. The stronger the internalization, which is to say the more exclusively the leader serves as the object in common for the group members, the greater the power the leader holds.

The psychology of this power hinges on the need for individual members to maintain their self-esteem and to defend against anxiety. Defenses operate at three levels. The first level deals with the anxiety aroused in response to perceived external danger and in response to the problems of managing impulses within the individuals. External danger can be real or the product of fantasies that are themselves projections of internal danger. The second level of defense exists in response to depression; for example, the underlying rage that is a reaction to the prospect that one is not loved or is in danger of being cast out of the group. The third level of defense is against the cataclysm of emotion that arises when one's identity is in jeopardy and one faces the prospect of annihilation. The annihilation symbolically stands as the destruction of the self. A pathological group exists when the balance of forces shifts toward defense and away from activity designed to accomplish real purposes. The real purposes of family as a group are the growth of its members and ultimately the members' achievement of independence.

The case of Arnold Kasper Haupt is a case of dependency and loss of identity. We should be aware in reading this case that the collection of the data occurred under unusual circumstances. Arno, or Junior as he was referred to throughout the case, was on trial for criminal conspiracy and faced a lengthy jail sentence, disbarment, and perhaps the destruction of all of his goals appropriate to his social status and level of education. The data for this case were collected because I was approached by the defense to act as an expert witness in this case. I agreed to undertake a study of the case holding in abeyance questions of appearing in court pending the results of my study. The attorneys, obviously, would not ask me to testify if at the conclusion of my study I found that they had no foundation in mounting a psychological defense on the grounds that Junior did not have the requisite state of mind to participate in a conspiracy because of his dependency on his father.

Under these circumstances it is apparent that Junior would have tried hard to convince me and the other psychological experts as to the merits of this defense. He would be inclined to tell his story in such a way as to prove the point that he simply obeyed his father's wishes and lacked independent will under the circumstances. Whether the story is valid will depend on your judgment as to its coherence and integrity. But bear in mind one fact: even if Junior was trying to influence my judgment and the judgment of the two psychiatrists who also appeared, the particular way he would try to influence us and the fact that he was following his father's orders in attempting to influence us would, if anything, substantiate any conclusion reached that indeed he was totally dependent on his father and probably incapable of making independent judgments. But this conclusion is yours to reach, just as it was for the jury to reach in arriving at its conclusion. Let's turn to the case before we engage in further interpretation.

THE UNITED STATES VERSUS ARNO KASPER HAUPT

THE INDICTMENT

The United States of America indicted Richard Cuthbert, Charles Towns, Arno Haupt, and Arno K. Haupt on 42 counts, charging that the defendants had been engaged between 1971 and 1975 in a criminal conspiracy to defraud the United States. The first group of counts

This case was prepared by Research Assistant Elizabeth C. Altman, under the supervision of Professor Abraham Zaleznik. Copyright © 1979 by the president and fellows of Harvard College.

charged that the defendants had "unlawfully, willfully, and know-ingly" devised a scheme to obtain money from certain hospitals with which they did business by causing the hospitals to submit, unknow-ingly, false reports for reimbursable expenses incurred in connection with their Medicaid and Medicare programs, the Hill-Burton hospital construction program, and a state modernization and construction program. The second group of counts charged that the defendants had committed various acts of mail fraud by using the United States Postal Service to carry out their scheme. Two other counts charged Arno Haupt and Arno K. Haupt with having perjured themselves in their testimony during a grand jury investigation of the fraud. The fi-nal count of the indictment was potentially the most serious charge in terms of possible punishment since it involved a relatively new federal law designed to enable the government to prosecute orga-nized crime. This law made it an offense to participate in a pattern of racketeering, through acts involving the use of the United States mails in furtherance of a scheme to defraud by an enterprise engaged in interstate commerce. Conviction on this count carried a possible penalty of a maximum of 20 years imprisonment, a massive fine, and forfeiture of control over, and interest in, the enterprise in question. Of the four defendants, only Arno K. Haupt stood trial. Cuthbert and Towns entered guilty pleas and agreed to become prosecution wit-nesses in exchange for a possible reduction of their penalties if they told the truth. The trial of the elder Haupt, father of Arno K. Haupt, had been postponed indefinitely because of his health. He was suf-fering from an advanced case of diabetes which had resulted in eye hemorrhages and near blindness. A member of the office staff had in-correctly but aptly begun referring to the elder and younger Haupt as "Senior" and "Junior," and the nicknames had stuck. Junior, at age 38, thus stood alone in facing the trial.

The Fraud

In 1971 the Haupts had purchased Hospitals Suppliers Service (HSS), a distribution house which handled hospital supplies. At that time HSS was divided into two divisions. The larger division, which han-dled about 80 per cent of the business, supplied soft goods to hospi-tals in the middle west. The smaller division, managed by Cuthbert and Towns, handled furniture and hospital equipment. There were two parts to the fraud. One consisted in simply inflating the manufacturers' prices by 20 to 30 per cent on the invoices sent to the hospitals. The second part of the scheme involved making profits through adding false freight charges. This was done either by overbilling or by charging hospitals freight charges which HSS did not incur since the manufacturers had absorbed them in the cost of the goods. At HSS such charges were called "phantom freight" or "free freight." The Haupts paid Cuthbert and Towns agreed commissions on the amounts contained in the invoices sent to the hospitals, usually 30 per cent for the furniture and equipment and 50 per cent for freight charges.

The scheme worked because the prices charged by HSS were within the hospitals' planned budgets and well within the current market prices for the goods in question. Seemingly no one in the recipient hospitals actually checked the invoice prices against the manufacturers' prices. The flexibility of such prices, the long lapse of time (sometimes up to 18 months) between the purchase of goods and the preparation of cost reports, and inflation, made such cross-checking difficult in any case. If any of the hospital administrators questioned a price on an invoice, he would call Cuthbert or Towns, who usually agreed to a reduction. The two men gave special attention to their customers and delivered the goods punctually and as promised so there were few complaints. During the trial a witness claimed that some hospital administrators knew about the inflated prices but tolerated them as long as they were within the budgeted amount.

From 1971 to 1974 Cuthbert and Towns encountered no difficulties in managing the fraud. Financially 1974 was their best year, but in October the first signs of impending disaster appeared. One of the hospitals with which they had a contract, Mt. Hope, had filed a petition for bankruptcy the previous year and had gone into receivership. Since Mt. Hope had an outstanding account of some $200,000 with one of the Haupt companies, this company, represented by Junior, filed claims against the hospital. In settling the claims, a dispute arose over the amount owed. When the hospital administrators looked into the records, they found that the costs under the cost-plus 5 per cent contract should have been some $45,000 less than what was actually charged. Junior settled the claim but did not investigate the source of the discrepancy, nor, at that time, did anyone else.

The details of the scheme were not fully revealed until 1975 when Cuthbert and Towns had already left the Haupts' employment. During a state investigation of an alleged financial scandal at another hospital, investigators accidentally uncovered evidence of the equipment and furniture fraud. They called in the FBI, and the FBI began an investigation which uncovered the evidence that led to the grand jury hearing in 1977 and the indictment of the principal suspects.

THE HAUPT ENTERPRISES

The Haupts retained the services of a law firm to defend Junior. The members of the firm, in preparing their defense, investigated the origins of the fraud, the Haupts' businesses, their management, and their controls. They accumulated documentary evidence that Cuthbert and Towns had begun the scheme before the Haupts acquired HSS in November 1971. The defense lawyers examined next whether their client knew of the fraud and actively participated in it. In looking into the business and its management, they discovered that HSS was only one part of a complex, convoluted organization put together seemingly piecemeal and without plan by the elder Haupt. Over the years Senior had invested in a series of ventures, many of which had proved to be unsound or had begun to lose money under his ownership. He made a practice of buying a new enterprise and draining off cash from it in order to pay back outstanding loans on his earlier investments. Since none of these ventures had proved to be sufficiently successful to carry the earlier ones through their difficulties, two of his major companies had gone bankrupt in 1965. In that same year Junior graduated from an Ivy League law school, and his father asked him to come to work for him in order to help him out of his financial difficulties.

Although Senior had decided in 1965 never to become involved again in any business he did not manage himself, he was attracted by HSS when it came on the market in 1971. Within a month of the purchase date, however, the Haupts discovered serious problems in HSS. Arthur Stapleton, a friend who served the Haupts intermittently as a controller and financial adviser and who had examined the inventory of HSS before the purchase, told the Haupts that half of the inventory was "worthless junk." Senior assigned Junior the task of working on HSS's financial problems. Junior, deeply engaged at the time in working on legal problems for various clients, took on the HSS problems as well.

In April 1972 Senior began to show signs of severe illness. He was unable to sit up for more than a few minutes at a time. When he underwent a prostate operation in June, his doctors discovered that he had diabetes. Because of his father's illness, Junior took on greater responsibilities in their businesses. The hospital equipment business in general had been deteriorating since the beginning of the year. A crisis occurred in mid-summer 1972 in Cuthbert and Towns's division. Junior claimed later that it was this crisis that made him aware of that division as a separate entity for the first time. One of the hospitals under contract to HSS owed $137,000 on an account that was overdue by some 120 days. HSS's major lending bank complained that 13 per cent of its loan to HSS was thus tied up in an unpaid account. Junior discussed the outstanding account with HSS controller Alfred Sharp, who explained that if HSS refused to give extended terms to the hospital it would go elsewhere for its equipment. Junior let the matter rest.

In August Junior asked the bank for more credit to cover receivables, but the bank informed him that it was not satisfied with the accounting at HSS and insisted on an audit by an accounting firm that had the bank's approval. In the course of the subsequent audit of HSS, the accountants sent Junior two letter agreements with the hospitals for him to include in the materials he was presenting to the bank. Junior noted that the letters referred to 5 per cent and 8 per cent profit margins. These were well below the 20 to 30 per cent levels he had been talking about with the bank officers. Junior took the letters of agreement to his father and pointed out the discrepancy in stated profit margins. He said that his father told him, "Look, you haven't seen these. If there's a problem, I'll take care of it. Forget about it." "And," Junior added, "I followed his instructions."

In January 1973 Senior acquired another hospital equipment business called Medequip, which was located on the east coast. He financed the purchase by leveraging money from HSS through Stuart, Inc. Just after he completed the purchase he received the financial report for HSS's performance from October 1971 to October 1972. It showed a loss of $450,000. Senior then decided the only way to get HSS out of its financial morass was to transfer most of the HSS operations to Medequip. Medequip was in a good financial position, and Senior was able to negotiate a loan of $700,000 from an eastern bank. He placed the sales staff under the control of Medequip and kept the accounts receivable under HSS. During the following year he transferred some $600,000 from Medequip to HSS in order to pay off the latter's debts.

But more troubles were on the way. Senior's eye hemorrhages became so severe that he began to lose his sight. He again called on Junior to give more of his time to operating the hospital equipment companies. Junior moved his office to the main building in May so that he could give more attention to what was happening. The following month the Haupts' major lending bank called its loan. Desperate for operating funds, Junior found a factor, FFI, which took over the eastern bank loan and added another $400,000 so that he had a line of credit for $1.1 million. He secured the new loan with the inventory and accounts receivable at HSS. But it was too late. The troubles of the contract division worsened. In October, creditors sent in accountants to examine the books at HSS. A lawyer for three of the creditors filed an involuntary bankruptcy petition against the company, and HSS became dormant for all practical purposes. The Haupts then set up a new company, Hospital Furnishings, which completely combined the midwestern and eastern businesses. Cuthbert and Towns were displeased with the new arrangement and demanded that they be allowed to run their own operation. The following spring Junior gave them full control over their division.

In 1974 came additional worries. In February the United States government indicted Senior for aiding and abetting an alleged income tax evasion. The case involved one of the men he had dealt with several years before in arranging loans through the Central States Pension Fund of the Teamsters Union. The charge was finally dropped in 1977, but the case took the time and attention of both Haupts while it was pending. The charge had no connection with the 1978 indictment for fraud, but the Haupts believed that the link thus established between Senior and the Teamsters Union was the major reason for the government's intensive prosecution of the hospital fraud case.

Their factor (FFI) continued to put pressure on the Haupts over the financial problems of HSS and Medequip and expressed doubts about the Haupts' ability to manage their companies. FFI finally told the Haupts that they could choose between having Medequip go into receivership or giving FFI possession of the company. The Haupts, wishing to avoid another receivership at all costs, decided to let FFI take possession. It did so in June and began auctioning off the inventory in the fall. In October the claims dispute between Mt. Hope Hospital and the Haupts took place.

The final collapse of the Haupts' hospital equipment business did not come until May 1975. By that time Cuthbert and Towns's division no longer had operating funds. The two men left the company in June to start their own business.

THE DEFENSE

Arno K. Haupt's attorneys were impressed by their client's apparent honesty. They believed him when he claimed that he had been unaware that a scheme to defraud the government was being carried out in his companies. But the attorneys felt that the intricacies and convoluted machinations of the Haupts' enterprises, although within the law and not without precedent in the business world, would probably cause the jury to believe such activities could only be the work of people with sinister motives. During their interviews with Junior they had become aware that a very unusual relationship existed between the elder Haupt and his son. They came to the decision, separately and then jointly, that Junior had been unable to perceive clearly what was happening in the companies. Although they realized their client was not suffering from a recognized mental disease or defect that would permit a defense on the grounds of insanity, they were convinced that by virtue of a highly unusual and peculiarly charged relationship he had with his father, Junior was disabled from connecting and understanding the available fragments of evidence of fraudulent activity. The attorneys decided, therefore, to base their client's defense on the grounds that he lacked the requisite degree of intent to be charged with responsibility for what occurred in the company owned by his father and himself.

The defense attorneys engaged the services of a psychiatrist and a psychoanalyst, Drs. Seymour and Bronislaw. Dr. Seymour restricted his examination to the defendant while Dr. Bronislaw examined the defendant, his family, his fiancée, and key employees in the Haupts' companies. The government, as required by law in such circumstances, appointed its own psychiatrist, Dr. Kazin, to examine the defendant.

ARNO HAUPT: THE DEFENDANT'S FATHER

The elder Haupt was born in Germany in 1911. His father made his living as a sculptor for many years, but when he married he taught himself engineering and mathematics in order to increase his income. His success was so great that when he emigrated to the United States in 1922, he was able to obtain a responsible job as a structural engineer. Senior remembered his father as an upright and fair man. Like most German fathers, he was distant and strict, but his son recalled he was excessively strict only about eating habits. Because Senior's father found it impossible to eat in the sloppy, communal conditions of the army mess he was discharged from the German army. Many years later he fainted when his older grandson reached across the table and grasped a piece of butter with his hand. Senior described his mother as being a much gentler person with a great love of music. She had never given her son musical training because her husband did not approve of it.

Senior remained in Germany to finish his schooling when his parents emigrated to the United States. He lived with his mother's sister, an artist, until he had finished high school and two years of law at the University of Berlin. He then joined his parents in Wisconsin where he completed his undergraduate and law degrees. Senior graduated in 1934 in the midst of the depression, yet he managed to find a good position in a large firm. He did so by writing to a German industrialist, Hermann Lohner, who was well known in the Haupts' hometown in Germany. Mr. Lohner had gone to the United States in the late nineteenth century where he founded a successful chemical business. Haupt wrote Lohner that business was entering a new era which would be characterized by increasing numbers of government regulations. As he was trained in administrative law and spoke several European languages, he felt he could be of great use to Lohner's company in dealing with the legal aspects of these regulations. He got the job, and immediately married a woman he had met at the University of Wisconsin.

Senior became vice president and chief counsel for Lohner Industries. He worked well with Lohner for 26 years, often travelling in Europe to help set up new businesses. He and Lohner shared similar attitudes toward business and work. In 1950 Lohner died, and a son, who was five years younger than Senior, took over the business. The two men were in constant disagreement. Senior disapproved of young Lohner's desire for money and his lack of interest in working hard. Senior recalled there was constant turmoil during their years together. He finally left the company in 1960. Although Senior denied that young Lohner discharged him for spending too much time on his own personal investments and legal work, clearly Senior had begun his own entrepreneurial activities while still working as Lohner's general counsel and employee.

When he left Lohner Industries, Senior felt there were few people in the United States who knew as much as he about how to structure deals in corporations. His interest in business, he recalled, went back to his childhood, dominated by the effects of the German inflation. As long as he could remember he had read the financial pages of several newspapers each day. No longer an employee of Lohner Industries, Senior was free to give full attention to his own enterprises.

In 1965 two of Haupt's companies went into receivership. Senior gathered together all the assets left untouched by creditors because they were heavily mortgaged and, with $200,000 that his mother inherited when his father died, organized a new company. He called it Stuart Inc., and placed it in his son's name. It was primarily a real estate company. Senior wanted to find a way to consolidate the various mortgages of these assets. A broker suggested that he apply to the Central States Pension Fund of the Teamsters Union for a loan. He did so, and the loan was approved. From this experience he got the idea of preparing applications for other companies seeking loans from the pension fund in exchange for a finder's fee if the loan was approved. In one case he was not given his finder's fee and he protested to the pension fund officers. It was the out-of-court settlement of this claim that led to his being included years later in the tax evasion indictment of a member of the Teamsters Union.

During this time Senior also began making investments in public companies which he sometimes sold or exchanged and started a business preparing companies to go public. Junior assisted him.

Haupt expressed great fondness for Junior, whom he and his wife called "Pepper." He said that he thought Pepper was made up of the best parts of himself and his wife, inheriting his father's intelligence and fantastic ability to work hard and his mother's health and her persistence, which in her case was so exaggerated that it was annoying. Senior said he had had a very pleasant relationship with Pepper ever since he was a very young child. He often took Pepper with him on his Sunday morning rounds to visit the supervisors of his real estate properties. Even then his son had been intellectually acute. Later he became an excellent student. Senior said he tried to avoid influencing Pepper and encouraged him to make his own choices in life.

Senior added that he treated his younger son in the same manner even though he had been a more troublesome child. Harrison Maitland Haupt, named after two of his mother's ancestors, was three years younger than Junior. Mait's school work was poor, his father said, and he never wanted to get up or go to bed when he was told to. His mother pampered him and, as a result, he was uncontrollable. At 14 he used to force his mother out of the driver's seat of the car, take the keys, and drive away. At 16 he ran away from home. At 17 he was arrested on the charge of carnal abuse of a minor. When Mait's case was heard before a judge of the juvenile court, his mother told the judge that her son should be put in a reformatory for what he had done. Senior said both he and the judge opposed her decision, but his wife remained adamant. The judge sentenced Mait to two years in a reformatory but then suspended the sentence and sent him to a psychotherapy center for six months. Senior felt the boy had never forgiven his mother for what she did to him.

In detailing his reaction to the powerless, Senior became animated over his idea for making a documentary film about the labor movement. The film, as he envisaged it, would begin with a scene of a fire that broke out in a Chicago factory in 1910. It would show female workers being burned to death behind locked factory doors. The doors were locked, he explained, to prevent the workers from stealing the goods they were making.

Senior also became highly emotional when he talked about government in the United States. He believed that the federal government knew cancer was caused by a reaction that took place when chlorine was added to water, but that it would do nothing to ban the addition of chlorine to public water supplies because it feared a panic would break out. Senior also believed the American legal system was becoming corrupt. The FBI was out of control and was worse than the Gestapo. And while the government tolerated invasions of privacy, it did nothing about controlling the radio waves that were soon going to destroy the world.

MARTHA HAUPT: THE DEFENDANT'S MOTHER

Martha Haupt traced her family back to early colonial times. Her mother, born and bred in the South, had always wanted her daughter to become a southern lady. Martha's father taught music at a conservatory in Madison, Wisconsin. She remembered him as a merry man with a strong sense of humor even though he was often strict with her and her two sisters. Since her mother was also musical, Martha's home was full of music and singing while she was growing up.

Martha lived at home while taking courses at the University of Wisconsin where she met Arno Haupt. She wanted to become a doctor, but her parents disapproved, so she left the university before completing her degree. She dated Arno Haupt for several years and finally, with considerable reluctance and hesitation, married him. The 44 years of their marriage were mainly unhappy ones for her. She felt her husband had been spoiled because he was an only child and a boy. His doting female relatives had encouraged him to be self-centered and demanding.

Because Senior devoted himself to business, Martha Haupt concentrated her attention on her two sons. She made sure they had music lessons; she arranged music parties for them so they could play their instruments with other children; she led the Cub Scout groups in which they were enrolled. She was always busy "programming their lives," as she called it. But then they grew up. Mait was thrown out of the house by his father; Pepper went away to college and law school and then he was constantly at work with his father. She was left to her housework which she hated and did badly.

Martha Haupt blamed herself for the many disasters that had fallen on her family. She blamed herself when her father lost his job at the conservatory because she had made a nuisance of herself in his department by trying to organize it properly. She believed it was her fault her husband had lost his job with Lohner Industries. She had said at a party that Mrs. Lohner "could use falsies" and her comment had gotten back to Mr. and Mrs. Lohner. She believed she was responsible for the fact that both of her sons had undescended testicles because she had prayed, while she was pregnant with them, that they would either be girls or be incapable of fathering children. She blamed herself when Mait was thrown out of the house because she had told her husband that the boy was running around instead of writing a term paper that was overdue. She thought she was responsible for the indictment against her husband and Pepper because for years she had written letters to the presidents of the United States—Johnson, Nixon, Ford, and Carter—telling them how to solve social problems such as alcoholism, drug abuse, and homeless children, as well as telling them how the hospital supply business should be run.

Martha Haupt felt her husband had "tricked" his son into coming into the business. She said her husband had always thwarted Pepper's ambitions. When Pepper was 13, she said, he announced that he wanted to become a theologian. His father said, "If you become a minister, I'll laugh you right out of the pulpit." When Pepper came home from law school he told her, "I've spent seven years studying law and I hate it," but his father made him come into the business to help him with legal work. It was his father who had programmed Pepper and his brother since they turned 17. He had turned the two boys against her. One night, shortly after Pepper came home from law school, Senior convinced him to move into his bedroom. Pepper put his mother's possessions into a shopping cart and moved her down the hall to a back bedroom. He then moved in with his father, "usurping" her place. He and his father had "married each other and the business."

Martha Haupt felt her husband had had no use for her for years. Since 1964 he had been impotent, and they had had no sexual relations. He was always telling her to be quiet and he denigrated her in front of other people. His mother had raised him to intimidate women, and when words did not suffice he would sometimes pinch her fingers, pull her hair, or punch her in the stomach. But, she said, when her husband started to go blind, he began to need her again. She scurried to the office, made him lunch, and then rushed back to the office to prepare supper. She considered all of this "a royal pain in the ass."

HARRISON MAITLAND HAUPT: THE DEFENDANT'S BROTHER

Junior's younger brother was as unlike him in appearance as he was in character. Junior was of medium height, overweight, and had very soft features. Mait was lean, taller than his brother, had long sideburns, and often wore an open shirt which displayed the hair on his chest and the chains he hung around his neck. He talked in a "macho" style that matched his appearance. He used the crude and violent words of street language with evident enjoyment.

Mait remembered his childhood up to the age of 12 as being a fairly happy time. He enjoyed walking and playing with his father up to the age of six or so and described his father as affectionate, serious, gentle, and hardworking. In retrospect he thought that the troubled period in his home, the years of bickering and anger, began in 1948 or 1949 when his father started staying away later and later to work on developing his own businesses. He felt his father's work habits probably caused his mother to become sexually frigid, and that her frigidity, in turn, caused his father's angry explosions. Physical violence was not a normal part of these outbursts, but Mait remembered vividly the few times his father physically attacked his mother.

Mait's own troubles with his mother began when the quarrels between his mother and father intensified. He did not mind learning piano, which he enjoyed, but he resented his mother's pressure on him to learn one instrument after another. He hated his mother's ideas for her sons' lives and he particularly disliked her Sunday afternoon "music for friends for fun." He rebelled against her efforts to create a "flowery" southern plantation style of life, and joined a tough, streetwise crowd. Mait's mother always distrusted him, he felt. If he had a girl home to listen to music in his room, she constantly poked her head into the room to see what was going on. When he took a girl to the movies, his mother followed them and sat a few rows behind them in the theater. Such distrust was irritating and embarrassing, but Mait was more seriously distressed by another incident. While he was taking a correspondence course on fireworks, he built a smoke bomb about the size of a cigarette and taped it to the inside of a small safe in his room. His mother saw the object and thought that it was a marijuana cigarette.

"She called the cops on me. The cops came into my house, broke my safe, and I felt intimidated and abused. This was one of the first incidents in my life where I felt she wasn't out to help me—she was out to get me." Still more serious in its consequences and its effects on Mait's feelings for his mother was her insistence that he be sent to a reformatory at the time of his trial. Mait said that the girl he was charged with abusing sexually was a 15-year-old runaway who had been living with a friend of his when he "shacked up" with her for a few days on the beach. The police had picked her up late at night on the street and found that she was on their missing persons list. When his mother appeared in court, she described Mait as a terrible, uncontrollable child, and Mait felt this had prevented him from being released.

Mait had had a miserable time during his brief stay in the youth house, but his experiences at the psychotherapy center were much better. He greatly admired the director of the center, whom he described as a "hell of a man" who would have made a "super father." Through his association with the director and his wife and the group rap sessions among the boys, where they worked out set "problems," Mait became more tolerant of his mother and learned to see her difficulties.

Even though Mait had feelings of affection for his father and felt he could go to him for help, his father's constant absence from home made a close relationship impossible. If he did go to him, his father gave him unrealistic solutions to his problems or supplied him with a quotation that was supposed to solve his problem. Mait did not harbor a grudge against his father for the angry outburst that caused Mait to run away from home at 16. Looking back, he thought his father had probably "tried to get a little bit" from his mother, and when "she wouldn't take care of him," his father had gone on a tirade that included him. When his father rushed into Mait's room and started shaking and abusing him, he "struck out, punched him a few times, knocked him down, and ran out of the house." He never returned to live there.

Mait felt that his father was far too weak toward his employees. He thought perhaps this weakness stemmed from his father's fear that he would lose people if he were tough with them. He was soft with them, and they took advantage of it. As a result his father ended up doing 99 per cent of the work, working 18 hours a day while "the other bastards were out on three-hour lunches boozing it up." He described his father's business style as one of precariously pyramiding businesses by drawing money from one to build up another. This way of doing business repeatedly created a sense of impending disaster and brought about a cry for help from his father. Mait had responded to such a cry in 1964 by going to work for him, but he found he could not tolerate the way his father handled the employees. If he, rather than his father, had been in charge, he would have "broken their legs" when they ripped him off. During the second year that Mait worked for his father he began to have breakdowns of uncontrollable crying and a feeling of utter helplessness. He started drinking and soon divorced his first wife.

Mait left his father's company and took up the kind of work he loved—mechanics, motorcycles, computers. His first business was a motorcycle franchise, but it failed because of his lack of expertise. Then he started buying gas stations and repair businesses and soon had a very successful $3 million business. He explained that his love of mechanical things went back to the days he spent with his grandfather. When his father's parents had come to live next to the Haupts, Mait had spent more time with them than at home. He passed hours watching his grandfather build and take apart mechanical objects and listened to him as he made complicated calculations. He also learned to be neat and organized like his grandfather instead of copying his father who "always had piles of paper and crap all over his desk." Mait developed a deep attachment to his strong and highly respected grandfather who had, nevertheless, a "hell of a sense of humor" and was always smiling. He knew that his grandfather had been very strict with his father, but when Mait knew him he had grown mellow with age. Mait's grandfather died just after Mait was released from jail for participating in the civil rights movement in Georgia. Mait broke down and cried in his wife's arms when he heard the news of his grandfather's death.

Mait felt it was curiosity that first attracted him to his grandfather and that his brother was never interested in his grandfather because he lacked curiosity. His brother was a conformist. When Pepper was young he always did what his mother said. Later he began to imitate his father, copying him in everything that he did. If his father called his mother a "bitch," Pepper would call her a "bitch." If his father read the paper, Pepper sat next to him and read the paper. If his father yelled at an employee, Pepper would do the same. Mait felt Pepper turned against his mother only because he wanted to imitate his father. He believed his older brother had never wanted to become a lawyer, but had become one because of his father.

Mait's own relationship with his brother varied like a wave. Sometimes it was close, sometimes distant, but he did not think his brother had ever been emotionally attached to anyone because he was essentially a cold person. Mait had heard stories that when they were young, Pepper had been extremely jealous of him. Their mother had been strict with Pepper because at that time all the baby experts advocated strict schedules for feeding and toilet training, but she had spoiled Mait when he came along later and had always given in to his temper tantrums.

Mary Mallott: The Defendant's Fiancée

Mary Mallott was the daughter of a real estate broker who had sold several pieces of farm and other property to the Haupts. Senior and Junior always were together when they came to do business with her father. On one occasion Junior asked Mary to go with him to a dinner and dance at a nearby lawyer's convention he was planning to attend. She accepted and enjoyed the evening. When the dance ended, Junior invited her to his hotel room, and although she was suspicious of what he had in mind, she went. Her fears were not realized, and their conversation, punctuated with a few kisses, continued until dawn.

Because she enjoyed Junior's conversation and found him to be one of the most intelligent people she had ever met, Mary was delighted when he began calling her after their first evening together. But she was dismayed when he started calling four or five times a day, interrupting her work and studies. When they began to see each other every weekend Junior called less frequently, and Mary's pleasure in the relationship revived.

Senior often came along when Mary and Junior had dinner together. At first Mary tolerated their discussions of business affairs, but she soon began to resent Senior's intellectual arrogance and she was bothered by the nature of the relationship between the father and son. During one dinner, she became so tired of hearing Senior talk about how intelligently he would run the economy and country if he were president that she said, "If you're so smart, how did you get yourself into a big court case?" Infuriated by her remark, Senior left the table. Junior ran after him to urge him to come back. After some 20 minutes, Junior returned alone and finished his dinner, but he remained deeply distressed by the incident.

Mary described the relationship between Senior and Junior as "weird." If Senior was not present, Junior talked about him constantly and telephoned him at least once an hour. She said that Junior admired him intensely even though his father treated him as an inferior. He often said to Junior, "You are not listening to me, sweetheart. You must listen to me." When Junior began to talk about marrying her and starting a family of his own, the question of his father's attitude kept intruding. When they chose an apartment for themselves in one of the Haupts' buildings, Mary said it would need repairs and renovations, but Junior told her they couldn't do them because his fa-

ther thought they weren't a good investment. Junior insisted that
when they had their own apartment his father would have to live
with them so they could take care of him and get him away from
Martha Haupt. Mary flatly refused.

Mary finally met Junior's mother when he very reluctantly
introduced them one afternoon in the company parking lot. At first
Mary liked Mrs. Haupt, but soon she couldn't stand her incessant
badgering about diet and health or her virulent anti-Semitism, which
was not shared by either her husband or her son. Later Mary visited
the Haupts' home, again against the wishes of Junior, and she "nearly
had a heart attack" at her first sight of the apartment. Newspapers
were everywhere—on the floor, on the chairs, on all the walls. The re-
frigerator was filthy and full of moldy food. The bathroom tub and
sink were black with dirt, and the smell everywhere was overpowering.

When Junior and Mary first began to have sexual relations,
Junior dropped several hints that it was his first such experience and
he asked Mary about her past experiences with sex. Mary was not
willing to discuss the past; she wanted to stay with the present. Mary
felt little interest in sex so she never complained that she did not have
orgasms with Junior. There were other compensations from their relationship. Junior's conversation was always interesting. He took her
to the best restaurants and hotels and always bought front row seats
at the theater and the opera. Even though Mary did not care very
much about expensive, material things, she appreciated his kindness
and his concern for her welfare. He supported her financially when
she decided to get a degree to teach history. Yet Mary had finally decided she and Junior could not get married until he had solved his
problems, both in the company and with his father.

ARNO K. HAUPT: THE DEFENDANT

Until Junior began discussing his work and home relationship with
the defense lawyers and the psychiatrists, he had viewed his life as
normal and in no way unusual. As he looked back over his life
through their eyes he began to interpret it differently.

Junior remembered his childhood with his father as happy
and secure. He found repose and peace in his father's presence as
they walked and talked together and he had only one disturbing
memory of those early years. When he was about six years old, he

went for a walk with his father on a sunny, quiet morning. When they came to a fence wide enough to walk along, he climbed up on it and began walking along it, balanced by his father's hand. Suddenly his father's support was gone, and Junior fell, cutting his head. He still had the scar. At all other times Junior felt his father had backed him and encouraged him in anything he wanted to do. Junior looked up to his father as a wise teacher and felt that he was sitting at Socrates' feet. One of the things he admired in his father was his dedication to work. Each night when Junior went to bed his father was at work at the desk just outside his own bedroom. When he awoke in the morning, his father was again at work. Junior admired his father's intellectual brilliance and had strong feelings of affection for him.

Junior's early memories of his mother were considerably less happy. Even though he acknowledged to himself that his mother was a warm-hearted person who had his best interests at heart, he had little affectionate feeling for her and he was in constant conflict with her. It was not that he actively disliked the musical parties she arranged or even that he objected to being constantly introduced to new instruments—the piano, violin, viola, cello, string bass, clarinet, saxophone, trombone, trumpet, tuba—but he resented his mother's constant pushing. She insisted that he always bring home A's from school and that he do better than all the other children. When he got a D and then an F in initiative, she was terribly upset. So Junior learned to copy a classmate who got A's in initiative by constantly raising his hand to be called on. Her unrelenting persistence annoyed and irritated him. He did what she said, but described it as "seething compliance." He was also annoyed by her terrible untidiness. Yet Junior felt none of the explanations he offered really explained his feelings of antipathy toward his mother. When his father attacked his mother, either verbally or physically, he tried to protect her, but he secretly sided with his father.

When Junior went off to college, he achieved some sense of independence from his parents. Because he wanted to recapture his father's early experiences, he decided to take a junior year abroad and study in Germany. There he fell in love, for the first time, with a German woman named Ingrid whom he met at the University of Berlin. Neither of them wanted to have a sexual relationship at the time, but they talked of marriage in the future. At the same time, he met a man, Werner von Stutterheim, who was some ten years older and a graduate student in physics. Junior admired Werner's brilliance, his self-confidence, and his ability to stand alone in his opinions and ideas. He compared the strength of his feeling for Werner to his feelings for his father. Werner and Ingrid did not get along well together, and Werner felt Ingrid was not the right woman for Junior. Junior took care that his two friends did not meet. When he came back to the United States, Junior ended his relationship with Ingrid.

Junior graduated from college with highest honors and a Phi Beta Kappa key. He was then accepted at an Ivy League law school where he had what he called an "undistinguished career." Junior was not quite sure why he had chosen law. After he graduated from law school and passed the bar exam in 1965, he made only one effort to find a job in a law firm. He accepted the job when it was offered to him, but he failed to turn up for his first day of work because his father had asked him to come work for him, telling him that he needed him to help solve the financial problems. Junior gave up his idea of having a separate career and his own apartment and moved back into his parents' home. He planned to move into the back bedroom, but there was an argument between his father and mother, and to "keep peace in the family" Junior moved into his father's bedroom.

All of these decisions seemed "normal, necessary, and desirable" at the time. They were meant to be temporary, but by the time of the trial Junior had remained in his father's business and bedroom for 13 years. The two of them spent virtually all of their time together, working 15 to 18 hours a day every day of the week, eating dinner together, and spending their hours of sleep together. Junior felt that he had become "an extension of his father's arm," the means for implementing his father's decisions.

Junior had his first sexual relation at the age of 33 with a woman employee. It did not last long. Three years later he met Mary Mallott. He did not feel for her the deep love he had felt for Ingrid, but he enjoyed her company and, somewhat reluctantly, he began to talk of marrying her. He knew his way of living was not fair to her, but he felt that changing his relationship with his father would take a great deal of work. Besides, he thought it would be difficult for him to desert his father now that he was nearly blind.

Junior had little to say about his feelings for his younger brother. He did not clearly remember how he felt, at the age of three, when his brother was brought home from the hospital, but he could remember that later he used to beat Mait up until he got big enough to defend himself. He said Mait was very bright, but he always did the opposite of what he himself did. He was studious; Mait was not. He got A's; Mait got D's and F's. He loved music and theatre; Mait probably didn't even know what an opera was. Junior thought his brother had once been very emotionally upset by the arguments at home, but that during his time in the psychotherapy center, when Junior was away at college, Mait had learned to be indifferent to the family problems and could walk away from them. Junior said he rarely saw his brother anymore, usually only when Mait came in to collect payments on the interest-free loan of $50,000 that Mait had made to him and his father at the time of their financial troubles.

THE TRIAL

The preparation for the trial, once the indictment had been handed down, took over a year. The trial itself, while originally expected to last for four or five weeks, took eight weeks to complete.

The assistant U.S. district attorney, acting on behalf of the government, opened the case for the prosecution by calling witnesses from government agencies, fiscal intermediaries, and hospitals affected by the fraud scheme. These witnesses described the way in which they administered the various programs for reimbursable expenses incurred in hospital construction or remodeling and their contacts with Cuthbert and Towns. The prosecuting attorney then called forward several employees of the Haupt companies and questioned them about the degree of the Haupts' involvement in the day-to-day management of their businesses. He asked the witnesses whether they had ever been present at meetings where either or both of the Haupts had been exposed to, or involved in, conversations or activities connected with plans to inflate manufacturers' costs or to overbill on freight charges.

Several of the witnesses testified that the Haupts had exerted close control over the daily management of the company. They reported that they had seen Senior open the mail, that Junior kept the checkbooks and company records in his law office, that one or the other of the Haupts personally signed all the checks paid by the company. Several witnesses testified they had been present at meetings where the inflating scheme or phantom freight charges had been discussed with one or both of the Haupts or that they had spoken directly to the Haupts about these matters. Some witnesses stated that they had seen one or both of the Haupts handling the phantom freight book. Some of the witnesses testified that the two Haupts were indistinguishable in the degree of control they exercised, that there were few disagreements between them, and that the father did not control or dominate the son.

The most damaging testimony came from Cuthbert and Towns. Cuthbert quoted from several conversations he had with the Haupts about the danger of getting caught, which hospitals could be cheated, and how much each hospital could be overcharged. He said he had described the free freight scheme to them, and that Senior, objecting to that term, had invented the phrase phantom freight. He said he and Towns had agreed with the Haupts that they would receive a 30 per cent commission on the cost-plus contracts and 50 per cent on the phantom freight billings. The remaining profit was to go to the company. Cuthbert claimed Junior had been involved in falsifying an invoice that was sent to a hospital when it questioned the prices charged by HSS. Cuthbert denied that he had been involved in any fraud scheme before the Haupts took over the company.

Towns admitted to having operated a fraud scheme prior to the Haupts' purchase of HSS but confirmed that Cuthbert had not been involved. Towns told the court he had discussed cheating the hospitals with the Haupts from the beginning and that he told them about the extra freight charges by March 1972. Like Cuthbert, he testified that Senior had invented the term phantom freight. Towns also quoted liberally from his alleged conversations with the Haupts. He told the court that when he warned Senior that they would get caught if they did not pay the manufacturers' long overdue invoices, Senior called out to his son, "Sweetheart, why are we not paying?" Towns said that in 1974, after the Mt. Hope crisis, Senior had suggested to him, "Let's all hibernate like bears for six months and let this thing pass over. Then we'll begin again."

The defense attorney questioned many of the witnesses about their agreements with the government to give testimony in exchange for not being indicted or in the hope of receiving a lighter sentence. He then brought out evidence that several of them had reasons to be hostile toward the defendant and his father. He questioned Cuthbert and Towns at length about the high expense accounts they had run up while working for the Haupts on an agreed expense account of only $3,500 a year. He asked them how they had been able to make deposits in the amount of $1 million in their bank accounts between the years 1972 and 1975 and where they had obtained the large sums of money they had invested in various other enterprises if they were earning, as they claimed, only $40,000 to $60,000 a year from the Haupts. They were unable to explain the differences between the amounts they claimed to have earned in commissions from the Haupts and the amounts they had at their disposal. The defense attorney questioned them about their agreements with the government to testify. Cuthbert replied that he had merely agreed to give truthful and complete testimony and added, during the redirect examination, that he expected to go to jail because he had pled guilty to several counts of the indictment.

The defense opened its case by questioning other employees of the Haupt companies about the nature of the relationship between the defendant and his father. In contrast to the earlier witnesses, they testified that the father and son often argued with each other, that the father was domineering and imposed his judgments on Junior, and that Senior often degraded and embarrassed Junior in public.

The defense then called Arno K. Haupt to the witness stand. In the course of questioning the defendant about the Haupts' enterprises and his relationship with his father, the defense attorney asked him about his testimony at the grand jury hearing. Junior told the court he had misled the grand jury by denying that he had control of the company checkbooks and records, that he had no knowledge of the cost-plus agreements, and that he had not heard the term phantom freight before preparations for the hearing began. He explained that at the time he thought he was telling the truth and he did not mean to mislead anyone, but later he recalled he had kept the checkbook and records at his law office until October 1972, he had seen the letter agreements in the fall of 1972, and he had heard the word phantom freight when he had discussed commissions with Cuthbert and Towns. He said that then he had not thought about the meaning of the term. At the time of the grand jury hearing, he added, he had been "living in a different world" because of the pressures he was under.

When the defense attorney questioned the defendant about his life since 1965, Junior answered that he had not taken any vacations, he did not belong to any clubs or organization. He said that his only recreation was going to plays and concerts. He said he had few friends, that his father was his best friend. Junior said that before he listened to Towns's testimony, he had never heard his father calling him "sweetheart," but since then he had heard him say it often.

The prosecuting attorney began his cross-examination by asking the defendant several questions about whether he had often acted in plays at college and about his education in English and German literature. He then went on to question him about his ownership of the Haupt enterprises. Junior replied that he owned these companies, but that they were his "father's creatures." His father was "the architect. He was the master. He was the one who figured out what to do. My job was to carry out those decisions." He ended the cross-examination with the words, "I didn't cheat the hospitals."

Harrison Maitland Haupt followed his brother on the witness stand. He told the court that he left home at the age of 17 because of an argument with his father, and that his father was a dominating, domineering person. He described the time he spent in the family business as "one of the most tense times I have ever been through" and said that the pressure was "almost unbelievable." Under cross-examination he said that on many occasions his father had tried to bend his mind and that was why he had left the business. During that time he had had a nervous breakdown and started drinking. He added, "It probably cost me my marriage at that time."

Martha Haupt then came on the witness stand. She told the court she thought her son went into law because his father was a lawyer, but he hated law and did not want to become a lawyer. She said her husband was dedicated to the idea that you have to keep a woman intimidated and that he was also dictatorial with his son. She ended her testimony with an account of being driven out of her bedroom.

After an extended discussion between Judge Rourke and the attorneys for the defense and the prosecution about whether it was proper for Arno Haupt to appear as a witness when he did not have legal representation for himself and when he was still under indictment, the defendant's father was allowed to testify. In the course of his testimony, he told the defense attorney that when Junior first joined him in 1965 he was a sort of "well-prepared legal clerk," but that later he began to take over and had done better than his father. Under cross-examination Senior denied that he had ever known anything about the cost-plus contracts, inflated or otherwise, that he had invented the term phantom freight, and that he had given false testimony at the grand jury hearing. He said he knew no more than the man in the street about federal support for the hospital programs. He described himself and his son as passive investors who left the management of the companies to their managers.

The prosecuting attorney asked Senior whether he would agree with the many witnesses who had characterized him as an extremely astute businessman. Senior replied, "As a businessman I am stupid or I would not be in this chair right now." When the prosecuting attorney then asked him if he would characterize his son as astute, Senior said that that would depend on which one he was talking about. He added, "The poor guy is not even married yet. I don't know whether he is astute or not." The prosecuting attorney then asked him questions about his relationship with his wife. Senior said she was always claiming to be ill and was constantly going from doctor to doctor. One time, he said, she was convinced that she had cancer and went to a "quack organization" in Boston and came back and told him she had three weeks to live. Senior said that he asked her, "Is that a promise?" and she replied, "No, that was a statement by the doctors in Boston."

Junior's fiancée, Mary Mallott, appeared briefly on the witness stand. She described the relationship between Junior and his father to the court. She called Senior "Adolf Hitler," and said that he was "constantly putting Arno down and imposing his thoughts and his own ideas on Arno and everyone around him." She described the state of the Haupts' apartment to the court. When the defense attorney offered photographs of the apartment as supporting evidence, the prosecuting attorney objected, and the judge sustained the objection.

The defense then called Dr. Kazin, the government-appointed psychiatrist, to the witness stand. He told the court he had found the defendant to be convincing and he believed in his sincerity. He said at times during the interviews the defendant had broken down and sobbed, and this was likely to happen whenever he expressed his exalted idea of his father or began to realize that he had given up the major part of his life to serve his father. In evaluating his findings, Dr. Kazin testified that he had two different impressions of the defendant. On the one hand, the defendant seemed to be extremely capable and showed no evidence of a mental disease or disorder in the generally accepted sense of that term. On the other hand, he felt that he showed a "remarkable, highly unusual character disorder which took the form of excessive dependence upon his father and a kind of persistent childishness into adult years." He found the defendant's respect for his father to be "grossly disproportionate in terms of what one would expect from a 40-year-old man" and he likened it to the "exaggerated respect or admiration for a God-like figure that religious people have."

Dr. Kazin concluded his testimony by saying:

When I read the indictment I got an impression that was strikingly at variance with my impression on seeing Mr. Haupt.

That's one of the main reasons I asked to see him again, to see whether the impression I got on the first interview held up on the second, and it did. Even though my conclusion was something of a surprise to me, I have a good deal of confidence in it.

The psychiatrist appointed by the defense, Dr. Seymour, was the last witness to testify. He said he had had 16 sessions with the defendant. In his opinion, the most striking feature that emerged from these was the discrepancy in the defendant between an "emotional baby" with an immature personality displaying many of the features of an infantile dependency relationship, on the one hand, and an intellectual capability, on the other hand, that was far in advance of his emotional development. He described the defendant as a "helpless, dependent little boy who could in no way challenge the father's assertiveness and control." Dr. Seymour related the defendant's story of falling off the fence as a child when he felt the loss of his father's supporting hand and told the court that the defendant had a recurring dream involving the threat of being mutilated or dismembered unless he assumed what he called the "contracted position."

Dr. Seymour said that the defendant's father tended to see his son still as a "little boy in need of nurture." He said that Senior had explained the bedroom arrangement as being based on the need for physical proximity between himself and his son so that he could teach, instruct, and advise Junior and give him the benefit of his own knowledge of world history and current events. Dr. Seymour described Senior as an "arrogant, pompous man who made a point of telling how smart he was, how brilliant his insights were, how compelling his knowledge was, and of making the contrast between the potency, as it were, of his mind and the relative weakness of his son."

The judge asked Dr. Seymour, "Doctor, is it your professional opinion that due to a mental condition existing at the time or times when the crimes charged were committed, the defendant was incapable of knowingly doing what the law forbids and purposefully intending to violate the law?" Dr. Seymour replied that in cognitive terms the defendant had the capacity to know, but that in emotional terms there would have been some compromise of his ability to make objective and independent assessments.

THE JUDGE'S CHARGE TO THE JURY

At the end of Dr. Seymour's testimony, Judge Rourke turned to the jury and told them, "You as jurors are the sole exclusive judges of the facts," and he warned them that the law does not permit jurors to be governed by sympathy or prejudice. He explained to them that since the defendant had pleaded not guilty the government had the burden of proving by competent evidence the charges made against him beyond a reasonable doubt. He said that both direct and circumstantial evidence had been presented during the trial, circumstantial evidence being proof of a fact or circumstance from which one may infer connected facts which reasonably follow in a man's experience.

Judge Rourke then reviewed the charges against the defendant. He told the members of the jury that they were to concern themselves with one count charging conspiracy and 29 substantive counts. He explained that conspiracy means an agreement or an understanding between two or more persons to violate the law. In order to find the defendant guilty on the conspiracy charge, he said that the members of the jury would have to find beyond a reasonable doubt that 1) some time between the dates indicated in the indictment an agreement existed between the defendant and two or more conspirators; 2) it was part of this agreement to defraud the United States or to violate at least one of the substantive statutes; 3) the defendant knowingly and willfully associated himself as a member with the conspiracy; and 4) any one of the conspirators knowingly committed at least one of the overt acts set forth in the indictment.

After a discussion of these substantive counts against the defendant, Judge Rourke addressed the jurors on the question of the credibility or believability of witnesses. He told them that they must consider the witnesses' relationship to the government or the defense, their interest in the outcome of the case, their appearance and conduct on the stand, and whether their testimony was corroborated or contradicted by other testimony and/or their own statements. He explained that expert witness testimony was unlike other testimony in that the witness is allowed to express his or her opinion. Opinion is allowed in this instance, he explained, because it is the opinion of a qualified expert on some particular technical matter, but such testimony is meant to be purely advisory. The members of the jury were to decide whether to accept or reject it. He also explained that the fact that the government had offered no expert testimony in opposition to the testimony of the psychiatrist appointed by the defense did not require the members of the jury to give more weight to the defense-appointed psychiatrist's opinions.

In closing, Judge Rourke told the members of the jury that they could not allow consideration of the punishment which might be inflicted on the defendant if he were found guilty to influence their verdict. The members of the jury then retired to reach a verdict.

COMMENTARY

Pathology also exists in this case study. It does not take a professional psychiatrist or psychoanalyst to arrive at this conclusion. Because of the blatant character of this pathology, or call it an eccentricity if you wish, the defense attorneys clearly believed that the best case for their client would hinge on their ability to demonstrate that this was a sick family, that Junior was totally dependent on his father, and therefore incapable of having that state of mind which would enable him voluntarily to enter into a conspiracy. It was clear from the testimony that fraudulent behavior had occurred. It was clear that Junior was involved in it to varying degrees so that his only defense seemed to be the psychological position of dependency. His father had brainwashed him, according to his defense attorneys, and Junior had lost all capacity to make independent judgments. If you and I were members of the jury we would find this defense difficult to accept. A man approaching 40, who graduated with honors from an Ivy League school and with a law degree from another Ivy League school, would have great difficulty accepting the notion that he was incapable of rendering independent judgment. If he chose to do what his father wanted him to do the choice was his. One could point to his decision to join his father's firm rather than an independent law firm following his graduation from law school as support of the dependency notion. But at a minimum it is evident that Junior was closely attached to his father. Whether it was pathological or not and of a sufficient degree to cross that line to render the principle of requisite intent inapplicable, is, of course, a matter for the jury to decide.

Here is an intriguing question. Putting aside the issue of where that line is to be drawn beyond which requisite intent disappears, where did the pathology exist? Was it a condition that was inherent in the family structure or was the family structure the result of individual pathology? Let's take up the question of the family structure first.

For structure to exist, is it necessary to have a leader? If so, who is the leader in this family group of four? A strong case can be made that Senior was the leader of this group and that the pathology inherent in it was a direct expression of his own sickness, which had begun a long time before he married Emily and fathered two sons. Emily also displayed certain pathological characteristics in her behavior but it is not clear the extent to which this pathology was a means of protecting herself from her husband. The basic structure of this family consisted of a strong pairing between Senior and Junior. Emily's position in the family was that of scapegoat while the second son, Maitland, was an isolate. He had no strong attachment to either his mother or his father. Indeed, one might make the case that for Maitland the problem was to establish a position in this family structure for himself. There seemed to be mythology underlying this group structure which revolved around an image of a chaotic world which had to be limited in its effects. The method of limiting it was through trying to gain control and to establish an order out of this chaos. The fact that this order involved certain grandiose schemes and unlawful behavior seemed to matter little. The great fear was if one were passive then chaos would reign. This mythology clearly grew out of the Senior Haupt's personal development and resultant pathology.

The fact that the Haupt family group was based on a pathological structure and mythology does not mean that the group itself lacked cohesion. In fact, the very nature of its cohesion maintained the structure of the group and kept alive its sick mythology. As with any group, the Haupt family had its leader, the father, Arno Haupt the senior. The pathology in the group stemmed directly from his underlying disturbance which arose as a result of his development. We have some clues as to what led to this problematic development but more importantly we have a very clear picture, or so it seems, of just how this pathology worked.

Arno Haupt, who is called Senior in this case, was born in Germany and came to the United States during his late adolescence. His parents came earlier leaving Arno to complete his studies in Germany. From all indications Arno Haupt, Sr., had developed early in his life rigid psychological defenses which were patterned after his own father who could not tolerate disorderly behavior. You will recall the instance in which his grandson, the defendant in this case, reached to grasp the butter with his hand. The grandfather fainted as a result of what appears to have been a massive anxiety attack. The more direct evidence of the rigidity and the obsessional quality of Senior's defense's consisted of his compulsive hard work, his tendency to isolate thinking from feeling, and his peculiar relationship to money and power. One of the more difficult problems in evaluating the significance of the types of defenses which Arno Haupt, Sr., demonstrated is whether they exist as a result of continuing psychological regression or as an attempt to maintain one's position in reality in response to inner psychological disturbances. At the time the data for this case were collected, Senior was involved in an obvious paranoid thought process. He was grandiose in his evaluation of his abilities and in his degradation of others. One does not have to be paranoid to devalue the president of the United States and his advisors, but if one is intent on pursuing a paranoid thought pattern, public officials serve as likely targets.

Senior's grandiosity focused on his business acumen. He held inflated estimates of his talents. He believed himself to be a genius in structuring deals, in "creative" financing, and in taking advantage of tax laws. The simplest explanation of his approach to business is that he took advantage of tax laws, of working capital manipulations, and of ease in setting up shell corporations to enrich himself and his family.

The defense attorneys believed Senior was a wealthy man. There is reason to doubt this evaluation. As in any game such as a chain letter in which funds are parlayed, new money must continuously be flowing in to pay off old debts. Sooner or later the day of reckoning arrives and the shell structures collapse of their own weight. The more important question to ask about Senior is why, with his talents, he was unable to build and operate substantial businesses with organization, sound structure, and continuity. It appears that at least one reason he was not able to do this was that his whole approach to business, including money, deal making, working over tax losses, was itself symptomatic of his psychological problems. Senior demonstrated a process called "counterphobia" where the individual creates or perceives danger in the outside world as a means of warding off the effects of internal danger. This counterphobic style becomes rigid defense and a style of relating to the outside world as a means of regulating anxiety and more specifically, substituting external for internal danger.

But it is not obvious what internal danger Senior had to

defend against. Nor is it clear how he drew his family into his defensive struggles. But before continuing with this theme, let's reexamine our inquiry of Arno, Sr.'s business style.

Arno, Sr. set himself up against visible external authority, the law, tax officials, bank officials, judges, and others. He engaged in a struggle with authority aiming to prove its stupidity and his own acumen. In this vein he ultimately worked out a path for his own self-destruction, that of his family, and especially that of his prized son, Arno, Jr.

In the end Arno, Sr., had his way. He involved the Federal Bureau of Investigation, federal prosecutors, judges, a jury, and a massive federal prosecuting apparatus to pursue him. Paradoxically he outwitted them all because his illness and impending blindness prevented the government from getting to him directly. They managed to get to him only through his son who, as a separate human being, probably meant very little to Arno, Sr. The clues to Arno, Sr.'s motives of revenge accumulate. His relationship to his father, while formally correct, appears more ambivalent in light of its demonstrated relation to Mr. Lohner, the head of the chemical company for whom Arno, Sr., worked and later Mr. Lohner's son, who succeeded his father upon the latter's death. Arno, Sr., fantasized himself in a relationship of son to a powerful father with his experience with Lohner, Sr. When Lohner, Sr., died, in fact even before Lohner died, Arno, Sr., found himself in a rivalrous relationship to Lohner's real son. The two clashed and Arno, Sr., was forced out of the business because of his business affairs outside of the Lohner's enterprise. Emily Haupt's explanation sounded more like a product of her own hostility and demeaned self-esteem than a measure of the reality in the case. We're entitled to ask whether Arno, Sr.'s pattern of business behavior that appeared before he left Lohner was not already a product of massive defense against depressive reactions. The appearance of manic-like activity, of grandiosity in thinking, may already have reflected his immersion in a deep psychological conflict.

Arno, Sr.'s relationship to his wife is instructive concerning the family group structure and underlying mythology into which the two sons were drawn in unique ways. According to Emily Haupt's statement, there was no love between her and her husband. Emily indicated that Arno, Sr., had been impotent for many years and that he had been verbally and physically abusive to her. In commenting on this behavior, Arno, Jr., the defendant, spoke of this with some enthusiasm indicating some identification with his father's abuse of the woman. For his part Arno, Sr., had no tender feelings toward his wife. You recall Arno, Sr.'s statement during the trial when his wife told him that she was going into the hospital, that there was some possibility that she had cancer and was going to die. Arno, Sr., responded, "Is that a threat or a promise?" It would not be too conjectural to state that the source of danger in Arno, Sr.'s psyche and consequently Arno, Jr.'s was the woman and her sexuality. For these two men, father and son, the woman, the mother, symbolized the chaos against which the group structure sought to defend itself. This was the organizing principle in the family collusion of father and two sons, but again the two sons acted out their collusion in very different ways.

Maitland, the younger son, was on the edge of delinquency for most of his adolescence and even into his adult life. He had enormous independence largely because he had to break out of the family, since there was no place for him in it other than as an isolate. Nevertheless, he acted out hostility toward women in his abuse of his mother and also in his promiscuous sexual behavior. Maitland symbolized overt impulsivity, lack of control, and the readiness to act out sexual and aggressive impulses.

Arno, Jr., symbolized just the opposite. Rigid in his defenses, he controlled his behavior resulting in very little experience with sexuality. At his age, approaching 40, he had been mostly celibate for his adult life. The fact that he moved into the bedroom with his father (the father kicked the mother out) might suggest some homosexual tendencies, but there is little evidence that he ever engaged in any kind of sexual activity, so we might conclude that he simply existed with a very low level of libidinal interest. It is striking that in the one instance in his life in which Arno, Jr., struck an independent course, he reverted to his habitual dependency on his father. You will recall that when Arno, Jr., went to Germany to study he was attracted to a woman who was also a student at his university. At the same time Arno, Jr., managed to develop a very strong dependency tie to an older graduate student who told him he should not pursue his interests in this woman. I would judge this represented a successful effort on Arno, Jr.'s part to carry with him, in a new setting, the existing psychological structure which was at its core a highly dependent relationship to his father and an ambivalent, if not hostile attitude toward women.

This psychological interpretation of the Haupt family

structure, its business activities, and its pathology leading ultimately to Junior's indictment and trial, brings us back to the question of Haupt, Jr.'s guilt or innocence. Was he so psychologically impaired that he was unable to be a willing participant in a conspiracy? The conspiracy itself was not in doubt: the question was whether he was a willing participant, willing to the degree that passed the line of what is known in legal circles as requisite intent.

The jury concluded that Arno, Jr., was capable of entering into a conspiracy and found him guilty. He was sentenced to five years in jail. Under the RICO provisions, the family was required to forfeit its assets. The judge ruled that if Arno, Jr., or the family would pay within a specified period of time, a sum equal to $100,000, that the assets would be restored to the family. The case was appealed. The appellate court found in favor of the lower court and Arno, Jr., began his jail sentence and was stripped of his status as a lawyer.

It is perfectly consistent to understand the psychology of Arno Haupt, Jr., and also to find him guilty of these crimes. We are dealing here with the problem of morality, of intent, and consequence. The law is extremely cautious about permitting psychological interpretations to sway or determine the jury's findings and for good reason. I do not doubt the validity of the interpretation I've just offered about psychological structure of the family and its effects on Arno Haupt, Jr. Nevertheless he lives in the world as it is and he must accept the consequences of his actions. There is a certain wisdom inherent in the jury system in which people of ordinary intelligence would find it very difficult to accept that a graduate of an Ivy League college and an Ivy League law school, who is practicing law and running a business, would be incapable of knowing what he was doing and making independent judgments as to whether it was right or wrong. The psychology of Arno Haupt, Jr., stands on its own. The law also stands on its own and in its wisdom attempts to place the greatest responsibility on the individual, where it properly belongs.

RIVALRY

WHEN ACTION OVERCOMES THOUGHT—THE FASHION SHOE COMPANY

Imagine that you are the consultant called in to advise Frank Faulkner on whether he should fire his president. The initial problem facing you is to determine why he wants a consultation in the first place. Does he want objective advice? Is he asking you to perform a task that is distasteful to him, such as firing an executive? Is he asking you to relieve his guilt feelings and give him support and approval? These are not mutually exclusive requests. But it is important to sense what is being asked of you, especially in this case of the Fashion Shoe Company, where there is apparent rivalry between the chairman of the board and his president.

It probably has occurred to you to wonder what, if any, relationship exists between rivalry and dependency in power relationships. The two seem opposites in a sense that surely rivalry can only exist if two or more people have a sense of power and experience little mutual dependency in their relationship. Here is a clue as to how latent or unconscious dependency wishes might give birth to intense individual rivalries.

Suppose you face a conflict over power and responsibility. Perhaps in reflective moments, you are overcome with a desire to be taken care of rather than to be the one responsible for others. In addition, suppose you are confronted with a difficult business climate and wonder if you have gone beyond the risk level prudent for your kind of business. Both of these hypothetical situations are familiar and all too human. They have been encountered numerous times in the course of growing up and taking on the challenges of a career. Yet these situations themselves produce a habitual response. In some cases, the response is to stop, look, and listen or seek some help and to reevaluate the strategy one is following.

Another usually less effective response is to rush into activity, to set up phantom terrors and antagonists in order to simulate one's sense of control.

Frank Faulkner took over Fashion Shoe Company when his father died. At a crucial juncture in his business, he appointed William Farnsworth to the post of president while he assumed the title of chairman of the board. Not long after this change, Frank wanted to fire William and in consideration of this impending decision, he hired a consultant. What is he looking for? What does he want from his consultant? And how did he get into the mess of wanting to undo a recent decision that was supposed to help his company grow and possibly lead to becoming a public corporation?

FASHION SHOE COMPANY

In June, 1968, Frank Faulkner took the newly created office of chairman of the board of Fashion Shoe Company. He was the controlling stockholder in a business which his father started about 35 years earlier. Upon his father's death in 1960, Mr. Faulkner, then 24 years old, became president and chief executive officer. In addition to the stock bequeathed to him, he purchased outstanding stock held by other family members and acted on behalf of his mother who owned the remaining 50 per cent of the shares.

Faulkner's plan in becoming chairman was to free himself from operating responsibility so he could turn his attention to a program of product diversification and corporate acquisitions. In addition to accelerating the company's growth, Faulkner hoped to "go

---

This case was prepared by Professor Abraham Zaleznik. Copyright © 1969 by the president and fellows of Harvard College.

public" as a means of increasing his wealth, providing for estate planning, and offering stock options to attract and hold able executives, who in his words were "professionals."

The company had had an enviable growth record in the 1960s. From a small business which manufactured ladies shoes for "private label" distribution, the company increased its sales and profits by more than 600 per cent. It introduced a "Fashion" brand name program, established marketing and design functions which were backed by national advertising in magazines and television, increased its full time sales force from about 10 to 60 men, and introduced sophisticated management control techniques including electronic data processing. In achieving this expansion, Faulkner had managed to attract executives from leading competitors who were interested in building a business under his leadership.

Mr. William Farnsworth, currently the company president, was the first "outsider" to join Fashion soon after Frank Faulkner became chief executive in 1960. He was an aggressive salesman with intuitive approaches to product design and marketing. Farnsworth succeeded in selling several major retail chains and he was also instrumental in developing several design innovations that provided product identification for the "Fashion" lines.

Farnsworth's appointment to the presidency occurred shortly after Faulkner decided to pursue acquisitions and ultimately to offer stock to the public. Faulkner describes the circumstances surrounding the naming of a new president as follows:

> There were three candidates for the job of president: Mr. Farnsworth, Mr. Garland (production manager) and the man who was the controller and treasurer. I called a meeting of these three men and told them of my plan to become chairman of the board. I said, one of you will be president and I want you to select the man. Go into a room and decide among yourselves who should be president.

Faulkner felt certain the group would name Farnsworth. The three candidates were about the same age but vastly different in background and personality.

Mr. Garland had been with the company since its inception, and had worked closely with Frank Faulkner's father. Since the business was largely manufacturing to customer orders for their own brand and using their own designs, the success of the business had depended upon meeting cost estimates, quality standards, and delivery promises. Mr. Garland was conscientious about managing the plant and assumed responsibilities beyond one's expectation of an employee. He had been devoted to Mr. Faulkner, Sr., and had customarily visited his house, both to talk business and to play with Frank almost as an uncle to nephew if not father to son. When Faulkner, Sr., retired from the business at age 48, Garland ran the business, checking by telephone with Faulkner, Sr., who lived across the continent from the plant and its offices.

Frank Faulkner was uncertain why his father had retired and moved so far from his business. The ostensible reason was a heart condition, but Frank felt it was just as possible that his father was a hypochondriac.

During the period following the retirement of Mr. Faulkner, Sr., and up until his death in an automobile accident, the company's sales and profits were on a plateau. Garland viewed his job as plant manager, producing for a selected number of retail accounts and servicing their needs for women's shoes to be sold under the store brand. While attending to costs and delivery schedules, Garland thought of his plant and the people it employed as members of a family. He knew all the employees by name and kept informed on all their personal joys and tragedies. He customarily opened his plant at 6:00 a.m. (a practice he continued to follow in 1969) and except for unusual circumstances, was the last to leave the building 12 hours later.

The company controller who came into the business about the same time as Farnsworth was a second candidate for the job of president. While Faulkner believed Garland had only moderate interest in becoming president, he believed the controller was ambitious and wanted the job. The controller was a tense, irritable person, who while conscientious in his work, was not the type of "professional" Faulkner would have wanted in the position of controller, let alone president.

The three men held their meeting and, by the process of elimination, named Farnsworth president, largely because of his experience in marketing and his personal aggressiveness. Shortly after becoming president, Farnsworth, with Faulkner's concurrence, asked the controller to resign because of shortcomings in his performance. Faulkner arranged through Fashion's public accounting firm to place the controller with another company. The controller did resign, but soon afterwards he became seriously depressed and killed himself.

Faulkner not only accepted the decision to name Farnsworth president, but also wanted to give him freedom to run the business. About six months after Farnsworth became president, Faulkner located new offices for himself in a sophisticated building a taxi ride away from the Fashion offices. Faulkner believed his move "uptown" would clear the way for Farnsworth to become president in fact as well as in title. This move would also, Faulkner believed, help him concentrate on long range planning and acquisitions. Faulkner took only his secretary and left the president and vice presidents, as shown in the organization chart (Exhibit 1), to carry out the program he had initiated for the Fashion Shoe Company.

The program consisted of the following steps undertaken about a year before Faulkner moved up to chairman of the board:

1. Designing new styles and new footwear lines and establishing a "Fashion" brand name through a magazine and television advertising program.
2. The upgrading of the line so it could be sold in better department stores and retail chains catering to higher income groups.
3. Building a new salesforce of bright young men who would be selected for their potential rather than past performance in selling to shoe buyers in prestigious retail outlets.
4. Opening a new plant (at some distance from the existing plant) in an economically depressed area which could supply a work force at wage rates below the current level in the industry. This plant was intended initially to manufacture the new lines, reserving the old plant for the more established lines of shoes.

The five vice presidents shown in the organization chart in Exhibit 1 were, with the exception of Garland, the type of "new breed" which Faulkner hoped to attract to the company. He viewed them as "professionals" who were intensely competitive and capable of exposing weaknesses in the organization as well as carrying out their own functions.

Markham, the controller, was the most recent addition to the group of vice presidents. He had had considerable background in management controls and had valued his experience in working as subordinate to "sharp and aggresive" general managers. In joining Fashion Shoe, he hoped to improve its reporting and controls but he

Exhibit 1
Fashion Shoe Company Organization Chart
June 1969

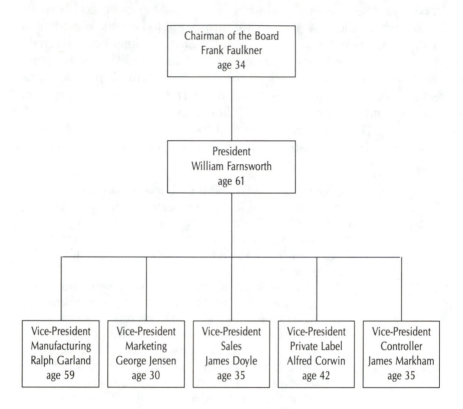

also looked forward to spending increasing amounts of time working with Faulkner in his acquisition program.

The next most "junior" vice president in length of experience with Fashion was James Doyle. He had been with the company less than two years, having been hired by Alfred Corwin. Corwin, currently vice president of private label, had been vice president of sales and marketing before he assumed this position. In bringing Doyle to the company, Corwin hoped to utilize Doyle's aggressiveness to build the salesforce needed to promote the Fashion brand line to prestige accounts. According to Faulkner, Doyle managed "to outmaneuver" Corwin and had forced a decision from Faulkner to rearrange job responsibilities and titles. This reorganization, which occurred in spring 1968, resulted in naming Doyle as vice president of sales, George Jensen as vice president of marketing, and Corwin as vice president of private label sales. These three vice presidents were, in effect, equal in status in reporting to the president where formerly both Jensen and Doyle held the title of "manager," reporting to Corwin.

In explaining this reorganization, Faulkner believed he would have lost Doyle if the title of vice president with its direct line of responsibility to the president were withheld. Faulkner had become aware of Doyle's expectations when he received a call from him at 5:30 a.m. Both men were in a hotel where the company was about to hold an important national sales meeting to introduce the new marketing plans and to stimulate salesmen to meet the sales targets established for them. Faulkner believed it was necessary for him to appoint simultaneously Jensen as vice president of marketing since Jensen and Doyle seemed competitive with each other. In Faulkner's words, "Jensen and Doyle don't like each other. They are both hungry, aggressive, and out to make a name for themselves. Where they both agree is in wanting to push aside and get rid of the tired old men."

Jensen was responsible for developing the product lines and marketing plans for each selling season. He worked with the company's advertising agency and was largely instrumental in moving into television advertising. When formulating plans for television, Jensen convinced Faulkner that the company should fire its advertising agency which, in Jensen's opinion, was unsuitable for work in television. Faulkner accepted this recommendation while aware of the fact that the head of the old advertising agency and Farnsworth were close friends and work associates of long standing.

Shortly after Faulkner moved his offices in early 1969, he began to feel uneasy about the implementation of the plans that he had formulated in conjunction with Farnsworth and the vice presidents. While dollar sales stayed even with comparable periods in 1968, they fell below the budgeted level. Of even more concern to Faulkner was the realization that profits would go below the amount realized in 1968. Faulkner recognized the impact on sales and profits of dropping "low end" accounts, increasing advertising and marketing expenses, adding men to the salesforce with an expected lag in bringing sales up to the level where the salesman would pay for himself, but he was concerned about Farnsworth's abilities in leading the "young tigers" who reported to him as vice presidents. Faulkner studied the figures into spring 1969 without taking specific actions. He began to act, however, when Farnsworth left the country for a spring vacation. Because he wanted to travel abroad with his family, Farnsworth had decided to take a three week vacation in spring 1969, when formerly he had taken only two weeks.

Faulkner spent two consecutive days in the Fashion offices and conducted interviews with executives and employees at various levels to get a closer view of what was accounting for the disappointing results of 1969. He conducted an "exit interview" with a product manager who had resigned. This product manager was critical of Farnsworth's leadership and especially critical of one of the sales managers who had been close to the president. Faulkner, upon learning that Jensen and Corwin were also critical of this sales manager's performance, decided to take "dramatic action" to indicate his concern about the sales and profit performance in early 1969. He discharged the sales manager.

Another decision that Faulkner made during Farnsworth's vacation was to close down the new plant. This plant had failed to meet its schedule. Earlier when Farnsworth had expressed optimism about the new plant meeting its quotas, Faulkner appointed a committee of three to monitor the new plant's progress. Jensen, one of the committee members, reported an impending "disaster." Faulkner went to the new plant with this committee and decided to close it down immediately.

During this same period, Faulkner conducted a "whirlwind" visit to various key accounts to establish once again his "feel" for the marketplace. Upon his return from this tour, one of the company's product managers came to Faulkner to report a conversation he had had with Garland, the vice president of manufacturing. According to this man, Garland had suggested that the product manager visit Faulkner to criticize Jensen's performance in heading the marketing department. The product manager said, in addition, that Garland had indicated that he would persuade Faulkner to name this product manager as Jensen's successor.

Faulkner felt angry upon hearing this report from the product manager. He was disturbed over the "political infighting" that seemed to have erupted, and especially at the possibility that the new plant had fallen a victim to "company politics." Faulkner asked the controller, Markham, to go to the factory with him to see Garland. He especially wanted Markham along because Faulkner felt "emotional" and doubted whether Garland should remain with the company.

According to Faulkner, he confronted Garland with the report from the product manager. At first, Garland countered this report with his own version, which was different from the one Faulkner had heard. Garland then said, "I was really testing [the product manager's] loyalty." Upon hearing this, Faulkner stated, he "pinned Garland to the wall." Faulkner continued, "Garland began to confess his sins and said to me, 'I'm with Fashion all the way. I'll keep my nose clean, I'm with you Frank.'" Faulkner decided not to fire Garland. He detected sincerity in Garland's statement and even though he still had doubts about him, Faulkner decided to keep Garland with the company, reflecting, "After all, I used to play with him as a kid—we have a strong emotional tie."

At the conclusion of his investigation, Faulkner prepared a detailed memorandum outlining his criticisms of the way the company was being run and the various decisions he had reached during Farnsworth's absence. He sent this memorandum to Farnsworth's house and it arrived there on the day he returned from his vacation.

Shortly after sending the memorandum to Farnsworth's home, Faulkner met a friend and business associate to whom he described his recent experiences as chairman of the board of Fashion Shoe Company. This friend suggested Faulkner call in a consultant who specialized in problems involving personality conflicts among executives. Faulkner accepted this suggestion and in meeting for the first time with this consultant, reviewed the events described in this case history. Specifically Faulkner asked the consultant to undertake a study and to recommend whether he should discharge Farnsworth, and if so whom he should select as the new president.

COMMENTARY

We often get some indication of what is going on in a power holder's mind by examining his timing and style as well as the substance of his actions. Taking a second look at a decision that is already made is not inherently wrong. But Frank's method of intervening suggests he may have been acting out of anxiety rather than purely rational motives. Why act when Farnsworth was on vacation? Why send him a letter to be read on his arrival home rather than wait for him to come to the office for a face-to-face meeting? Why engage subordinates in a conspiratorial-like investigation instead of a deliberate, carefully drawn study in which a wide range of participants is included, especially his president, William Farnsworth.

The timing and style of Frank's actions cause us to suspect that a great deal was going on in determining his actions beyond the realities of his business situation.

There are two lines of interpretation one can take. The first explains the panic reaction Frank was undergoing as a direct result of the adverse business results experienced during the first year of the new program with Farnsworth acting as president. Obviously, the year was a big disappointment for Faulkner, but perhaps more importantly to him, it forecast a serious business climate, one that he had not consciously realized, let alone anticipated.

A second line of interpretation imposes a deeper psychological perspective, one that at times will strain credulity and require (at a minimum) a careful examination of evidence. This interpretation begins with the notion that Frank had been, for many years, engaged in a deep-seated rivalry with his father. The fact that his father was dead doesn't diminish the significance of this longstanding developmental rivalry. Frank himself alluded to certain ambivalent attitudes towards his father. He wondered about his father's passivity, suggesting worries about his health and his father's unwillingness to maintain an active business life. Frank took over the business when his father died and managed to gain control of his mother's shares so he dominated the corporation. In his own words, Frank seemed to divide the executive world into two types: the young tigers and the old ineffective people. He encouraged a conspiratorial event in which his head of sales and marketing, Corwin, had been "killed off" by his younger subordinate. Why would Faulkner entertain a business conversation upon receiving a telephone call from Doyle at 5:30 in the morning? This call led to reorganizing the sales and marketing department and then demoting Corwin and elevating Jensen and Doyle, both of whom had been subordinates to Corwin. It may have been a very good business decision on its own terms, but again we must examine the style of the activity as well as the substance. It is the style that raises questions about Faulkner's inner motives. Was he encouraging a conspiracy, an enactment of a drama in which younger men destroy the older man?

If there is any truth to this interpretation, then we should inquire into the appointment of Farnsworth as president. Was the appointment motivated, at least partially, by Faulkner's hidden yet dominant need to continue reenacting a drama in which a younger man destroys an older man? However one interprets Faulkner's behavior during the period when Farnsworth was away on vacation, it suggests a kind of anxiety-driven need to undermine the older man's position.

These two lines of interpretation, the first based on realities of the business downturn and, second, the psychological reenactment of young vs. old, are not mutually exclusive. They could coexist and indeed one would amplify the other. Following this thought, it would appear as though the business downturn hastened the rollout of the psychological drama of the younger man overcoming the older. The business downturn produced a great deal of stress for Faulkner. His habitual response was to take flight into activity, instead of the more careful approach of waiting until Farnsworth returned and engaging him in the study of what was wrong in the business and what remedial steps should be taken. Apparently Faulkner needed a scapegoat for the business reversals, the forces of which were probably well in place before the decision to appoint Farnsworth president.

When business troubles loom on the horizon it is extremely important to maintain a firm grasp on reality. The appearance of fantasy, either directly motivating the action or in response to the stress of the impending business troubles, prevents rational action and effective approaches to solving the business problems. Reality and fantasy can remain independent of each other. When they begin to cross over in ways that are out of control, the dangers to a business enterprise increase in severity.

We began this chapter with some questions concerning what Faulkner wanted from his consultant. That is not clear, but one can appreciate the complexity of the consultant's job. He could easily become another target of Faulkner's rivalrous feelings or a temporary palliative to the guilt feelings that Faulkner undoubtedly had as a consequence of his behavior. It would be essential for the consultant to maintain a neutral position and not stimulate either rivalry or overt dependency. If dependency took hold, it would not be long before Faulkner would react to his own feelings and become even more panicked and ineffective.

WHEN THOUGHT INHIBITS ACTION—THE BRANDON CORPORATION

Dependency and rivalry appear to be polar opposites in relationships of power. In the case of dependency, one power figure is dominant and becomes the object of need fulfillment on the part of subordinates. In rivalry, an unbalanced situation exists. The actors in the drama struggle to achieve ascendancy, to become the central figure, or object, upon whom others will depend.

The elements in the struggle are diverse, but fall into two broad types. First, there are the external, or purely situational, elements that affect the distributions of power. Position in the hierarchy is an example of an external element. So is title, compensation, job definitions, and the other symbols of power defined by the formal organization. So long as the actors accept the legitimacy of structure there should be no cause to engage in rivalry, at least from the standpoint of elements external to the participants.

Alas, as we have discovered, life is not so simple as to allow for clear definition of a power structure that achieves consensus as to rights, responsibilities, and entitlements. As known to anyone who has ever appointed someone else to a position of responsibility, such as in leadership succession, no one will question the right of the appointing agency to name a person to the position. The question is, why the person selected and not someone else, including candidates who were excluded from consideration, or if considered passed over for the job. If the candidate's credentials are unassailable, those left behind, so to speak, soon recognize the legitimacy of the appointment and put their disappointment to one side in the interests of serving their own needs as well as meeting the expectations of the organization.

But appointments are never clear cut, which explains why people leave a corporation soon after someone else is named to a position coveted by others. "Why him and not me" is the question often asked as contenders and candidates ponder their fate in the quest for position and power. If this question cannot be answered soon in the logic of the situation, trouble looms. People will leave to pursue their interests elsewhere, or if they remain in doubt about the answer to the question, manifestations of rivalry will soon appear.

Another type of rivalry often appears, but it stems from internal elements. Examples of internal elements are: unbridled ambition, deep-seated envy, little tolerance for waiting one's turn, inability to live comfortably with any structure, hostility toward authority of any kind, grandiose estimates of one's own ability, and conversely the propensity to attack the ability of others.

Introspective people have a tendency to look for internal motives to explain (to themselves and others) the causes of rivalries. For those with little inclination to look inward, the propensity is just the opposite: situations count while motives are meaningless. Neither position is tenable. Situations count and motives provide the energy to propel the drama of rivalry. Situations require definition and all actors are capable of making their own definitions, without necessary regard for objectivity. Inner motives and their manifest discontents are like impulses looking for a place to settle. Hence situations and motives join forces for the staging of rivalry.

Norman Podhoretz, the editor of *Commentary*, wrote an insightful and shrewd book called *Making It*. The book is a personal memoir on ambition and the hazards of working one's way up the ladder of success and achievement. His ladder was not business or corporate hierarchies, but the ladder of esteem, according to which individuals in the literary world weigh and measure accomplishment. This is a bitchy world, guaranteed to fire discontent as one peruses reviews and best-seller lists, and listens to gossip about the rise and fall of authors. This memoir illuminates what goes on in the corporate as well as the literary world.

Podhoretz draws a distinction that speaks to the point of rivalry, at least the type generated by internal motives rather than external situations. The distinction is between jealousy and envy.

I have just finished reading a novel by a Japanese born British subject. The novel is called *The Remains of the Day* and the author is Kazuo Ishiguro. The book is about a very British gentleman's gentleman, a butler who is obsessed with his professionalism and the detachment he seems to believe is a necessary piece of equipment in the successful practice of his craft. To read this splendid novel is to experience the horror of the inability to feel, the incapacity for love, the insensitivity to human communication. This book is brilliant, combining humor and horror in delineating the commonplace. The construction is marvellous in its compactness, flow, and suspense. The novel exemplifies the gift of projecting the universal in the particular. What an experience reading this book!

But the truth be told, the reading produces jealousy. I wish, deeply wish, that I were capable of such a wonderful piece of work. Alas, I am not. But while I am jealous, I am not envious. Here Podhoretz hit on a truth. To be jealous is a vital, and possibly even constructive emotion. It accepts desire without depriving the author of his gifts. Envy, on the other hand, is antisocial. It covets what the author has. It wants to take it away from him. It is not enough to admire him, to wish we had the talent it takes to produce such a wonder of insight. Envy commands that we must take it away from him, make it our own possession, hoard it, and consequently end up not being able to use it because beneath this covetousness lies a fear. If we use it and display it, someone will want to take it away from us. Thus the tragedy of rivalry: to end up having something of value and not being able to use it by the very nature of the motive that allows us to snatch away someone else's gift.

Perhaps all I'm really saying about rivalry is what a friend once told me: there are no complicated situations, only complicated people. Thus, Charles Warner, the chairman of Brandon Corporation, found himself in confrontation with his president and chief operating officer over chain of command, authority, and the supposed limitations on spontaneity in hierarchical relations. Was it the situation, or the people, or both that fired this conflict? Sort out the elements of this rivalry, if in fact you want to call it that.

BRANDON CORPORATION

On February 11, 1983, Charles Warner, the chairman and chief executive officer of the Brandon Corporation, met with his president and chief operating officer, Frank Reynolds. The meeting took place late in the day and at Reynolds' request. Mr. Warner had had some prior indication that Mr. Reynolds was upset because Reynolds did not attend a product development meeting that Warner had convened earlier in the day. Before starting the product development meeting, Warner asked the sales vice president, who reported to Reynolds, where he was. The sales vice president replied that Mr. Reynolds would not be attending the meeting.

Reynolds was visibly upset and angry during his meeting with Warner late on Friday afternoon. He threatened to resign and showed Warner a list he had prepared that detailed, in writing, the ways Warner had broken the chain of command and, according to Reynolds, damaged his authority and standing in relation to his subordinates. The list cited the fact that Warner had called a product development meeting including as participants all of the people who reported to Reynolds. As a further indication to Reynolds that his authority had been subverted, he angrily reminded Warner that the chairman had negotiated a new arrangement with one of the Brandon Corporation's key licensees in Europe without Reynolds attending the negotiations, or reviewing and approving the terms of the new arrangement. Reynolds felt the chairman had acted arbitrarily, without regard for the integrity of the chain of command, and in a manner that had diminished Reynold's capacity to continue as president and chief operating officer.

While this meeting was not the first time Warner had confronted anger in his president and chief operating officer, nor the first time Reynolds had threatened to resign, the anger appeared to Warner as both more intense and sustained so that the prospect of having to deal with a resignation appeared more real than on pre-

---

This case was prepared by Professor Abraham Zaleznik. Copyright © 1983 by the president and fellows of Harvard College.

vious occasions. Warner had decided while listening to the complaints of his chief operating officer that he would ask Reynolds to hold in abeyance any decision to change his relationship with the Brandon Corporation until both he and Warner could discuss further and in more detail their relationship and the difficulties Reynolds experienced in working with Warner. He asked Reynolds to adjourn the meeting and to use the weekend for reflection on what had occurred recently to disturb him and what they should do next to improve the situation. Warner said he planned to think long and hard about how he had upset Reynolds and how he might go about avoiding such situations that involved Reynolds' authority and his working relationship with subordinates. Warner further proposed a meeting for an early hour on the following Monday morning.

Reynolds responded favorably to Warner's suggestion and indicated he would not reach a firm conclusion as to what he would do, which Warner took to mean that Reynolds would hold in abeyance his decision to resign. They both agreed to meet Monday morning and shook hands and left for their respective weekends. Upon arriving home, Warner called Reynolds to restate their commitment to a "cooling off" period. Reynolds had not yet arrived home, but Warner continued calling until he reached Reynolds who reassured the chairman he intended to reflect, he would delay any decision on resignation, and he would be at the Monday morning meeting with Warner.

The Brandon Corporation was a medium-sized manufacturing company that designed, produced and sold a line of specialty electrical products. The products, mainly control devices, were used in the assembly of large pieces of equipment. Brandon's customers designed and manufactured the equipment, which usually specified the Brandon products as subassemblies or parts. There was only one major competitor in Brandon's business. Because of design innovations, which resulted from Warner's initiatives and expertise, the company had improved its market share significantly at the expense of its competitor and had enjoyed a number of years of success in its markets. The company's balance sheet was exceptionally strong. As a result of its improved market share, the company's profits and cash flow had increased and the balance sheet showed extraordinary liquidity and a very low debt-to-equity ratio.

A significant change had occurred in the fall of 1982, when Brandon's main competitor started a price war with the obvious aim of recapturing the market share it had lost to Brandon over

Exhibit 1
Brandon Corporation Executive Organization Chart

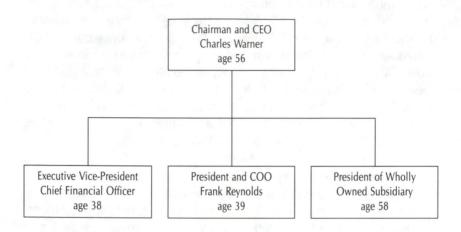

the past five years. While Warner fully intended to meet the price competition, he had no idea how long the price war would last and how deeply the competition would cut into the company's profits and cash flow. It was in response to the price war that Warner had grasped an opportunity to make a favorable deal with his European licensee and had called the product development meeting. The night before he had called the meeting, Warner thought of a number of possible product innovations which he was eager to present to his executives in marketing and engineering. Warner felt strongly that the company's long-term success in the price war depended upon its ability to present new and improved products even though in the short run it had to meet its competitor's prices. He could hardly restrain his enthusiasm and therefore had hurriedly called the product development meeting without first consulting Reynolds. Exhibit 1 presents an organization chart that shows job function and lines of authority for the top management of the Brandon Corporation.

Besides dealing with the intense competitive problems through pricing and product improvement, Warner had undertaken in conjunction with his chief financial officer and an outside investment banker, investigation of opportunities for acquiring companies. The Brandon Corporation was owned privately with all the corporation's shares in the hands of Warner and his immediate family. Warner believed the company should expand by buying other privately held concerns in businesses that either related to or complemented Brandon's activities. At age 56, Warner had no intention of selling out to another company, nor of retiring. He spent many hours discussing the company's future with his chief financial officer. The two of them had hired the investment banker after conducting interviews to decide which of several leading investment bankers would be in the best position to help the Brandon Corporation. This work entailed considerable travel for the two executives, extensive research work on the part of the chief financial officer, and many hours during which Warner and the chief financial officer met to discuss the long-range plans for Brandon. Warner expected Reynolds to devote himself to managing the company day-to-day while he in turn would concentrate on ideas for product innovation in existing markets, and the problem of acquisitions.

Warner was aware of how difficult it can be to recruit, develop, and motivate key executives in a privately held company. He felt that if executives met his standards for ability and performance that they would constantly be tempted to leave and join a publicly held corporation where scope of responsibility and financial incentives might be considerably greater, and perhaps include participation in stock option plans. To meet this problem, Warner had consciously and carefully arranged a compensation package for key executives that he believed would enable the Brandon Corporation to keep talented executives despite the drawbacks of working for a privately held corporation. The compensation package consisted first of salary and bonus that together represented at least 40 per cent more money than these executives could reasonably expect to realize working for another company, either publicly or privately owned. In addition, there were the usual perquisites alongside a deferred compensation plan that raised the compensation value beyond the 40 per cent premium to perhaps 75 or 100 per cent above the market. The deferred compensation plan became fully vested after seven years and the plan was in its first year in early 1983. The only executives who participated in this compensation program were the president, the chief financial officer, and the president of Brandon's wholly owned subsidiary. This subsidiary manufactured and sold a product that was totally independent of the corporation's main lines and therefore operated apart from Brandon. Warner had complete confidence in the president of this subsidiary and viewed him, along with the president and the chief financial officer of Brandon as his key executives for whom he had developed the special compensation package.

Charles Warner joined his father's business in 1949 when he graduated from college with a bachelor's degree in business administration. His father had founded the business, and at the time Warner joined it, the company was very small as measured in sales, profits, number of employees, and product lines. It specialized in one product line which provided the family with a good income, but with few prospects for growth in sales or profits.

In 1957, Charles Warner formed a new company called the Brandon Corporation. Warner decided to establish this company so that he could pursue new market and product opportunities that went beyond the scope of his father's business. Charles Warner and his father each owned 50 per cent of Brandon. The elder Warner received his 50 per cent share in exchange for his willingness to countersign a note for $25,000 held by a bank that had loaned Charles the money necessary to start the business.

By 1961, the Brandon Corporation was barely surviving. Despite the problems, Charles Warner decided that he wanted complete ownership of the business. His father balked at the suggestion that he should turn over his 50 per cent of the Brandon shares to his son. Nevertheless, he transferred his shares to Charles who immediately put his father on the Brandon payroll where he remained until his death.

Reflecting on his desire to own 100 per cent of the Brandon shares, Charles Warner said, "Brandon was my idea. I founded the company, and I couldn't live with the division that way and getting my sister and her family involved in the company." Warner had been conscious of the fact that should his father retain the 50 per cent ownership, his estate might become burdened with taxes upon his father's death. In addition, Charles Warner faced the prospect of having his sister own shares in Brandon which she would inherit when the elder Warner died.

In 1973, Charles Warner suggested that his father consolidate his business in the Brandon Corporation. According to Charles Warner, his father was by that time sympathetic to the activities of the Brandon Corporation and felt that by merging his company with Brandon, his business would continue. Charles Warner said, "Father realized I would take care of him in a dignified way and as a result he became enthusiastic. He came into the office every day and saw young people. This kept him in good health. The last two years of his life, I insisted that he not drive his car. I had one of our employees who lived near father pick him up in the morning and drive him home from work at the end of the day." The elder Warner died in 1981 at the age of 92. After his father died, Charles Warner realized he would be the last member of his family who would run a business. His children had made definitive career plans which excluded the possibility of ever coming into the Brandon Corporation and succeeding their father.

During the 1970s, the company was successful in expanding its product line and in opening new markets. However, it experienced severe difficulties in controlling quality and manufacturing costs and it appeared threatened by a number of years of unprofitable operations. Charles Warner recognized he needed help in running the company. He sought advice from the president of his wholly owned subsidiary who recommended Warner hire as president and chief operating officer an individual who had once worked for the president of the subsidiary. Warner accepted this advice and hired the man, who remained for a couple of years but then decided to resign and go into business for himself. Warner once again sought the advice of the president of his subsidiary who recommended another executive from his industry. Warner hired this man who stayed with the company several years. This president brought to the company rich experience in the technical aspects of Brandon's product and made many changes that worked to the advantage of the corporation. However, he also displayed bizarre behavior in his relationships with women and was totally indiscreet, making no secret of the fact that he enjoyed extramarital affairs and that he encouraged his subordinates to do the same. Warner, after an extreme display of poor taste on the part of his president, decided to discharge him and at that point elevated Frank Reynolds from the position of vice president of sales to president and chief operating officer.

Frank Reynolds joined the Brandon Corporation in the early 1970s. He had graduated with a degree in engineering, but had worked in a large corporation in its marketing department, utilizing his technical background to master his understanding of product design and applications as a salesman. He advanced in his work and joined the Brandon Corporation on the advice of the president of its subsidiary, for whom Reynolds had worked in the large corporation. Reynolds soon received promotions and he became vice president of sales two years after he joined the company. Reynolds performed well in this capacity but he became dissatisfied working for the president who was later asked to resign because of indiscreet behavior. His dissatisfaction reached the point where Reynolds tendered his resignation to Charles Warner, indicating that he was willing to stay on long enough for the company to find a successor to the position of vice president of sales. Warner was very reluctant to see Reynolds leave the company and decided to offer him the position of president and chief operating officer in order to keep him in the company. Reynolds accepted, whereupon Warner asked for and received the resignation from the incumbent.

In the position of president and chief operating officer, Reynolds recognized a number of opportunities for improving the company's performance. Costs and product quality were out of control and the company was losing money at an alarming rate. Reynolds acted decisively in making personnel changes, and in instituting procedures which considerably improved product quality and costs of manufacturing and distribution. The company became profitable and entered an aggressive program in which product innovations and marketing programs increased the company's market share and enabled it to accumulate cash and equivalent liquid assets for its future program of acquisitions.

Warner and his other two key executives recognized Reynolds' contribution and attributed his competence as an executive to certain personality characteristics. In their eyes, for example, Reynolds was an extremely well-organized individual who identified a problem, figured out how to solve it and then without deviating from his course implemented the solution. He was openly aggressive in his style, and was quick to display his anger at subordinates and even Warner should events appear to interfere with his program for action. Reynolds himself in commenting on how he worked in comparison with Warner said, "Charles is an idea man and I implement. He comes up with a lot of ideas and then I have to talk him out of his bad ones after figuring out which ones are good."

Frank Reynolds was born in a rural community, the second of four children. His older brother was a machinist who had dropped out of college and gone into machine shop work. His sister, younger by three years, taught school and was unmarried. The youngest brother worked for the Brandon Corporation in the sales department. This brother dropped out of college and Frank arranged to get him a job in a Brandon manufacturing plant. When the younger brother applied for a promotion, Frank Reynolds rejected the application on the grounds that his brother was unqualified for the job. Reynolds took this occasion to tell his brother that he should leave work, go back to school and complete his college degree and then go to work. Reynolds also offered to support his brother through the completion of college, an offer the brother accepted. The younger brother completed college and came to work once again for the Brandon Corporation, but this time in the marketing field following the career path of his older brother Frank.

Frank Reynolds enjoyed a close relationship with his parents, especially his father. By a program of careful savings and investments, Reynolds had accumulated a substantial equity. He bought two farms in partnership with his father. His parents lived on one farm which the father managed in his retirement. The father had been a teacher and football coach in a high school, and upon his retirement both worked and lived on the farm. Frank Reynolds and his family, which consisted of his wife and two children, visited the farm at least one weekend a month and for holidays and in this way maintained a close relationship with his parents. Managing the farms and other investments required Frank and his father to confer during these monthly visits and on other occasions. The older brother was somewhat estranged from his parents, although he too was married and had children. Frank, commenting on his brother's relationship with their father, said, "They are too much alike in their personality to get along."

Reflecting upon his recent angry exchange with Charles Warner, Reynolds felt he had been successful in running the company. At age 39, he believed he had to make a decision about his career, particularly in meeting his desire to own and manage his own business. Reynolds regarded his acumen in saving and investing with considerable satisfaction. He was proud of the equity he had accumulated through his investments and believed he had the assets to strike out on his own. He also believed it was in Charles Warner's best interests to sell the business and realize cash from the equity represented in it. He recalled advising Warner directly to sell when it seemed that a large publicly held company might be interested in acquiring Brandon. Warner at that time told Reynolds that he had no intention of selling the business and that he had no desires other than to continue as chairman of Brandon, to expand the business through developing new products, and through acquiring other companies.

COMMENTARY

Frank Reynolds is making the case for the situation causing the conflict. Specifically, he is appealing to the logic of chain of command. He is president, while Warner is chairman. He is in charge of operations, while Warner is (or should be) concerned with strategic planning. To Reynolds, Warner is the key to the situation: Warner's inability to play by the rules of chain of command. Thus Warner must not call meetings with Reynolds' "direct reports," nor must he communicate with them directly, since it violates the imperatives of maintaining clean lines of authority in the organization. In the same vein, Warner cannot conclude a royalty arrangement until, and unless, Reynolds reviews it and gives it his O.K.

What is so striking in this case is Reynolds' inability to look into himself and see that this rigid conception of what an organization is about is his way of engaging in a rivalry with his boss. Reynolds needs to dominate: witness his successful dominance in his parental family, and his paternal stance relative to his younger brother. He is somewhat patronizing in his comments about his boss. Suggesting that Warner sell the business implies a position that is not his to take, and silently expresses some contempt for Warner, if not outright envy of his position.

Warner's position is his own. He built his business, and while he too became dominant in relation to his father, he maintained a respectful stance even while he sought ownership control when he bought his sister's shares.

There are at least two aspects of this case that are puzzling and raise intruiging questions. First, why is Warner afraid of Reynolds? Second, is there some latent conflict in both of these men that exacerbates their opposite tendencies: Reynolds' activity and overt aggressivity, and Warner's passivity and avoidance of conflict?

You may be surprised at the possibility that Warner is afraid of Reynolds. The surprise is in raising the question, not in answering it. After all, you may ask, doesn't Warner have complete control of the situation? His ownership of the company does give him complete control. The question I am raising has little to do with control in the legal or formalistic sense. What is Warner's state of mind regarding his control? If he *felt* he had control, he might possibly approach Reynolds, not with an apologetic "standstill agreement," but with some humor. For example, suppose Warner said to Reynolds something like this: "It looks to me that you want all the fun of this job, of working with engineers, salespeople, factory people, customers, etc. Suppose we switch jobs. You become chairman, and I'll become president. You sit in your office and think, while I talk to people and have the fun of working on problems with them. Would that suit you? Would that be a good way to run the company?"

You may not find my brand of humor appealing. If not, try something more direct than a humorous hint about what life is like, or should be like, in a business dedicated to first-rate performance. Here is how Warner could deal directly with Reynolds: "Frank, you've got some strange notions about life in an organization, especially this one. I don't believe we should run this place according to the rules of chain of command. You evidently do, so we have a disagreement. I want to talk to anybody I feel like talking to and whenever I feel like it. I want you to do the same. It will make our work more interesting, it will be more stimulating for our people, and in fact make it easier for you and me to talk business, solve problems, and run this company. If you are convinced we should follow the chain of command to the letter, then you and I aren't going to get along, and you should leave this company. If the idea of working closely with me, of talking with anyone we feel like appeals to you and you are willing to experiment with how we work together, then let's go to it and forget about strict lines of reporting and who has what kind and how much authority."

Authority figures should not be afraid of their subordinates. The fact that they are from time-to-time testifies to how complicated things become when the legacies of past relationships involving power result in guilt and anxiety becoming the primary motivators. The behavior is defensive, equivocal, and at times devious, rather than spontaneous, direct, and optimistic.

What is the evidence to indicate that Warner's cautious and conciliatory stance in the face of Reynold's anger is a result of residual problems in accepting and dealing with his power? Before I can even attempt to answer this question, let's simply accept for the moment that this formulation is correct. How does this legacy of the past actually work in the present? More specifically, suppose Warner had to overcome a latent rivalry with his own father in order to accomplish what he had in building his business. Also, suppose this father-son rivalry is seldom overcome once and for all. Like Hamlet's doubting, the continuing effects of even the most normal rivalry of son toward father lead to a tentativeness toward power, even the power one has earned legitimately.

Even the slightest feeling of temporariness produces the Hamlet-like effect of doubting, of caution, and the compelling need to equivocate, to permit thought to overcome action. It's as though one occupies the throne, but only on condition that the suitcase is packed and ready for a quick trip, because the occupant of the throne is an object of other lustful power contenders' envy. They want what you have, and they will get it through fair means or foul. Thus, no matter its legitimacy, under circumstances of inner doubt, power becomes the victim of ambivalence—at once the object of desire and danger. The end result at its extreme is paralysis, the inability to act. Obviously, Warner is nowhere near the extreme case of the doubter for whom thought dominates action. Nevertheless, in his relationship and response to Reynolds, he acts as though he is arrested by lingering doubts about the legitimacy of his power.

Of course, the truth of the matter is I don't know, nor I suspect do you, what the approximate relationship is between Warner's history with his father and his response to Reynolds' anger and threat. Warner acts *as if* he is a man for the moment dominated by the past. There is such a disparity between his actual power and his felt dependency on his subordinate as to require some explanation. The version I have presented depends heavily on a model drawn from psychoanalytic theory and clinical experience. This model doesn't assure the truth of the explanation. It suggests a truth, consistent with the facts we are able to accept, and so we have to leave it at that and await fresh evidence either to support or refute the idea that there are ghosts abroad ready to do us harm. Instead of living in some surreal spiritual world, these ghosts inhabit us. They are simply the equivocal, unsettled, yet haunting images of the past that we are inclined to project on to the present.

MASCULINITY AND FEMININITY—MARIGOLD PRODUCTS, INC.

Almost without exception, the discussion of rivalries in organizations among members of the opposite sex produces strong emotions and personal reminiscences of uncomfortable situations. While I was preparing to write this chapter, I was flying to a business meeting. An attractive and bright-looking young woman sat next to me and we began a conversation as the plane took off. It turned out that she was a computer specialist on her way to make an important presentation to her boss and his staff on product development. Having just purchased a Poqet computer I eagerly showed her the product and asked for her opinion on certain features of its operation. She immediately took to the machine and began to demonstrate its operating features, referring to the manual. I was fortunate enough to find myself in a tutorial on the use of my new travelling computer. In case you've never encountered this machine, it weighs about one pound, operates on two double A batteries, and once I get WordPerfect on a ROM card, I will have solved my problem of writing comfortably while travelling, without lugging a seven or eight pound machine with restricted battery life.

While listening to her explanation of the machine, it occurred to me that she might help me "get into" this chapter by giving me some fresh perspectives on the Marigold case, which is the next case study.

I narrated briefly the story of Marigold, and again I was delighted with how quickly she grasped the problem. But I noticed that what she picked up on was the "action" question: What should Donald Holden do about the fight going on between the director and assistant director of the human resource department? She talked about whether it was right for an assistant to undertake initiatives without consulting her boss. She was also concerned about Holden's seeming inaction in letting the problem reach the point where the two people were attacking each other and becoming visible antagonists to division heads and other managers.

As far as I could tell, what she had to say about this case reflected a great deal of "organizational savvy." Furthermore, she seemed to think in the same ways as any number of men with whom I have discussed this case. She did not bring to the discussion of organizational issues special perspectives one might expect from a woman. After all, the rivalry was between a man and a woman. What, I asked her, did she make of the fact that the director, the man in this case, was very passive about his job, and allowed the woman, the assistant director, to move aggressively to the point where she openly announced that she wanted his job, and suggested that he would do better being the assistant, reporting to her?

She began reflecting on this situation and made some further observations about the responsibilities of a subordinate, of the need for moving quickly to prevent a situation like this from occurring, but then I noticed a change in her facial expression. She became less animated and more pensive. She began to "drift" and talk about her relationships with men, or as she put it, "her love life." It turned out she had a penchant for men who were passive and had difficulties making commitments. She also, with some frequency, found herself in a peculiar situation where men who wanted to marry her seemed dull while the men who excited her, and it was clear she meant sexually, seemed to be the passive types who couldn't for the life of them make decisions—to fish or cut bait, to break off the relationship, or make a commitment and marry her.

Now I don't make it a habit of drawing people out, friends or strangers, particularly on intimate matters like their sex life. The reason I don't is purely civil: it's just not nice to probe into another person's psyche, to let a friend or stranger get overextended, reveal things that later they wished they had not, leaving them embarrassed and chagrined at the possibility that they appeared naive.

On occasion I break this rule of mine. I remember sitting on an airplane next to an elderly man. I noticed that he was crying and I asked him what was wrong. He told me that his wife died and he described their relationship, their life together, and how his friends in trying to comfort him would say, "You had such a wonderful life together, you should be thankful for what you had, and you should get on with your life, instead of lingering over the past. What more could you want?" He had a ready answer to this question: "Just one more day with her."

It is sometimes difficult to know when it is an act of kindness to listen, and when it crosses that subtle line between friendship and probing into areas that had best be left alone to the privacy of the person's thoughts, or work with a therapist.

But let me get back to my new acquaintance and her reflections as we flew to our respective business appointments. I left off just as she shifted in her mood and became reflective, undoubtedly as a result of the Marigold case as I had briefly described it to her. She had responded initially as a good orgnaizational person is supposed to. The director had failed to conduct regular performance appraisals with the assistant director, she observed. Had he done so, he would have nipped the problem in the bud. As I indicated, she drifted off of this sane organizational talk and began to reflect on her "love life." I couldn't help but wonder if Freud didn't have it right when he observed that the conflict of passivity and activity precedes the conflict between masculinity and femininity. See for yourself!

MARIGOLD PROCUCTS, INC.

As the Christmas holidays approached, Donald Holden felt under increasing pressure to solve a problem in the personnel department of Marigold Products. Holden, chief operating officer of the company, disliked the alternatives facing him as well as the pressure to act during the holiday season. But he realized that the situation had to be

This case was prepared by Professor Abraham Zaleznik. Copyright © 1987 by the president and fellows of Harvard College.

resolved because of the effects on the people involved and other executives operating divisions within Marigold.

The director of personnel administration and his assistant director were fighting. The director had been with the company for over 30 years. He was the first head of personnel, and in fact had built the department as the company grew and found it necessary to expand personnel services. The director was in his fifties, married with three daughters. His wife was a successful teacher and his daughters were completing school and in the early years of their careers. The assistant director was in her early forties. She had graduated from high school and left her parents' farm to find a job in a city some distance from where she grew up. She was the only one of her siblings to have left home. Her brother, a little more than a year younger, ran the family farm while an older sister married a farmer and lived nearby. The assistant director had married and later divorced her husband. Her daughter was in college, living in the dormitory while her son was in high school and living with her. Of the two children, her daughter was "more independent," while her son "needed propping up" from time to time.

The assistant director had worked as an administrative assistant before joining Marigold. The director of personnel had recruited and hired her as a general assistant, to replace a woman who had been his assistant but who had been asked to run personnel services for one of the large divisions of the company. This assistant left the company soon after her transfer. While the new assistant had had no personnel administration experience, she had a good record as an administrative assistant and seemed eager to work in the personnel field. Over a four year period, the assistant director had increased her scope of responsibility to include recruiting management people for the company's division heads. Formerly, each division recruited its own people, but the assistant director had convinced division directors that she could help in recruitment and preliminary screening. Increasingly, division heads and other executives asked her to find management people to fill job openings.

As the assistant director became more active in working with division heads and their staffs, the director became concerned that executives were asking his assistant for help and not coming to him. He suggested to the assistant director that she share this work with him, but she was reluctant to comply because she felt that the executives had confidence in her and not in her boss. The director and the assistant director then had a number of acrimonious exchanges. The director wanted the assistant director to sign a statement outlining the principle of shared responsibility for executive recruitment, but the assistant director refused. She proposed, as an alternative, that she should run the department and recruit for the divisions while the director should concentrate on external matters such as community relations.

The director believed that the conflict could easily be resolved if Holden would issue a directive outlining the responsibilities of the director and the assistant director following the content of the document the director had asked his assistant director to sign. The assistant director also believed the conflict could be resolved if Holden were to appoint her as the director of personnel administration, a job she felt she could perform more ably than its incumbent. She had presented this view to Donald Holden and he asked her what she thought should happen to the present director. The assistant director responded that he should be designated as the assistant. She expressed confidence in her ability to get the director to work cooperatively and amicably as her subordinate.

The director and assistant director were barely on speaking terms. Divisional executives became reluctant to bring work to the personnel department sensing the prospect of being caught in the middle of a battle between the two executives. The director felt under pressure to keep close to what was going on in his department while the assistant director resented his "looking over my shoulder and wanting to be involved" in her activity. The director believed he was being pushed out of his job. The assistant director believed that the director was not doing his job and that he felt under siege only when he observed what his assistant was able to accomplish, particularly in providing recruiting services to the divisions. Individually, the director and the assistant director believed the conflict would be resolved once Donald Holden, the chief operating officer, made a decision to name him or her, respectively, to be in charge of the personnel department.

COMMENTARY

Nothing amuses me more than observing people, whether in a class or not, wrestling with so-called action questions. What should Donald Holden do this Christmas season as the director and his assistant go at it in their dispute over the management of the human resources department? All I can say to that question is that I would fire the assistant director on the theory that there is a moral problem in this case that supercedes the host of practical questions it raises. This moral question poses no special intellectual problem. In my view few action questions pose a significant intellectual problem. There may be dilemmas, such as do you really want to fire the assistant, who by all measures of *her* action as assistant showed initiative, competence, the ability to learn, and, moreover, met the test of the marketplace: the division heads and other managers she supported as a staff executive were completely satisfied with her work. To add insult to injury, or so it would seem, firing her would leave the department in the hands of a man who seemed to show little initiative and outreach in supporting line executives.

My reaction to these dilemmas is simply to acknowledge them, but to place the moral question as the governing issue that would determine my decision to fire her. It is morally unsupportable to undermine one's boss, even if he (or she) is lazy, not measuring up, lacking in expertise, or whatever the shortcoming. If I could not tolerate working for such a boss, and I doubt that I would be as tolerant as she, I would probably leave the job. But before it came to that, I would take my boss into my confidence. I would describe the initiatives I thought *we* should take in adding to our support of management. I would (or hope I would) enlist his cooperation and enthusiasm for the project, get his advice and help, and, in general, create a collaborative instead of an antagonistic relationship growing out of my desire (not so hidden) to be in business for myself.

If I were Holden, I would establish the importance of this moral question by firing the assistant director. I would then begin to worry about my human resources department, and wonder whether I had the right person in the director's job. What would worry me especially is the placement of responsibility on someone with as little professional training and experience as the assistant director. It is wonderful to observe how rapidly she could learn, but as admirable as this quality is, what really did she bring to her job in the way of professional background, experience, and competence? I would ask myself, "What is going on here with the director? Is he professionally up to the standard we need in a field that is getting more rather than less complicated?" These and other questions would be on my agenda following my decision to meet the moral issue head on.

Having said all this, and I know there is plenty of room for disagreement, which is why case discussions get so lively, let me come back to a concern of mine as we began to consider the Marigold case. What is so complicated and so intellectually challenging in the "action" questions? My answer is little or nothing. You and I can engage one another for a long time discussing the dilemmas of being practical, of trying to solve day-in-and-day-out the myriad problems life in an organization presents. The real question for any executive is this: How do you frame the issues facing you so that you can *learn* from experience? What teachers should be doing in their classrooms is less manipulating the students to "keep them interested" and more engaging this job of enabling managers to learn from experience.

To enable in this direction is to provide experience with a theory. And as you well know by now, my theory of choice when it comes to human relations in organizations is psychoanalysis.

To me the intruiging problem the Marigold case poses is the way unconscious conflict becomes an interlocking event. The director appears to be overwhelmed by his own passivity. His conflict over his passivity appears to center on the woman, the object of his fears, I would say, more than his desires. How does he characteristically present this conflict to the world at large, or to anyone who is interested enough to pay attention? He is like a moth inevitably drawn to the flame, which will end up destroying him. He appears to be in the grip of a compulsion to repeat his problematic experience, to give an independent life to his aggravation over the woman, the mysterious and fearful object.

Now I am not a traditionalist who believes that men should be active and women passive in all matters of relations between the sexes. To live a decent and productive life, men and women must be both active and passive, whether we are talking about sexuality (and I mean the real stuff) or work. But the image of what is passive and active tends to blur, particularly in this case as in many others in life, including my airplane companion's problems with her "love life." For reasons difficult to fathom, (unless one understands the workings of unconscious mental life) active and passive take on multiple and nefarious meanings that are difficult to shake off.

Examine for a moment this same problem, the balance between active and passive modes, in the life of the assistant director. In an admirable way, she became different in her family, the only one among her siblings who managed to make a break from her past, to build a different life for herself. It takes a lot of aggression, which underlies the active mode, to accomplish what she had in her life. But unfortunately, she had to go it alone. Her marriage failed, and she was raising two children by herself, also an admirable accomplishment, one requiring a great deal of courage and resourcefulness. Oddly enough, she tells us that her daughter shows the same aggressive qualities. On the other hand, her son needs bucking up. Is this configuration an accident? Or, does it reflect the way psychological conflict passes from one generation to the next?

In the Marigold case, two individuals with mirroring conflicts come together to enact not just an organizational problem, but a lifelong and yet-to-be-solved personal problem of the relationship between the sexes.

Interestingly enough, the senior executive in this case, Donald Holden, is drawn into this lifelong conflict in ways that he does not perceive, let alone understand. I suspect that his inactivity while the problem between the two antagonists appeared and heated up related to a passive trend in his personality that served him no purpose. Passive trends can be useful; properly applied, they encourage observation and reflection. In the end they generate creativity because they encourage thinking, which ought to be the prelude to acting. Something appears out of balance, not only in the case of the two antagonists, but also in the case of the senior executive.

Return for the moment with me to the idea of the "action question." As I have indicated, the typical action question is, "What would you do if you were (so and so) to solve the problem of (whatever it is)?" I'm convinced this question and others like it are trivial. As I have stated, in the forms in which they typically appear, they present little intellectual challenge. Moreover, if they persist and remain on the agenda, it suggests that something has gone awry, as I have shown in my interpretations of the Marigold case. And as in most cases when life goes awry, accept the information that it is time to look past your nose, to deepen the inquiry, and to use all the theory at your command to help you see what is going on.

IDENTIFICATION WITH THE UPPERDOG— GENERAL AUTOMOTIVE SUPPLY

Let's shift perspective slightly as we approach this case study. We have been considering the problem of rivalry—where one or more people covet the same position or object. If I have been convincing up to now, you should be prepared to entertain the notion that, probably, no rivalry exists *de novo*, without precursors, without some marker that forces individuals implicated in the rivalry one way or another to face their history. If this idea depresses you, take a second look. The fact that we are carriers of history, our own especially, creates opportunity. For example, there is opportunity to learn from experience, to see the world through different lenses, to overcome the boredom of simply following blindly a decision model that could be inaccurate.

The General Automotive Supply case revolves around its chief executive, Maurice Fortier. It would be fair to say at the outset that Fortier settled for himself the problem of rivalry, in this case two or more individuals coveting the same power base, by manipulating key subordinates into conditions of psychological dependency. On the surface, he appears to epitomize the image of a strong leader. Strong he is without a doubt. But is he a leader? Turning the question around, is he really a manager, and is his idealization of management a fairly complicated and deeply ingrained response to his own personal problems with rivalry and, perhaps, envy?

If you have not already become familiar with the distinction between managers and leaders, take the time to locate and read "Managers and Leaders: Are They Different?" This essay appeared in the *Harvard Business Review* (May-June, 1977). It will help you engage the question of how the uses of power serve as mechanisms for ordering one's life and relationships with others, as well as controlling one's inner world. This notion of regulation and control, (another way of describing the concept of psychological defense) suggests that one of the uses of power is to create a structure that is addressed simultaneously to the reality of the world as one sees it, and the reality of one's psyche as one experiences it. These two realities should be mutually enhancing. Unfortunately they often work at cross purposes, locking the power holder into rigid patterns of behavior to avoid changing his or her world view and inner reality.

The General Automotive Supply case is subtle. There will be aspects of Fortier's character and behavior that you will find admirable; other qualities in the man will put you off. Instead of reacting either favorably or unfavorably, suspend judgment for a time so that you can answer the question: What makes this man tick and who are his self-determined protagonists and antagonists?

GENERAL AUTOMOTIVE SUPPLY COMPANY

Monsieur Maurice Fortier, for 15 years the president of General Automotive Supply Company, was recognized in the business community as a strong leader whose image was closely associated with the prosperity he had implanted in the company. He was a vivid example of one who seized opportunities to express himself in the service of organizational purpose. Fortier's relationship to the organization can be traced back to the conditions existing when he took over the company, the type of organization he had built around himself, the nat-

This case was prepared by Research Associate Pierre Laurin under the supervision of Professor Abraham Zaleznik. Copyright © 1987 by the president and fellows of Harvard College.

ure of his personality, and his ideas about managing a corporation. A description of his activity in the company is presented here to provide a basis for analysis of one man's selective orientation toward a particular style of management.

COMPANY HISTORY

The General Automotive Supply Company (GAS) was a Canadian wholesale company operating in the automotive parts and surplus industry. It was founded in 1924 by Monsieur Lucien Beauregard.

The company grew steadily and slowly from 1924 until 1935, when Beauregard initiated a program of rapid expansion. After World War II this expansion caused serious financial difficulties since, according to many executives, the company had not been able to control its relatively widespread activities. One of the largest Canadian banks, which ranked as a major creditor, assigned one of its officers to review the operations of the company. It then formed a committee to supervise policy and operations and to remedy the company's financial problems. Finally, to forestall liquidation, Beauregard resigned from active management, placed his stock in a trust as a guarantee to the creditors, and agreed to the naming of a new president. The committee selected one of its members, Maurice Fortier—a company vice president—as the new president of General Automotive Supply.

Fortier had entered the company in 1940 after obtaining an M.A. degree in commerce. In his first assignment he supervised accounts payable, including the routine clerical work. After three years in this position, he began a study of accounting practices for store operations which gave him considerable familiarity with store problems. His investigations focused on the conditions under which certain stores lost large sums of money while others were performing well. He made a number of recommendations which came to the attention of the president.

When the Automotive Electric Systems Company was bought in 1945, Beauregard offered three opportunities to Fortier: First, he could become special secretary to the president. Fortier refused this job because in his opinion it lacked opportunity for personal initiative. Second, he was offered the position of sales manager. He refused because he felt that he lacked experience in sales and marketing, and that the personal risk was too high in the light of his inexperience. Third, he was offered the position of general manager of the Automotive Electric Systems subsidiary, which he accepted. Fortier believed that this company had good technicians but that it was weak in administration. He said, "I began to look into the operations of the company to find out where order and organization needed to be restored."

When Fortier left this subsidiary in 1950, it showed a good profit and increased sales.

In the meantime, Fortier had been appointed to the control committee, which included the founder and several representatives of the creditors, and in which he became very active. His suggestions centered upon restricting expansion and putting order into the company's activities, as, for instance, in the centralization of purchases. Based upon these experiences, the creditors, with the founder's approval, offered Fortier the presidency in 1950.

Fortier began to correct the problems that he considered responsible for the financial difficulties. He stopped the production of a mass of reports and figures, and introduced a new method of margin control by requiring store managers to show the purchase cost of each item appearing on customers' bills. He instituted close control of purchases and inventories, with the aim of reducing working-capital requirements. He even took measures to change the behavior of office personnel.

Fortier had another issue to deal with after becoming president: his relations with the founder's family. Beauregard had eight children. Two sons seemed initially interested in a career in the business. Fortier encouraged this, but insisted they earn their positions through demonstrated competence. He urged them to start at the lower positions and to work their way to the top—provided their abilities justified advancement. The two sons did not enter the business, but instead worked in other ventures.

Beauregard died in 1955 and distributed his shares of stock equally among his eight children. The family continued its representation on the board of directors and, according to Fortier, maintained confidence in his leadership in the light of his successful record.

Fortier stated that he recognized the stockholders' privileges, but not at the expense of good administration. As an example, Fortier understood a shareholder's efforts to help friends by requesting special consideration for them as potential suppliers, but told the shareholders to address this type of request only to him personally and not to his subordinates. Fortier said:

> I told the family I was ready to pay attention to their requests and make a decision on the basis of what I judged was best. If they did not agree, well, it was their business. They were perfectly entitled to administer it themselves if they wished. I was pleased with this job, but I did not need it. I was perfectly independent and could go elsewhere.

As of 1967, only two of Beauregard's children were members of the board of directors. The creditors' representatives had been replaced by businesspeople with experience in a variety of fields; one company officer, Gene Hart, was also a member of the board.

POLICY AND PLANNING

Each year Fortier called in his top executives for a two day session to discuss the company's general orientation. The industry was undergoing competitive changes which made things far more difficult for wholesalers like GAS. The big automobile manufacturers attempted to capture a greater volume of the aftermarket business, edging out some of the independents. They began to "round out" their brand names on original equipment to include any make of car. They had also introduced longer warranties on cars in order to keep the motorist at their dealers' garages. Mass marketers, such as department stores and oil companies, began to invade important segments of the aftermarket and tended to bypass middlemen.

Fortier recognized these dangers but saw many possibilities for innovations in the unaffected sectors of the industry. Very much aware of how loosely certain industry practices were performed, he decided to develop specialized services that competitors could not easily duplicate. His market coverage and his capacity to manage large inventories of various auto parts were used to group and distribute European car parts across Canada.

Most of the competitive developments affecting the whole industry were at the retail level; these included service bays in department stores, expanded service stations, and more business for car dealers from auto manufacturers. For the moment Fortier discarded the idea of opening retail stores or service centers to the motorist since he did not think he could better the service already rendered in this field by professionals. He had opened a truck repair center because in that case he could provide highly specialized services.

In seeming contradiction of the independent middleman's shrinking role, Fortier was interested in developing distribution warehouses. He believed that despite changes in the industry there would always be a need for an organization with a large assortment of auto parts readily available. To accomplish this, the existing warehouses began to develop business with independent wholesale stores in addition to their GAS captive outlets.

ESTABLISHING A WAREHOUSE

The following describes the planning process for the establishment of a warehouse on Canada's west coast and a problem concerning the sales forecast that emerged from it.

Gene Hart, head of the warehousing subsidiary (GAW), had sponsored the project. British Columbia on the west coast was the third most important market for automobiles in Canada—after Ontario and Quebec—and enjoyed a fast-growing economy. Distances between cities were large, and wholesalers were remote from the manufacturers concentrated in the east. There was already a company operating a distributing warehouse and wholesale stores in the province, but Hart was convinced there was room for GAW. Conversations with wholesalers in the area persuaded him that chances to meet competition would be better if the company started by offering the whole array of company products than if it progressed piecemeal. This contrasted with the Toronto warehouse (which started by supplying only the GAS stores) and the eastern maritime warehouse (which specialized in certain lines).

Hart's plans had been accepted, and a large building had been bought. The purchase was considered a bargain by Denis Tremblay, vice president of technical services, after a trip to evaluate the deal. A former manager of the competing company in the west had also been hired as future manager.

While the treasurer was visiting Toronto, the president spoke with Tremblay. The subject was the space allotted for each product line:

Fortier: Well, Denis, I haven't made all the computations you have, but it seems to me that you're planning a lot of space for mufflers.

Tremblay: You needn't worry. Profitability was the base of all my computations, and the people in Toronto assured me that the man in charge is the sort to play it close to his chest. Marcel [the treasurer] is with them now to prepare the budget.

Fortier: [Grinning] Ha ha! The guys over there *will* find we're not bumbling ahead with our eyes shut.

On his return from Toronto, the treasurer expressed concern about the sales forecast. First, the diversity of products to be carried put the break-even point rather high. He was also worried about Hart's market penetration forecast. He anticipated difficulties in realizing the sales figures proposed by Hart, considering that these sales would consist exclusively of new business with new customers.

A few days later Fortier expressed his feelings with his usual candor about the situation reported by the treasurer:

> We've moved backwards in this whole business. We should have done a market survey first. Now it's too late. We thought we had a market survey, but in fact we did not. We did not proceed very intelligently about this business.

Fortier then explained his belief that they had a market survey:

> We founded our estimate on our general basis of evaluation such as the number of jobbers over there, the talks we had with manufacturers, and so on. I let Gene Hart enthuse me. He's not a scientific sort of guy. We needed other sales measurements than those we had. There's no reason to get nervous, however. I would apply drastic measures if I thought we had made a mistake, but we are not fundamentally mistaken. We'll simply have to work harder than expected on the market penetration. Fortunately, our big competitor also operates wholesale stores in the area, and he competes with his own customers. We hope to take advantage of that situation.

Exhibit 1

General Automotive Supply and Its Subsidiaries

4 Companies	8 Warehouses	92 Stores	70 Machine Shops
General Automotive Supply (GAS)		59 Stores covering the Province of Quebec	52 Machine Shops: 47 General 5 Specialized
		19 Stores covering the western part of Ontario	
		5 Stores covering the Ottawa region	
General Automotive Warehousing Company (GAW)	5 Warehouses: Montreal,Quebec, Toronto, Ottawa, Eastern Maritimes		
Automotive Electric Systems Company (AES)	1 Warehouse: Montreal	8 Stores spread across the Province	18 Specialized Machine Shops
		1 Warehouse and Store, Montreal (Tool and Equipment Division)	
European Automotive Products Company (EAP)	2 Warehouses: Montreal Toronto		

EXECUTIVE RELATIONSHIPS

The General Automotive Supply Company and its three wholly owned subsidiaries operated eight warehouses and ninety-two wholesale stores from headquarters in Montreal. Exhibit 1 shows the distribution of the company's activities for each corporate entity.

The top management of GAS and its subsidiaries consisted of seven executives reporting to Fortier. (The allocation of responsibilities among top management personnel is represented in Exhibit 2.) Although the company had no prepared formal organization chart, the exhibit summarizes information provided by top executives.

Exhibit 2

Organization Chart

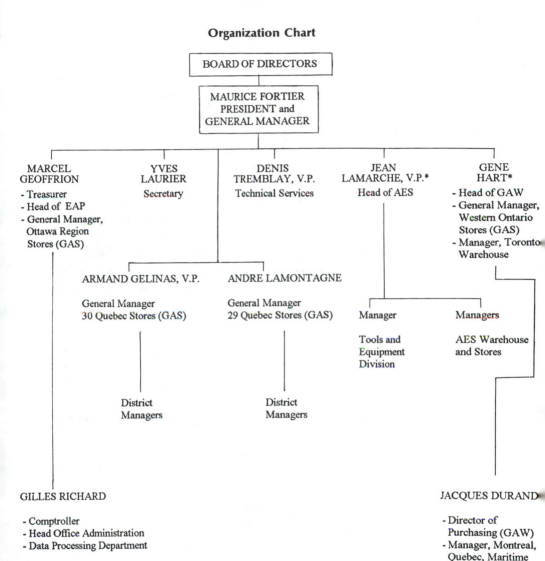

BOARD OF DIRECTORS

MAURICE FORTIER
PRESIDENT and
GENERAL MANAGER

MARCEL
GEOFFRION

- Treasurer
- Head of EAP
- General Manager,
  Ottawa Region
  Stores (GAS)

YVES
LAURIER

Secretary

DENIS
TREMBLAY, V.P.

Technical Services

JEAN
LAMARCHE, V.P.*

Head of AES

GENE
HART*

- Head of GAW
- General Manager,
  Western Ontario
  Stores (GAS)
- Manager, Toronto
  Warehouse

ARMAND GELINAS, V.P.

General Manager
30 Quebec Stores (GAS)

ANDRE LAMONTAGNE

General Manager
29 Quebec Stores (GAS)

Manager

Tools and
Equipment
Division

Managers

AES Warehouse
and Stores

District
Managers

District
Managers

GILLES RICHARD

- Comptroller
- Head Office Administration
- Data Processing Department

JACQUES DURAND

- Director of
  Purchasing (GAW)
- Manager, Montreal,
  Quebec, Maritime
  Warehouses

---

*   All the Executives worked at the head office except Jean Lamarche, who operated
from a different building in Montreal, and Gene Hart, who was located in Toronto.

The president was at the head office about two-thirds of the time. He came in about 8:30 in the morning and worked in his office throughout the day, going out only occasionally to see an executive. Once he came in, he would look over the papers on his desk and ask for explanations from or give orders by telephone to his subordinates. Sometimes he asked them to come in to discuss the matter with him. He would then call in one or two additional executives if he judged the issue warranted it. He was easily reached by his executives by telephone.

The various administrative issues were dealt with by meetings with the persons concerned, rather than by written reports. For example, when the vice president of technical services was asked if he was preparing reports on the different studies he was undertaking for the president, he answered, "No, I'm not. He wouldn't have time to read them, and I wouldn't have time myself to write them."

All the executives were unanimous in insisting, however, that a person had to be well prepared before discussing a matter with the president. The following remark by an executive is typical:

> The idea is to arrive with a layout of arguments for and against the matter under discussion: one-two-three-four. You have to be well prepared to discuss things with him. He will not tolerate any weakness. If there is something amiss, he will send you back to study the question until you come perfectly up to the mark.

Fortier himself had statistical records for almost any matter to be discussed. He would often, before or during a meeting, take out a record from the files and return it immediately after using it. He did not let documents pile up, and his desk was always clean of papers. One morning, while clearing his desk, he explained, "I hate to see a clutter. I spend my time pushing out papers."

Fortier expressed some aversion to group meetings:

> I don't like to work in group meetings. It is a waste of time. There's always one personality who dominates the meetings, and the others are inhibited. You can't shake them or tell somebody in the presence of others, "What you're saying does not make sense." When you discuss things with somebody in particular, you can know what he thinks of the situation. If he's reticent, you can get him to say what he thinks by direct questions. You can give him your opinion frankly, without running the risk of hurting him in the presence of others.

The following episode describing a decision-making activity involved the president, Denis Tremblay, and Philippe Nantel, head of the data processing department.

The First Meeting

The matter supposedly to be considered at the meeting was Nantel's salary. It turned out, however, that the discussion focused on department structure for the coming year. Fortier first inquired if Nantel was on schedule according to a timetable of the unfinished steps in the present phase of the process. As there was some delay, Nantel explained at length what had been done since their last meeting on this issue. Conversation was interrupted by phone calls, and Nantel took the opportunity to talk about personal matters with Tremblay. After a few questions, Fortier appeared satisfied with the explanations.

Fortier: Fine! That's all right then. Now let's talk about the department organization for 1967. When we're all set with the theoretical part of this work, what will we do? We have computer programs which provide a ready-made logic with which to organize our operations. We will work within the framework of these programs, but corrections will have to be made. Now what will we do with the department? What will we do with Venne and Duval?[1] Or if you'd rather, what can we do without them?

Nantel: We've made up programs ourselves in the past.

Tremblay: I was wondering if the best way to proceed wouldn't be to go by outside contracts and fix exact deadlines.

Nantel: If a major problem comes up, we're better off going outside.

Fortier: [To Nantel] Tell me, what does your work actually consist of? See to it that machines operate all right? Integrate machines and people? What is it?

Nantel: So far I've focused especially on inventory.

Fortier: I know you like that.

---

[1]Jean Duval, assistant to Nantel and former head of the department, and Guy Venne, computer analyst and programmer.

Nantel: For instance, when the machine goes wild over inventory control, I locate the trouble and make the necessary adjustments. Now with the new programs, the accounting system will be integrated with inventory control. This will involve Richard [the comptroller].

The president had listened attentively, but now interrupted on a note of disapproval:

Fortier: Duval cannot function in these areas. What I want from you is for you to tell me who in the long run will get the programs done. These will be small programs. Will it be necessary to pick up someone from outside each time, or will we have someone here on a full-time basis? If we have somebody in permanently, he's the one to take care of that. The question now is what will we do? Venne happens to be here at the moment, but we'll be losing him. He's good—very good, in fact. He's extremely capable in mathematics. If the work here starts getting trivial, he's going to look elsewhere. [Pointing at Nantel] If he should leave tomorrow, what would you do?

Nantel: It wouldn't be a disaster. I would go to Univac . . .

Fortier: You've got to do some thinking about that. Maybe we should start planning what he can do. Is that clear? I'm not day-dreaming now. [Raising his voice and speaking more quickly] There will come a point at GAS when we no longer need Venne. We have to know when that will be, tell him when, at what precise time. After that, if it's necessary to give him partial contracts, that's okay. Or maybe we'll need him permanently. This guy has to organize his life. Now, I think we need somebody inside to coordinate activities in the data processing department. But I'm the one who's doing all the talking. What about you?

Nantel protested and brought up objections as to what Duval could do.

Fortier: [Interrupting resolutely] Please! I'm not the one who will give Duval his instructions. [Lowering his voice] I understood that Duval was interested in mathematics, but that he's no good at it. You [Nantel] will have to organize all these details about your employees. I want you to make a chart of your department and let me know how you intend to organize it.

Nantel: Duval has started to set up programming. He's done well so far.

Fortier: I know he's been brought in to set up programs, like the payroll procedure for example. But from that to say that he can set up elaborate programs! . . . [Shrugs skeptically] I want some propositions about Monsieur Venne and the extent to which we can make our procedure sophisticated.

Nantel: Huh! . . . There are a number of improvements which could be made.

Fortier: [Impatiently] That's not the key problem. You're running in circles. The problem is that we need a man who's capable of understanding a program and who has enough talent to set up additional programs, even if they aren't so brilliant as Venne's. These programs could be shown to Univac before being used. The question is not to wait months to see if a guy [Duval] fits or not. So who will do it? It'll be you or somebody else, but it's time now to think about the way it will be organized.

The telephone rang. Tremblay and Nantel remained silent during the phone conversation. After Fortier hung up, Nantel spoke:

Nantel: Look, Monsieur Fortier, I have to take care of personnel, organize tasks, and make up schedules. If I have to do programming as well, I'll never be able to keep up.

Fortier: There's an important nuance to consider in this question. Is it you who will be in charge of the programs, or is it going to be a man who will supposedly work for you? It's a great advantage for a department head to be able to execute programs, since he's less vulnerable. In addition, you earn a bigger salary. If you depend on someone else, he can take the bit in his teeth and ask you for a raise.

Nantel: [Nervously] It's definite, Monsieur Fortier, that if Duval stays in the department, I cannot set up programs because he thinks that's his responsibility. On the other hand, Duval takes care of a number of things in the department. Without him I'd have trouble with other departmental tasks.

Fortier: Don't quote names. We need a guy to take care of the programs and make them work properly. You have to organize your department so this will be done. This is what I call a chart for 1967. So far everything has been fine. Now suppose we're through with delays, what's the next move? Toronto? Quebec? If you give it a lot of thought, you may decide to hire someone.

Second, the diagnostic period is over. We know our problem. We know how to solve it. The question now is to sell our managers on an idea which cost us $100,000. We won't have to start all over again elsewhere with the work we've done here. What we will have to do is to figure out *how* to make the appropriate changes. It'll be necessary to explain the system to each manager. One will say, "Business doesn't work that way, I have such and such a problem, I work under such and such conditions." We'll tell him, "Well, all right. We'll take that into account, but on the other hand, we're not going to set up a whole new program just for you." In sum, what has to be done is to implement the program elsewhere. I'd rather you took charge of that than Duval.

Nantel: I agree with you that the programs only need to be touched up and that the whole system is all right now. But to reconsider the logic of a program, you need time to think.

Fortier: If you take care of that, you make the link between the problem and the technique. We're actually avoiding the issue. If we don't have some guy in the GAS organization who can rescue us when something serious happens, I mean a guy who really knows the programs, then there's something wrong. [Stopping momentarily, he continued more softly, encouragingly] Do you see any possibility of thinking about that? Do you think it would help you make your recommendations about the organization chart? Do you see what I mean? I'm not asking you to wear yourself out, but I do ask you to consider quite clearly what we must do next.

The number one problem is that we cannot bind ourselves to Venne. He's a very capable man, but what remains to be done won't be much of a challenge to a man of his caliber. We're like the guy who would try to kill a fly with a shotgun. He won't miss it, but he will waste bullets in all directions. This is why we cannot think of Venne in the long run.

Fortier then explained in concrete detail the type of problems which would arise, underlining how Nantel could handle them. Nantel watched him while he was talking, shaking his head. When Fortier had finished, Nantel (obviously nervous—it showed in his voice) responded.

Nantel: Any programmer could do these things. You wouldn't have to pay the price of a man like Venne. The issue would be simply to tell him precisely what we want. Venne is the one who designed the system. Actually, I know our needs specifically and I could initiate his work. Now, if in your mind it's the programmer who's important, I'll give up the other matters and take up programming. If it's the total system which is important, that's another matter.

Fortier: I want you to tell me what is best for the GAS Company. My concern is the fear that a technician is leading the department because he's a good mathematician. *You* are in charge of the department and I want you to stay in charge. Prepare your recommendations for me on the department organization and I'll follow them up. What I want to avoid is having the programmer become the brain of the operations, and then come in one day for a couple-thousand-dollar raise, and have you tell me, "Give it to him, we need him to keep the system running." Programmers today are in demand everywhere. Just read the ads of job offers and the promised salaries. We can't afford to have "prima donnas" who can do any-

thing they please at GAS. Aren't I right? [Nantel nodded.] You see what I want?
Fine.

Nantel left the office and the president asked Tremblay to stay.

Fortier: He seems pretty worried.

Tremblay: I think he's concerned about the problem raised by Duval. If he [Nantel] became programmer, it would cut the floor out from under Duval's feet. I don't think Nantel is interested in doing programming.

Fortier: I don't want him to do programming at any price. It seems to me I told him that very explicitly. What I don't want is prima donnas within the place. As to the salary question, I'd prefer to wait to see what he will do.

Tremblay: You have to be careful with him. Sometimes he flies off on a tangent and it's hard to bring him back.

Fortier nodded and began to discuss something else. After Tremblay had left the office, the president said (referring to Nantel):

I want him to take the initiative and solve his problem himself. Men have this tendency to define problems and then think they've solved the problem by defining it. Yet that's only the beginning. It's a problem I often have with my subordinates.

One day later, Nantel revealed that after leaving the president's office he had spent a lot of time thinking about the issues raised at the meeting. He admitted he had been careless in letting himself be bound too much to one man (Venne). He described four alternative solutions to the problem raised by the president. Each represented a different combination in the planning of his own time and in the use of Duval's, Venne's, or an outside programmer's services. He would propose to hire a programmer from outside and to use Duval somewhere else at the head office. He would meet Venne himself and let him know that the future problems of the company would not require his services. He said, with some regret, "I admit this is a rather drastic solution, but I'm afraid that's the only possible one for the good of the company."

He enumerated without hesitation the reasons for his choice, and gave a thorough description of how he conceived the division of labor between a programmer and his department head. He then explained why he thought he had the qualifications to direct a programmer and why his assuming the functions of both department head and programmer would be detrimental to the company and to himself, even if he could do programming. Asked why he had not brought up these considerations at the meeting with the president, Nantel reflected:

> Well . . . I don't know. I couldn't. Maybe today I can take a cold, hard look at them and analyze them better. When I left my boss's office yesterday, I was really upset. These things boiled around in my head all night . . .
>
> One of the things I didn't like yesterday and which really offended me is that the boss seemed to imply that my salary could be reduced if I didn't combine both jobs. This I just will not accept. I was depressed after the meeting, but not discouraged. I'm aggressive by nature.

THE SECOND MEETING

A second meeting took place two days after the first, with the same people. Nantel had met Tremblay a few hours before the meeting. Tremblay was the first to arrive at the president's office.

Tremblay: Nantel is quite concerned. He seems very disturbed at the idea of combining the jobs of programmer and department head.

Fortier: Why should he be disturbed? It's the result of our discussion the other day. He didn't understand?

Tremblay: Well . . . maybe that's it. I'm sure myself that I fully understand. It's about this programming question. I'm wondering if we understand enough about what makes up programming. It's a matter which requires a lot of time and attention, but. . . . [Nantel came in before he could finish his sentence.]

Fortier: If you would excuse me for a moment, it won't be long. I have some letters to read.

He read the letters on his desk while Nantel explained to Tremblay the content of a handwritten report he had prepared on the matter to be discussed. The president rubbed his hands, as though anticipating something very satisfying.

Fortier: To the attack, men! [Pointing to Nantel] Where are you going to begin?

Nantel: I begin?

Fortier: All I know is that I don't.

Nantel: Okay then. Let's say there are two problems.

The telephone rang. Nantel reread his notes during the call (five minutes) and then continued.

Nantel: I was saying, there are two problems. In fact there are three. The first is the programming question; second, the problem of Jean Duval; and . . .

Again the telephone interrupted the conversation for two minutes.

Fortier: Excuse me. One would swear it's on purpose.

Nantel: [Laughing nervously] I don't have a fourth problem.

Since there was no reaction to his statement, he went on, wearing the same uncomfortable smile.

Nantel: It's just that after the first phone call, I had one more problem. [With more self-assurance] I would not favor the alternative of taking on programming myself in addition to what I already have to do. I have developed sufficient understanding of the programming field to let me work with someone other than Venne. We still have some work to complete on inventory problems. I think when we've finished up the inventory programs, we'll no longer need Venne.

      In the present situation, even though I'm not the one who wrote the programs, I'm the one who gives the instructions to do so. I know what to ask from a program and what to do with it. I also know how to work with another programmer. It would not be profitable to have an ace like Venne in programming since I can control the process myself.

Fortier: This is precisely why I want a guy who knows programming to be in charge of the department. Otherwise, the programmer can tell you that X hours are necessary to establish a program. If you aren't in a position to control the background on which it is based, you're completely dependent on him.

Tremblay: [Nodding at Nantel] He knows what he wants from a programmer. He knows the equipment. If he's in doubt about the time required, he can always consult Univac. They will help him. If this is the only problem . . .

Nantel: [Continuing in the same tone] When I speak of exerting control . . .

The telephone interrupted for another two minutes.

Nantel: There is actually a control problem with Venne. At the last pay, he had an 88-work-hours claim, and he spent only 35 hours here. I'm obliged to place complete confidence in his claims for the time spent working at home.

Tremblay: We certainly lack control on this point.

Fortier: That's what I've been telling you: a guy must know the field in order to exert control.

Nantel: He tells me he's worked 53 hours at home. I have to believe it's true.

Fortier: [Softly] Nothing prevents your telling him, "From now on, all the work has to be done here." It's true he hasn't much time left here. And even if he works here, it isn't certain you can control his activities. These guys have a talent for finding problems; they don't lack imagination. But this is secondary. The main point is, do you have to be responsible yourself for these problems or not? Personally, I believe that the crucial point is knowing whether or not you will be under the dominance of someone else's expert knowledge. Don't forget that you have only a single man working with you. It's different from having 15 specialists working with you. If one defects, you can turn to the 14 who remain. What bothers me is the scarcity which exists in this field. I know that the analysis surrounding programming is much more important than the programming itself. The problem is that for the next 15 years these guys [programmers] must be considered as well as you. Now, if you think you're capable of controlling the process, it's up to you.

Nantel: In the coming months I must focus on the analysis of inventory problems. [With a smile] Even though you do say I like that.

Fortier: [Seriously] Why do I say you like that?

Nantel: You said that last time. [Becoming serious] This analytic activity represents a lot of work, and I'm doing my best to manage the department well.

Fortier: [In a soft, encouraging tone] My offer doesn't stem from the fact that you don't work enough. On the contrary, I find that you work *too* much. No; you see, my concern is that it will be more difficult for some time to have programmers than to have guys who will tell them what to do, even if the last task is more difficult. We've been pushed to the wall twice with specialists . . . [Raising his voice, he relates the two instances] So, I don't want any more of these prima donnas.

Nantel: If a programmer is really a prima donna, he will not stay at GAS because the problems to come won't be much of a challenge.

Fortier: That's all right. So in summary, what do you recommend?

Nantel: First, to engage a programmer when Venne finishes the inventory programs.

Fortier: Do you think you can interest a programmer in us in spite of the lack of scope?

Nantel: I discussed this with Venne without referring to any precise case. There are young programmers who are interested in gaining experience with these problems. Unless something happens to prevent it, Venne should leave in six months. We could hire someone a month before Venne leaves.

Fortier: What else?

Nantel: Actually, Jean Duval is a lot of help to me in accounting, while I focus on inventory problems. Once this stage is finished, the final result of my recommendations will be for Duval to leave and for the department to have an additional secretary.

Fortier: You mean, a programmer, Duval gone, and one more secretary. You'll feel better about that?

Nantel: Actually, Duval, Venne, and I get in each other's way.

Tremblay: [To Nantel] Concerning your effectiveness program on payroll, did you succeed in lowering the number of your personnel?

Nantel: We now have two fewer secretaries.

Fortier: Two fewer, eh? That's great. Now, is Venne on time according to what you saw this morning?

Nantel: He didn't come in this morning. He had to see a relative in the hospital.

Fortier: Tell me, what is your impression of him so far?

Nantel: [Hesitating] My impression . . . is that the delay . . .

Fortier: [Interrupting vigorously] Do you want to know my impression? It's that if you don't keep a close watch on him, he'll always be late. If you do keep a close watch, his pride will be hurt. This will excite him. [He pauses, then adopts a neutral tone] As for Duval's case, if we hire a programmer, we'll have to put him somewhere else.

Tremblay: I tried to place him somewhere at Univac, but it didn't work out.

Fortier: It didn't? Well, we'll try everything here. Maybe we'll find an opportunity. Think about it. You have time ahead of you. Well, I think that's okay.

Nantel nodded and left the office; Tremblay stayed to discuss something else.

MANAGEMENT PHILOSOPHY

Fortier's beliefs were an important part of his personality. The opinions he held about issues as general as education or as intrinsically organizational as training were closely related and formed a salient aspect of his life. His commitment to the company rested on a deep conviction that capitalistic organization represented the best of the imperfect systems to realize development of resources; his particular use of the power provided by the organization was grounded on strong moral and religious beliefs. Fortier was, in sum, a man who invested highly in something with which he chose to get involved, without ever committing himself to something in which he did not strongly believe.[2]

ATTITUDE TOWARD PEOPLE

Fortier believed that resources at an individual's disposal were numerous, but that most people preferred security to problematic undertakings. The possibilities of what an individual can do are extraordinary, but there are so few extraordinary individuals. People are afraid of change; they are afraid to take responsibilities. He believed that the majority do not really want to improve themselves if this requires effort: they don't want responsibility. They simply want a safe, secure job and someone to tell them what to do. It is a primary objective for many people in a business organization to protect themselves from risk, from being held responsible for anything which might go wrong. Yet they like to feel that their job is useful, that they contribute something. They like to feel that they are important and that the enterprise needs them in some way. The dependent person can be an excellent employee in a well-structured position, however; he works long hours, he is thorough, loyal, follows policies, and has few bad habits.

---

[2]M. Fortier's reflections are taken from a written lecture he delivered at a university and from general conversations.

Now I have here among my personnel some who are weak. Maybe it's my fault, too. You have to be modest in these matters.

ATTITUDE TOWARD MANAGEMENT

Fortier took pride in considering the GAS Company as a school. He believed in sending young recruits into the field to measure their skills against a wide variety of difficulties. He also believed in the permanence of human traits and dealt with the issue of employee evaluations and promotions accordingly. In order to avoid having employees develop expectations out of line with their capacity, he would insist that they be told where they stood in the company.

> For instance, if we see that X has reached the limit of his capacities, we should tell him at the review period: 'Well . . . you're all right in your present position, but I honestly don't think you can go further at GAS.' So the guy knows where he stands. Lack of ambiguity toward one's status contributes to peace of mind in work.

ATTITUDE TOWARD THE COMMUNITY

Fortier was devoted to many organizations with religious or purely philanthropic goals. He stated that there were other needs in life than the material, and he considered it his duty to invest time in what was not material. He also encouraged his staff to do the same. One of GAS's top executives who was sitting on the board of an institution for rehabilitation of ex-convicts narrated how he had taken a young man from the court, hired him, paid his bail when he got into trouble again, and gave him a second chance after a good reprimanding.

In addition to his attachment to the French Canadian community, Fortier also had numerous contacts with the English-speaking community. He was willing to use his influence to promote what he considered legitimate interests of the French-speaking group.

PERSONAL HISTORY

Fortier's report on his personal history stresses the importance of fighting in a life which presented so many obstacles and difficulties, but also acknowledges the support he received at home and the capacity he developed to organize an orderly attack on problems. He was the third child and eldest son in a family of seven children.

> The atmosphere at home was one of discipline, accompanied by a lot of love. My father was prone to anger, but it was an anger we accepted easily. He had a strong temper, having in sum the faults of his qualities. My two elder sisters were there to deaden shocks, as was my mother. Women are different from men in playing this sort of role.
>
> My father was in the middle-income bracket. We didn't lack money for essentials, but we could not afford to waste money on luxuries. We were not spoiled as children. I learned to know the value of money quite early.
>
> As a boy I spent a few summers in youth camps and there I learned to fight, not only physically, but psychologically as well. I went to English-speaking Irish camps where I, as a French Canadian, was in the minority. I learned to defend myself. I also became very involved in sports and participated in all kinds of activities. I liked to fight, but I also liked to get involved in well-organized sports, not disorderly games. I was an active participant in the organization of teams.
>
> After school I went to college and then to a university. I took part in a number of associations and was elected president of several student organizations. I was a delegate in Europe, representing a student association. I fulfilled my functions seriously and did not waste my time gossiping. I was also capable of enjoying myself. All in all, I can say that I had a happy childhood.

Fortier enumerated without hesitation the principles he learned at home:

> My parents both had good educations. I am speaking now of education, not necessarily of instruction. In fact, my father finished only the ninth grade, but he was the most learned man in the village at that time. My mother came from a background which laid more stress on instruction. She worked constantly and did not like to go out.

As for the principles instilled at home, first there was a horror of vulgarity. Everything which was not sane or in good taste had no place in our home. Then there was an advanced sense of civic duty. I have been taught how to live in society, to respect other's property, for example, or not to litter the highways. There was also a sense of orderliness. My father was always on time for anything he had to do. Finally, the dedication to work. This is the example I constantly had before my eyes.

Fortier regarded the education received at home as the most important factor in determining people's attitude toward work. He himself related his home experience to his actual attitude toward life and work:

I learned at an early age that life is tough. My father had become an associate in a manufacturing company and was an example of a man who made a career for himself under difficult conditions, but who had kept his desire to succeed, the attachment to what he was doing, and the energy to achieve his goal.

My father early made me understand how complicated are human problems. During the depression he was in charge of a manufacturing department, and people came to him with their problems, their fears, their jealousies. I remember I once proposed a drastic solution to get rid of these problems. He explained to me that things were more complicated than that. He made me understand that it is necessary to have a shelf position in the minds of people, a little like the soap salesmen who try to keep a shelf position in the supermarket.

In sum, my father had the proper qualities for a businessman. There is no question in my mind that given the choice between a father who is a farmer and one who is a businessman, I would be willing to pay 50 per cent more to have a father who is a businessman.

The desire for excellence and for good human relations are in my opinion the key factors guiding a man on the road to leadership. You have to want to become president to achieve it. Knowing is not everything; you have to want to know. This quality is not acquired through study.

ATTITUDES OF SUBORDINATES

In a study that was limited to the people in the head office at GAS, all executives were unanimous in mentioning at some point that the president was an outstanding man. He seemed to embody an achievement in which they were proud to participate. To many of the senior executives, Fortier's takeover had meant the start of a new career in a prosperous company. "Thanks to the president, we are now working for a company which is doing well. Fortier completed the founder's great ideas admirably. When he took the reins of the company, he used his experience to show us what needed to be done. We have been eager to follow him. The president is a perfectionist who is able to get the best out of each man."

Fortier also appeared to possess the strength of character that inspires admiring devotion—as illustrated in this comment by a younger executive:

> When I met M. Fortier to discuss possibilities of employment, I was immediately enthusiastic about him. To me, he was the ideal businessman as we conceive him as students. I did not have to deliberate long. I had debts, but it was not the economic side I considered first—not even the nature of the company's operations. I've been attracted by the leadership of the president.

The following comments by two subordinates illustrate how the same reported behavior from M. Fortier could provoke different reactions. One remarked:

> The degree of control to which I am subjected corresponds to my idea of what should exist. I have the opportunity to profit greatly from the president's experience and knowledge. He makes numerous suggestions and quite often he leads me to consider certain points I had not thought about. This does not come necessarily as an order, but as a suggestion about which it's necessary to think.

Another said:

> As you know, the boss has a strong personality. Unfortunately, this affects people's creativity negatively. They tend to take less initiative and they would rather work within the framework defined by the president. There is a lot of effort to decentralize—

even too much, as in marketing—but people can't help feeling the president is the one who dominates and takes responsibilities. At the head office the atmosphere is permeated by the president's personality. People are afraid of him. This restraint of creativity is the ransom we have to pay for profiting from an extraordinary man like Fortier.

Commenting on the issue raised by this last sentence, another executive attempted to explain how the president's assertive behavior affected certain types of subordinates:

> You will realize that the organization here is centered around one man. The boss, however, has a tendency to decentralize more and more. He is also becoming less intransigent. In the past there was a terrible fear of the boss around here. It was really the fear of God the Father. This was due, I think, to his strong personality.
>
> The result is that you tend to have submissive and docile subordinates. Is it the type of executive the boss really wants? I don't think so. I think, on the contrary, that he likes to have people who stand on their own two feet in front of him. The only thing is that his behavior transmits the message that he wants the contrary. But this depends a lot on the people with whom he is dealing.

Executives had to adapt to Fortier's style of interpersonal relations, however. According to one:

> The president thinks quickly and expresses himself directly. His suggestions are always good. He is sharp in his remarks, and if you make a mistake, you hear about it, but next time you're more careful. Thus he makes me think a lot before acting. I don't like to give him something which is not exact. On the other hand, he is a very busy man and expects quick as well as exact answers. I proceed more slowly and am not so hurried as he. This causes tension from time to time, but in general I could say that I made up my mind about this a long time ago.

The last excerpt exemplifies the mixed character of the feelings expressed at GAS, and points to specific reasons for one executive's displeasure and also for his attachments to the company:

You have here a company which is unique because of its extraordinary leader. He is difficult to work with since he is very exacting and has the great qualities and faults of a leader.

First of all, he pushes integrity to the extreme. For him one cent is one cent and one dollar is one dollar; it is yours or it's mine, there are no positions in between. He is intransigent but also extremely just. He tries to give to each what is due to him and does not indulge in favoritism.

He needs to know everything about the company and expects us to know everything as well. He regularly calls us during the day to inquire about details on this and that aspect of operations. To know that he can call you each half hour for precise requests and information about questions you might have temporarily forgotten puts a man under a lot of pressure. You must always be ready to answer all kinds of detailed questions. You must be prepared to argue, otherwise he doesn't like it. There is nothing he hates more, I think, than seeing someone surrender on a point without even bringing in an argument. This creates tension and puts pressure on a man. I don't think he realizes how much pressure he exerts on his staff. He's very severe on himself and so he is in turn on others.

The president works to be happy. His work capacity is extraordinary. He made a trip to England last year. He left on a Saturday afternoon, and came back Monday at eleven. On Monday afternoon he had people meeting with him in his office. You need an iron constitution to do that. He's beginning to be particularly worried about his health. He's afraid to hear about illness.

On the other hand, he's very humane. If you are tired, for instance, he'll send you on a holiday and pay for you to rest and recuperate. The door is always open for the guy who was absent because of illness. Sometimes he adopts a very tough attitude toward employees, sometimes the contrary. He wonders sometimes why you don't fire X in your department, while at other times if you mention you fired somebody, he'll express compassion for the victim. It reminds you of a grandfather's attitude toward grandchildren—not a father, but a grandfather. He'll tell you, "Maybe you went too fast, he has a family" . . . and so on.

You see that here a man is not a number. The atmosphere is very good. It is almost familial. If somebody is in trouble he is supported 100 per cent by the company. You always have somebody to whom you can commit yourself. Our offices are always open. If X [a vice president] next door, has some personal problems, he will drop by and we'll talk it over. The same is true for me if I have some problems. I'll discuss my worries and come out feeling relieved. I'll not see the things the same way after that. It's a little like a large family in which you impart your problems to your older brother. . . .

People sometimes ask us how we manage to continue working for a man as tough as Fortier. First, there is the fact that most of the executives have invested a lot in this company, and it would be difficult to start over again elsewhere. But there is also the fact that GAS is going forward and that the problems of the industry are extremely interesting. There is no routine here. There are always new things happening . . . . [A silent pause] Well! Who knows? Maybe we like to be hustled under an avalanche of work!

COMMENTARY

In introducing this case study, I suggested that Fortier is a strong man, but not a leader in the sense that I described leaders in the essay, "Managers and Leaders: Are They Different." Fortier appears relatively weak in the substance of the business. His acuity in marketing appears limited. For example, he remained detached from the decision to open a West Coast distribution center. The objectives for opening this West Coast warehouse were vague, as was the market research purportedly conducted to help decide whether this investment was sound and timely. In contrast, note Fortier's intense involvement in, and close supervision of, the organization of the company's computer operations. Admittedly, management control in GAS's business is very important. But why supervise this decision and enter into detailed review of the problem, the alternatives, and the recommended solution? Why remain detached in the marketing aspects of the business?

One explanation is that Fortier chooses to work on those problems in which he feels confident. His confidence extends from the technical issues of management controls (after all, that is his business background) to his ability to dominate his subordinates and to control their behavior. In contrast, he appears less confident in marketing, and less able, or willing, to dominate Gene Hart, who appears on the organization chart in Exhibit 2 as head of General Automotive Warehouses (GAW).

How Fortier achieves dominance is an interesting aspect of this case study. He creates uncertainty and ambiguity in the minds of his subordinates, especially among those subordinates who are located in the head office. His interchanges with Nantel, the head of the data processing department, clearly demonstrate that Fortier works hard at achieving psychological dominance of his subordinates. For example, he prevents Nantel from presenting his findings and recommendations in an orderly fashion by permitting frequent telephone interruptions. It is apparent that all Fortier need do to prevent telephone interruptions is to instruct his secretary not to accept calls while he is in a meeting. The effect, if not the purpose of the interruptions, is to keep subordinates in a highly stressful environment.

It is significant to note the presence of a third party during the meetings with Nantel on data processing. The head of technical services, Denis Tremblay, was present but seemed to have no role or direct involvement in the proceedings. Why was he present? To add further to Nantel's stress? To create more embarrassment in having someone witness his clumsy handling of Fortier's interrogation? Or was he there as Fortier's witness, and possibly as the transmitter of the image of Fortier as a tough, demanding, and unrelenting prober in solving business problems. Interviews with subordinates demonstrated the effects of a corporate mythology about Fortier as the paternal, stern, yet caring boss. This image of Fortier in the minds of his subordinates controlled their behavior. Fortier had no need to elaborate this image himself; key subordinates projected it based on the kind of behavior Tremblay witnessed.

Cursory examination of Fortier's organization chart (shown in Exhibit 2) generates some puzzling reactions. For a man concerned with order and control, the chart appears contradictory. Evidently, Fortier did not mind mixing functions that cut across line and staff responsibilities. His treasurer, Marcel Geoffrion, also headed the European Motor Products Company and the Ottawa Region stores of GAS, while continuing to have the corporate controller reporting to him. In turn the controller, who also had data processing reporting to him, seemed nowhere in evidence during the discussions about the reorganization of this department.

While Gene Hart was nominally in charge of purchasing, his subordinate, Jacques Durand, the director of purchasing, worked in the head office in Montreal while Hart worked in Toronto, suggesting that this important function came under Fortier's direct supervision, despite the organization chart.

One could conclude that Fortier simply cared little for the

significance of formal organization. While this interpretation appears warranted, it fails to throw light on what Fortier intended when he created an ambiguous formal organization.

In this case, the effect may well have mirrored the intention: to keep subordinates off balance and under stress by making their duties, responsibilities, and zones of influence ambiguous and overlapping.

We have to look beyond the actual behavior into Fortier's world view and personal history to grasp the significance of rivalry and his need to dominate others. A good starting point is to examine how Fortier came to power in GAS. You will recall that GAS encountered financial difficulties under the direction of the company's founder, who was an entrepreneur intent on expanding the business. The rate of expansion exceeded the ability to generate working capital and maintain bank borrowings. In came the banks and forced the founder to place his shares in escrow, remove himself from management, and relinquish power to Fortier, the banks' choice as the work-out man.

Fortier understood the nature of the company's problem. There was no shortfall of sales; the store locations were in favorable markets. The problem, he reasoned to himself, was to control margins, costs, and inventories in order to increase cash flow and diminish the pressure for additional working capital. Fortier was a clear thinker, and an expert in managerial controls. He succeeded in turning the company around, and in restoring ownership to the founder's family and heirs. At that juncture, the heirs decided to keep Fortier in office. After all, he had preserved their assets, and by choosing him, the family could avoid rivalry in determining who among the heirs should be given power. Fortier was the right man in the right place at the right time in the turnaround. While conditions had changed, family dynamics weighed heavily in maintaining Fortier's power base in GAS. He had accomplished what many power holders aspire to: he had reversed dependencies. The owners needed him, while he behaved as if he did not need them. It takes acuity in the ways of power for Fortier to have achieved this position of relative independence. It also took considerable self-esteem, or narcissism if you prefer, to have played out the game as he had perceived it.

Fortier derived his self-confidence from a coherent and strongly held world view, which, while it simplified reality, permitted him in his culture to function with a minimum amount of anxiety.

There are six key elements to this world view. First, there is the conviction that the world is chaotic and it is his job in life to bring order. Second, he is convinced that the world needs structure and that his abilities allow him to introduce structure. Third, the world presents obstacles, and he is accustomed to overcoming obstacles. Fourth, the world is divided into two populations: the few and the many. Fortier perceived himself to be one of the few and, therefore, presented with special opportunities as well as responsibilities. A fifth element in this world view places the many in a dependent position, while the few elaborate their sense of independence. Finally, as a sixth element, Fortier believed that he must keep people at a distance. As a corollary, he also believed that he could tolerate the lack of intimacy in his human relationships.

These six elements in his world view are reconstructed from his behavior as well as his self-reflections. They appear to be derived in part from his cultural background, and in part from unique aspects of his personal history. Obviously, the two are interrelated.

Fortier grew up in a family of French Canadians during a period in Quebec's history that preceded French nationalism, separatism, and cultural pride. The French Canadians were truly subordinate to the English Canadians in politics, economics, and opportunity for upward mobility. The land, the church, and a select few professions channeled the opportunities for young men (women counted for little in the world outside marriage and the family). Business was a residual choice for talented men who had no opportunities in owning land. Certainly corporate business, dominated as it was by the Anglo community, presented few attractive alternatives. To become a doctor, lawyer, and in the case of the youngest son, a priest, was the circumscribed world for talented young men during the time that Maurice Fortier grew up, attended school, and selected his life's work.

Fortier's choices in life were anomalous in the culture of French Canada of his youth. But this is not a surprising outgrowth of his personal history. His father steered him in the direction of business, and indeed, his father fostered an identification with English Canadians rather than French Canadians. His father sent him to an Anglo boys' camp, which must have tested his nerve and determination to survive in an alien environment. This experience produced a remarkable feeling of having overcome obstacles, of achieving independence, and gaining a sense of personal responsibility. Fortier's identification with the "upperdog" led him to detach himself from the values of his cultural group, yet he had no desire to assimilate within the Anglo community, a task that would have presented him with an obstacle impossible to overcome. Yet implied in his assertiveness and dominance of subordinates (all French Canadians, with the exception of Gene Hart) was a latent hostility and disdain for his cultural and ethnic group.

In his self-reflections, Fortier appeared unconflicted about his identifications. Largely because he remained with his group, and assumed responsibility for them, much as a father in relation to his children, Fortier could function free of guilt. Whatever disdain he felt for his fellow French Canadians would produce few guilt feelings because in fact he had not abandoned them. He enacted paternal responsibility in conformity with the elements of his world view.

Fortier did not appear to be a man struggling with envy. Ordinarily, an individual who identifies with the upperdog envies the group to which he aspires while disparaging the "underdog" of which he is a part. In Fortier's case, the lack of envy, at least on the surface, reflected his pragmatism. Not prone to waste his energy on matters outside of his control, Fortier had learned to live in the world as it was. Visions of what might be, which are so characteristic of leaders and so unavailable to managers, presented him with few opportunities for frustration, discontent, or painful awareness of the gap between what might be and what is.

Monsieur Fortier was a man fulfilled. He had overcome the painful dilemmas of rivalry. He was a successful father in his own house. The only possible fly in the ointment he had conjured up to smooth his way through life was the prospect of a change in the economic and competitive environment of his business, such as aggressive marketing on the part of automobile manufacturers to keep their customers coming back to dealers for aftermarket parts and service, or the competitive threat of mass retailers offering automobile maintenance and repair to their retail customers. There is reason to doubt Fortier's business imagination and herein lay the vulnerability to his intricately balanced formula for a life as a manager.

CAN A NICE GUY FINISH FIRST?—THE WATKINS AND WORSTER AGENCY

Immediately after World War II, a discernible shift occurred in how managers think about themselves. Led by university researchers in the human relations movement, managers came to believe that ideally a professional manager should be as concerned about people as about the tasks at hand, that he or she should be a person-centered rather than a task-centered executive. In conjunction with this new ideal, managers became interested in the techniques of communication, participation, and the democratic distribution of power. This era also saw a shift toward decentralization from the centralization that had characterized formal organizations of the pre-war period.

The "bull of the woods," the authoritarian boss, and the directive leader seemed outmoded. Practitioners and academics alike asserted the claim for this new image of the professional manager on pragmatic rather than on purely humanistic grounds. The growing conviction that supported democratic organizations assumed that people would be motivated to work hard if they felt they were an integral part of the organization. Their involvement would lead to innovation as well as higher productivity. After all, those

CHAPTER

10

closest to the task should be better able to fix things when they go wrong, and to accomplish the task more efficiently, than power hoarders several levels removed from the work.

This new movement countered the theories of scientific management, with its specialization of function and centralization of control. Yet the new breed of managers emerging from the depression of the 1930s and the agonies of World War II sincerely believed in the new democracy in corporate America.

Questions soon arose concerning the pragmatic foundation of power sharing and participation. Did these ideals really result in higher productivity and increased innovation? The evidence was conflicting, ambiguous, and in some cases negative. But perhaps the most disquieting evidence to appear suggested that there were some latent motives supporting the image of the new manager. A variety of hidden agenda indicated that the "nice guy" image screened some well-honed techniques of dissembling and manipulation. Furthermore, the new corporate democracy could be used, in conjunction with the special language of idealization and intellectualization, to deny or disguise one's own intentions. In other words, there is more than one way to skin a cat. Or, at the risk of mixing metaphors, "you attract more bees with honey than with vinegar." Managers were no less controlling under the new ideals than under the old. The goal was the same, but the methods had shifted. Be a nice guy, make people feel good about themselves, get them to like you, and above all divert their attention from reality toward a collective myth, enabling the manager to operate with a free hand.

A man, whom I have fictitiously named John Goode, ran the northwest office of the Watkins and Worster advertising agency. His story appears in the case study you are about to read. The Watkins and Worster case presents a detailed narrative of work and life in the agency under John Goode's direction. Do you believe that John Goode was a genuinely nice guy, sincere in his concern for people, in his warmth, humor, and unpretentiousness? Conversely, was he one of those wolves in sheep's clothing, who dissembled, manipulated, and controlled in the interest, perhaps, of protecting the agency, as well as his power? What are the risks and consequences facing the genuine nice guy? What risks and consequences face the manipulator disguised as a nice guy? If you are wondering what these questions have to do with rivalry, you will soon discover how

Exhibit 1

W&W Accounts in the Northwest City Office

Name of Account	Product	Relative Volume of Billing*
Conn Milk Company	Full line of dairy products and miscellaneous food products	11
John Fisher Company	Fisher Deviled Crab and other canned seafood	5
The Durifilm Company	Plastic packaging films	2
First National Bank	Commercial banking	1

*These volume figures give relative size of billings and not absolute dollar amounts. Illustrative in interpreting the volume figures, the Conn account was 11 times larger in dollar billing than the First National Bank account.

Source: Interview data.

vying for power dominated the flow of work in this agency. You will also discover what being a nice guy, sincerely or manipulatively, does to the underlying dynamics of rivalry for power. Here is John Goode's story.

WATKINS AND WORSTER AGENCY

Watkins and Worster (W&W), a large, well-established advertising agency, was headquartered in New York and had several regional offices. One of these, Northwest City, had been in existence for about a year, employed 26 people, and served four W&W accounts: Conn Milk Company, John Fisher Company, the Durifilm Company, and the First National Bank. Exhibit 1 describes these accounts' relative characteristics.

This case was made possible by the cooperation of a business firm which remains anonymous. It was prepared by Research Assistant Hal Spear under the direction of Professor A. Zaleznik. Copyright © 1970 by the president and fellows of Harvard College.

John Goode was account supervisor of all Northwest City accounts. Until recently, he had been the account executive on the First National Bank account as well. The Conn Milk Company account, supervised by George Lorenz with Bill Jones as associate account executive, was one of the major advertising accounts in size of billings of all companies located in the Northwest City area. Its advertising media were regional newspapers, TV, and radio. The Fisher account, with Marie Ayers as account executive, advertised mainly in national women's magazines. The Durifilm account, supervised by Bruce Fahey, placed advertisements mainly in packaging and food trade journals. The First National Bank account, also supervised by Bruce Fahey, advertised in Northwest City newspapers.

The W&W organization chart (Exhibit 2) shows the major functional divisions of the office. A client was normally served by at least an account supervisor and an account executive. Copy and art—the "creative" services—developed the individual advertisements, and the production department worked with outside suppliers and oversaw the production of film and radio commercials. The media department bought time and space. Although ultimate responsibility for the work on a given account rested with the account executive, the control department coordinated the detailed activities and collected cost information for each account. In the Northwest City office, a home economist, not assigned to any specific account, was expected to prepare food recipes for promoting various products. Any specialized promotion work, market research, and certain other minor functions were done in the appropriate New York offices.

THE FLOW OF WORK

The regular account work began with a marketing plan establishing the detailed outline of a sales program for each of a client's products. Produced largely by the account executive, but in coordination with the account group, the plan generally did not include the creative services content and had to be approved by both the New York office and the client.

Once this approval had been secured, the account coordinator wrote job orders for specific tasks and assigned time deadlines. The coordinator continued to check with individual departments to maintain schedules, frequently transmitted materials to and from var-

Exhibit 2

Organization of the Northwest City Office

ious departments, and worked with the account executives as problems arose.

As the time approached for a specific advertising campaign to begin, the account executive called an account group meeting, made up of the account executive, the account supervisor, a supervisor from each service—copy, art, media, production—and the account coordinator.

The W&W Operations Manual stated that "account group meetings should be called whenever *combined thinking* is likely to contribute constructive ideas." Further, account executives were responsible for calling the meetings, and supervisors of each of the service departments attended "primarily as specialists in their own fields, but should participate in the general discussion of account strategy."

According to George Lorenz, account group meetings in the Northwest City office were held with wider participation than in the New York office. Account group meetings in the Northwest City office usually included, in addition to the required people listed above, the following: other account executives if they were not busy with work on their own accounts; the copywriter, if working on the campaign being discussed; the home economist (at Fisher account group meetings); and the secretary of the account executive who was holding the meeting. Exhibit 3 presents selected data on those personnel in the Northwest City office who attended account group meetings most frequently.

There did not seem to be any formal rules or universal customs regulating what should and what should not be discussed during the meetings. Rather, it appeared to be up to the account executive to determine the agenda as well as the degree to which an idea should be worked out in the meeting or left up to the responsible individuals after the meeting. The frequency of meetings varied greatly, but a rough average for the Conn and Fisher accounts appeared to be about once a week; the Durifilm account group met less frequently; and the First National Bank account group met infrequently.

John Goode stated that his original decision to have frequent meetings with broad participation was based on a desire to inform the personnel in the office about the various phases of each account. He said, "The important thing is that these people feel they are a part of this group, that they see where they fit in, and that they see their work as important."

Exhibit 3

Data on Northwest City Office Personnel

Name	Position	Salary	Service with W&W	Age	Education (beyond high school)
ACCOUNT MANAGEMENT					
John Goode	Regional Manager, Vice President, and Account Supervisor	$65,000	1 year, 8 months	52	College
Marie Ayers	Account Executive	$45,000	1 year, 8 months	46	Secretarial school
George Lorenz	Account Executive and Vice President	$42,500	3 years, 4 months	34	College
Bruce Fahey	Account Executive	$33,000	1 year, 2 months	37	College
Bill Jones	Associate Account Executive	$34,000	1 year, 7 months	30	College
COPY					
Carlton Fromm	Copy Supervisor	$33,000	1 month	38	College
Dan Rittner	Copywriter	$30,000	1 year, 10 months	30	College
ART					
Phil Mascetta	Art Director	$35,000	1 year, 10 months	41	Art school
Jim Cooper	Artist	$20,000	1 year, 6 months	32	College
MEDIA					
Helen Fowler	Media Supervisor	$22,500	1 year, 6 month	35	Secretarial school
CORPORATE SERVICES–GENERAL					
Florence Langen	Office Manager	$18,500	1 year, 11 months	49	Secretarial school
CORPORATE SERVICES–CONTROL					
Mary Navin	Account Coordinator	$18,000	1 year, 8 months	31	Secretarial school
PRINT PRODUCTION					
Al Berklund	Production Manager	$23,000	3 years, 10 months	30	College
(PROMOTION)					
Doreen O'Mara	Home Economist	$15,000	6 months	28	College

Source: Company records. Salary information given to researcher by John Goode.

READINGS OF ACCOUNT GROUP MEETINGS

The material in this section was recorded by the case researcher. Before attending the first account group meeting, the case researcher received two descriptions of the custom of levying fines for the infringement of "ground rules." One came from Mary Navin, account coordinator:

> There is a system of fines. It's two dollars if you come late, one dollar if you interrupt the meeting by taking a phone call there, or one dollar if you're excused. And it's a quarter if you disagree with the account executive.

The other description came from Phil Mascetta, art director:

> It started a while back. They had it in another agency I worked at. Everyone seemed to be scrambling around at the meetings here. John or maybe George or myself might be late, held up by a phone call, perhaps, that would mean a few people would be sitting 20 minutes waiting. So we started the fine system, and it worked. Then we added to it for interrupting, contradicting, and so forth. Of course, we're not very consistent; we sometimes forget. But I really have to jump to it; since I started it, they jump on me if I'm late. I'd say all have contributed about equally to the kitty.

Excerpts from Meetings on March 12

On the morning of March 12, John Goode scheduled a short talk to the entire office staff, immediately prior to a Conn account group meeting scheduled for 10:00 a.m.

John: I've got two or three things I want to talk about this morning. [George's voice in background saying, "Quiet!"] I'll give you the good news first. A year ago you may remember that we were beaten out by Smith & Company[1] for the publicity and public relations part of the John Fisher account. They were hired and didn't deliver. Fisher examined their work side by side with our advertising contributions. Last week they fired Smith & Company and hired us. This will increase the size of our Fisher account by 50 per cent.[2] We're happy to be able to make this announcement right on the heels of having gotten Supermobile [an auto-

---

[1]A competitive advertising agency.

[2]Marie Ayers, account executive of the Fisher account, was out of town and absent during this meeting.

mobile account] at our New York office. This is *our* Super-mobile. That's about all I had to say, with one exception. We gave our Fisher presentation to the plans board in New York; our Conn plans too, but that didn't include the creative work, while the Fisher included both the marketing and the creative plans. The kudos which were sung down there have now made it necessary for us to produce this thing on a little more polished basis. It's to be circulated to all offices of W&W as an example of an excellent handling of an account; creatively, and in the use of research in the development of the creative work. So everybody that had a part in it, meaning everyone here, can be very proud of the fact that this is going across the country as a representation of W&W's best. And it comes from Northwest City, of which we are very proud. [John then talked for a few minutes of his plans to give a series of presentations to the whole office staff.]

Well, that's all I had this morning. I thought you'd want to hear the good news about our new piece of business. It should bring smiles to some faces around here.

George: How much do you want to fine him, Phil? He ran over two minutes. [Some laughter among general conversation.]

John: Everybody's here. . . .

George: [Interrupting] No, the thing is, I'm fining you, John, for delaying the meeting.

John: There's going to be an account group meeting so those scheduled for the Conn account can just stay where they are.

As the main group of people broke up, there was general talk in the room. George asked Doreen [the home economist] to stay for the meeting, although she ordinarily did not attend Conn account group meetings. After about two or three minutes, George started to open the Conn meeting. A notice had been circulated to the account group members concerning the agenda for the meeting. The agenda read: "Discussion of promotion campaign for Conn's Flavored Drink."

John: How long do you intend to take for this meeting?

George: We have a half-hour time limit.

John: O.K., fine, because I have a luncheon date.

George: You're welcome to leave any time.

John: Yeah, I know, but I don't want to have to pay for it. [Several laugh.]

George: To begin very quickly, yesterday at the Fisher account group meeting we discussed having a cross-ruff[3] promotion between Conn and Fisher in which we would band small cans of Fisher to half-pints of sour cream, and large cans to pints, to offer a combination for a dip. Fisher was quite interested in it, but in talking with the Conn sour cream product manager, he gave every indication that somewhere between 70 and 80 per cent of their sour cream sales are to Jewish people—not necessarily Orthodox Jews—but the feeling was that banding shell food and sour cream together would be an insult to some people.

Now, Conn felt that because of Fisher's domination of its particular market and good distribution, this would be advantageous to them, so they asked us to work up a cottage cheese/Fisher Deviled Crab promotion. That is, Conn has. This might very well be the fall cottage cheese promotion campaign. This would be very advantageous for Fisher. And I think it would be advantageous for Conn because if it *wouldn't* be advantageous for Conn, we aren't going to do it. But I'd like to request you, Doreen—and I don't know how to handle the billing, where to charge the time to, and frankly, I don't care, because it all goes into the same pot on this, so you can charge it to Conn, I guess—I'd like a half-dozen variations on dips involving cottage cheese and deviled crab.

John: Do you want to stick to just the two ingredients?

George: Well, no. I want those to be the base ingredients. And what I'm after is "devilish dips" or something of that sort and from that we should work up later, after we've had the base, and make up the recipes and have both Conn and

---

[3]Word used in advertising trade to mean an effort wherein two products are being used to help sell each other.

Fisher try them. Then we should work up a "Devilish Dip Booklet," banding methods, and pricing with Fisher. Now, Marie isn't here, so it's hard to discuss this. But this would mean support of this thing, including a TV commercial showing dips being made, point-of-sale, the works. Conn seemed to think this was a wonderful idea.

John: On cottage cheese?

George: Yeah.

Phil: [Just arrived] No sour cream in this at all, just cottage cheese?

George: No.

John: No, before you came in, George explained that this was a conflict between ethnic use of sour cream and shell food.

George: So that is an assignment, Doreen, if you will take it. The main thing is to get a taste test on a bunch of dips. I think six or eight dips would be adequate. And if it goes, it would mean a hell of sales jump for Fisher. It would be a good deal, because a banded combination of this sort with the price-off deal, the way Conn sells cottage cheese . . .

John: I want to put in just one request, George. If Mary will, in all her assignments, indicate that "rough roughs" are to be done copywise and artwise for examination before we go any further.

George: Oh, yeah. We can.

John: Then we can discuss it with both Conn and Fisher so they can see we're not putting a lot of unnecessary detailed hourly development work on this beyond the basic thought that will go into . . . .

George: The basic plan exists.

John: Now what you want . . . .

George: All I'm looking for, John, is . . . . We have been talking about a premium or a consumer purchasing inducement to go with cottage cheese. This is Fisher Deviled Crab. This is wonderful from our standpoint as an agency and from Fisher's standpoint while Conn gets the benefit. The only

contribution we would want is in the form of a price con-
cession on the deviled crab.

John: I'm not talking about. . . .

George: Now, as far as the other piece is concerned. . . .

John: You've given Doreen an assignment; you've asked for recipes and so forth. [Conversations continue indistinctly for a
few sentences between George and John.]

George: Well, that's all. All Doreen has to do is come up with a
half-dozen recipes that we can use. . . .

John: Art and copy aren't doing anything?

George: Nothing yet. We're too far ahead; it's a fall campaign.

John: O.K.

George: Later, we'll come up with TV commercials, the works. But
that will be when we get to the fall plan. We have too
many that are coming up before the fall plan. After all, that
runs in September. We don't want to start it until the fifteenth of August, do we?

Bill: We still have the same relationship? It's perfect, the small,
the eight-ounce and the large and the sixteen-ounce?

George: Yeah. Keep it in that proportion, Doreen.

Doreen: All right.

George: [Picking up a piece of paper that indicated he was turning
to a new subject] Now, I want to run through this flavored
drink promotion just once and see where we stand on this
thing.

George then spoke for about four minutes, explaining the
issues involved in this campaign which was to be based on advertising on the Conn-sponsored TV show "Mounties on the Trail," and on
newspaper and point-of-sale advertising. The promotion involved (1)
a free, plastic "Mounties" belt, attached to every package of flavored
drink bought during a certain period; (2) a premium requiring proof
of purchase (George did not specify the kind of item to be offered as
a premium); and (3) a lottery conducted in each store that sold the
product (proof of purchase of the product would not be required to

enter the lottery in which some item, such as a barbecue set, would be raffled off in each store to the entrants of the lottery).

George began by describing aspects of the selling campaign.

George: We supply the store with pads of entry blanks and the consumer is not required to purchase anything in order to enter this thing. But we have learned through experience that about four out of five people who wish to enter feel that they can win only if they purchase, and will purchase the product involved. The primary reason for this is to take these metal ice tables on which to display the product, build a western corral, "Mounties on the Trail" atmosphere stuff and . . . [Telephone rings. Mary answers.]

Mary: George. George, it's for you.

George: Who is it?

Mary: I don't know.

George: Excuse me just a second. [His voice heard indistinctly in background for a while.]

John: Incidentally, on this purchase ratio for the store deal that George is working on, on the Super Tea test we've had better than 2,500 entrants which we checked through . . . [George can be heard in background saying, "I'll be right out." He hangs up and waits as if to say something.] . . . er, from the time they entered until the time they left the store. We checked at the checkout counter and they averaged 17 of 20 purchases.

Bill: Is that right? That many?

George: Bill, would you pick this one up? I gotta take a call from New York. I'm going to excuse myself so there'll be no fine.

Al: [With a few others] Ohhhh-hhh.

John: You're outvoted. Sorry.

Al: Getting pretty dramatic around here.

Helen: In fact, there was an interruption *and* leaving . . .

John: Yeah, that's true.

Al: Helen, thank you. Two!

Phil: A phone call's an interruption and leaving is another one.

John: O.K. Go ahead.

[George leaves.]

Bill: Well, we promised that this would only be a 30-minute meeting. So, why don't we get through this thing. We've gone. . . George has gone through the giveaway, the self-liquidating aspects of it, and the raffle. Why don't we go right into the creative. The only thing. . . this starts the first of June, so we haven't got the gun right on top of us on this one, so we should. . .

Mary: Well, you do according to the schedule. Tomorrow. . .

Bill: You can't get ahead of it. You really can't beat it. [John and others are heard laughing.] So we're right under the gun [More laughter] and away we go. Uh, but. . . . I think with the group here we should look at this thing very carefully. [Most of the people are looking at a "rough" of a newspaper ad which was tacked up on the bulletin board behind Phil and John. The ad shows a young boy in a cowboy outfit drawing two six-shooters, with a headline concerning "the fastest growing guns in the Northwest."] My comments on this one. . . . I don't know. . . . I scratched that gun, the fastest growing gun thing once, but it's gotten back in there. I don't know why. But I think it is in very poor taste.
   Dan, why don't you read what you have written? All this material's due tomorrow and this is what has come out of the art department so far. The rest of the copy is there as I understand it now.

Dan: Yeah, it's there.

Bill: How did this "fastest growing guns" thing get back in there?

Dan: I never knew it was taken out.

Bill: Well, then, does anyone else feel that this is distasteful? I do.

Dan: Why?

Bill: Well, I know Conn wouldn't buy it in the first place; I don't think we should, in the second. This "fastest growing guns in town"—people don't want their kids to be associated with being. . . .

Phil: I think it's a guy being. . . .

Bill: Quick on the draw. This is a bad relationship from Conn to be in with parents, I'm sure.

John: You're appealing not to the youngsters, but to the kids; uh, I mean. . . .

Bill: To the parents.

John: Parents.

Bill: Yeah.

John: This is for parents, a printed ad; and the kids come into the TV more heavily. I have a basic question before we start in on the headline, Bill. With a premium ad in the newspapers, the major thing we're selling is the premium. At least we should be, if we utilize it the way our experience has shown over and over again that you must do to make it a success. This thing—the premium—doesn't come in until down at the bottom; it isn't played up in the headline; there isn't anything that says there's something that is a free premium on here unless you read the whole ad.

Bill: Yeah. Sorry, I got sidetracked on that.

John: So that the ad in itself, for the purpose we decided and that George reviewed for us again this morning before, uh, it doesn't come off at all, it's completely. . . .

Bill: I think, Phil, we'll have to get away from. . . .

Phil: Yeah, I agree, but why was this asked to be played down?

Dan: Yeah, George just said that they intended to subordinate it and that the job the ad was to do was to sell the Conn flavored drinks to adults on a copy platform which I have here, which is embodied in this copy, uh. . . .

Bill: This is absolutely true, but. . . .

Dan: Now. . . .

Bill: We're trying to illustrate the ad somehow. We're going to have an illustration in the ad . . . .

Dan: It was my thought to have the belt buckle shown, but not big, down at the bottom, and maybe have it shown on the figure of the boy.

[Mary is heard indistinctly saying something about a holster.]

Bill: Why don't you go ahead and read your copy platform.

Dan: Here, this is the actual copy for that ad which embodies the points. [Reads ad copy which stresses health, flavor, and convenience.] Then we go into this little box . . . which I won't read . . . .

Helen: Why does the milk ad have to be appealing to adults mainly? Why couldn't we shoot for the kids in that, too? Instead of using a child, what about using Cap'n Jim?[4]

Bill: Well, I think the child is somewhat wasted. I think we're devoting an awful lot of space to something that doesn't mean a darn thing as far as selling flavored drink goes. I think John's point about . . . .

John: [Interrupts] To go back to the basic objective, George has stated—apparently after the fact—the objective of the whole thing, that our newspaper ad must be directed toward selling chocolate drink, or flavored drinks. If we're going to put money into a premium, and we're going to use the premium as a means of moving chocolate milk, we know perfectly well that to try to straddle a fence like this isn't going to do either job any good. We either go out and sell chocolate milk with the bare mention of that fact that there's a premium there and knowing beforehand that we don't expect the premium to move the product, or, if we're going to use the premium as a lever to move the product, then we've got to sell the premium. We know that is so; this is a basic fact that we proved so many times, we don't even have to give it a second thought. Now, which is our objective? This is a promotion built around a premium.

[4]A character in the "Mounties on the Trail" TV show

We're going to put point-of-sales effort on it. The Conn organization is going to sell this premium. Therefore, I feel that this advertising direction that is taken in this newspaper ad, Bill, is completely off base.

Bill: Well, the only way that they could be criticized, John, would be with exclusive distribution in stores and at retail. If they're going to buy a flavored drink, they're going to buy the one that's in the store.

John: [While Bill is speaking] Why have a premium?

Bill: Well, to get them interested in buying chocolate milk, we're shooting for people who are now using either a mix or are not using flavored drink at all—are using white milk or not drinking milk because they don't like it.

John: All right, the way we would sell chocolate milk would not be to sell it for gunmen; we'd sell it for . . . .

Bill: For health, or . . . .

John: For health, for flavor, for ease and convenience because the kids love it, because is has a soda fountain flavor, and that sort of thing. And not because he's drawing guns.

Dan: Well, yeah. I didn't intend it to be taken as seriously as everybody has taken it. We have some awfully cute illustrations of kids in cowboy outfits and guns and the idea was to show this little kid—who obviously is not going to grow up to be a gangster—having fun with a cowboy suit on. And the headline was intended to be light, not heavy. It was taken wrong, so obviously it is wrong and should be changed. I . . . .

John: I would say that the illustration here looks as if he is kind of . . . [Mary laughs.]

Dan: That looks pretty grim, I admit.

John: Can we start with something that is important to the quality of the product we're trying to put over, so that their attitude toward that product will rise and be reinforced with the illustration? Could you . . .

Bill: You mean take it out of the soft drink . . .

John: Well, let's say you had three kids in cowboy outfits sitting at the counter in the kitchen and your headline is sort of a "fountain at home—no fuss, no bother, always so good" or something—"Conn-flavored milk."

Bill: Yeah, or you could have three kids western style at a bar thing with their feet up on a rail with the guns hanging up, you know, just back views of them in the soda-fountain-at-home idea. I think the product advantages here are two, primarily. One, health, and the second, convenience. I mean, if parents have trouble getting the kids to drink milk, this is an easy way of doing it. It's already in the carton; there's no mixing.

Phil: Shouldn't we say somethin' like that, then?

Bill: Well, I think Dan has it in the copy.

Dan: It's all in the copy.

Phil: Do we have to stick to straight flavored drinks? Can we mix 'em with ice cream for sodas?

John: Well, you can have the mother being the soda fountain attendant or something of this sort. And one of them saying, "Make mine strawberry." The other one saying, "Chocolate," and so forth—so you can get the flavors in there and then play up the headline, the advantages of buying the prepared flavored milk. Something along that line. But you're sure how you want to pitch this and not go out for the premiums? You don't think the premium's strong enough?

Bill: No. My feeling on the premium is that a premium is a good secondary device to interest kids in buying flavored drinks. But if we're shooting primarily for adults in this thing, they aren't particularly interested in getting the kid a belt buckle. So to me, the prime advantage in the ad should be definitely on the product itself.

Dan: Well, let me add a little bit longer view. I think that George said this may be our last opportunity to promote that product. I think one of the things we should do is to promote the product. We do have a good start. . . . [Voice becomes indistinct.]

Bruce: Which raises the point which has been bothering me for the last five minutes or so. Maybe I didn't hear it when it was stated, but what is the marketing problem here and what are the marketing objectives?

Bill: The marketing problem is . . . it has changed within the last 12 months. This product returns as much margin to Conn as does white fluid milk. This product has been limited to about six or seven weeks in the summertime where the sales go crazy, and then right back down again to a level even below what it started out at. I mean, because of the seasonal aspect of the product, it tapers off very quickly going into the holiday season, and it's really not much more than a nuisance item for the rest of the year.

Bruce: Why is it only a six- or seven-week seasonal product? It's not like bock beer, is it?

Bill: No. Oh, no.

Bruce: You can have it all year long?

[George returns to the meeting, which continued for about 30 minutes.]

Transcript of the First Part of the Fisher Account Group Meeting, March 17

The following material is from the tape recording and the researcher's observations.

Phil: About time to start collecting fines?

Marie: Yes, it is.

Phil: What's the right time?

Marie: Ten o'clock.

Phil: [To Bruce] You just made it under the wire.

Bruce: May I be excused? I have got to get some stuff together for the First National Bank book, which closes on the nineteenth.

Phil: [To Bill] You're about one second late.

Marie: [To Bruce] The meeting won't be complete without you, but go.

Bill: Huh? Say, I was going by my clock. Who has the official time?

Marie: It's thirty seconds past ten.

Phil: You owe two bucks.

Marie: No, he doesn't. Sit down, Bill.

Phil: Well, I have about five minutes after.

Marie: You're not late.

Voices: [Indistinctly] Don't let him get out of it. Come on, pay up.

Phil: Don't act like that, Marie. We can't make money if you let these characters get out of it.

Marie: We need his creative thinking at this meeting today. We have to have them in a good mood.

Phil: Come on, it's after ten.

George: It's not after ten. I just called the time signal.

Marie: Here we go again.

George: Pick up the phone.

Phil: Sneaky.

George: Damn right, I'm sneaky. [Phil in background repeating, "Sneaky."] I can't afford you and your bad habits. Dial the TIME number.

[Several voices are indistinct as multiple conversations go on. George is dialing the telephone number that gives a time signal. Bill, Mary, and possibly others discuss a premium idea for the Conn account while George dials.]

George: It is now 30 seconds after ten o'clock.

Phil: So? You haven't been here 30 seconds. [Mary and Bill continue discussion concerning Conn premium.]

Phil: Now, here's someone, right here.

[John enters. Conversations continue as George hands the telephone handset to John.]

George: Someone wants to talk to you.

John: Hello.

[Long pause. A smile appears on John's face. George laughs loudly and long.]

George: That's what I call living proof that the fine is owed. [Laughs again]

[Several talk at once, including remarks about the fines.]

Marie: The main purpose of this meeting is to discuss commercials for the Northwest area—radio commercials.[5] But before we start on that, I have a nice little letter to start the morning with, from Fred Mays [a Fisher executive]. He says: "Having in mind the discussion we had last year about the preparation expenses for Fisher Deviled Crab magazine advertising,"—Mr. Berklund—"I'm delighted to see that you got under the estimate by nearly $12,000. Please express my thanks and congratulations to all your associates for such a fine job." [Applause]

Marie: Carlton, you have some material, I believe, on radio commercials.

Carlton: Well, I have the . . .

Marie: We checked the radio stations first on whether there would be any objection to starting off by saying something about "go to the devil," or "my wife gave me the devil" and there's no objection if it's used in good taste.[6] So . . .

Carlton: I have the estimates here on these jingles if you'd like to hear those, if you want to. The cost is . . .

Marie: Well, let's hear the commercials first.

Carlton: Well, I did three on "she gave me the devil," and Dan has some on "the devil with cooking"—right, Dan?

---

[5]Reference is to a campaign just being initiated on the Fisher account.

[6]Helen had stated at a meeting the week before that she thought use of the "go to the devil" phrase would be unacceptable over radio stations.

Dan: Yes.

Carlton: I assumed and maybe wrongly, I don't know, but I assumed last week that you objected, Marie, primarily to the fact that we did not get to the sales story fast enough in the other commercials I presented.

Marie: Yes.

Carlton: So these go into the sales story a lot faster. Takes you about . . .

Marie: These are 20 seconds?

Carlton: No, no. These are minute spots, but they go into the sales story in perhaps 15 seconds at the outside. This first one is about two little boys. [Carlton reads the following, imitating different boys' voices.] "Your daddy just give you the devil?" "Sure, I asked him to give me the devil." "You diiiidd?" "Yeah, Fisher Deviled Crab." [Carlton then reads, in his normal voice, the announcer's part of the commercial which emphasized flavor and convenience of Fisher Deviled Crab.]

Carlton: The other one is two women, fundamentally the same thing, about how one's husband gave her the devil, and why did he give her the devil, and so forth. The announcer makes the point that more women would be wearing minks if, when they gave their husbands the devil, it was Fisher Deviled Crab . . . .

Marie: Um, hm.

Carlton: But it's a little play back and forth and it only takes about 10 or 15 seconds to establish that and then you go right into the selling copy . . .

Marie: Um . . . what . . . um. I'd like an opinion on that. Let's go round the room. Mary, how does it appeal to you?

Mary: I don't think that if I were just listening to the radio I'd hear them. I mean they'd be on, but they wouldn't impress me so that I'd listen.

Marie: Um, hm. Phil?

Phil:	I think they're all right. There's one thing that confused me there on that mink . . . how it tied in.
Marie:	Well, that's a detail. I don't . . . I'd like to discuss just the basic, general idea.
Phil:	Generally, I think they're all right.
Marie:	John?
John:	I think it's in poor taste to have the children doing it.
Marie:	Yes. But do you think the basic idea of using the devil as an attention-getter at the opening and then going into "sell" is right?
John:	Yeah, I think that's all right—the way it's used in the second one—but I don't care about the first one.
Marie:	George?
George:	[Starting very quietly] I don't like them at all. I don't think they make a memorable point for Fisher Deviled Crab at all. They give good name identification for the devil, but I think you're fighting something here, Marie, where you're going too much against a lot of other deviled products. Deviled eggs, for example. And I think just the devil association is not enough. We've gone, in my opinion, a little too far.
Marie:	Um, hm.
George:	[To Carlton] I don't think your sale . . . your selling power carried through after that introduction, old friend.
Marie:	Dan?
Dan:	I think that the devil, "gave me the devil," is a memorable phrase. It's a phrase in the popular idiom. Uh, I think, I don't agree with George's point. I don't think we're selling this against any branded devil products at all.
Marie:	Um, hm.
Dan:	And I think we can stand alone with the deviled crab idea. On the other hand, we can probably use a little bit more reinforcement of the selling points of the use idea.

Marie: Um, hm.

Dan: The Fisher Black Devil?

John: Because we found that in the research, if you remember, on name brand identification, that Black Devil is known almost better than the word Fisher.

Marie: Um, hm.

John: And it's a well-known brand identifying . . . it commonly.

Marie: Yes. Al?

[George talks with John in lowered tones as Al speaks.]

Al: I like the first one—the two kids, which could be done in a pretty off-beat voice, I think. And I think it had a lot of sell, George, that commercial, the meat of it. But that Black Devil idea, is just a devil to stop. As you said just the other day, George, you hear one piece of profanity on the radio and it stops you dead. And then after that, maybe you can say Black Devil. After the initial stop is there.

Dan: Well, it isn't really profanity.

Al: No, but it's . . .

Phil: You're not a Southern Baptist?

Dan: No, I'm not. [Phil and some others laugh quietly.] I admit.

Marie: Bill?

Bill: The go-to-the-devil part of it I don't like, but I like the devil association; I think that's a good one. I think you've built it, so why not use it?

Marie: Um. If . . .

John: Could we, could we take a series of incidents in the early colonial days when the witchcraft business was going on? Uh, there is many, there are many tales of burning at the stake and so forth and we could start off with a factual "In 1665 Mary Hutchinson was burned at the stake, to shake the devil out of her." [Several murmur "Wow!"] "But when they have the devil in them today," or something, I don't know . . .

Dan: Oh, what the devil, I burned the steak!

George: Would you really like one of those genius-ly creative ideas that I give you every once in, say, once in two years?

Marie: Yes, surely.

George: If you're going to play the devil, play it big. Have two peo-ple. For instance, two men talking. And you open up with a man saying, "My wife told me to go get the devil." Then the other fella says, "The devil, you say?" "No, she said 'The devil with cooking!'" "What the devil do you mean?" "She told me to get Fisher's deviled crab. She doesn't want to cook."

Marie: Well, George...

George: And then, I mean if you're gonna stress the devil, bring him in in several different ways and come off it, into your straight "sell."

Marie: Well, George, basically this is the same idea, basically, that uh, that Carlton is giving us...

George: Use the devil as if he were mad at him; just once.

Marie: Yes, well, now, I'd like to add my opinion. Mine is *for*, too. I think basically the idea would accomplish what we're try-ing to accomplish, and that is to get that devil image planted in the person's mind—and in the opening, with somewhat of a shock treatment—if we did that, then went into our "sell." And all that, of course, would have to be worked over. But if we're in agreement that the basic idea is right, or if the majority are at least, I suggest that we get together with the creative people. Carlton, if you and Dan and I can get together and work up a list of the objectives, of the specific objectives we want to accomplish, and then perhaps you can do some more refined commercials, and then let's discuss them again.

John: I think one thing, one thing I would like to add in qualify-ing my being for it. I would like it better if it was used in some such way as Bill mentioned, or George mentioned, or even woven into an incident, rather than "Go to the devil," or something of this kind.

Marie: I don't think...

John: Because while it's a shocker, I think, ...maybe it's, maybe it's...

Marie: A pleasant shocker we need. Not an objectionable one.

John: Yeah. I don't think when it gets to be...it's not on the pleasant side. I think you can use the devil without...

Marie: Being offensive.

John: Telling somebody to go to the devil.

George: May I make another suggestion?

Marie: Um, hm.

George: I think these are extremely flat commercials. I'd suggest that before you even attempt to refine this technique you take these sample commercials and make a tape of them with a half-dozen off-the-air commercials exactly like it, showing no particular creative brilliance. Just another group of commercials that'll fill a minute at the end of a program or somewhere else. Put these up against them and see just how really terrible they can be.

John: I'd suggest we get the Conn commercials.

[Marie and several others laugh, drowning George's words.]

George: But this is another example of the same thing.

Marie: Well, this is a rough draft and, as I said, we're discussing a basic treatment.

George: You're being much too kind to the copy people, Marie. It leads to biting the hand that feeds...

Marie: But we don't want to cut off something that isn't finished, when it's just in its...

George: What did you do with the musical treatment business?

Marie: Well, we have that for consideration, too. We're trying to bring out all the ideas we can, and then choose which is the best. Now, in addition to this treatment, Dan Rittner, I believe, has another one.

Dan then read another copy idea for the Fisher product. The meeting ended after another 20 minutes.

COMMENTARY

There is little question in my mind that John Goode was a nice guy. He was low-keyed, non-threatening, protective, humorous, supportive, and all the other good adjectives that describe the kind of person who reduces tension in a group rather than one who increases tension. For an example of a tension producer, take a second look at the account executive, George Lorenz, who was critical of other people's work, markedly aggressive in how he presented his views, and not averse to creating adversaries either in other account executives, such as Marie Ayers, or in some of the creative people such as Dan.

At the risk of exaggerating, it would almost appear as though John Goode and George Lorenz were engaged in a minuet in which one moved in relation to the other. The more aggressive George became, the more John Goode acted to relieve tension, to play the part of the nice guy. Was this minuet an accident of nature, or was there possibly some causal connection such that John's passivity increased George's aggressivity, and vice versa? Surely it was in the nature of the two men, their respective character structure, to differ in their behavior. But as in a marriage, the behavior of one of the partners elicited the complementary behavior of the other.

The relations between these two men become even more intriguing if one takes into account some critical aspects of the power structure in the agency. George was in charge of the office's big revenue producer. His success, so to speak, made the agency successful. He was the provider, also in a manner of speaking, for the creative people. His work offered diversity in media, in advertising content, and in the possibilities for expression, advancement, and reputation for creative members of the staff. The possibilities were so attractive as to conjure up a picture of all of the creative people becoming attached, beholden to, and identified with George's work at the expense of other clients and their respective account executives. If this potential attachment and dependency were insufficient to cause a modicum of fear in Goode's heart, consider this possibility. Suppose that in the normal course of doing his job, and doing it well, George Lorenz became the man the client, Conn Dairy, believed in. For this client, Watkins and Worster and George Lorenz became synonymous. George would not have had to behave deviously for this perception to have fixed itself in the client's mind. With this perception of George Lorenz as the agency, George was fair game to be picked off by competitors, lured to their agencies with the expectation that when George moved, his business moved with him. So maybe John's role as a nice guy addressed itself to an unpleasant reality of George dominating the agency not only internally, but also externally in the competition for clientele. If you find this line of analysis of some interest, you should be asking yourself the following question: What does being a nice guy have to do with dealing with internal competition, with dampening or suppressing rivalries among staff? To answer this question we have to examine very closely the form and substance of John's niceness.

John seemed to take a special interest in rewarding members of his staff. At the beginning of account group meetings, he commented favorably on performance, client relations, or signs of special recognition from the home office. From the sample of behavior we have observed, the rewarding comments were usually directed toward the less powerful account executives and creative staff. This behavior had at least two intentions and effects. First, the flattery counterbalanced George Lorenz's clout in the agency. It also asserted, albeit gently, the position of the northwestern office as a part of the larger parent. Seeing the office as a part of a major advertising agency amplified the staff's consciousness, even pride, in being a part of a major advertising agency. Carrying out this performance among people who may have tended toward cynicism required the utmost sincerity. There was only one instance I could find in the account of life in the Watkins and Worster Northwest Office where staff laughed at and not with John Goode. You will recall that John was holding forth on an advertising approach to a tie-in campaign linking Conn's cottage cheese with Fisher's deviled foods. Acting out of character, Goode launched forth with an idea of tying the imagery of the campaign to the days of the Salem witch hunts. In looking for the "devil," Goode associated to Anne Hutchinson, who had been tried for being a witch, although he mistakenly calls her Mary.

As a rule, whenever Goode turned his attention to the substance of the agency's business, he usually referred to research studies that showed, for example, that you either promoted the product or the premium, but never both. It was not as though John offered his expertise or authority to buttress a position he had taken regarding a marketing plan, or an advertising campaign. It seemed that he relied on distant, objective studies to support his position. With this tactic, he gained some safety (after all, research data appears stronger than one's opinion or intuition), but he lost the kind of respect that goes with personal persuasion, and putting one's ego on the line.

Coming back to the "devil" theme in this joint promotion, John plainly ran out of gas. It was the sort of gaffe one observes as a singer on stage begins to go out of tune providing first embarrassment for the audience and then, in reaction, laughter, the kind of guffawing clearly designed to reduce anxiety. It is interesting that John took a chance and behaved out of character. It is especially interesting that he took this chance when George Lorenz was out of the room.

John Goode's forte was being a nice guy, a tension reducer, a pourer of oil over troubled waters. He was not a leader in the sense that he had gained the respect of his people through his command of the substance of the business, or his ability to bring business into the agency. A rainmaker he was not. A convener, a moderator, a nice guy he definitely was.

But to cast John Goode in the role of a manager rather than a leader is not meant to disparage him or his work. The problems of keeping the agency together, and preventing vicious rivalries from undermining its morale as well as its image in the northwest market, were formidable. The more interesting question is whether there was conscious intent in Goode's behavior, or whether his role was an outcome of his personality; that he did what he did as an outgrowth of his character that left him with little choice but to be a nice guy.

It is difficult to answer the question of what determinants underlay Goode's behavior. It is my own conviction that people do what they do out of the necessities of character. In my experience, being a nice guy, or for that matter a tough guy, is a response to personal development. Character, defined as an individual's habitual mode of acting, is addressed to the regulation of both inner and outer reality. It serves as a stabilizer and maintains personal equilibrium, while defining the person to relevant people in his or her environment. To say that someone acts out of character ("It's so unlike him to do this or that") is to suggest that the person becomes unrecognizable to others. But while character is at best preconscious, if not unconscious, it does not mean there is no awareness of intent and consequences. People have an infinite capacity to serve their own interests as well as to rationalize their behavior. It is for these reasons that character is so difficult to change. We are accustomed to taking advantage of who and what we are. We are also accustomed to making the most of it, to find all sorts of reasons why who and what we are become exemplary traits.

It would be unfair to John Goode to say his behavior as a nice guy was totally reflexive. I believe he understood its advantages, and considered it a rational response to the power politics of agency life, and the realities of his talents, which, unfortunately, did not include the gifts of a first-rate marketer. He did what he had to do, and took full advantage of his abilities and limitations.

In reading the Watkins and Worster case, you may have been struck by the presence and persistence of a ritual, beyond Goode's habit of trying to find something good to say about people, the northwest office, or the parent agency in New York. At the beginning of meetings, much joking appeared, especially around the ritual of fining people who came late to meetings. You probably noticed that this ritual bifurcated the group. The more power an individual had, the more he or she tended to be fined, while the less powerful tended to be the administrators of the ritual. Thus, George Lorenz and John Goode paid fines, while the so-called creative people managed the fining ritual.

To understand this behavior, its motivational aspects as well as its consequences in group psychology, I shall ask you to engage in a momentary digression. The understanding of ritual owes much to social anthropology. While it may be suspect as science to use a theory for its own confirmation, we need not stand on ceremony (no pun intended) when it comes to gaining insights into human behavior.

Social anthropologists have made some keen observations about the function of rituals that apply to literate as well as preliterate societies. Much in any group will divide people as well as bring them together. There is much in group experience to arouse fear, such as the fear of known danger as well as fear of the unknown. In business, there is realistic fear of competition, of economic recession, of finding one's product or job suddenly obsolete. In preliterate societies, there is fear of enemies known and unknown, and of nature, whose wrath can destroy crops, fishing boats, and bring on illnesses and death. We rely on knowledge and science to help bring fear into proportion. The more we know, the more we can control and overcome fear. The same holds true for savage societies. A fishing expedition in a lagoon causes tribesmen relatively little anxiety. An impending storm poses little danger, since there is sufficient warning to move the boats back to shore. But when the fishing expedition will occur in open waters, there is much cause for anxiety, yet the expedition must proceed to put food on the table. To succeed, the anxiety must be controlled, or the fishermen will fail.

The conditions I have described call for the enactment of ritual to assuage the gods and to relieve anxiety. Thus anthropologists have observed that impending events of little uncertainty are apt to proceed with no ritual. Conversely, events fraught with uncertainty are preceded with ritual.

In the same vein, conflict within a group can endanger the safety of its members. Dealing with conflict favors a ritual in which sham conflict replaces real conflict. Joking behavior is a close kin of ritual designed to replace real with sham conflict. If one accepts the joke (after all, words do not hurt in the same way as weapons) tension is lessened and the danger of splintering the group minimized.

A formula seems to emerge. Whenever one observes ritualistic behavior, look for sources of anxiety and examine the ways in which the introduction of ritual serves to allay the anxiety. Following this formula, what function did the fining ritual, and the joking associated with it, serve in maintaining group cohesion? What were the divisive and conflictual elements that, if left unattended, could result in the splintering of the group?

The fining and joking reduced the social distance between the power figures in account management and the creative staff. For once, those who tended to be initiators became passive to the superficial aggressivity of those who imposed the fines. In other terms, the fining and joking momentarily inverted the hierarchy. The real power figures accepted the temporary dominance of the less powerful. As a result, tensions seemingly lessened, perhaps enabling individuals throughout the hierarchy to carry on their customary working relationships.

Group cohesion often requires the obliteration of rivalries and the dampening of aggression. People prefer feeling good about themselves in a warm and friendly group than enduring the tensions that go hand in hand with aggressive hard work. Yet this cozy feeling exacts its price, and places leaders face-to-face with a dilemma. Should a leader go along with the socially adept moves to foster cohesion, or should leaders consciously disturb these moves in the interests of fostering excellent work? The choice habitual nice guys make is clear. Fortunately, the choices can be expanded to more than simply being nice and ultimately ineffectual, and being an SOB and fostering first-rate work. We should all remind ourselves of some of the old virtues, such as civility and good manners. It is possible to focus on tasks, to allow rivalries to surface, and to make ample room for the display of aggression in work, while demonstrating the virtues of civility and courtesy. To convert a situation in which it appears one has only to choose between being a nice guy who accepts less than excellent performance, and an SOB who is a strict taskmaster, into a situation where it is possible to be respectful of others while being demanding in the quality of work, requires something more than the reflexive styles of behavior that grow out of character development. John Goode's story is that sometimes, perhaps all too frequently, we behave out of necessity and not cultivated choice. Could Socrates have had this observation in mind when he advised leaders to "know thyself"?

THE
PSYCHODYNAMICS
OF LEADERSHIP

CHARISMA AND GUILT IN LEADERSHIP— ANDREW CARNEGIE

On February 26, 1901, the banker J. P. Morgan gave Andrew Carnegie a check for $480,000,000 and said, "Mr. Carnegie, I want to congratulate you on being the richest man in the world." Indeed, Andrew Carnegie was the richest man in the world and, probably, one of the most powerful.

Consider this problem: Can one become rich and powerful without feeling guilt? Your first reaction to this question probably is laughter. But a moment's reflection should convince you there is a serious problem here that needs to be resolved. What may make leaders different from the rest of us is their relative freedom of action in situations that ordinarily are guilt provoking. For example, try firing someone and see if you are inclined to do what many power figures do, which is to get someone else to do the dirty work. Strange as it may seem, it is easier and requires less emotional stamina to initiate massive layoffs, than to lay off one particular person.

To make my position even clearer, consider this assertion: The ordinary state of mind in using power (accumulating it is another matter that we shall consider in due course) is a sense of guilt.

The guilt can be provoked as a result of doing things that hurt others, even though the actions are rationalized as "the greatest good for the greatest number." Simply holding power and wealth in greater proportions than what one expected, or when compared with other people relevant in one's life scheme, ordinarily brings about some sense of guilt.

People like to make comparisons. They ask, "how am I doing relative to what I expected, and how am I doing compared to my neighbors, friends, classmates, siblings, and perhaps even powerful objects from the past, such as a parent or an admired (perhaps even feared) hero. Even if the active comparisons produce little guilt, they may provoke its close cousin, shame. The two emotions are different and often provoke dissimilar reactions. Yet for our purposes the differences are not as important as the possibility that the accumulation of power and wealth requires a state of mind, call it a sense of freedom, not only that these accumulations are possible, but that they are justified, that one is entitled.

We are a species that loves to keep score. "How am I doing" is the universal preoccupier, even though most of us are not bound to an instant evaluator such as a baseball player's RBI, or a Standard and Poor 500 index. To keep score literally reports how we are doing, which is sufficient to itself. But apart from the objective scorekeeping, there is a subjective evaluator that is just as important as its objective counterpart. In comparison with expectation, and in comparison with "relevant others" am I keeping up, ahead of the game, or falling back?

To be obsessed by such questions, as many wealthy and powerful people are, may indeed be neuroticism at its worst. But even in the absence of neurotic struggles with the subjective evaluator, there is an implicit goal to gain the upper hand and be in control, so that actions taken, decisions made, and issues resolved occur in a context where the individual power holder feels free of constraint and, in effect, is not a prisoner in his own house.

The sense of guilt is the normal condition that is attendant to the accumulation and uses of power and wealth. The absence of manifestations of guilt is the issue worth investigating because it is an unusual state of mind. There is little question that liberation from the conventions of guilt permits freedom of thought and action characteristic of outstanding leaders. Unfortunately, it is also a condition that leads to hubris and the many abuses of power that we shall deal with in this part of the book.

People are raised to feel guilt (and shame as well). These affects are conditioners for living amicably and cooperatively in society. Remember the golden rule: Do unto others as you would have them do unto you. A transgression of this rule should result in feelings of guilt. Perhaps even more importantly, anticipating an action that violates this golden rule is ordinarily sufficient to stop the person from committing this act. The thought gives rise to guilt, a painful enough experience to cause the actor to think twice.

We are left to wonder then how powerful people find the freedom to do what they please. Andrew Carnegie presents a case study of a leader who found within himself the permission to organize his life, structure his business, and act in relation to his associates according to his definition of what was the right thing to do, and with lesser or no regard for how they defined their goals, needs, and desires. You will find in this narrative a few instances in which traces of guilt appear, but they did not appear to be sufficiently strong to alter Carnegie's course of action. If you agree with this first observation, that Carnegie functioned free of the sense of guilt, ask yourself why. Explain Carnegie's ambition, his clear-cut dedication to accumulating wealth and power, and his ability to slough off would-be obligations and reciprocities inherent in human relations. Where did Andrew Carnegie get the permission to achieve wealth and power?

ANDREW CARNEGIE

A man who has been the indisputable favorite of his mother keeps for life the feeling of a conqueror, that confidence of success that often induces real success.

Freud

THE BEQUEST

The man who dies thus rich, dies disgraced.

Carnegie, 1889

Research Assistant Audrey J. Cohen prepared this case from published sources under the supervision of Professor Abraham Zaleznik. Copyright © 1975 by the president and fellows of Harvard College.

Andrew Carnegie's death in 1919 was a major news story around the world. There was much speculation about the size of his fortune and the terms of his will. The *New York Sun* estimated that Carnegie was worth $600 million; the newspaper believed that he had given away $250 million and had left the remainder for his family.

> But when the will was opened, the shelves were nearly bare. The *Literary Digest* helpfully listed for its readers an itemized account of Carnegie's principal benefactions, which came to the precise total of $350,695,653. Of what remained of his fortune to dispense by his will—a sum of $30 million, which was less than one-tenth of his fortune, two-thirds of even that went to the Carnegie Corporation of New York. Of the remaining $10 million, $4 million were set aside to provide yearly pensions of from five to ten thousand dollars to Dunfermline (Scotland) relatives and to his old friends.
>
> Except for the real estate that Carnegie had owned, there was no other monetary bequest at all. Instead he wrote, "Having years ago made provisions for my wife beyond her desires and ample enough to enable her to provide for our beloved daughter, Margaret, and being unable to judge at present what provision for our daughter will best promote her happiness, I leave to her mother the duty of providing for her as her mother deems best. A mother's love will be the best guide."[1]

PHILANTHROPY: THE DREAM FULFILLED

In 1899 Carnegie had written an essay entitled "Wealth." In it he considered what a wealthy man could do with his fortune. There were three alternatives: to leave it to his family, to bequeath it in his will for public purposes, or to administer it during his lifetime for public benefit. Carnegie considered the first alternative despicable.

> Beyond providing for the wife and daughters moderate sources of income, and very moderate allowances indeed, if any, for the sons, men may well hesitate. . . . The thoughtful man must shortly say, "I would as soon leave to my son a curse as the almighty dollar," and admit to himself that it is not the welfare of the children, but family pride, which inspires these legacies.[2]

On the second alternative Carnegie wrote:

It may fairly be said that no man is to be extolled for doing what he cannot help doing, nor is he to be thanked by the community to which he only leaves wealth at death. Men who leave vast sums in this way may fairly be thought men who would not have left it at all had they been able to take it with them.[3]

He chose the third path.

. . . in this we have the true antidote for the temporary unequal distribution of wealth, the reconciliation of the rich and the poor . . . the surplus wealth of the few will become, in the best sense, the property of the many, because administered for the common good, and this wealth, passing through the hands of the few, can be made a much more potent force for the elevation of our race than if distributed in small sums to the people themselves.

This, then, is held to be the duty of the man of wealth: To set an example of modest, unostentatious living, shunning display or extravagance; to provide moderately for the legitimate wants of those dependent upon him; and, after doing so, to consider all surplus revenues which come to him simply as trust funds which he is called upon to administer. . . the man of wealth thus becoming the mere trustee and agent for his poorer brethren, bringing to their service his superior wisdom, experience, and ability to administer, doing for them better than they would or could do for themselves.[4]

Carnegie took seriously the self-imposed task of being a philanthropist. He believed in donating his funds on a planned, rational basis, and chose to concentrate his fortune in the area of education. He founded over 2,800 free public libraries, including the entire New York City system; he created numerous foundations to administer his wealth when he realized that it was too large a task for one man to perform. Among these foundations were the Carnegie Institute of Pittsburgh, the Carnegie Trust for the Universities of Scotland, the Carnegie Institute of Washington, the Carnegie Foundation for the Advancement of Teaching, and the Carnegie Corporation of New York.

There were at least two underlying motivations for Carnegie's choosing the third, rather than the second, alternative. First, he enjoyed the publicity and praises he received. One of his desk drawers was labelled "Gratitude and Sweet Words" and in it he kept flattering magazine and news stories about his benefactions. Carnegie never insisted that his name be inscribed on the many libraries he created, "but certainly he never objected to its being done, and, upon request, he would provide the library with a photograph of himself, which would hang in the place of honor just inside the main door."[5] Similarly, he received a great deal of satisfaction from his close association with important college presidents and the most powerful leaders of government, both in the U.S. and abroad. Carnegie took it upon himself to promote peace in the world. He believed that he, Theodore Roosevelt, and Kaiser Wilhelm II of Germany controlled the future of international affairs.

> Carnegie had a wonderful fantasy, in which this unlikely trio of himself and his two heroes would meet together, Carnegie would outline his program for world peace and the President and the Kaiser would enthusiastically accept it. Then and there, war would be doomed, the lion would lie down with the lamb, and all the world's spears would be beaten into plowshares.[6]

If Carnegie relished the prestige which came with being generous and associating with influential people, he also enjoyed the sense of being moral. Throughout his life his favorite mottos reflected this desire: "Thine Own Reproach Alone Do Fear," "The Kingdom Of Heaven Is Within You," and "The Aids To A Noble Life Are All Within." It was in this spirit that Carnegie founded the Hero Fund and endowed it with $5 million. He wrote about the Fund's purpose:

> We live in a heroic age. Not seldom are we thrilled by deeds of heroism where men or women are injured or lose their lives in attempting to preserve or rescue their fellows; such are the heroes of civilization.[7]

The fund awarded wages and medals to persons who performed acts of courage—acts which originated in the desire to do good.

Not all of Carnegie's gifts, however, served primarily his need for flattery or virtue. Carnegie was extremely attached to Dunfermline, Scotland, the town of his youth. Before 1900 he had already given this town its first library and swimming baths, and the town had reciprocated by presenting him with his first "Freedom of the

City." By 1903 Carnegie wanted to do more for Dunfermline. He bought the Pittencrieff estate, for centuries the home of the aristocracy, and donated it to the town. He gave $2.5 million to the Carnegie Dunfermline Trust which was charged with

> the purpose of providing the means of introducing into the daily lives of the masses, such privileges and enjoyment as are under the present circumstances considered beyond their reach, but which if brought within their reach are calculated to carry into their homes and their conduct sweetness and light. . . .[8]

Carnegie placed special emphasis on the effects this Trust could have on children; it should bring into their lives, especially,

> some charm, some happiness, some elevating conditions of life which residence elsewhere would have denied, that the child of my native town, looking back in after years, however far from home it may have roamed, will feel that simply by virtue of being such, life has been made happier and better.[9]

With this trust, Carnegie proved himself in a town where he had once been nobody; he truly recaptured, and remade, the past.

EARLY CHILDHOOD

Andrew, born in 1835 in Dunfermline, was the eldest child of William and Margaret Carnegie. A sister Ann was born in 1840 but died the next year. Tom was born in 1843.

Descriptions of William and Margaret vary considerably. William was quiet and shy, fond of reading books and taking solitary walks through the country. His trade was weaving; he loved to sit at the loom and create beautiful cloth. Margaret, in contrast, possessed great strength of will, determination, and courage. She was outspoken, hard-working and "fiercely possessive of all that she could call her own."[10] Margaret tended to the realities of life more successfully than her husband.

> It was she who handled the family finances, hoarded the precious pennies, and tended the family garden. With a tough resil-

iency that her husband lacked, she accepted life for what it was, a competitive struggle.[11]

Andrew appeared to be a healthy, happy baby, unafflicted by colic or other disturbances. He had a voracious appetite and,

> at the age of one would be finished with his oatmeal porridge, which he would scoop up with two spoons, one held tightly in each hand, before his mother was ready to serve his father.[12]

While he was still very young, Andrew enjoyed watching his father weave at the loom. The child waited eagerly for his father to return from work.

Many years later, one of the neighboring children recalled watching Andrew playing by himself as a small child. He would be sitting on the floor with pennies from his mother's cash box. The play he seemed to like best was "tae get hand o' as many pennies as he could, build them up on the top o' each ither, an' knock them o'er wi' his haund."[13]

When Andrew was five, he protested against going to school. His indulgent parents decided that the boy would only attend school when he wanted to. When Andrew was eight, the parents arranged for the boy to meet the schoolmaster with the hope that he would then ask to go to school. Andrew's formal education lasted for only five years.

In his autobiography written in the 1900s Andrew recalled memories about his parents and his town. He wrote of his mother:

> . . . Margaret was my mother, about whom I cannot trust myself to speak at length. She inherited from her mother the dignity, refinement, and air of a cultivated lady. Perhaps some day I may be able to tell the world something of this heroine, but I doubt it. I feel her to be as sacred to myself and not for others to know. None could ever really know her—I alone did that. After my father's early death she was all my own. The dedication of my first book tells the story. It was: "To My Favorite Heroine My Mother."[14]

He remembered his father this way:

The change from hand-loom to steam-loom weaving was disastrous to our family. My father did not recognize the impending revolution, and was struggling under the old system. His loom sank greatly in value, and it became necessary for that power which never failed in any emergency—my mother—to step forward and endeavor to repair the family fortune. She opened a small shop in Moodie Street and contributed to the revenues . . .

I remember that shortly after this I began to learn what poverty meant . . . and then and there came the resolve that I would cure that when I got to be a man.[15]

When Andrew was 13, the technological changes in the weaving industry put his father out of work. William would return from visits to the manufacturers and tell Andrew that he could earn no more money. Whereas William was devastated and incapable of forming alternative plans, Margaret once more took charge of the family's destiny by deciding they should emigrate to the United States.

It was she who made the final decision to move, she who arranged the public auction—the roup—to sell their furniture, she who urged Will to find a buyer for his one remaining loom.[16]

Andrew seemed on the whole to share his mother's hopes, not his father's doubts. Only in leaving Dunfermline, the town he loved, did he feel remorse.

I remember that I stood with tearful eyes looking out of the window until Dunfermline vanished from view, the last structure to fade being the grand and sacred old Abbey.[17]

Andrew remained very attached to Dunfermline and the memories of his youth throughout his life.

When the Carnegies moved to America in 1848, they faced the poverty they had known in Scotland as well as unfamiliar surroundings. Once more William learned that his trade was an anachronism. Margaret returned to stitching shoes so that her family could eat. The continued poverty, however, did not weaken Andrew's self-esteem. Rather, his confidence was growing. One biographer referred to his being

carefully nurtured by the special kind of privilege that he had enjoyed throughout his childhood. In spite of the harshness of his world, he had always been peculiarly protected from it—in part by an overly solicitous mother and an indulgent father and in part by his own personal charm, combined with an aggressive nature. He had seen pinched hunger in the faces of his playmates in Dunfermline; . . . and he now lived in the slums of a back alley of Pittsburgh. . . . But in all of these experiences he had been more an observer than a participant. There had always been for him the bowl of hot porridge on the table, the clean collar in the dresser drawer, the plum duff with the sailors on Sundays. The protective shield of personal privilege that he enjoyed in childhood distorted his observation and warped his later recollections of his early environment, so that as a man he would actually extol the virtues of poverty.[18]

EARLY CAREER

My childhood's desire was, to get to be a man and kill a king.

Carnegie, 1897

Andrew's early career was marked by initiative and risk-taking. He seemed alert to all possibilities that would bring him both monetary and psychological rewards. Indeed, his rapid succession of jobs demonstrated his intense desire to become a man.

Andrew's first job was as a bobbin boy earning $1.20 a week in a textile mill where his father was working. Soon, he was offered a higher-paying job as a bobbin boy in another factory. The owners adopted Andrew emotionally and helped him become a clerk. Andrew saw the opportunity of learning double-entry bookkeeping and studied it after hours.

In 1849, a friend of the family recommended Andrew as a messenger boy in the Pittsburgh telegraph office. Andrew got the job and worked at becoming indispensable. He now used his free time to learn about the telegraph. One day a special call came in before the regular operator was at work. Andrew replied that he would take the message. He later received praise, not blame, from his boss. A year later, Andrew was a regular operator, taking all messages by ear! He soon was receiving all overseas press dispatches for all the newspapers of Pittsburgh.

Throughout this period, Andrew's ties with his mother continued to be strong, and those with his father steadily deteriorated.

> Both Andrew and his mother would have had to have been most unperceptive not to see how removed from, if not insignificant to, their present and future plans Will had become. . . . Andrew had become, under his mother's tutelage and encouragement, the main support of the family, and they all knew it.[19]

In 1855, William died, a tired and demoralized man. This loss, however, did not radically alter the family constellation.

> Will's death did not bring Margaret Carnegie and her elder son any closer than they had been before. Their relationship was already fixed and would remain so for as long as Margaret should live. Carnegie would continue to look to his mother for guidance and support in each undertaking, and she would not only give what was expected of her, but she would demand the right to give it. Some commentators have suggested that at this time Carnegie made a definite promise to his mother that he would never marry as long as she lived, but it is doubtful if any such formal pledge was ever made. It was not necessary.[20]

What Andrew had lacked in his relationship with his father, he found in Thomas A. Scott, the newly appointed superintendent of the Western Division of the Pennsylvania Railroad. Mr. Scott needed a telegraph operator and he chose Andrew. While Carnegie enjoyed sending messages that would transfer freight and move locomotives and people, he especially

> liked the daily contacts with Thomas Scott. He was flattered that Mr. Scott would ask for him by name, and he knew from the first meeting that here was "an extraordinary man, . . ." one to whom the term "genius" in his department may be safely applied.[21]

For six years, Andrew worked directly for Scott and regarded him as a hero. Scott, similarly, was fond of Andrew and emotionally adopted him as his son. He addressed him as, "my boy, Andy." It was through Scott's praise of Andrew that the young man became known in the higher echelons of the Pennsylvania system.

Their relationship, however, was often strained because of Andrew's initiative. For example, one day when Scott was out of the office, Andrew received news of a very bad accident on one of the lines which prohibited any of the freight cars from moving. Andrew felt confident about what orders should be given. Realizing that the wrong orders could lead to more serious consequences, he nevertheless relayed his messages with the familiar T.A.S. signature attached. When Scott finally arrived, Andrew told him what he had done.

> All was right. He looked in my face for a second. I scarcely dared look in his. I did not know what was going to happen. He did not say one word, but again looked carefully over all that had taken place. Still he said nothing. After a little he moved away from my desk to his own, and that was the end of it. He was afraid to approve what I had done, yet he had not censured me.[22]

Later, Andrew learned that Scott was boasting of Andrew's initiative as a proud father. Andrew recalled:

> This satisfied me. Of course I had my cue for the next occasion, and went boldly in. From that date it was very seldom that Mr. Scott gave a train order.[23]

Scott was also responsible for introducing Andrew to the world of capitalism. He mentioned the opportunity of investing in Adams Express stock, a company in which he already owned shares. Evidence shows that Scott advanced Andrew the necessary funds. Interesting, however, is the untrue account Andrew presented in his autobiography. There, he recalled that his mother mortgaged their home in order to allow him to purchase the stock! This investment proved sound, and soon Andrew was investing in more and more companies.

In 1859, Scott was promoted to the vice presidency of the Railroad. Andrew, aged 24, took over Scott's position as superintendent of the Western Division. His salary was now $1,500 a year!

During the Civil War Andrew served in the war department in Washington. After successfully managing vital transportation needs, he returned to Pittsburgh and his business ventures. Although still salaried by the railroad, the bulk of his income was now coming from his investments: the Central Transportation Company (sleeping cars), the Columbia Oil Company, the Pennsylvania Oil Company, the Western Union Telegraph Company, the Iron City Forge, and the Third National Bank of Pittsburgh, to name just a few. In 1863, Carnegie filed his income tax return. At the age of 28 he had nearly

$50,000 annual income derived from a wide variety of investments. This income represented almost one million dollars worth of capital! Even Carnegie was amazed by his remarkably fast rise to fortune. Soon after the Civil War ended and Carnegie no longer was serving national goals, he resigned from the Pennsylvania Railroad and devoted himself to expanding his financial interests. From 1865 to 1874 Carnegie's business involvements included sleeping cars, bridge building, telegraphy, and others.

In 1867 Carnegie's brother married. Carnegie decided to move to New York City where he would be closer to the financial community. His mother moved with him. In the St. Nicholas Hotel Andrew provided his mother with all the luxuries which she had never known before. Their furnishings were "worthy of Windsor Castle."

What was Carnegie's reaction to his wealth? Unlike many of his peers, he did not choose to forget his past. Rather, he desired to use his wealth to return to the land of his childhood. In 1865, Carnegie urged Scott to use his Washington influence to get him a consular post in Scotland. The appointment was never made, so Carnegie travelled to Europe for five months at his own expense.

In December 1868, after Carnegie drew his financial balance sheet, he added this accompanying statement.

Dec. '68
St. Nicholas Hotel
New York

Thirty-three and an income of $50,000 per annum! By this time two years I can so arrange all my business as to secure at least $50,000 per annum. Beyond this never earn—make no effort to increase fortune, but spend the surplus each year for benevolent purposes. Cast aside business forever, except for others.

Settle in Oxford and get a thorough education making the acquaintance of literary men—this will take three years active work—pay especial attention to speaking in public. Settle then in London and purchase a controlling interest in some newspaper or live review and give the general management of it attention, taking a part in public matters, especially those connected with education and improvement of the poorer classes.

Man must have an idol—the amassing of wealth is one of the worst species of idolatry—no idol more debasing than the worship of money. Whatever I engage in I must push inordinately therefore should I be careful to choose that life which will be the most elevating in its character. To continue much longer overwhelmed by business cares and with most of my thoughts wholly upon the way to make more money in the shortest time, must degrade me beyond hope of permanent recovery. I will resign business at thirty-five, but during the ensuing two years I wish to spend the afternoons in securing instruction and in reading systematically.[24]

The years from 1871-73 were trying for Carnegie emotionally, for he had increasing difficulties in his relationship with Scott. Although not directly employed for the railroad, Carnegie had continued close personal friendship with his first benefactor; they were investors in many of the same enterprises. Now, however, Carnegie's independence and self-preservation required that he reconsider his feelings.

In 1871 Pullman notified Carnegie that the Union Pacific Railroad quickly needed $600,000 cash. Carnegie convinced Thomson of the Pennsylvania Railroad to furnish enough securities to secure a loan of $600,000; by rescuing the Union Pacific, Carnegie and Thomson would be in a position to dictate their interests to the directors of the panic-stricken Union Pacific. The Pennsylvania had good reason for desiring this power. It was in the midst of an expansion program. It already controlled routes from Chicago and from St. Louis to the East Coast. Since Scott, an executive of the Pennsylvania, was on the board of directors of the Kansas Pacific which ran from Kansas City to Denver, the Pennsylvania had a dominant voice on this line. However, the Pennsylvania did not control any routes to the Far West. If Thomson could influence the Union Pacific and join the lines of these three trains together, then the Pennsylvania would be the first truly transcontinental railroad.

The financing was soon arranged. Carnegie, Pullman, and Scott were elected to the board of directors of the Union Pacific, and Scott became president of the board.

In exchange for the loan, the Union Pacific gave to Thomson 30,000 shares of its own stock with a face value of $3,000,000. Thomson turned the shares over to Carnegie for safekeeping. The four partners in the transaction—Carnegie, Thomson, Scott, and Pullman, were given the option of buying any or all of these shares at the current market price. The public announcement that the Pennsylvania was backing the Union Pacific and that Scott, a respected railway man, was the new president, sent the market price of Union's stock upward. The four partners could easily make sizable profits by buying the shares at the agreed option price and selling them on the market.

The original directors of the Union Pacific, however, were appalled to learn that at least Carnegie and Pullman actually sold their shares on the market. The Union Pacific considered this behavior treacherous and retaliated by dismissing all three men from the board. This dismissal hurt Scott the most. The only one of the three whose career was closely associated with the Pennsylvania Railroad, Scott had now lost his chance to extend the control of the railroad to the Far West. H. F. Clark, Cornelius Vanderbilt's son-in-law and a representative of the rival New York Central Railroad replaced Scott as president of the Union Pacific. Scott was personally hurt by the public humiliation and his career suffered. From this time he harbored ill feelings against the men who betrayed him, Carnegie and Pullman.

When Carnegie later described this incident in his autobiography, he altered the facts. He recalled that it was Scott, not he, who succumbed to the temptation of selling the shares.

> . . . While I was absent upon . . . business Mr. Scott decided to sell our Union Pacific shares. I had left instructions with my secretary that Mr. Scott . . . should have access to the vault . . . but the idea that these should be sold, or that our party should lose the splendid position we had acquired in connection with the Union Pacific, never entered my brain.[25]

In 1872 Carnegie had his last business dealing with Scott. Scott was in need of money and advice for a venture that Carnegie considered too speculative: a new railroad line from the Louisiana-Texas border to San Diego. The following year brought a financial crisis in the country. Scott and his associates who had gone ahead with construction of the new line were now in a desperate situation. The only salvation was to have friends endorse bank loans. Scott, who had been of so much help to Carnegie, approached him now for endorsement. Carnegie answered:

> I decline. I was then asked whether I would bring them all to ruin by refusing to stand by my friends. It was one of the most trying moments of my whole life. Yet I was not tempted for a moment to entertain the idea of involving myself.[26]

Moreover, Carnegie refused to ask his friends to help Scott, and Scott's company became bankrupt. When Carnegie's bankers heard that Carnegie had been unwilling to help Scott, they concluded that he too must be in financial difficulties. They called him to question the security of their loans to him. Carnegie was financially solvent, and thus could have agreed to aid Scott. This incident suddenly and completely severed the ties between Carnegie and his former benefactor.

Guilt over this betrayal plagued Carnegie for many years. In his autobiography he wrote that, "it gave more pain than all the financial trials to which I had been subjected up to that time."[27] After Scott's death, Carnegie rationalized his former behavior by intellectually arguing against financial arrangements based on friendship. In 1885 he addressed a graduating class of Curry Commercial College on "The Road to Business Success." One danger he urged them to avoid was

> the perilous habit of endorsing—all the more dangerous, inasmuch as it assails one generally in the barb of friendship. It appeals to your generous instincts, and you say, "how can I refuse to lend my name to assist a friend?" It is because there is so much that is true and commendable in that view that the practice is so dangerous.[28]

One historian commented on this episode.

> In any event, the pain, if not a sense of guilt, persisted, and even when Carnegie was an old man, writing his autobiography, he could not ignore this episode as he did many other unpleasant incidences of the past. He felt compelled to recount the whole story and once again justify his decision. His concluding sentence to the story showed that the pain was still there; "I fear Mr. Scott's premature death can measurably be attributed to the humiliation which he had to bear."[29]

THOMAS CARNEGIE

Paralleling Andrew's relationship with Scott was his relationship with his brother Tom. As a boy, when Andrew dreamed of starting his own company, he always included his brother in his fantasies. At the age of 15, Andrew declared to Tom that they would someday be in business together in the company "Carnegie Brothers." Before that dream was realized, however, Andrew helped Tom gain practical experience in telegraphy and counselled him on his early investments in oil.

Although the two brothers worked closely together, their temperaments were quite different. Andrew was exuberant, optimistic, and extroverted. His emotions were readily apparent; everybody who dealt with him felt as if he knew Andrew well. Tom, on the other hand, was reserved, quiet, and more cautious. He kept his feelings to himself. While Andrew resembled his mother, Tom was similar to his father in mood and demeanor. When Will died, Tom felt the loss the most keenly.

The differences in temperament between these two brothers became even more clear in their work relationships. When Andrew became superintendent of the Western Division of the Pennsylvania Railroad, he immediately appointed Tom, age 16, to be his personal secretary. Unlike Andrew, who took initiative under Scott, Tom was never so impetuous or personally ambitious. He did his work conscientiously but never stepped over the limits of his responsibility. Later, when Andrew had left the railroad and had reorganized the Keystone Bridge Company, he again asked Tom to work for him. In 1865, Andrew sailed to Europe for a nine-month tour. Tom, age 22, assumed complete responsibility for Andrew's business involvements at home. Correspondence between the two brothers portrays the nature of their relationship.

Andrew, enthusiastic about an English manufacturing process which fused steel facing onto iron railroad rails, continually urged his brother to expand the bridge works and iron mills at home.

> We must pull up and develop the Union Mills sure. . . . How is the Brick concern doing? . . . Am glad to see you are pushing around after trade, but my dear boy, the South is our future market. The Freedom Iron Co. made most of its large profit from Southern Trade. . . . I beg to urge upon you the importance of sending a first class man to Nashville, Memphis, Vicksburg, etc. at once. . . Will you please carry out these views regardless of expense or anything else?[30]

At the same time, he wanted Tom to insure that the companies stayed financially solvent.

> The Carnegie family, my boy, are destined always to be poor, but

> I am poorer than I expected if $8,000 in debt. We must work
> like sailors to get sail taken in . . . .[31]

Letter after letter arrived carrying contradictory advice. Tom, in the meantime, was faced with the problem of a stagnant, post-war economy. Credit was tight, businessmen were cautious about expansion, and unemployment was high. Just keeping the companies alive at their present size required long hours and hard work.

In addition to the real problems that Tom had to face and that Andrew did not understand, Tom was subject to his brother's personal criticisms. Andrew would ask why Tom was not doing better and doing more. Although he continually rhapsodized about an Italian sunset or a piece of art, Andrew assured Tom that he was not simply enjoying his vacation but also working to extend his business acquaintances abroad. Nevertheless Tom, worn down by managing large and varied business interests, did get exasperated by Andrew's preference for travelling and giving suggestions rather than implementing the ideas himself. Seldom did Tom complain, but after several months of receiving unsolicited advice and gratuitous blame, even his patience was tried. One of Andrew's replies indicates that at least once Tom had spoken out in his own defense.

> You wonder if we ever think of one who has notes to meet, etc. Indeed, we often do, and the more I feel myself drinking in enjoyment, the deeper is my appreciation of your devoted self-denial and the oftener I resolve that you shall have every opportunity to enjoy what I am now doing. I'm sure you have had a trying game of it and often you must have felt disposed to throw up the game and write me advising my return, but I trust the skies are brighter now . . . and am happy to believe matters are hereafter to be easier upon you. It is a heavy load for a youngster to carry, but if you succeed, it will be a lasting benefit to you. Talk to Mother freely; I always found her ideas pretty near the right thing. She's a safe counsellor, safer than I, probably, who have made money too easily and gained distance by carrying full sail, to be much of an advisor when storms are about, or sail should be taken in.[32]

The letter had its effect of appeasing Tom. When Andrew later suggested that he end his tour early to return to business at home, Tom insisted that he stay and complete his travels. Tom assured Andrew that the responsibility of management was not too great a burden.

In the 1870s when Andrew wanted to expand into steel, Tom regarded the idea with skepticism. He and other junior partners of Andrew, Phipps and Kloman, raised doubts about the tremendous cost of the equipment, the difficulty in obtaining ore, and the lack of a well-defined market. Andrew was undaunted. He was going to form a new organization with new partners and new financial backing; if his former partners wanted to join him, there would be places for them in the new company. Tom, Phipps, and Kloman did eventually decide to invest although they still were dubious of the strategy. Even when the steel business was at the height of its success, Tom maintained his office in the old iron mill.

Criticism and differences over strategy marked the relationship of the two brothers through the next decade. The elder brother repeatedly blamed the younger for not achieving higher profits. He described to Tom how Phipps watched the costs of production in the Lucy Furnaces and the rolling mills and implied that Tom would do better if he did the same. Because Andrew's expansionary policies were always successful, Tom's inclinations to proceed more slowly and cautiously were subject to continual ridicule. Notwithstanding these tensions, Tom's career remained dependent on Andrew's. Indeed, when Andrew founded Carnegie Brothers and Company in 1881, he appointed Tom chairman of the board. Andrew had no official position in the management of the company even though he owned 55 per cent of the capital. As he explained, names and titles meant "simply nothing" to him.

The contrast between Andrew's style of leadership and Tom's personality began to effect Tom's health. Although married and a father of nine children, he started drinking alcohol in excessive quantities. By 1886 he was depressed and despondent, both physically and emotionally ill. Andrew visited him in Pittsburgh and learned that

> Tom was not responding to treatment—he seemed to have lost any real desire to live. Carnegie, who had never really understood his younger brother, had found him in the last few years even more withdrawn and inaccessible. The truth was that Tom had been drinking heavily over a period of five or six years, far in excess of anything that his family, and especially Andrew, knew about. Tom had never been an active supporter of Andrew's

grandiose dreams of business expansion. Left to his own devices, he would have conducted a small, sound, conservative
business operation in Pittsburgh. He had always resented the
constant pressure from Andrew to acquire more and more. He
had been mistrustful of Andrew's reckless gambles, and in the
early years he had tried, with occasional success, to hold his
older brother in check. But the gambles he could not stop had
paid off, and the business had expanded beyond Andrew's wild-
est dream and Tom's worst fears. Tom felt more and more iso-
lated and unnecessary. Although he still had loyal
support—from the other partners, the plant superintendents, and
even from the workers—which Carnegie never had, Tom had
lost all real influence in directing the company's policies and operations. Perhaps it was for this reason that he sought escape in
drinking. Now, stricken with fever, he had neither the physical
strength nor the will to recover. Andrew on his visits could do
nothing to arouse Tom's spirits or encourage his recovery.[33]

By that fall, Tom was dead.

PERSONAL LIFE

While Carnegie's business life was flourishing, his personal life remained static. Only when he was 17 did he learn about sex. His
teachers were the men on the operating crews of the railroad, a nota-
bly vulgar and crude group.

It would not be strange if from this introduction Carnegie would
regard the sexual experience as being something coarse and vulgar, like swearing or chewing tobacco. His disgust for and rejection of all that he observed and learned from these men, causing
him to turn too readily to the "sweet and pure surroundings of
home," offer an explanation for his later development.[34]

Carnegie was by no means an isolate. He knew many
women socially and enjoyed their company. However, for many years
he never was emotionally involved with any woman except his
mother. For example, he often called on Rebecca Stewart, Thomas
Scott's niece. While other employees of the railroad speculated on a
possible romance, Carnegie thought differently.

> She played the part of elder sister to me to perfection . . . We were much together, often driving in the afternoons through the woods. She was not much beyond my own age, but always seemed a great deal older. Certainly she was more mature and quite capable of playing the elder sister's part. It was to her I looked up in those days as the perfect lady.[35]

Until Margaret Carnegie's death in 1886, she and her son Andrew lived together and travelled together. Even though Andrew had to make many business trips to Europe by himself, he looked forward to spending the summers with his mother in their country home in Pennsylvania. After Tom married and had his own family, Margaret depended more and more on Andrew. She "became more possessive of her older son and more demanding of his attention."[36]

It was not until 1880 when Carnegie, age 45, met Louise Whitfield, age 23, that his mother, then nearly 70, felt threatened by another woman. Relations between the two women were bitter and vicious. Nevertheless, in September 1883 Andrew and Louise were secretly engaged. Carnegie was unwilling to commit himself to a marriage date, and by the next spring the engagement was broken. Several months later, they became engaged once more. Again, the question of when they would marry was unresolved. In the meantime, Margaret suffered an attack of pneumonia. Carnegie wrote Louise of his mother's ill health.

> Mother *seems* really better; it is miraculous. I trust yours is also better. Everything does hang upon our mothers with both of us. Our duty is the same—to stick to them to the last. I feel this every day . . . .[37]

Louise's mother was eager for the marriage, so Carnegie recast the facts by implying that she, too, was an obstacle to the wedding.

The combination of these psychological problems, his brother Tom's alcoholism and ill health, and numerous business activities, exhausted Carnegie. By October 1886 he was spending his days in bed with typhoid. Tom died, and in November Margaret died. Andrew reacted to his mother's death by avoiding all memories of her life. For many years he never referred to her aloud. He put away the miniature picture which he had kept on his desk; he took down and stored in his attic the large oil painting of Mrs. Carnegie in old age. From this time Andrew recognized and feared death.

> That anything so wondrous as life should have its end was a mystery to which he could never be reconciled. In his active days, when the vital pulse was running its strongest, the idea of death became more than an antipathy—it was a horror, and all suggestions that thing to mind he instinctively turned from.[38]

After Margaret's death, Andrew turned with more energy to life. By the end of November he was writing to Louise:

> It is six weeks since the last word was written and that was you as I was passing into the darkness. Today as I see the great light once more my first word is to you . . . . Louise, I am now wholly yours—all gone but you . . . . I live in you now. *Write me.* I only read yours of six weeks ago today. Till death, Louise, yours alone.[39]

After many weeks of recuperation, Carnegie returned to New York. In April 1887 he and Louise married in a small ceremony. Carnegie presented his wife with a home; for the first time Carnegie was his own master.

STEEL: THE NEED TO CONTROL

In 1881 Carnegie founded Carnegie Brothers and Company, Ltd., and in 1886, Carnegie, Phipps and Company. Both of these steel companies represented complete and separate units from blast furnaces to rolled rails and structural beams. Both were fantastically successful. Annual net profits equal to 60 per cent of the capitalization were usual. Carnegie never occupied a managerial position in either company or a formal position on the board of directors. Because he always owned more than 50 per cent of the stock in these private partnerships, however, he was in fact the sole decision-maker on matters of importance.

Much to the annoyance of his partners, Carnegie never believed in paying substantial dividends; he continually reinvested the profits in expansionary activities and technological improvements. Since Carnegie controlled such a sizeable amount of the stock, even a small dividend would give a substantial yearly income. The largest holdings his partners ever owned were 11 per cent for Phipps and 6 per cent for Frick. By 1895, his partners were getting old and worried about ever realizing the profits for which they had worked so hard. Phipps expressed his feelings in the following letter:

> . . . Would much prefer increasing our cash capital and have it ready to pay retiring Partners . . .
>
> Quite sympathize with Jack's wish for money—he is tired—discouraged with expansion. Hope tells a flattering tale, never otherwise with us. We get in sight of div[d], then like Philip Nolan ("man without a country") he sees his native land—then a new ship, a new voyage—and never each time a new and deeper disappointment, so with our div.[d40]

As late as 1899, when profits amounted to $21,000,000, a sum almost equal to the capitalization of the Carnegie Steel Company (the product of the reorganization of the two partnerships), dividends remained small.

In addition to limiting dividend payments, Carnegie's ironclad agreements insured that all the other stockholders would be friendly to his interests. The ironclad agreement was originated by Phipps in 1887. The year before, both Tom and Andrew Carnegie had been severely ill. Phipps feared that both men would die and that the company would have to buy back the shares from their estates. Since these two men owned such large interests, (17 and 54 per cent respectively) the company would not have enough free capital to compensate the heirs and would inevitably become bankrupt. The first ironclad agreement attacked this problem. Drawn up by Phipps and legal counsel, the document allowed the company to purchase, at book value, and over an extended period of time, the shares of a deceased partner. The time allowed increased with the number of shares; in the case of Andrew Carnegie's death, the company would have 15 years to purchase his interest. Because of Andrew's majority interest, even junior partners agreed that the ironclad agreement was a necessity.

Phipps, who held as many shares as Tom Carnegie, and second only to Andrew, also conceived of the ironclad as a way of forcing the sale at book value of the interest of any partner whom the controlling parties (two-thirds in number and in interests) wanted out of the company. Both senior partners had memories of being brought to court by a former junior partner who wanted more for his shares than book value. Phipps and Andrew Carnegie never wanted to be in that situation again. Indeed, after the ironclad agreement went into effect, Carnegie was even more careful than before not to over-capitalize the book value of the company.

Through 1895 book value accurately represented the value of a partner's interest. When Carnegie used the agreement to rid the company of such men as Miller, Kloman, Shinn and Abbott, and Leishman, feelings were certainly bad but financial arrangements were essentially fair. After 1895 rapid annual growth in earnings and the acquisition of extremely rich iron ores were not reflected in the capitalization of the company and the book value. As each year passed, book value grew smaller and smaller in relation to the actual value of a partner's ownership. In 1899, this discrepancy would prove to be disastrous to the Carnegie Steel Company.

In addition to dictating dividend policy and the choice of partners, Carnegie kept himself fully informed on operating details within the Carnegie Steel Company. He was seldom in Pittsburgh since he spent six months in New York City and the remainder of the year in Scotland, and he rarely attended board meetings. Nevertheless, he demanded and received amazingly full minutes of all board meetings. He wrote to the company's secretary, Mr. Lovejoy:

> Some suggestions I made to Mr. Frick are, I think important. . . that the votes of each member, pro and con, in the board shall be recorded; that no new undertakings be gone into except by a two-thirds majority of the total number of the Board, nor new methods adopted; and their [sic] are several other points which may be important.[41]

In another letter to Lovejoy he added:

> The minutes should, in addition to this, record every reason or explanation which a member desires to give. If this were properly done then any of us looking over the minutes would be able to judge of the judgment displayed by the voter, which of course would affect his standing with his colleagues. It would bring responsibility home to him direct. The minutes cannot err in being too full, the fuller the better. They can err in being too much curtailed.[42]

Partners realized that Carnegie's desire to reward or punish them would be based on their contributions in these discussions. After board meetings, they would await Carnegie's reply, "Thoughts on Minutes." These responses, received within a week to a month, were often as detailed and copious as the minutes themselves. No matter where Carnegie was geographically, he was quick to spot problem areas in his company.

Because of his close scrutiny of details within the company, he was always ready to blame and praise. Of the many executives in the steel empire, only Schwab survived to the end; all the others died, resigned, or were forced out. Carnegie also knew the names of supervisors in all areas of the company and personally judged their contributions. The hope of being recognized and rewarded by Carnegie himself motivated these men toward increasing efficiency and loyalty. Carnegie

> knew precisely which (men) were producing and should receive the rewards. This is what made his partnership system highly effective. The Millers and the Browns, toiling away at the mills at Duquesne or Homestead or Braddock, worked with the knowledge that at any moment they might feel the golden touch on their shoulder. So they worked harder and lived in hope.[43]

Carnegie did reward good achievements. He wrote to Frick in 1896:

> Every year should be marked by the promotion of one or more of our young men. I am perfectly willing to give from my interest for this purpose . . . .[44]

Since one-sixth of one per cent or even one-ninth of one per cent could easily become worth a million dollars, Carnegie's system was very successful. There was never a shortage of men willing to enter the competition. Every year they had to work harder and longer hours; every year the goal seemed to be farther away. Life in the Carnegie empire was a perpetual race which taxed physical stamina, mental powers, and emotional energy. Men kept working, though, in the hopes of being recognized and rewarded.

Carnegie's style of management involved much more than the need to control. He embodied distinctive attitudes toward labor and toward key subordinates. An examination of two crises—the

Homestead labor strike and the break with Frick—will highlight important aspects of his personality. In both situations he displayed a great deal of ambivalence, and, as a result, he suffered greatly at their outcomes.

HOMESTEAD, 1892

In his writings Carnegie glorified workers and his dealings with them. He wrote in 1884:

> The right of workingmen to combine and to form trade unions is no less sacred than the right of the manufacturer to enter into associates and conferences with his fellows, and it must sooner or later be conceded. . . . My experience has been that trade-unions upon the whole are beneficial both to labor and capital.[45]

In his autobiography, he added: "For 26 years I had been actively in charge of the relations between ourselves and our men, and it was the pride of my life to think how delightfully satisfactory these had been and were."[46] Homestead destroyed this sense of satisfaction.

The Homestead plant was the largest open hearth steel mill in the United States. When the Carnegie Steel Company purchased the plant in the 1880s, it acquired a long history of labor difficulties, for the Amalgamated Association of Iron and Steel Workers was one of the most well-organized, powerful unions in the country.

Frick assumed control of all of the plants in the Carnegie empire in 1892. Known as the toughest antilabor man in the industry, he wanted to show the union that he was running Homestead. Since production of pig iron had grown faster than demand, Frick had no qualms about closing the plant during a confrontation with Amalgamated.

In the spring, Carnegie and Frick had many discussions about Homestead. Shortly before Carnegie left for Europe, he told Frick to post a notice at the plant that was in effect an open disavowal of unions at all of the plants. If the workmen should strike, he instructed Frick to close the plant and wait for the men to return to work. He specifically did not want to bring in strikebreakers or hire new men; he had been publicly committed to this principle for at least six years, for in 1886 he had written:

> I would have the public give due consideration to the terrible temptation to which the working man on a strike is sometimes subjected. To expect that one dependent on his daily wage for the necessaries of life will stand by peaceably and see a new man employed in his stead, is to expect much. This poor man may have a wife and children dependent upon his labor. No wise employer will lightly lose his old employees.[47]

Frick refused to post Carnegie's notice since he did not want to battle with all the unions in the Carnegie empire at once. Also he sensed, more than Carnegie, that refusing to recognize the union at Homestead would precipitate serious troubles. Frick wanted the public to think that labor, not management, started the fight. Instead of outright denial of the union, Frick's strategy was to offer terms so severe that the union would never accept them.

Phipps and Lauder, two other partners, joined Carnegie in England to rediscuss the Homestead plant. Carnegie now changed his plans; he sent new instructions to Frick that put the new position as more subtly anti-union.

In previous summers, Carnegie and his family lived at Cluny Castle in Scotland. Since the castle was being repaired in 1892, Carnegie rented Rannoch Lodge in the Central Highlands of Perthshire. This lodge was in one of the most remote, inaccessible areas of Scotland. There was a railroad stop ten miles away, but no coach road with public transportation to the lodge. Visitors had to be met and brought by private carriage to Rannoch.

> This summer Carnegie did not expect the usual crowd of visitors and the gay festivities that he had always had at Cluny. He had left his address only with Frick, his secretary, and a few close friends in New York, and he did not issue his usual generous invitations to friends in Britain to visit him "at any time."[48]

Frick, in the meantime, prepared for the worst. He built a stockade around the entire plant and down to the river. He entered into negotiations with the Pinkerton Detective Agency whose men he had previously employed to protect strikebreakers.

The union wished to renew the contract of 1889. Specifically it asked to keep the sliding scale for steel billets based on a $25 market price even though the billets had fallen to $24. All other parts of the proposal were the same. The union was confident that the only source of disagreement could be on the basis for the sliding scale payments. It had the backing of 3,000 nonunion members in Homestead as well as its own members. The Association also believed that Carnegie had stated that he would not use strikebreakers in the event of a strike.

Frick proceeded in his plan by proposing wholly unacceptable terms. Both the Association and local newspapers realized Frick was fighting the union, not the terms of the contract.

Carnegie was now sending messages to Frick which indicated his reasons for breaking the power of the Amalgamated: its refusal to adapt to new technology and its high wages. Historians have argued that Carnegie was mistaken in making both of these charges.

Even though the workers and Frick were not coming to any agreement, the union believed that Carnegie would intervene as he had earlier against Frick in a coal field's strike. The deadline of June 24, 1892, passed, yet there was no message from Scotland. On June 25 the company posted a notice that managers would deal only with individual workmen, not with the union. The workers replied by hanging Frick in effigy. Several departments were closed on June 28 and, by June 30, the whole plant was closed. Both union and nonunion men stopped working.

Frick now called on the Pinkerton guards. He asked that 300 men sail up the Monongahela River by night and enter the plant to "protect" it. Frick wrote to Robert Pinkerton:

> As soon as your men are upon the premises, we will notify the Sheriff and ask that they be deputized either at once or immediately upon an outbreak of such a character as to render such a step desirable.[49]

The workers from Homestead took turns watching the river, the plant, and all roads leading to the plant for they expected Frick to bring in strikebreakers. They had the support of the municipal government since the mayor was one of the skilled workmen and an ardent supporter of the strike.

For four days the tension built. Frick brought the sheriff of Allegheny County and a few of his deputies to Homestead to provide added protection for the company's property. When the sheriff was unexpectedly asked to deputize the company's guards as official law officers, the sheriff denied the request. He and his aides were escorted out of the plant. Frick's legal advisor now assured management that it had every right to bring in private guards.

Early on the morning of July 6, 1892, the Pinkerton men arrived on barges. A bloody twelve-hour battle took place between these hired men and the workmen. Several men were killed.

Homestead was not the most violent fight between labor and management in American history. The reason it attracted such enormous concern was that it occurred within the Carnegie empire. Unlike Frick and Pullman, Carnegie had a reputation of praising

> the dignity of labor, the sanctity of a man's job, of profit sharing and the Gospel of Wealth, and of democracy triumphant.[50]

How did Carnegie let this catastrophe happen? Did he know of Frick's plans to hire Pinkerton guards? Why didn't he return to the United States and take charge?

When Carnegie first heard of the battle, he panicked. He cabled Frick that he was coming to Pittsburgh immediately. Lauder and Phipps were still in England and wanted to keep him there. They knew that Carnegie would be furious with Frick and would cause a confrontation with him. They wrote to Carnegie urging him to stay where he was. Carnegie realized he had to choose between returning to the plant and losing Frick or remaining in Scotland and losing face. He decided to remain in Scotland, furiously angry with his key subordinate. He resented the fact that Frick ignored his instructions not to bring in strikebreakers and that, after following his own sentiments, Frick bungled the job. Eighteen hundred and ninety-two was a national election year in the United States. Democratic newspapers in the United States and abroad seized upon the Homestead debacle as a indication of the evils of unregulated, protected Big Business. Carnegie had to combat external as well as internal attacks on the management of the Carnegie Steel Company.

Homestead remained a bitter memory for Carnegie.

> Nothing I have ever had to meet in all my life, before or since, wounded me so deeply. No pangs remain of any wound received in my business career save that of Homestead. It was so unnecessary.[51]

Moreover, in recalling these events in his autobiography, he unconsciously absolved himself of any guilt.

> He came to believe that he was on a coaching trip and not at Rannoch when the trouble broke out; that he was not informed of the riot until three or four days after it had happened, rather than within twelve hours; that he actually thought the men being hired when the gates to the plant opened again were his old employees returning to work; that O'Donnell's and Reid's [union] proposals came too late for him to do anything that might have achieved an amicable settlement. . . . In time, Carnegie even became convinced that the workers had sent him a telegram that read, "Kind master, tell us what you wish us to do and we will do it for you."[52]

When Carnegie returned to the United States in January 1893, he visited Homestead. Before both new and old workers, he read the following speech:

> I have not come to Pittsburgh to rake up, but to bury the past. It should be banished as a horrid dream, but the lessons it teaches should be laid to heart for future application. For 26 years our concerns have met with only one labor stoppage. I trust and believe that this record will be equalled in the next 25 years. When employer and employed become antagonistic, their antagonism can only be described as a contest between twin brothers. No genuine victory is possible for either side, only the defeat of both. . . . I made my first dollar in Pittsburgh and expect to make my last dollar here also. I do not know any form of philanthropy as beneficial as this; there is no charity in it. I have hoarded nothing, and shall not die rich apart from my interest in the business. Unless the Pittsburgh workers are prosperous, I shall have nothing. I have put all my eggs in one basket right here, and I have the satisfaction of knowing that the first charge upon every dollar of my capital is the payment of the highest earnings paid for labor in any part of the world for similar services. Upon that record I could stand.[53]

MR. FRICK

In some respects, Frick's background was similar to Carnegie's. Born in 1849, Frick was the son of an impecunious father. His mother came from a wealthy family and, at an early age, Henry learned to admire his successful grandfather instead of his unsuccessful father. Henry emulated his grandfather's drive and hoped to supersede his wealth. At school Frick only enjoyed mathematics since it was the sole subject he considered relevant to business. When he turned 17, he left school to acquire practical training. He held a variety of jobs: a clerk, a salesman, and then a bookkeeper in his grandfather's distillery. At the age of 21, he invested on borrowed money in 123 acres of coal land and formed the Henry C. Frick Coke Company. Within a year Frick had tripled the number of ovens from 50 to 150 and had expanded his ownership of coke lands. By 1877 Frick was personally worth one million dollars. He was determined, however, to achieve even greater financial success.

From the beginning of their careers, Carnegie and Frick used different styles.

> Carnegie had always worked as a member of a group; Frick for the most part had ploughed a lonely furrow. While Carnegie, in his early teens, was soliciting his friends to entrust their hard earned savings to an uncertain enterprise, his younger contemporary was walking from farm to farm, persuading the crafty husbandman to sell or lease the acres on which his seeing eye had detected outcroppings of coking coal.[54]

Henry Clay Frick's business involvements with Carnegie began in 1881. At that time, the Frick Coke Company was reorganized with Carnegie as one of the investors. By 1883, and at Frick's request, Carnegie was the largest shareholder in the Frick Company. Frick continued to run his company and his managerial excellence impressed Carnegie; when Tom Carnegie died in 1886, Andrew Carnegie had both stock and a management position open. He offered Frick 2 per cent of Carnegie Brothers for the book value of $184,000. Phipps would hold the stock in trust for Frick until the accumulated dividends equaled the purchase price; it was an easy, inexpensive way to become a partner.

In 1889, Frick replaced Phipps as chairman of Carnegie Brothers and Company. His interest was also increased from 2 per cent to 6 per cent, again without Frick's having to supply any cash. Frick and Carnegie admired each other because they shared common visions. Frick, for example, agreed that only a small fraction of annual profits should be paid out as dividends; most of the funds should be reinvested in technological improvements. Frick also strove to reduce costs and increase profits; in one year, he nearly doubled the profits of Carnegie Brothers and Company from $1.9 million to $3.5 million.

Notwithstanding these shared policies, Frick and Carnegie had many conflicts. Carnegie often acted without considering the opinions of other persons whose interests would be affected. For example, in 1894 Carnegie decided to consolidate the Frick Coke Company with one of its competitors, W. J. Rainey and Company. Without consulting Frick or even informing him of his plans, Carnegie met with Mr. Rainey and seriously discussed the proposed consolidation which would result in the new Frick-Rainey Company with Rainey executives obtaining important positions. When Frick heard of this meeting, he was incensed. Besides being completely excluded from the negotiations, Frick believed that the consolidation, while beneficial to the steel company, was certainly not in the best interests of the coke company. Moreover, he disliked Rainey and feared him as a rival among Carnegie's associates. Frick submitted his resignation from the partnership.

Although Carnegie convinced him to change his decision, Frick remained sensitive to actions which discriminated between the two companies. For example, Frick argued for good relations with the Pennsylvania Railroad, which was generous with its rebates to the Coke Company; Carnegie argued that the railroad was charging exorbitantly high freight rates to the Steel Company. Frick did not share Carnegie's enthusiasm for labor. The Homestead strike made the differences in approach highly visible.

The two men differed in temperament and personality. While Carnegie would converse with his associates on a wide number of issues and had an enthusiastic, often jovial demeanor, Frick was always somber, serious and cold.

> His associates could never remember Frick's telling a joke or indeed conversing on any subject not related to the business at hand. His concentration on business affairs appeared to be almost monomaniacal in its intensity, and quite frightening to ordinary men.[55]

A close associate of both Carnegie and Frick has written:

Carnegie was the Napoleon—that is the commander and intuitive genius, who planned campaigns and executed them with a rapidity and boldness that swept all enemies from his path; while Frick had the calm qualities of a von Moltke—long-headed, deliberate, a great tactician—a man who acted from carefully reasoned premises, while Carnegie struck out boldly, burning all his bridges behind him, not necessarily knowing himself the stages of his reasoning by which he reached his results. In fact, he didn't reason much—he acted on impulse; but his impulses were usually far more accurate than others' logical processes. But both were very big men—too big to enjoy each other's presence in the same organization.[56]

The two men shared no common interests outside of work.

> Frick took almost no interest in politics, other than the direct effect of governmental policy on business; seldom read a book not related to the science of coke and steelmaking; was something of a social recluse; and was not actively interested in philanthropy. Frick's only interest outside of his business and his family was one which Carnegie did not share—the collection of great art, particularly of the late medieval and Renaissance periods. What responsive chord of appreciation was struck in this business ascetic's soul by the rich, sensuous canvases of Titian, Tintoretto, and Velasquez is difficult to say, for Frick, unlike Carnegie, always kept his feelings and most of his thoughts to himself.[57]

By 1898, the Carnegie Steel Company dominated the steel industry in the world. Profits for that year equaled $10 million, an increase of $3 million over the previous year, and represented nearly 50 per cent return on the total capitalization. Estimates for the following year's profits were almost $20 million. Carnegie wanted further expansion, yet most of his partners wanted to realize more of the profits in the form of dividends. In any case, the organization of 1892 no longer sufficed.

From May 1897 to October 1898 Carnegie had been living abroad, and had not returned to Pittsburgh once. Now, he decided that he would sell his interest in the company. There were two possible methods. First, the other partners could buy out Carnegie's interests in both Carnegie Steel and the Frick Coke Company, and combine both firms into one. The same partners would remain in control but would greatly increase the capitalization. Secondly, they could sell Carnegie Steel and Frick Coke to outside parties who would undoubtedly sell shares to the public on the New York Stock Exchange. Carnegie, who hated detaching ownership from management, favored the first method; his partners preferred the second since they would realize a greater return for their interests. Frick and Carnegie agreed that the price to outsiders would be $250 million for Carnegie Steel and $70 million for the Frick Coke Company. If no outside parties were available, the partners would reorganize into the Carnegie Company, Ltd. This new company would purchase all the property and business of the H. C. Frick Coke Company for $35 million and all the property, assets, and business of the Carnegie Steel Company for $125 million.

After discussions in the beginning of 1899, most of the partners agreed that the reorganization scheme was best. Now, however, Frick, Carnegie, and a few other partners realized that selling the companies for $320 million would be financially more desirable than the reorganization plan. Carnegie decided he would prefer to sell to outsiders.

Early in April Frick and Phipps announced that an anonymous syndicate was willing to purchase the two companies for the stated price. Suspicious of this proposal, Carnegie demanded that, for a 90-day option, the syndicate deposit $2 million in cash, of which an amount equal to his 58.5 per cent be in his name. If the sale were not consummated in 90 days, the syndicate would forfeit the deposit.

Frick and Phipps discovered that this deposit was a serious obstacle. In order to continue the negotiations, they put up nearly 14 per cent of the money themselves. They also waived the deposit necessary to cover their interests and convinced the other junior partners to do the same. Carnegie, in the meantime, took the proposal in good faith and handwrote his farewell address to the business world.

On May 10, Carnegie received a cable describing the syndicate's plans. William H. Moore of Chicago, with the backup of John W. "Bet a Million" Gates, sought to form a gigantic steel trust. Not only did Carnegie abhor large consolidations, but he hated Moore and Gates, for they had notorious reputations for Wall Street speculation. Carnegie scornfully referred to these two gamblers as the "Chicago adventurers."

Carnegie noticed that part of the syndicate's proposal referred to spending $10 million of the expected stock sale for bonuses for finalizing the sale and for lawyers' fees. Of this amount, Frick and Phipps would receive $5 million for having arranged the option; in effect, they had become members of the loathsome syndicate. Carnegie now had two reasons to be angered at the treacherous behavior of these two partners.

By early June it was apparent that the syndicate would not be able to raise the required funds in time. Frick and Phipps travelled to Scotland to see if they could arrange an extension for the option. The answer was definitely no. Carnegie also decided to keep the deposit left by Phipps and Frick as well as the part left by Moore. Carnegie used the money for renovations for his home in Scotland, Skibo Castle; several years later, when his break with Frick was complete, he delighted in showing visitors the crenelated splendor of Skibo and saying, "The whole thing is just a nice little present from Mr. Frick."[58]

Relations with Frick went from bad to worse. Soon after the Moore fiasco, Frick and Carnegie engaged in their last battle. This crisis concerned the price at which Carnegie Steel would purchase coke from Frick Coke. Clearly, the financial interdependence of both companies argued for a settlement of the controversy. For every ton of coke which Carnegie Steel bought, Carnegie took the major share of the profits; for every ton of steel that Carnegie Steel sold, Frick's interest in that company became more valuable. Frick Coke Company continued to charge Carnegie Steel the market price, but the steel company refused to pay any excess over $1.35 a ton.

Carnegie returned from Europe in November 1899 and the two men started negotiating about the price of coke and the reorganization plan. Frick, fed up with the whole process, read the following statement before the Board of Managers of Carnegie Steel.

> . . . Why should he (Carnegie) whose interest is larger in Steel that it is in Coke, insist on fixing the price which the Steel Company should pay for their coke? The Frick Coke Company has always been used as a convenience. . . . The value of our coke properties, for over a year, has been, at every opportunity, depreciated by Mr. Carnegie and Mr. Lauder, and I submit that it is not unreasonable that I have considerable feeling on this subject. . . . He threatened, if the minority stockholders would not give their share of the coke to the Steel Company, at about cost, he would attempt to ruin them.[59]

Frick and Carnegie were both interested in acquiring the same piece of land. On this subject Frick added:

> He also stated, I am told, while here, that he had purchased that land from me above Peters Creek; that he had agreed to pay market price, although he had his doubts as to whether I had any right, while Chairman of the Board of Managers of the Carnegie Steel Company to make such a purchase. He knows how I became interested in that land, because I told him, in your presence, the other day. Why was he not manly enough to say to my face what he said behind my back? He knew he had no right to say what he did. Now, before the Steel Company becomes the owner of that land, he must apologize for that statement.[60]

What was Carnegie's reaction to this speech?

> The silence from New York was nearly deafening in its ominous heaviness. Carnegie made no direct reply to Frick, and of course made no apology for any remarks he had made while in Pittsburgh. He waited a week to see if the board would approve of the minutes as they stood without repudiating the remarks of the chairman. On 27 November the board approved of the minutes without a demur. Carnegie realized that he himself would have to act quickly and decisively if Frick were to be put in his place, and that place would surely be out of office.[61]

Carnegie called on Frick and asked whether he would voluntarily resign as chairman of the board of Carnegie Steel. Frick replied in the affirmative. On December 5 Frick's resignation was accepted unanimously by all present at the specially convened board meeting. "The junior partners felt that Frick had now been adequately punished. Carnegie, though, was not yet satisfied, for three issues remained unresolved. First, Carnegie Steel still was purchasing coke at a price Carnegie considered unreasonable. Second, Frick was still chairman of the board of the Frick Coke Company. Third, Frick still was the third largest shareholder (6 per cent) of the Carnegie Steel Company; this interest would affect any plans Carnegie had for reorganization.

Carnegie solved the first problem by enlarging the size of the board of managers of the Frick company and filling the positions with friends. Their votes would allow the company to reach an agreement with the Carnegie Steel Company over the question of the price of coke. Carnegie also toyed with the idea of purchasing the entire Frick company for $35 million, but decided against it.

The key problem was Frick's 6 per cent interest. The ironclad agreement of 1887 was still legally binding. Its present status was confused since another ironclad agreement had been drafted in 1897 and signed by all the partners except Phipps. This last agreement sought to increase book value so that it more accurately reflected the growth in the company's earnings and to alter the schedule of payments required to buy back a partner's interest. Although Carnegie had used the 1897 ironclad in January 1899 to buy back some shares from an ill shareholder, he now chose to repudiate its assumed legality. If Frick did not allow Carnegie to dictate his wishes to the Frick Coke Company, he would force Frick to sell his shares in the Carnegie Steel Company at a much undervalued price.

The newly expanded board of the Frick Coke Company voted to sell coke to Carnegie Steel for $1.35 a ton. Frick furiously left the meeting to ask his lawyer about getting a court injunction to prevent the Frick Company from making any deliveries of coke under these conditions.

> Carnegie called on Frick the next morning at his office, ostensibly to persuade him not to seek a court injunction but to accept the settlement as an accomplished and irreversible fact. It was the last face-to-face meeting the two men would ever have. Frick sat in stony-faced silence while Carnegie, holding all the trump cards, tried with sweet reasonableness to obtain Frick's cooperation. Finally, having heard Carnegie out, Frick said, "And if I don't accept this contract and am successful in enjoining the Frick Coke Company from making any deliveries to Carnegie Steel, what then?"
>
> Well, then Carnegie replied, the company would have to make use of the ironclad agreement and take over Frick's interest in Carnegie Steel at book value. The threat of the ultimate weapon had at last been used.[62]

Carnegie succeeded in getting most of the associates in the company to sign a resolution that Frick sell back his interest by January 31, 1900. Frick brought the issue of the coke price and the valuation of his shares to the courts. He engaged D. T. Watson, the lawyer who had drawn up the first ironclad agreement in 1886, and John A. Johnson as his attorneys. Carnegie also tried to get Johnson, but discovered that the opposition had hired him first. The Court of

Common Pleas in Allegheny County heard the case which became extremely complex. Newspapers throughout the country ran features about the trial, the antagonists and the companies. The specifics of the case were forgotten as the public gained information for the first time on the huge profits of the Carnegie Steel Company. The press was gaining facts with which to reawaken anger against trusts.

By the middle of March, both men realized that they could not really win. If Carnegie convinced the court that his company was only worth book value, he would never be able to sell it for $250 or $300 million. If Frick won and forced the dissolution of the Frick Coke Company and the liquidation of its assets, he would lose more money there than in the undervaluing of the 6 per cent. Frick and Carnegie accepted the compromise solution: both companies would consolidate with an increased capitalization. Frick and all the other partners would keep the same proportion of the new stock. Both sides met in Atlantic City to settle the details. Since Carnegie would not allow any of his loyal partners to meet Frick, however, Lovejoy and Phipps had to represent Frick at this meeting.

FAREWELL TO STEEL: THE DREAM ACQUIRED

> Mr. Carnegie, I want to congratulate you on being the richest man in the world.
>
> **J.P. Morgan, 1901**

Carnegie recovered from the battle with Frick with renewed enthusiasm and optimism. He was talking of investing in new railroad lines and new manufacturing facilities. Carnegie controlled so many resources now that industrialists in other fields started to panic. They looked to J. P. Morgan to save them. In January 1901 Morgan arranged a secret meeting with Schwab to ask if Carnegie would now sell his company. Schwab first proposed the idea to Louise Carnegie and, the next day, to Andrew Carnegie.

> It was not an easy night for Carnegie, for he was pulled strongly in both directions. There were the new railroads, the plant at Conneaut, and the unquestionable promise that within ten years at most—probably within five years—as much of the world of steel as he wanted would be his. He stood where few men have, on the edge of total triumph in his field of endeavor, and he was

being asked to step aside voluntarily before that triumph was complete.[63]

Andrew Carnegie was now 65. He did not know whether he would live to complete the work which still lay ahead of him. Certainly he could not be sure that he would have time to engage in the other work which truly interested him, the business not of getting but of giving. Louise wanted him to retire from the demands of making more money; she thought he should devote the remaining years of his life to philanthropy. Carnegie realized that his pride was satisfied; he had frightened the mighty Morgan and now could name his price for his company without entering into negotiations and politicking. The more Carnegie considered the two alternatives, the more he believed in retiring from an active business life, provided that Morgan would accept his price and his terms.

The next morning Carnegie scribbled a few numbers on a scrap of ordinary paper. Schwab took the paper to Morgan who agreed to the price: $480 million. On February 26, 1901, the contract between the two men was made final. Carnegie now controlled the largest amount of liquid assets in the world. On March 2, Morgan successfully filed the prospectus of the United States Steel Corporation, the first firm capitalized at over one billion dollars.

COMMENTARY

What is the evidence to indicate that the question of guilt, its presence or absence, is important in understanding Carnegie's achievements as a leader? While posing this question, we should not ignore the many talents Carnegie developed and used in his business career. He had a strong financial imagination. He understood how money can make money through careful investment. He also understood the principles of economy of scale and vertical integration in the steel industry. His acquisitiveness was highly focused, without wasted effort in fields of endeavor that showed little economic potential. Carnegie had his feet on the ground. While much is made of vision in leadership, too little may be made of focus. The ability to remain grounded in reality, to focus attention on the elements of advantage in any economic situation, to remain committed to allowing the elements of advantage work in one's favor probably accounts for as much success in business as vision. To foresee a future is vision.

To understand and apply focus is clarity of thinking and persever-ance. Much of what executives do, and that Carnegie did almost to an extreme, is to prevent other people from diminishing focus, by their predilection for their own ideas.

Anyone who does not listen to other people's ideas is a fool. The other side of this coin is that if one is easily persuaded, fo-cus disappears. Carnegie's style of leadership assured focus. For one thing, he insisted that policy discussions result in written minutes to which he responded in writing so records of ideas and decisions were not at the mercy of collective memory. He was anything but mercu-rial in his attachment to business. He was a financier, but he selected and remained dedicated to the iron and steel industry. For diversion, he travelled, rebuilt a castle in Dunfermline, his birthplace, and evi-dently read extensively. But for business, there were no diversions or adventures. He was not the type of entrepreneur who flitted from business to business as a bee flits from flower to flower in making honey.

Ideas and focus are an unbeatable combination. This combination can only work if the individual is unencumbered by the baggage of guilt. So we return to our original question.

Andrew Carnegie acted in a number of instances in ways that ordinarily provoke guilt reactions. Four situations come to mind. The first is how he dealt with his mentor, Thomas A. Scott of the Pennsylvania Railroad. Scott early on recognized Andrew's tal-ents and gave him opportunity as rapidly as Andrew learned the op-erations of the railroad. Even when Andrew unadvisedly grasped initiatives beyond his responsibilities and demonstrated capabilities, Scott adopted a benign attitude and could not help but admire An-drew's ability to learn and willingness to take initiative. Clearly Scott reacted as a good father to a determined son and, in effect, por-trayed the characteristics of a successful father opposite to Andrew's experience with his real father. As Scott advanced Andrew, he began to teach him the art of investing so that Andrew became indepen-dently wealthy at an early age.

Carnegie turned on his mentor first when he sold his shares in the Union Pacific Railroad, causing Scott to be fired from the presidency and casting a cloud over the reputation of the older man. Then, when Scott needed financial support, Carnegie refused to lend him money. As a result, Scott suffered financially and sev-ered his ties with Carnegie.

Carnegie did feel some guilt after these events. In his

writings, he repeatedly tried to explain away the facts, even in one case distorting the facts so that he would appear blameless. Yet there was insufficient anticipatory guilt to prevent Carnegie from acting against his benefactor. There is no obvious or ready explanation of Carnegie's behavior. Perhaps the lack of guilt reflected a basic flaw in Carnegie's psychology: an inability to put himself in the position of people presumably close to him, and following the paths of empathic attachment, to take their interests as his own. Another possibility is an underlying competitiveness that Andrew Carnegie experienced toward men who, while clearly not antagonists, could not find a place in his mind and heart, yet whose interests were as dear to him as his own. Later when we examine Carnegie's relationships to his brother and partners in the steel business, we may find further evidence of empathic failure. Finally, Carnegie's attitudes toward money may have overridden his concerns for human relationships. Carnegie was determined to accumulate wealth. The rules by which he pursued his aims could have acted as moral imperatives, also overriding concerns about people. We shall have more to say about this aspect of Carnegie's character and the times in which he lived and worked when we consider the influence of the Protestant Ethic on human behavior.

Thomas Carnegie was eight years younger than his brother Andrew. Under the circumstances of their father's displacement and emotional depression, Andrew evidently occupied a surrogate position in the life of his younger brother. Andrew brought Tom into business and made him responsible for running the steel business. This responsibility weighed heavily on Tom, particularly as a consequence of Andrew Carnegie's method of controlling the business while he took long leaves of absence during his travels in Europe and stays in Scotland. Carnegie insisted on detailed minutes of board meetings. He wrote detailed commentaries and gave his views (really directives) concerning the problems revealed in the minutes. Carnegie's directives could not be lost in bureaucratic shuffling. Consequently subordinates, especially Tom, whose obligations to Carnegie were direct and intense, were obliged to act on those directives. Follow up was assured through further reports and minutes that Carnegie read carefully and responded to in considerable detail.

The burdens that fell on Tom could not be relieved easily in the confidences of work associates or in the ease of talking things over with his older brother and chief. Andrew Carnegie was simply not available except on his own terms, and at a distance.

We have no direct evidence of how Tom reacted to a letter from Andrew, who wrote in a more personal and caring tone to his brother, sympathizing with his burdens, but advising him that sure relief was at hand if he confided in their mother and accepted her advice. We have no direct evidence of his reactions and had best not try to imagine, in the context of Tom's experience, how potentially damaging and demeaning it is to be told to seek out Mother to relieve the stresses of business responsibility. What we do know is that Tom became increasingly depressed, took to alcohol, and died.

Andrew Carnegie's relations with his partners followed a pattern of close control and psychological distance that we saw in his dealings with his brother. The use of minutes and written commentaries applied to all subordinates just as they did to Tom. In the absence of blood ties, the ironclad agreement served Carnegie as the chief mechanism for controlling his partners' behavior. They were all given shares in the business to reward them for their performance. The ironclad agreement prevented them from selling their shares except when they left the company. The price established for the sale markedly undervalued their asset. The promise of riches was always in the future, but the penalties of departure kept them closely tethered to their job and their boss. Long before the popularization of golden parachutes, Andrew Carnegie had invented golden chains.

The psychological mechanism he used he did not invent but probably understood very well. To gain control over someone else, promise a large reward of uncertain magnitude with an equally uncertain time for realizing this very large promise. This psychological control was at the heart of the ironclad agreement, enhancing the mystery and awesomeness of Carnegie's formidable presence.

Carnegie's ability to control his subordinates depended on still another element. Simply put, Carnegie was more shrewd, had greater negotiating talents, understood maneuverability more than others, and operated with far more coolness than his would be rivals. He outwitted Frick, who was no slouch when it came to looking after his interests. Carnegie's coolness under fire simply permitted him to overpower Frick and decide on his own time when to end the battle for control, which enabled him to emerge from the fray, in J. P. Morgan's words, "the richest man in the world." Carnegie's ability to control others depended in large measure on his freedom from guilt.

In summary, the four guilt issues are (1) Scott (2) brother Tom (3) the ironclad agreement (4) the Homestead strike and his relations with his associates.

The final event we should consider in the panoply of issues of potential significance in understanding guilt in Andrew Carnegie's career as a leader is the Homestead strike in Pennsylvania. Carnegie disclaimed responsibility for the Pinkerton attack on the strikers with its bloody aftermath. Yet it is unlikely that Frick and other partners acted on their own in hiring the Pinkerton agency and in staging the strikebreaking attack. Carnegie appeared truly distressed. In his letter to the workers, he tried to absolve himself of responsibility, yet given his method of control, he himself must have known that he was implicated.

We suggested earlier that the capacity to accumulate wealth and power may depend on talent, opportunity, and the inner sense of permission—that one is entitled, and indeed expected, to succeed. While Carnegie showed some remorse and inner conflict over the problematic events surrounding his relationship to Scott, his brother Tom, his partners, and his employees, he was not immobilized in taking action, nor did he seem burdened by responsibility and power. Where did he find permission that led to his freedom of thought and action?

Reviewing Andrew Carnegie's life history, especially his formative years, focuses attention on his relationship to his father and his mother. His father fell upon hard times when his craft as a weaver had been overtaken by technology in the textile industry. The skilled weaver, equipped with his own loom, had been displaced by power-driven looms installed in large mills. The family's luck scarcely improved with the move to America, since the conditions in the textile industry were no less changed by technology in the United States than in England and Scotland.

As the father's condition deteriorated, Andrew's mother seemed to become stronger. She made the decision to move to America, and apparently invested her hopes for the family in young Andrew. He did not let her down.

Andrew's attachment to his mother remained strong until her death. He did not marry until his mother died. Andrew surpassed his father as the head of the family. Far from feeling guilt over this psychological event, he appeared absolved under the influence of his mother who not only gave him permission but also created a standard for him that he lived up to the rest of his life.

Families exist in a culture, and in acting as agent for the culture transmit values and ideals from generation to generation. In a similar vein, mothers' child-rearing practices gain support from the wider culture, particularly if the parents feel strongly attached to the aims the culture seeks to perpetuate.

During Andrew Carnegie's formative years in Scotland and the United States, the ideals of capitalism, free enterprise, and individualism were probably at their peak in Western Civilization. Scholars such as Max Weber wrote sociological treatises on the influence of the Protestant reformation on the rise of capitalism. In his famous and much quoted book, *The Protestant Ethic and the Spirit of Capitalism*,[64] Weber argued that the secular and rational components of modernization embodied in the culture of capitalism derived from the Protestant ideals of duty and predestination. It was no longer a matter of means to ends that propelled men to work hard, to be frugal, and to accumulate wealth. It was their *duty*. Salvation could not come from doing good works and, in the vernacular, buying one's way into heaven and eternal life. Salvation was a matter of predestination, of having been selected (and therefore being special). The signs of this selection were in worldly activity and in achievement.

Andrew Carnegie's life reflected the vision of the Protestant Ethic. Through his abilities, his labor so to speak, he accumulated wealth. He eschewed wealth for its own sake, and acted out his convictions by using his money for philanthropic ends. His foundations have supported education, public libraries, and other causes to improve the life and well-being of the masses. Compared with the influence of his mother's child-rearing, investment in Andrew's achievement, and inculcation of the virtues of the Protestant Work Ethic, the argument that he provided for philanthropic causes to assuage a sense of guilt, first over having displaced his father, second over his brother Tom's demise, third, his treatment of his benefactor Scott, and finally over the bloodshed during the Homestead strike, would be stretching the point. He may indeed have assuaged latent guilt feelings by turning over the bulk of his fortune to public causes. But in the main, there is sufficient weight to the argument that he was unconflicted in his accumulation of wealth, and that part and parcel of the impact of the Protestant Ethic was to permit and encourage young men to follow the path Andrew Carnegie took as his life's work, to put aside any curiosity we might have about his unconscious motives propelling him to give away his fortune. He believed this was the right thing to do, and he acted on his beliefs.

Andrew Carnegie was a remarkable leader in industry and finance. These arenas provided ample scope for his considerable talents. But standing beside talent is an array of psychological factors whose presence or absence affects the force and focus that drive talents. The sense of guilt can be a major inhibitor in applying one's talents and achieving the necessary focus that usually assures success. The capacity for guilt is a normal outcome of child development. This capacity is a civilizing force. It makes for compassion, empathy, and all the other virtues that help people live with one another. The capacity for guilt and its presence as a legacy of childhood can inhibit significantly the quest for power. The incapacity for guilt is the factor that not only leads to freedom of action, but also leads to sadistic behavior on the part of leaders. This dual effect of the capacity for guilt reflects only one of the many human dilemmas of leadership. The detailed study of the lives of important leaders will reveal, one by one, some of the other human dilemmas and how they played themselves out in the history of enterprise.

Endnotes—Chapter 11

1. Joseph Frazier Wall, *Andrew Carnegie* (New York: Oxford University Press, 1970), pp. 1042-1043.

2. Andrew Carnegie, "Wealth," *North American Review*, vol. CXLVII (June 1889): 653-664, and vol. CXLIX (December 1889): 682-698. Reprinted in *Carnegie, The Gospel of Wealth*, ed. Edward C. Kirkland (Cambridge: Harvard University Press, 1962), p. 20.

3. Ibid., p. 21.

4. Ibid., pp. 23-25.

5. Wall, *Andrew Carnegie*, p. 819.

6. Ibid., p. 924.

7. Ibid., p. 894.

8. Ibid., p. 849.

9. Ibid., p. 850.

10. Ibid., p. 33.

11. Ibid., p. 44.

12. Ibid., p. 37.

13. Ibid., p. 38.

14. Andrew Carnegie, *Autobiography of Andrew Carnegie* (Boston: Houghton Mifflin Co., 1920), p. 6.

15. Ibid., p. 12-13.

16. Wall, *Andrew Carnegie*, p. 68.

17. Carnegie, *Autobiography*, p. 26.

18. Wall, *Andrew Carnegie*, p. 83.

19. Ibid., p. 95.

20. Ibid., p. 129.

21. Ibid., p. 114.

22. Carnegie, *Autobiography*, pp. 71-72.

23. Ibid., p. 69.

24. Burton J. Hendrick, *The Life of Andrew Carnegie* (Garden City, NY: Doubleday, Doran and Co., Inc., 1932), vol. I, pp. 146-147.

25. Carnegie, *Autobiography*, p. 164.

26. Wall, *Andrew Carnegie*, p. 302.

27. Carnegie, *Autobiography*, p. 174.

28. Wall, *Andrew Carnegie*, p. 305.

29. Ibid., p. 306.

30. Ibid., p. 236.

31. Ibid.

32. Ibid., p. 237.

33. Ibid., p. 418.

34. Ibid., pp. 118-119.

35. Ibid., p. 138.

36. Ibid., p. 399.

37. Ibid., p. 416.

38. Hendrick, *Life of Carnegie*, p. 255.

39. Wall, *Andrew Carnegie*, p. 419.

40. Ibid., p. 638.

41. Ibid., p. 671.

42. Ibid.

43. Ibid., pp. 665-6.

44. Ibid., p. 665.

45. Ibid., p. 542.

46. Carnegie, *Autobiography*, p. 228.

47. Wall, *Andrew Carnegie*, pp. 581-2.

48. Ibid., p. 546.

49. Ibid., p. 556.

50. Ibid., p. 560.

51. Carnegie, *Autobiography*, p. 232.

52. Wall, *Andrew Carnegie*, pp. 575-6.

53. Ibid., pp. 566-7.

54. Hendrick, *Life of Carnegie*, p. 290.

55. Wall, *Andrew Carnegie*, p. 669.

56. Ibid., p. 670.

57. Ibid., p. 716.

58. Ibid., p. 732.

59. Ibid., p. 741.

60. Ibid., p. 741.

61. Ibid., p. 742.

62. Ibid., p. 753.

63. Ibid., p. 788.

64. Max Weber, *The Protestant Ethic and the Spirit of Capitalism*, trans. Talcott Parsons (New York: Charles Scribner's Sons, 1958).

THOSE WHO ARE WRECKED BY SUCCESS—HENRY FORD

Until now, this book has not strained your sense of the world and how people in it behave. Even in considering the role of guilt in leadership in the case of Andrew Carnegie, the interpretations stayed close to the facts of the case. The levels of inference were not too distant from the narrative of Carnegie's life and work.

With the case of Henry Ford, and the cases to follow in this part of the book, I ask you to suspend disbelief until I have made a three step argument. The first step is to establish that the particular leader we are observing suffered from significant psychological symptoms. I recognize this first step may be hard for you to take. There is a general conviction that very important people don't get sick, at least mentally sick. To take a leaf from Henry Kissinger, who said that power is a great aphrodisiac, I would add that power is also a great buffer. It protects from mental illness. However, the protection lasts only as long as the power holder maintains a firm grasp on the sources of his power and continues successfully to internalize and consolidate the power base. This is a large caveat.

CHAPTER

12

What it means is that a failure in internalization and consolidation has the same psychological effect as the loss of power, which creates vulnerabilities to depression, whose consequences can be extremely debilitating. But as I shall demonstrate, actual and subjective loss are two sides of the same coin. People who lose power get depressed. People who feel a loss of power, even without a change in objective conditions, will react as though the loss were real. And, indeed, the loss is experienced as real in all its intensity and with all its ramifications in inducing pathology.

The second step in my argument is to show the dynamic process by which a psychological event leads to symptom formation. I will rely on facts to establish that a psychological event did occur. In the life of Henry Ford, the great founder and leader of the Ford Motor Company, the psychological event was his success in designing, manufacturing, and selling the Model T. Until about 1916, Ford performed brilliantly. He established and maintained a focus for himself and the company in producing a car for the mass market. Once he had achieved this enormous success, he displayed symptoms such as megalomania, and obsessional fixation on the product he had built. It seemed as though no appeal to reality could shake his conviction that he had built *the car* for the farmer and the masses. His fixation on the Model T almost ruined the company he had built.

The third step in the argument is to reveal, if possible, the antecedents in his personal history that led to the equivalent of the loss experience. In other words, what were the sources of his vulnerability, and more particularly, why did he regress at the peak of his success? As you will see, guilt probably played an important role in his experience with success. Unlike Andrew Carnegie, the permission Ford needed to accrue power and money was at best tenuous and difficult for him to accept.

In short, this chapter leads us directly into the realm of psychopathology. Attempts at using psychoanalytic methods and theory to interpret the life themes of great men and women have produced mixed results. I shall also discuss what can go wrong in explaining a great leader's life from the window psychoanalysis provides for understanding the dynamics of the mind. But for now, let us turn to the case study, the life of Henry Ford and the development of the Ford Motor Company.

HENRY FORD AND THE FORD MOTOR COMPANY

By 1914-1915, the Ford Motor Company had become the largest automobile manufacturer in the world. The huge plant at Highland Park was the most modern and the best equipped car manufacturing plant in existence. As such it was the subject of serious study both in the U.S. and abroad. Henry Ford was acclaimed as a mechanical genius, and after the announcement of the five dollar day, as a philanthropist and near miracle worker. Around him stood the best men in the industry; they were young, able, and ambitious.

Yet from this point until Ford's resignation in 1945, the company slid, at first almost imperceptibly and then with increasing speed, into a morass of despotic, one-man rule, and the repercussions of the organizational collapse were evident in every area of company functioning. The most crucial contributing factor to the decline was Ford's adamant refusal to break with the Model T. From its "birth" in 1908 to its "death" in 1927 few changes in the car were permitted.

The Rouge, the vast plant along the river in Dearborn, became a nightmare for its employees. While Ford for many years shunned away from publicity, this attitude changed suddenly. The announcement of the five dollar day, and his involvement in a settlement for peace of World War I (the Peace Ship adventure) were the first indications; his acquisition of the weekly publication the *Dearborn Independent* reinforced the change in his attitude. It continued with a senatorial nomination and thoughts of running for the presidency, and developed further with a vicious and prolonged anti-Semitic campaign in his newspaper; then came battles with the unions, Wall Street, and the New Deal. In September 1945 Henry Ford was finally compelled to resign the presidency in favor of his grandson, Henry Ford II.

THE MODEL T

In August 1906 the editorial of the magazine *Motor Age* showed remarkable foresight in the following article:

Most of the material in this case originates from the doctoral dissertation of Dr. Anne Jardim, *The First Henry Ford: A Study on Personality and Business Leadership*, which was supervised by Professor Abraham Zaleznik. Copyright © 1969 by the president and Fellows of Harvard College.

Exhibit 1

The Life Cycle of Henry Ford and the Ford Motor Company
Childhood and Early Career

1863	Born in Dearborn, Michigan
1876	Death of his mother
1879	Departure from the farm to work in Detroit
1882	Return home
1888	Marriage
1891	Return to Detroit to work as an engineer for the Edison Illuminating Company
1896	First automobile completed
1899	Employed by the newly formed Detroit Automobile Company
1901	Dissolving of the Detroit Automobile Company
	Founding of the Henry Ford Company
1902	Departure from the company
1903	Founding of Ford Motor Company
1903–07	Production of seven models

Growth and Power of the Ford Motor Company

1905	Founding of the Ford Manufacturing Company
	Announcement of plans for mass production
	Establishment of an experimental tractor shop
	Death of his father
1907	Consolidation of the Ford Motor Company and the Ford Manufacturing Company
	Construction of the Highland Park plant
1908	Introduction of the Model T
1913	Announcement of termination of the contract between the Dodges and the Ford Motor Company
1914	Announcement of the five dollar day
1915	Plans announced for the construction of a blast furnace and tractor plant along the River Rouge
	Peace Ship
1917	Production of the tractor
	Ford Plant transformed for war production
1918	Henry Ford's resignation of the presidency in favor of Edsel Ford (reappointed after Edsel's death)
	Candidacy for the senatorial election in Michigan
1919–25	Construction of the Rouge
1920	Beginning of the anti-Semitic campaign
1927	Abandonment of the Model T
	Manufacture of tractor transferred to Ireland
	Apology to the country's Jews
1945	Resignation of the presidency in favor of his grandson, Henry Ford II

The simple car is the car of the future as only a few years will show and the maker who will begin on the policy of extreme simplicity will have his reward in an ever-increasing business and possibly small but satisfactory and steady profits. . . . The present-day design of the motor car does not tend toward extreme simplicity. . . . The simple car will not only be the car for the masses but will be easier to make, more satisfactory to sell and more sensible for the ordinary man to use. The average man wants a simple car, the simplest that can be made, and such a car will prove so popular, as to bring sufficient credit and remuneration to its maker. A golden opportunity awaits some bold manufacturer of a simple car.[1]

Of all the manufacturers who had begun to build cars, Henry Ford was the only one who realized that the majority of the population was unwilling to spend more than $1,000 for a car, and that the economies necessary to enable the production of low-priced cars could only occur if the number of models would be reduced to the bare minimum to obtain maximum standardization. And standardization was what he implemented until the adoption of the "any color so long as it is black" policy.

To sense that the future of the automobile industry lay in the cheap car was not as simple as it might appear. In 1902, cars selling at $1,375 or under represented approximately two-thirds of the total production. By 1906, however, cars in the price range $2,275 to $4,775 represented 45 per cent of total production and by 1907, in a complete reversal of the 1903 position, cars costing less than $1,375 formed only one-third of the total sales. Given these figures, it was far from easy to foresee in 1905 that the demand in the high-priced range would have less than two per cent of the total market by 1916."[2]

In 1879 at age 16, Henry Ford left his father's farm for Detroit's machine shops, but after three years he returned home. He worked irregularly on the farm spending the bulk of his time operating and servicing steam engines for neighboring farmers. In the early 1880s, he built a "farm" locomotive which was essentially a tractor powered by steam. This locomotive ran 40 feet only once, and although it never ran again, Ford continued to experiment.

It was Ford's impression that too much hand labor was spent on the farm.

To lift farm drudgery off flesh and blood and lay it on steel and motors had been my most constant ambition. It was circumstances that took me first into the actual manufacture of road cars. I found eventually that people were more interested in something that would travel on the road than in something that would do the work on the farms. In fact, I doubt that the light farm tractor could have been introduced on the farm had not the farmer had his eyes opened slowly but surely to the automobile."[3]

In September 1891, accompanied by his wife of three years, Ford left the farm which his father had given him when he married, and returned to Detroit to work as an engineer with the Edison Illuminating Company. Ford seemed to have spent his time on the job picking up information whenever possible and experimenting with engines. In these early years Ford's concern lay with the engine, but hardly at all with the automobile.

At the end of 1898, Ford completed his second car (his first car had been completed two years earlier). Within the year several prominent Detroit businessmen had agreed to back him and the Detroit Automobile Company was formed. This second car, which might have put the Detroit Automobile Company on its feet, was never put into production. While the shareholders held on, Ford designed failure after failure. In 1901, the formal notice of dissolution for the company was filed. In the meantime, Ford was building racers and in October 1901 his car won a race. At the end of November, his early backers agreed again to finance him. This time the Henry Ford Company was organized with Ford as a shareholder for the first time. This company was to manufacture a small car, but Ford had "the racing fever," which resulted in a disagreement with the other shareholders. Ford left the company in 1902.

In August 1902 Alexander Malcomson, a coal merchant, signed an agreement with Henry Ford to establish an automobile company which began operations in 1903. The agreement required Ford "to devote his time to the construction of a commercial automobile for exhibition purposes." The partnership was to continue until the car was built and capital raised to form a manufacturing company.

Ford was still unable to freeze a design, (between 1903 and 1907 there were seven models produced) but the assembly method of operation (realized through a contract with the Dodges) meant that substantial contracts had to be set up months in advance, and because of his business manager Couzen's persistance, Ford was compelled either to have his design changes ready or to defer them to a subsequent model. With deadlines to meet and hard-headed businessmen to contend with, the cycle of failures, which had started with the Detroit Automobile Company, was broken.

In May 1905, Henry Ford called reporters in to announce grandiose plans—to reach the masses by selling 10,000 cars at $500 each.[4] In November of that year, Ford took a step toward control of the company's manufacturing operations with the formation of the Ford Manufacturing Company (a concern quite separate from the Ford Motor Company) in which Ford, with 2,550 of the 5,000 shares issued, had, for the first time, majority control. In the same month plans were announced for the Model M. For its production, the basis was laid for the assembly line idea. In the same year, Ford established an experimental tractor shop in a barn a short distance from the Ford plant.

On October 1, 1908, the Model T was introduced and took the market by storm. The car was strikingly successful in the vast agrarian market. The price cuts which became Henry Ford's equivalent to an annual model change expanded demand down the line to even the lowest income groups.

> The Model T was sold on service—it was rugged and reliable and could be easily fixed by men accustomed to handling machinery; it was sold on price at $440 in 1914, a gap of nearly $500 existed between the T and its nearest competitor, and it was sold for cash on the barrelhead by the company. If they needed it, Ford dealers were compelled to arrange their own financing, and since the largest market segment prepared to pay cash was the farm belt, this was the market which was most intensively cultivated. The T, more than any other was the farmer's car.[5]

With the expansion of the company's manufacturing facilities and the price cuts permitted by the economies of scale, the production climbed from 1800 cars in 1905 to 534,100 in 1915 to 2,049,400 in 1925.

Throughout the years Ford turned a deaf ear to suggestions for improvements in the Model T. Complaints started to pour in from Ford agents—the car's brakes were unreliable, the planetary gear shift hopelessly unsatisfactory in the light of the advances made by the company's competitors. In spite of this, the last Model T had to be similar to the first one!

A good example of Ford's refusal to adopt improvements of the Model T occurred after his return from his first visit to Europe. During his absence, his most trusted subordinates, Wills, Sorensen, and Martin, developed a new model which in design was lower and 12 to 15 inches longer than the Model T. Ford tore the car to pieces! An eyewitness account reads:

> He had his hands in his pockets and he walked around that car three or four times, looking at it very closely. It was a four-door job, and the top was down. Finally he got to the left-hand side of that car that was facing me, and he takes his hands out, gets hold of the door, and bang! One jerk, and he had it off the hinges! He ripped the door right off! God! How the man did it, I don't know!
>
> He jumped in there, and bang goes the other door. Bang goes the windshield. He jumps over the backseat and starts pounding on the top. He rips the top with the heel of his shoe. He wrecked the car as much as he could.[6]

However, time was working against the Model T. Rising incomes, installment selling, and trade-in plans made the consumers receptive to more expensive cars and made annual model changes more attractive. The sales figure for Ford cars made this trend increasingly clear. In 1924 Ford controlled two-thirds of the market; by the end of 1926 his share had fallen to one-third, and the general feeling in the industry was that his excess production capacity ran to nearly 40 per cent.[7]

A joke about the Model T once told to President Wilson by Henry Ford had macabre connotations:

> "Once when passing a graveyard," he told Wilson, "[a man] saw a huge hole being dug and asked the grave-digger whether he intended to bury an entire family." "No," said the grave-digger, "the grave is for just one person." "Then why is it so big?" The digger explained that the dead man had been a very queer fellow; he had specified in his will that he should be buried in his Ford because the Ford had pulled him out of every hole so far and he was certain it would pull him out of this one.[8]

Ford tried to meet the demand for a closed car by putting a cumbersome body on the Model T without essentially changing its open-car design, but the annual model change he completely rejected:

> "The Ford car," he said in 1926, "is a tried and proved product that requires no tinkering. It has met all the conditions of transportation the world over. We are developing broader markets in South America, Australia and Europe. Within ten years, Russia will be a big customer. . . . The Ford car will continue to be made in the same way. We have no intention of offering a new car. . . . We do not intend to make a 'six,' an 'eight' or anything else . . . we have experimented with such cars as we experiment with any things. They keep our engineers busy, prevent them from tinkering with the Ford car."[9]

Finally, on May 26, 1927, the Model T assembly lines at Highland Park and the Rouge shut down. In the same year the manufacture of the tractor was transferred to Ireland.

THE NEED FOR CONTROL

Ford's leadership style was characterized by his need for control. Ford's fellow shareholders were the first ones to face this tendency; later it was felt by company executives, the government, and the unions.

Ford's first battle began in 1903 against the Electric Vehicle Company, which had acquired the Selden patent. This patent covered in the broadest terms the application of the compression gas engine to road or horseless carriage use. It implied that the holder had the power to impose a monopoly on the industry. After a long series of court hearings, the patent was finally held invalid.

Slowly but persistently, Ford was getting rid of the other shareholders in the Ford Motor Company as well as in the Ford Manufacturing Company. These two companies were consolidated on April 29, 1907.

As production of the car started to increase, the company inevitably outgrew its existing plant. In 1907, the company acquired 57 acres at Highland Park, on the outskirts of Detroit, and there the actual implementation of standardization and mechanization took place. The principle of the Ford method of production was the process line, in which the car moved through a sequence of men and machinery from the raw state to the finished product. The company's engineers were free to concentrate on production methods instead of the annual model change, and were able to break down operations into the simplest steps eliminating the learning curve. Ford was so far ahead that no other manufacturer could catch up with him. Even if they were to freeze their designs, none had the volume to allow the highly specialized machine tools, and given the policy of model changes, the limited time in which specialized tools would be in use, pushed their costs even higher than those of hand operations.[10]

It was with justification that the presidents of Packard, Paige Motors, Hupp Motors, and the chairman of the Dodge Company later agreed that competition with Ford in 1913 was impossible.

The massive stream of cars which flowed from Highland Park moved to the company's branch houses as well as directly to its dealers. The branch houses were retail offices which stocked parts and finished cars for sale to individual buyers as well as for delivery to dealers. The advantage of the branch system over the wholesale distribution method used by Ford's competitors lay in the close supervision of the company's dealers; the company retained absolute control over the prices of cars, parts, and accessories, and could enforce the standards of service which were required by the dealers' franchises.

In 1913, John F. Dodge announced his resignation from the Board of Directors of the Ford Motor Company and gave one year's notice of the termination of the contract between Dodge Brothers and the Ford Motor Company. From 1903 the Dodges, in addition to ownership of ten per cent of the company's stock, had been prime suppliers of parts. They were committing their entire output to a single customer whose private and public position was to exploit the economies of scale, economies made possible by the scope of his own operations, in order to reduce the price of the Model T. The Dodge plant was not subject to the close control the Ford Company wielded over its other suppliers and Ford would undoubtedly soon refuse to pay the double profit the Dodges earned from Ford dividends and from the volume orders for parts.[11] Rather than wait for Ford to terminate the contract, the Dodges took the initiative.

In June 1915, Ford announced that he planned to build a blast furnace and tractor plant on a site of more than 1,000 acres along the River Rouge. In the following month, a further announcement was made: the new venture would be a partnership under the name of Henry Ford and Son. Financed by Ford himself, it would not be interfered with by "absentee stockholders who do not labor but merely invest their money." The new venture resulted in a lawsuit by the Dodges after they discovered that Ford was planning to use the engine of the Model T to produce a tractor and that he would cut down the dividend payments to expand the business and reduce the price of the Model T even more. Because of the price cuts, Ford cut the profits for 1917 in half. The Dodges requested an injunction to restrain the program of expansion, as it would also imply duplication of production facilities (with their facilities), and to implement the distribution of 75 per cent of the current cash surplus— approximately $39 million.

The Supreme Court finally decided that a special dividend equal to 50 per cent of the fiscal 1916 cash surplus, less dividends paid in fiscal 1917, be distributed.

Though the company was still in a position to afford its plans for expansion Henry Ford set his plans for expansion momentarily aside and started a series of moves intended to get rid of its stockholders. He resigned the presidency of the Ford Motor Company in December 1918 with the intention of devoting his time to building up other organizations, and his son, Edsel, became his successor. He stated in an interview with the *Los Angeles Examiner*:

> As I do not believe in subsidiary companies I cannot resort to that method which many financiers employ. My only recourse is to get out, design a new car which can be sold cheaply and which will be in all details up to date. The only other venture I have gone into is our tractor company and this will be the method of handling; that is through Henry Ford and Son Incorporated. In this company, all the stock will be held by my family.[12]

Within weeks of the Los Angeles interview the stockholders, one by one, afraid of the implications of his statements and remembering the "Dodge Affair" opened negotiations for the sale of their stock.

ESCAPADES

In 1912, Ford was 59 years old, and his business career was to continue for another 33 years. The Model T was finished and he was in the process of winning control of the company and building it into the largest and most intensively integrated plant in the world—in order to build still more Model T's. Side by side with these developments came Ford's involvement in the public realm, which began with the declaration of the five dollar day in January 1914. The announcement of the five dollar day came simultaneously with an announcement of a reduction in working hours from nine to eight hours a day. In addition, the company stated that it would arrange its annual production schedule in such a way that layoffs would be made at harvest time "to induce our men to respond to the calls of farmers for harvest hands."[13]

Ford's popularity after his announcement of the new working benefits was short lived, and because of his "escapades" the general public began to ridicule him.

Henry Ford developed a pacifist's view of the world. In April 1915, he said that if the United States entered the war, rather than accept a single order for cars which might be used for military purposes, he would see his factory burned to the ground. In September, he had given $1 million to fight preparedness, and a few days later had announced that he would increase the gift to $10 million.

Louis Lochner, an American associated with the Fifth International Peace Congress and Rosika Schwimmer, a Hungarian feminist writer, visited him. They proposed a campaign aimed at arousing the public demand for peace which might encourage President Wilson to summon a conference of the neutral nations.

Ford agreed to help and during a luncheon with a group of prominent pacifists Lochner made the half-serious suggestion that a ship should be chartered to take the peace delegates to Europe. The effect on Ford was immediate. That afternoon the *Oscar II* was chartered amid the protests from participants, and two days later when Ford met with Wilson it was already Ford's peace conference. When the president said he approved the idea of continuous mediation but that he could not be tied to one project only in the quest for peace, Ford decided that Wilson was a "small man."[14]

The arrangements for the voyage and the ridicule began: "Great War Ends Christmas Day, Ford To Stop It," said the headlines of the *New York Tribune* on November 24, 1915.

Invitations to join the expedition were sent and inevitably the refusals came streaming in. The ridicule which surrounded the departure of the Peace Ship continued undiminished during the voyage. When the ship docked in Oslo, Ford discussed with the amazed reporters, not the prospects for peace, but his farm tractor:

> Machines and not men would now be the drudges; he had not patented his invention and he would attempt to prove to the arms manufacturers that they could make a large profit by building tractors rather than guns.[15]

On the following day, Ford left Norway for the U.S. Tentative plans had been made for establishing a Conference for Continuous Mediation made up of like-minded men and women in the neutral countries. While Ford continued to finance the Conference from Dearborn, the extent of his support was steadily reduced. On February 7, 1918, financial assistance was brusquely terminated. In the meantime, "the transformation of Henry Ford from Peace Angel to Vulcan was effected in less than a week."[16]

On February 3, 1917, Wilson severed diplomatic relations with Germany and two days later Ford announced: "In the event of a declaration of war, I will place our factory at the disposal of the United States Government and will operate without one cent of profit."[17] Ford never lived up to that statement.

In the first months of the war, Ford suggested a one-man submarine: "Carrying a man apiece, they will run out below the biggest battleship afloat, touch off a bomb beneath it; and blow the ship out of existence."[18]

Ford's involvement was a passing thing; by the war's end, he was already engaged in other "causes."

A good example of Ford's superficial involvement in his "causes" was the trial of a libel suit which Ford had begun in 1916 against the *Chicago Tribune*. His pacifist stand at that time was construed by that newspaper to mean that he opposed the calling of the National Guard which had taken place in June 1916 in the face of unrest on the Mexican border. A Ford spokesman had in fact stated that any Ford employee who answered the call would forfeit his job. No such measure was taken by the company, but the *Tribune* published an editorial which called Ford an anarchist and an ignorant idealist. The trial took place in 1919 and was decided in his favor, but the jury of farmers made it a hollow victory. The million-dollar claim for damages was settled for an award of six cents.

During the course of the trial, the extent of Ford's ignorance once the automobile was set aside was painfully delineated by the counsel for the newspaper:

Counsel: "There have been several governments overthrown in Mexico during that period, haven't there?"

Ford: "I think there have, but still you can go down and travel."

Counsel: "Were you able to travel in 1915 and 1916?"

Ford: "You are able to travel now."

Counsel: "I said in 1915 and 1916."

Ford: "Got 300 tractors there in the last six months."

Counsel: "Did you hear my question? I move to strike that out as not responsive."[19]

On June 14, 1918, Ford's candidacy was announced for the senatorial election in Michigan. The campaign was notable chiefly because of the candidate's lack of participation:

"The president has asked me to become a candidate for United States Senator from Michigan," Ford said in September. " I know nothing about parties or party machinery and I am not at all concerned about which ticket I am nominated on . . . I shall not spend a cent nor make a single move to get into the Senate. I shall not have a campaign organization, nor pay any campaign bills. . . . I do not care anything about parties or politics or politicians. I would not walk across the street to be elected president of the United States. I certainly would not make a public speech to get the nomination or to be elected."[20]

Ford had in fact never made a public speech in his life, nor did he attempt to do so during the course of the campaign. The obvious result was defeat.

The intimacy politics called for, the endless involvement in planning, the day-to-day assessments of tactics, the need to appeal to other men's self-interest in the give and take of negotiations, all held little attraction for him. In the 1920s when there was a serious movement afoot to nominate him for the presidency, F.L. Black, a staff member on Ford's newspaper, asked him whether he really wanted to be president. Ford answered: "I'd like to be down there for about six weeks to throw some monkey wrenches into the machinery."[21]

After his defeat Ford turned on the victor of the senatorial election with an energy never exhibited before. Truman Newberry, the successful Republican candidate and a member of a prominent Detroit family, was hauled through the courts on charges of corrupt practice and bribery brought out by the instigation of a corps of private investigators hired by Henry Ford. Though finally cleared of charges by the Supreme Court, Ford maintained that "Wall Street interests" had bought Newberry his seat.

In November 1922, Newberry resigned from the Senate. In his letter of resignation, Newberry referred to the "political persecution" which he had to live with from the day of his election and to the "hundreds of agents who had hounded and terrified men in all parts of Michigan."

The ridicule which had begun with the Peace Ship had followed relentlessly on the heels of all of Ford's public actions. Although he was widely admired among farmers and factory workers, other than his own, and although he was looked up to by pacifists and prohibitionists alike, these were not the people who controlled the newspapers or wrote the wounding editorials. In self-defense Ford now adopted two seemingly separate strategies: he made himself far less accessible to the press by literally withdrawing behind a wall of secretaries and publicists, and he bought his own weekly newspaper, which would continue under its original name as the *Dearborn Independent*.

For the first one and a half years of its existence the newspaper confined itself editorially mainly to the support of Wilson and the League of Nations, but from the beginning, Ford had seen it as an instrument of enlightenment:

> "I am going to print the truth," he told Upton Sinclair in 1919. "I am going to tell the people what they need to know. I am going to tell them who makes war, and how the game of rotten politics is worked. I am going to tell them how to get the idle land into use above everything. I am going to tell the young men to find useful things to do, because that is the way to be happy in this world."[22]

In 1919 Ford's anti-Semitic attitude gained attention and

coincided with a feeling in the press that Ford had the idea the newspapers were persecuting him. Ford himself was quoted as saying:

> There is a good part, not all, of the American press that is not free. It is owned body and soul by bankers. When they tell it to bark, it barks. The capitalistic newspapers began a campaign against me. They misquoted me, distorted what I said, made up lies. . . . The invisible government got at its work.[23]

The first *Independent* article which was exclusively dedicated to anti-Semitism appeared on May 27, 1920. Under the banner, "The International Jew: The World's Problem," the paper announced:

> There is a super-capitalism which is supported wholly by the fiction that gold is wealth. There is a super-government which is allied to no government, which is free from them all and yet which has its hand in them all. There is a race, a part of humanity which has never yet been received as a welcome part of humanity and which has succeeded in raising itself to a power that the proudest Gentile race has never claimed—not even Rome in the days of her proudest power. It is becoming more and more the conviction of men all over the world that the labor question, the wage question, the land question cannot be settled until first of all this matter of an international super-capitalistic government is settled. . . . If all this power . . . has been gained and held by a few men of a long-dispersed race, then either they are supermen whom it is powerless to resist, or they are ordinary men whom the rest of the world has permitted to obtain an undue and unsafe degree of power. Unless the Jews are supermen the Gentiles will have themselves to blame for what has transpired and they can look for rectification in a new scrutiny of the situation and a candid examination of the experience of other countries.[24]

For 20 consecutive weeks the series continued. The threat of the "International Jew" was said to lie in the covert leadership Jews held all over the world; their master plan was to so demoralize the lives of Gentiles by war, revolution, and disorder that the control of world politics, finance, and commerce would fall into their hands. Given this all-encompassing conspiracy, everything and anything found its own good place. Morals had declined because Jewish money interests were working "to render them loose in the first place and keep them loose." Rents were skyrocketing because "the Jewish landlord" was at work. The short skirts of the flapper era "came out of Jewish clothing concerns." Gambling, pornography, even nightclubs—"every such activity has been under the mastery of the Jews."[25] The anti-Semitic articles were to continue through 90 issues of the newspaper. Reprinted in book from under the general title of "The International Jew," they were published in four volumes and also translated into German. By March 1923, the Munich correspondent of the *Chicago Tribune* reported that the books were "being distributed by millions throughout Germany to aid Hitler's campaign against the Jewish people in Germany."[26]

Like the Peace Ship, as abruptly as it had begun, the campaign would later be abandoned. On July 6, 1927, Ford released a sweeping retraction of, and apology for, the *Independent's* anti-Semitism:

> I deem it to be my duty as an honorable man to make amends for the wrong done to the Jews as fellow-men and brothers, by asking their forgiveness for the harm I have unintentionally committed, by retracting as far as lies within my power the offensive charges laid at their door by these publications, and by giving them the unqualified assurance that henceforth they may look to me for friendship and goodwill.[27]

PERSONAL HISTORY

Ford's memories of his childhood are striking for the closeness and immediacy with which his mother is recalled—and for the hesitation, indifference, and even hostility which characterize his recollections of his father.

However, Ford's earliest memory, one which he recorded himself (a very remarkable circumstance taking into account his dislike for dealing in written work) concerned his father.

> The first thing that I remember in my life is my father taking my brother, John, and myself to see a bird's nest under a large oak log twenty rods east of our home and my birthplace. . . . John was so young that he could not walk. Father carried him. I being two years older could run along with them. This must have been about the year 1866 in June.[28]

Henry Ford was born on July 30, 1863, in Dearborn, Michigan. William Ford, his father, was a farmer who had inherited 200 acres of his father-in-law's farm. This had put him in comfortable circumstances. William would reach the respectable age of 79, dying in 1905. His wife died in childbirth, when Henry was 13 years old. In one of the interviews Ford had with his first biographer he said about his mother:

> She was of that rarest type of mothers—one who so loved her children that she did not care whether they loved her. What I mean by this, is that she would do whatever she considered necessary for our welfare even if she thereby temporarily lost our goodwill. . . . [29]

Later in his life he pointed to the old farmhouse where he had been born and brought up and which he had restored: "You see that home across the street there? That's my mother's home. My father just walked into that place. That belonged to my mother."[30]

In an interview for the *American Magazine* Ford talked about his mother more extensively. The interview took place in the old farmhouse.

> As a tribute to his mother Henry Ford has restored the home she loved. It stands today exactly as it was in 1876; if not with the same furniture, with exact reproductions. There is no evidence that she is no longer here. . . . We were in her kitchen—the kitchen as it was when she was here doing for her children; spotless and orderly as she always kept it, not missing her presence, but radiant with something you could feel—a son's reverence for her. . . . I never had any particular love for the farm. It was my mother on the farm I loved. . . . You know, farm work is drudgery of the hardest sort. From the time I left that front gate as a boy until now my only interest in a farm has been to lighten its labors. To take the load off the backs of men and put it into metal has been my dream. If I can do that I shall have rendered in a real service to humanity—the sort of service she tried to teach me to perform.[31]

Reading the interviews of Henry Ford with his biographers and with journalists one might get the impression that he had fought a real battle with his father: first, over his mechanical bent; second, over his wish to leave the farm; third, over his belief in the future of the automobile. He painted a picture of himself as the persecuted small boy who repaired watches and clocks for the neighborhood, free of charge, after having stolen out of the house at night, against his father's commands.

However, this story has been flatly contradicted by Ford's eldest sister, Mrs. Margaret Ruddiman: "His father never forbid him to repair neighbors' watches. I never knew of him going out at night to get watches and bringing them back to repair them. Those are largely imaginative stories."[32]

The same imagination is shown in Henry Ford's account of his departure from home. When Ford left the farm for Detroit at age 16, it was not, Mrs. Ruddiman said, a dramatic instance of "the farm boy running away from home in order to pursue his life's work."[33] Yet this is Ford's account: "Without saying a word to anyone, I walked nine miles to Detroit, rented a room in which to sleep and sought employment in a machine shop."[34]

Once again Mrs. Ruddiman felt it necessary to contradict Ford's story:

> I wish to make clear the fact that we knew that at some time Henry would go to Detroit to learn more about steam engines and machinery. However, no time had been set and we did not know just when he would feel that he should begin his work and study. I am sure that father and Henry had discussed his leaving and the time had been left up to him. Of course father was disappointed that Henry did not wish to continue life on the farm, but if learning about machinery was what he wanted to do, father would not hinder him.[35]

One of Henry Ford's early acquaintances from Detroit confirmed this statement. "One morning I brought some valves into the office and while there I saw Henry Ford's father, and Henry was with him. I didn't know who they were but the next day Henry came to work. . . . ."[36] The people he went to work for were in fact old friends of Ford's father.

In 1882 Henry Ford returned to his father's farm and was to remain there for nine years. He was then 19, and had received his mechanic's papers. Mrs. Ruddiman said that the reason for his return was that he "wanted time to think and plan."[37]

Henry Ford's picture of his father who supposedly was unwilling to help him with the development of the automobile is also

questionable. Mrs. Ruddiman recollects: "It is true that my father offered to put money in the first automobile but my brother wouldn't
take money from my father or any member of the family. . . . I don't
know why my brother told my father not to invest money in the first
car, but he did just that."[38]

The discrepancy between Henry Ford's and his sister's stories was repeated in their account of his first trip home with his car:

> His first trip he took with his car was to his parents home, one of
> the employees remembered Ford telling him. He thought he re-
> ally had something and his dad got mad about it. He didn't like
> it at all. He thought it was something that would scare all the
> horses off the road. . . . He could never get his father interested
> in this idea—his father wanted him to be a farmer. The first
> trip when he went home to his dad, his father. . .was very
> disappointed.[39]

As must now seem inevitable, Mrs. Ruddiman's version
differs:

> It was characteristic of father that he would not ride in the car on
> his first day. He was as interested as all of us in the fact that here
> was the horseless carriage about which we had been hearing.
> He looked it all over and listened with interest to Henry's expla-
> nation of it, but he refused to ride in it. . . . Despite his refusal to
> ride in the car on that first Sunday, father was very proud of Hen-
> ry's achievement. He talked about it to us at home and he told
> his neighbors about it. . .and on later trips of Henry's to the
> farm, father rode in the car.[40]

It was only in the 1930s when Ford was in his seventies
that he eventually admitted to Ann Hood, a schoolgirl with a journalistic talent, that his father was "kind and just but a man of few words,"
yet his mother loved his father "with the deep love of a woman who
never had parents." He respected his father he said, but it was "to his
mother that he turned for love and understanding."[41]

The main disciplinarian in Ford's youth appeared to have
been his mother. In contrast to her dominance was his father's mild-
ness, even though one could get a different impression out of several
statements made by Henry Ford. Ford's relationships with other men
were characterized by the absence of intimacy. He could not establish friendships. A quotation out of the biography of Dean Marquis,

an Episcopalian clergyman who was hired by Ford to run the sociological department (personnel and labor relations) and who left at bitter odds with Henry Ford in 1921, illustrates the atmosphere he created inside the company:

> The Ford executive had added to those two uncertainties in life—taxes and death—a third that is discharge. Of the man climbing up in the Ford organization it may be said that he has but a short time to live and is full of misery. He cometh up and is cut down like a flower. He never continues for long on the job.
>
> A judge of national repute once said to me, I have a great admiration for Henry Ford, but there is one thing about him that I regret and can't understand, and that is his inability to keep his executives and old time friends around him. The answer is that it is not a matter of inability, but disability. He can't help it. He is built that way.[42]

The absence of close ties to men inside the company was paralleled by a similar absence outside and by a rejection even of his own brothers.

One of his top executives, Sorenson, wrote:

> He lived a life so secluded, that few ever saw him in his own home. I know of only two members of the Ford staff who ever spent a night with the Fords. One was our English manager, Lord Perry, I was the other. . . . Sometimes a boyhood friend or two would see him at his office, but I never knew him to look them up. . . . I knew his two brothers, William and John, but never saw them in his home. They hated him, either because they envied him or because they expected him to do more for them. . . .[43]

Another associate reaffirms Sorenson's statement:

> Mr. Ford was quite a strong family man, but the interesting part was that he didn't get on too well with his own immediate family. I'm quite sure that he didn't get along with his brothers, Bill and John, anywhere near as well as he did with his wife's family . . . he felt more friendly toward his sister than he did toward his two brothers.[44]

In a magazine article in which Ford discussed the four women in his life—his mother, his wife, his mother-in-law, and his sister. Mrs. Ruddiman was credited with being "a real sister" to him after his mother's death, and Ford did help her during his lifetime on a modest financial scale. But for his brothers he did little in comparison with what was done for his wife's large family and there was nothing whatever left to them in his will.[45]

Ford's behavior was characterized both by hyperactivity and his inclination to impulsive action. In his description of Ford, Dean Marquis would later note:

> A still picture of Henry Ford would be impossible for the simple reason that there is something in him that is never still. He thinks quickly and he acts quickly, and he is always thinking and acting. His normal state seems to be that of mental agitation, and it is an agitation that is contagious. In his presence no one is ever entirely at his ease, at least that is true of his employees. You come to feel certain of but one thing, and this is that with any work which he has to do, the unexpected is bound to happen. There is about him the fascination of an unlimited uncertainty. No living being knows what he is likely to do or say next. . . . As in every other man, there is in Henry Ford the mingling of opposing elements. In him, however, the contrast between these elements is more pronounced than in the average man. Phenomenal strength of mind in one direction is offset by lamentable weakness in another. Astounding knowledge of an insight into business affairs along certain limits stand out against a boasted ignorance in other matters. Sensational achievements are mingled with equally sensational failures. Faith in his employees and, at times, unlimited generosity toward them are clouded on occasion by what seems to be an utter indifference to the fate and feelings of the men in his employ. There seems to be no middle ground. . . . [46]

EXECUTIVE RELATIONSHIPS

Between 1919 and 1925, construction at the Rouge and the vast plan for integrated manufacture had cost Henry Ford at least $360 million. The company owned iron mines, timberland, and sawmills in Michigan's Upper Peninsula; coal mines in Kentucky and West Virginia; glass plants in Pennsylvania and Minnesota; rubber plantations in Brazil. Raw materials and finished products alike were carried in Ford ships, or over a Ford railroad in Ford freight cars. The Rouge produced coke, iron, steel, castings, engines, and bodies for Highland Park and the outlying assembly plants, and it built the company's tractors; starters and generators, batteries, tires, artificial leather, cloth, and wire were all Ford made. Ford production in 1925 was 20 per cent greater than the entire industry's in 1920.[47]

The underside of the strategy of expansion is the need to create a structure and to establish mechanisms of control. Ford Motor Company met neither of these needs. As late as 1933 a *Fortune* report noted:

> The Ford Motor Company has passed its formative period and needs an administrator at least as much as it needs a creator . . . . Taken as a whole, the company reflects most sharply the strengths and weaknesses of its founder. There are too many people who will do what Mr. Ford thinks and there are not enough people who can influence what Mr. Ford thinks.[48]

"What Mr. Ford thinks" had initially been the company's greatest strength: the decision that there should be no change in the Model T had led to enormous economies of scale; in turn, these had made price reductions a phenomenally successful marketing policy, and expected demand had encouraged further integration in the interest of additional economies. In the end Henry Ford had come to control the processes of production from the raw ore to the finished car.

Ford's thinking applied to personnel precipitated disaster. At the executive level the Ford Motor Company had no structure of authority derived from position: gradations of the power structures were defined by a man's closeness to Ford.

The Ford Motor Company, Henry Ford often said, offered no titles to any man. "The Ford factories and enterprises have no organization, no specific duties attaching to any position, no line of succession or of authority, very few titles, and no conferences."[49]

During the period 1920-21 a rapid turnover in executives took place:

> There was a great deal of apprehension because virtually every day or every few days, purges were going on. Departments were being eliminated overnight. These purges were not conducted on a scientific basis. Departments were completely wiped out.[50]

Decision-making lay secure in Ford's hands. The executive exodus had cleared the ranks of a large share of independent men. Those who remained, the closest to Ford and thus the most powerful, were implementers of his decisions rather than contributors to their formulation. It became increasingly clear to Ford executives that they worked not for a company with a definable purpose to which they could contribute, but for a single eccentric individual—Henry Ford.

In the company, authority was respected only where it was recognized that the executive who exercised it held Ford's personal favor and support. It was equally recognized that Ford's shifting moods might without warning upset the balance of the moment. For a Ford executive, each day might bring new groupings of power to contend with, and the *de facto* executive structure resulted in continuous conflicts. One executive made the comment:

> He constantly played man against man. Mr. Ford's idea was that both men would work harder because if one man lagged he would soon lose status. . . . He would give one of the men a job to do and at a later date he would give the other a job along the same lines and before long they both realized they were working on the same job.[51]

Conflict, Ford believed, was the most effective way not only of stimulating competitive effort, but of sorting out weak executives who were of no use to the company. Ford refused to accept or even to acknowledge the necessities of organization. The effects of this style of leadership were obvious. He became more and more manipulated by the people who surrounded him: Liebold, Bennett, and Sorensen.

The power which Liebold, Ford's private secretary, exercised was his by default. Since Ford alone could make a decision, the channels through which a request finally reached him assumed extraordinary importance and Liebold controlled outsiders' interviews with Ford. He handled Ford's personal finances and he kept a close watch on company affairs. He had direct control over Ford's corps of secret detectives whom he did not hesitate to use in the service of his own prejudices. An anti-Semite himself, he encouraged Ford's anti-Semitism. It was Liebold who often acted as "executioner" and discharged people.

However, Liebold's power was fleeting while Sorensen's became more prominent. Sorensen's power base was firmer than

Liebold's, as it was centered in Ford factories, while Liebold's power was related to a large extent to the anti-Semitic campaign. Sorensen was destroying potential rivals in the manufacturing organization. The elimination of rivals was part of Sorensen's price for submission to Ford. Like Liebold, he did as he was told. He said himself that he never tried to change Henry Ford's ideas and evidence is that he never did. But in order to carry out those ideas Sorensen had to overcome opposition which as often as not was of his own creation: by continually giving proof of his unswerving loyalty, he could damn another man in Ford's eyes by the mere insinuation of disloyalty, and he used Ford's ambivalent attitude toward his own son to his personal advantage.

Ford's attitude toward his son, Edsel, was characterized by an ambivalence so extreme that throughout his life it laid him open to the grossest forms of manipulation. One of the executives mentioned: "Henry Ford was constantly trying to train Edsel Ford in the way he thought the responsibilities of Edsel's job should be discharged. He felt that Edsel had to be harsher, act faster, and he turned into a personality something like Sorensen's. Mr. Ford didn't think that Edsel was tough enough."[52]

Ford's method of hardening his son played perfectly into Sorensen's strategy.

> Mr. Ford would get Sorensen to do something against Edsel's will. Edsel couldn't have helped but know what was going on because we knew it ourselves.[53]

Edsel Ford was in fact fighting for the company's future and in doing so he further strengthened Sorensen's position. "Mr. Ford" said one executive later, "was unmerciful in embarrassing Edsel, in disagreeing with him, in not accepting Edsel's well-thought plans for bettering conditions within the company.... He was always opposed to anything that Edsel brought up that was progressive."[54]

In the later part of Ford's life, in the period where he developed disagreements with the government over the New Deal and the National Recovery Act and then with the United Automobile Workers over recognition, he came more and more under the influence of Harry Bennett, an ex-boxer who was head of the Ford Service department. Bennett's ties with the Detroit underworld were notorious, along with his involvement in Dearborn's corrupt politics, and he was the leading figure in the terror that enveloped the Ford plants in the thirties. A responsible labor leader writing in 1938 described the miasma of threat and intimidation for which Bennett was responsible.

> There are about eight hundred underworld characters in the Ford Service organization—they are the Storm Troops. They make no pretense of working, but are merely 'keeping order' in the plant community through terror. Around this nucleus of 800 yeggs, there are however between 8,000 and 9,000 authentic workers in the organization, a great many of them spies and stool pigeons and a great many others who have been browbeaten into joining this industrial mafia.[55]

At first a loyal subject, Bennett rapidly became Sorenson's rival. Bennett developed a stranglehold on the organization. In the words of an executive:

> The stranglehold was this. He had control of hiring and firing. He had control of the payroll department. He had control of transfers. He had control of transportation and communication. He had to approve all travel vouchers.
> That meant that one could not hire, fire, raise, or transfer a man. I could not make a long distance call, I could not send a telegram if he did not wish me to do so.[56]

In the 1930s, when the United Automobile Workers' drive to organize closed in on the Ford Motor Company, Ford turned to Bennett and his "service" department, and Sorensen was slowly superseded as he himself had superseded Liebold.

> Bennett was one of those fellows who in the presence of Mr. Ford was more or less like a lamb. He would jump in the Detroit River . . . if Mr. Ford told him. He reversed that policy if it was anybody else and tried to dominate them a hundred percent— the kind of domination you get when a man is quoting somebody else.[57]

In 1944 Sorensen himself fell before Bennett's axe. By then Edsel Ford was dead and Henry Ford was in a state of near senility. For over a year after the declaration of war in 1941 he had refused to acknowledge that there was a war:

He often told newsmen in my office that there wasn't war—it was all newspaper talk to get Americans excited and spend our money on munitions.[58]

Under severe family pressure, Ford in 1945 was finally forced to resign. His grandson, Henry Ford II, became president. In a legal deposition made in 1950 Henry Ford II said that Bennett was relieved of his responsibilities "about five minutes after I was made president."[59]

The rebirth of the Ford Motor Company had begun.

COMMENTARY

Henry Ford's particular talent revolved around concrete materials, such as the internal combustion engine, and mechanical processes involving the conversion of energy and motion. He had displayed his talents while on his father's farm, learning to repair farm equipment and watches. He was a tinkerer in the classic sense of that term. The French would have called the young Henry Ford a *bricoleur*, which presents a nuance not quite contained in the English term "tinkerer." A *bricoleur* fixes things, but the word implies a certain ingenuity in using the materials at hand to do the fixing.

A tinkerer works by trial and error. In contrast, as one moves up the scale of talents, there is increasing reliance on abstract knowledge, or more plainly, theory. An engineer uses theory to rapidly select more alternatives, and a scientist is even farther toward the abstract end of the continuum of talents. But even in the realm of science, there are gradations in the level of abstraction at which the scientist works. For example, the physicist may be experimental, which involves planning and manipulating objects along with observation and measurement. Then there are theoreticians, who work almost exclusively in the realm of abstract relations and principles.

There is a story of a young boy whose father took him to meet the great scientist, Albert Einstein. The youngster played the violin, as did Einstein, and the two discussed how the instrument makes sound. At a particular juncture in their conversation, the boy suggested that he demonstrate a principle involved in their discussion. Einstein shook his head and said, in effect, if it could not be worked out in theory, then it fell short in producing the aesthetics of knowledge.

Theory interested Ford not at all. He was the essence of the concrete thinker, who worked by doing, and in the doing, manipulated physical objects. The fact that he turned his interests to the motor car is not surprising. The romance of the self-propelled vehicle, of the possibility of a horseless carriage, captured the imagination of many young men in the United States and Europe.

It is important to recognize Ford's considerable talents not only to explain some of the reasons for his success, but also to understand its limitations. More importantly, we can now see why his particular talents were of little use in assuring his growth as an industrialist and a human being.

Ford fell victim to his success. Why this was so is one of the mysteries of his life, and undoubtedly, the life of other talented people. This victimization begins with what appears to be the outbreak of significant symptoms of mental disturbance after he had achieved his success with the Model T.

The introduction of the assembly line reduced the costs of producing a car, savings that Ford passed on to the consumer with consistently lower prices. Ford had realized a dream: producing a car for the farmer. Its simplicity in design, ease of maintenance and repair, and ability to traverse rutted and unfinished roads met the needs of rural America, although the car truly was a product for the masses, urban and rural alike.

Being a concrete thinker prevented Ford from seeing his product in an abstract sense. Even in venting his rage over Edsel's attempts to build a new and improved model, Ford could not find words. Instead, he literally ripped the mock-up apart with his bare hands. Some ability to think abstractly might have permitted Ford to imagine an automobile in the many functions it could perform, in the satisfaction of many of the consumer's needs. Abstract thinking might also have allowed Ford to see his organization in many different lights—for example, as a place for advancing product development, technology, and manufacturing processes.

In addition to the limitations imposed upon him by the nature of his talents, Ford's fixation on the Model T and his obsession for keeping the product in its fixed and final form both reflected a disturbance in his mental functioning. He also exhibited other symptoms, such as grandiosity, megalomania, and hostile reactions suggestive of a suspicious nature, if not paranoid apprehensions. His anti-Semitic campaign in the *Dearborn Independent* provided him with an outlet for his suspicious and hostile reactions.

That he endured significant humiliations, brought on by his grandiosity, suggests he operated under the burden of significant blindspots. It was not unrealistic for him to enter politics, but that he had so little conception of what running for office entails, and even less conception of the responsibilities of office, made him vulnerable to ridicule. His ill-conceived venture with the Peace Ship and the grandiose notion that he could bring an end to World War I were manifestations of unrealistic thinking. He had bargained away his sense of reality in exchange for a buffer against massive depression. But depression caused by what? Common sense would suggest that people who fail in a venture become depressed, not people who succeed. Is Ford's reaction to success a totally aberrant phenomenon, or is it comprehensible, and even more commonplace than superficial observation would suggest?

In the climb to the top, the would-be power holder operates with uncanny sharpness, and all appearances indicate a well-organized, purposeful individual. Once having achieved the pinnacle, the power holder becomes vulnerable to certain frustrations not yet experienced, or if experienced, tolerated in the dedication to achieving goals. There are commonplace frustrations, such as not being able to see results as rapidly as one would like. President Truman, who was famous for the sign over his desk ("The buck stops here") remarked about his successor, President Dwight D. Eisenhower, "Poor Ike. He'll order people to do this and do that and he'll discover nothing gets done." Truman was referring to the differences in the experience, and expectations, of a military as contrasted with a political leader. The frustrations of not having one's program and decisions implemented are real, but there are also other hidden frustrations that can be deadly to the well-being of a powerholder. It seems probable that "being wrecked by success" was an outcome of Ford's unrealized, and unconscious, hopes.

While it may seem improbable, Ford built the Model T for his father. The critical notion here is the use of the car as a means of correcting a perceived fault in his development and his relations with his parents. This interpretation seems improbable because of Ford's overt hostility toward his father. He manifestly worshiped the ground on which his mother stood (the restoration of the farmhouse was a monument to his idealized version of who his mother was and what his relation to her was like) while he denigrated the image of his father. If it had not been for Mrs. Ruddiman (Henry Ford's sister), we would have been left with this sharply-drawn contrast between a good and giving mother and a harsh, unsympathetic father.

In her oral history interviews, which are in the Ford Archives in Dearborn, Michigan, Mrs. Ruddiman presents a different picture of their father. Far from being unsympathetic to his son's talents and ambitions, the elder Ford helped, including getting young Henry his first job in Detroit.

Rewriting personal history is commonplace for power holders, even to the extreme of inventing one's life. Facts count for little. What become facts are those necessities of the mind designed to maintain a balance, often precarious, between desire and conscience.

What is indisputable fact is that Ford's mother died when he was 13 years old. How did he experience this loss, and what were its consequences for his personality organization? This question becomes more complicated because of the possibility that Ford had already, as a much younger child, experienced loss of his mother upon the birth of younger siblings. The idealized image of the mother would appear to have been a means of recapturing the lost mother. The hostility toward his father, despite evidence that the elder Ford was a kind and understanding father, was misdirected yet psychologically useful. He probably carried a great deal of rage toward his mother that had become displaced onto his father. The Model T, as the car for the farmer (the father), served as a symbol of a restored relationship with his father, and consequently, as a restored relationship, at a deeper level, to the mother whom he had lost.

Psychic symbols can have considerable relevance in our lives, but they never measure up to reality. A car is just a car. One can view it concretely, as a convenience for getting from here to there, or abstractly, as a product in a consumer market, as a manifestation of technical understanding, or in many other forms. The ability to think abstractly is valuable because it helps avoid the mistakes of investing emotionally more than one should, or of holding expectations that can never be realized. The car never could have been restitutive of lost objects, nor could it have restored a past that, if it had existed, was transitory.

The tragic side of this misplaced investment was the near destruction of the Ford Motor Company as it lost position in the marketplace, allowing General Motors and other car makers to capture market share with flexible product designs, pricing points, and market positions. Even more tragic is the failure of Ford's relationship with his son Edsel. Ford would never let his son be the kind of son that, perhaps, Ford wanted to be to his father. Instead, Ford played out his hostility to his father by elevating Harry Bennett, a crude gangster so unlike his real son, to a position of considerable power in the Ford Motor Company. Perhaps reflecting Ford's own state of mind, the company became a seedbed of infighting, paranoid suspicion, and self-serving behavior. A police state and a fascist political body were far cries from the enlightened view of the corporation that was being promoted by industrialists such as Alfred Sloan of General Motors, and leaders in the human relations movement such as Professor Elton Mayo of the Harvard Business School.

After Edsel Ford died of cancer, his widow deposed the elder Ford and turned control of the company to her son, Henry, and a group of outside executives and advisors. Henry Ford II went a long way toward redeeming the presence and vision of the Ford Motor Company. Soon after taking office, he fired Harry Bennett, brought new blood into the company, and helped rebuild it into a successful corporation.

One of the lasting ironies of this story of a man (and a company) wrecked by success is the ill-fated introduction of a new automobile in the 1950s. The car was to represent a new, forward-looking design. Instead, it became an object of ridicule and was soon removed from the product line. The car was called the Edsel.

Endnotes—Chapter 12

1. Editorial, "Simplicity Apparently Not the Objective," *Motor Age* vol. X, no. 6 (August 9, 1906): 8.

2. Ralph C. Epstein, *The Automobile Industry: Its Economic and Commercial Development* (Chicago: A.W. Shaw, 1928), pp. 76-77.

3. Henry Ford, *My Life and Work* (Garden City, NY: Doubleday, 1923), p. 36.

4. *Detroit Journal*, 9 May 1905.

5. Allan Nevins and Frank Hill, *Ford: The Times, the Man* (New York: Scribners, 1954), vol. I., p. 509.

6. George Brown, *Reminiscences*, Ford Archives, pp. 110-111.

7. "Ford to Fight it Out With His Old Car," *New York Times*, 26 Dec. 1926, sec. 8.

8. Louis P. Lochner, *Henry Ford: America's Don Quixote* (New York: International Publishers, 1925), p. 23.

9. "Ford to Fight it Out With His Old Car," *New York Times*, 26 Dec. 1926, sec. 8.

10. Memorandum of conference with Oscar C. Borhnoldt, July 1926, accession 96, box 1, Ford Archives.

11. *Detroit News*, 4 Nov. 1916. [Ford estimated that the Dodges had made $10 million profit on their $27 million worth of sales to Ford Motor Company.]

12. *Detroit News*, 20 Nov. 1915.

13. Harry Barnard, *Independent Man: The Life of Senator James Cousens* (New York: Scribners, 1958), p. 131.

14. Lochner, *America's Don Quixote*, p. 25.

15. Nevins and Hill, *The Times, the Man*, p. 45.

16. Ibid., pp. 52, 55.

17. Ibid., p. 55.

18. Ibid., p. 56.

19. State of Michigan in the circuit court of the county of Macomb, Henry Ford vs. The Tribune Co., vol. IX, p. 5976.

20. "Why Henry Ford Wants to Be a Senator," *World's Work* (September 1918): 522.

21. F.L. Black, *Reminiscenses*, Ford Archives, p. 21.

22. Upton Sinclair, "Henry Ford Tells Just How Happy His Great Fortune Made Him," *Reconstruction*, vol. I, no. 5 (May 1919).

23. "Henry Ford at Bay," *Forum*, (August 1919): 141.

24. Reprinted in the *Detroit Times*, 9 June 1920.

25. Nevins and Hill, *The Times, the Man*, pp. 314-315.

26. *New York Times*, 8 July 1927.

27. Ibid.

28. Ford Archives, accession 572, box 1.

29. Allan L. Benson, *The New Henry Ford* (New York: Funk and Wagnalls, 1929), p. 15.

30. Edward B. Litoyot, *Reminiscenses*, Ford Archives, p. 30.

31. Edgar Guest, *American Magazine* (July 1923).

32. Margaret Ford Ruddiman, "Memories of My Brother Henry Ford," *Michigan History*, vol. 37, no. 3, (September 1953): 243.

33. Ibid., p. 255.

34. Bensen, New Ford, p. 34.

35. Ruddiman, "Memories," p. 255.

36. Fred Strauss, *Reminiscenses*, Ford Archives, p. 30.

37. Ruddiman, "Memories," p. 259.

38. Margaret Ford Ruddiman, *Reminiscenses*, Ford Archives, p. 94.

39. Gustav Munchow, *Reminiscenses*, Ford Archives, p. 94.

40. Ruddiman, *Reminiscenses*, pp. 268-69.

41. Ann Hood, *Reminiscenses*, Ford Archives.

42. Samuel S. Marquis, *Henry Ford: An Interpretation* (Boston: Little, Brown, 1923), p. 52.

43. C.F. Sorenson, *My Forty Years With Ford* (New York: Norton, 1956), p. 12.

44. J.L. McCleod, *Reminiscenses*, Ford Archives, pp. 402-403.

45. William L. Stidger, "I've Been Helped by Everybody," *True Story Magazine* (1933).

46. Marquis, *Interpretation*, p. 160.

47. Nevins and Hill, *The Times, the Man*, p. 257.

48. "Mr. Ford Doesn't Care," *Fortune*, (December 11, 1933): 132- 133.

49. Ford, *My Life and Work*, p. 92.

50. L.E. Briggs, *Reminiscenses*, Ford Archives.

51. Black, *Reminiscenses*, p. 128.

52. Ibid., p. 53.

53. J. Galamb, *Reminiscenses*, Ford Archives, p. 131.

54. T.F. Gelli, *Reminiscenses*, Ford Archives, p. 109.

55. Benjamin Stolberg, The Story of G.I.O., p. 116. Cited in Nevins and Hill, *Ford: The Decline and Rebirth* (New York: Scribners, 1962).

56. L.S. Sheldrick, *Reminiscenses*, Ford Archives, pp. 87-88.

57. Frank Reichs, *Reminiscenses*, Ford Archives, p. 104.

58. Black, *Reminiscenses*, Ford Archives, p. 102.

59. U.S. Southern District of New York District Court, deposition of Henry Ford II in Harry Ferguson and Harry Ferguson Inc. *vs.* Ford Motor Company *et al*, January 1950, Ford Archives.

THE CASE OF AN OBSESSIONAL LEADER—FREDERICK WINSLOW TAYLOR

In our collective naivete, we tend to see in highly talented people more than is there. For example, because Henry Ford built a great car and a factory to produce it in vast numbers, and because he dramatically introduced the five dollar a day wage for his workmen, he became a folk hero. The popular press projected onto him the image of miracle worker. He was mentioned for high political office and his opinion was sought on diverse issues of public concern. Yet in back of this image stood an uneducated man incapable of dealing flexibly with ideas, and so unaware of himself that he believed the image, and acted on his grandiosity until he was successively humiliated in the courtroom, the press, and ultimately in the minds of the same masses of people who had worshipped him as a hero.

Ford's fall from grace can be traced to unconscious conflicts that had served him well as he labored to develop the car for the farmer. These same neurotic struggles proved his undoing as he became evermore fixated on the Model T. Humanity has a tendency to reproduce and relive old psychological conflicts. For talented and powerful people, these conflicts soon enter the public arena in the

CHAPTER

13

works they help stimulate, and also in the disabilities inflicted upon many innocent participants in the work of these gifted leaders.

Henry Ford's career overlapped significantly that of another important leader in industrialization and modernization. Frederick Winslow Taylor, known as the father of scientific management, produced a complex web of ideas and practices that revolutionized the factory.

Taylor was a focal point for industrial conflict. He fought with workers and managers alike to establish his system in the name of industrial harmony. Despite all the vilification, Taylor remained committed to scientific management as a system of ideas that would bring rationality to the workplace. The harmony that he expected to follow his scientific management was inherent in the method itself. His system required no transformation in motives or attitudes except for the acceptance of all the tenets and practices of scientific management as an orderly, impartial organizer of the factory.

Many myths surround the life of Frederick Winslow Taylor. One myth is that Taylorism, as scientific management came to be called, sought to take the initiatives and control of the workplace away from the craftsmen as well as the unskilled workers. There is truth to this myth, but what is mythological is the belief that scientific management was hostile to workers. The fact is that scientific management took control away from management as well as workers, and placed it in the hands of specialists in industrial engineering. Factory managers could not establish the plan of work any more than the workers. Procedure belonged to the "efficiency experts," who themselves were trained in the methods of scientific management. These methods included breaking down tasks into their smallest components. Measuring the time required to complete the steps, which had been subjected to careful study to eliminate unnecessary movement, led to establishing the physical set up for each job and the flow of work for the factory as a whole. Once implemented, there would be little reason for conflict, since wages were based on production through piece rates, and the standards were to be established objectively to result in "a fair day's pay for a fair day's work." Exploitation of the worker had no place in this system. If management appeared to be exploiting workers, such as by changing piece rates as workers achieved standard, the explanation lay not in the system, but in its abuse by ill-informed or greedy managers and owners.

The practices of scientific management took hold in industry after an equivocal start. Factory management resisted the approach almost as vehemently as workers. But the efficiencies realized through the organization of work following the principles of scientific management overwhelmed resistance. Yet Taylorism failed in its major objective of creating harmony in the workplace. The turbulence surrounding scientific management matched the inner turbulence Taylor experienced as an adult bent on a mission of industrial reform, and as an adolescent casting about for a line of work that would somehow bring some peace and harmony into his inner world. The method failed in this regard, just as it failed as a panacea for the industrial conflict of the late nineteenth and the first half of the twentieth century.

Frederick Taylor was a troubled man, suffering for most of his life from the debilitating effects of an obsessional neurosis. His life exemplified how a gifted individual could use his suffering to drive his talents. The aim of curing the human problems of an industrial civilization merged with his efforts to find a cure for the illness he had endured for most of his life. Here is the story of his life and his work, and how the two merged.

FREDERICK WINSLOW TAYLOR

Frederick Winslow Taylor, universally known as the "Father of Scientific Management," died on March 19, 1915. Within a few years after his death, his place in the industrial history of the world seemed to be assured, for he had laid, almost singlehandedly, the foundations for both the science of management and the wholly new profession of industrial engineering. Such eminent contemporaries as Walter Lippman, Louis Brandeis, and Dean Edwin Gay of the Harvard Business School unhesitatingly called him a "great man." New business schools such as Harvard and Dartmouth adopted Taylor's system of "Scientific Management" as the core of their curriculum. The spread of his ideas was not limited to the United States. By 1918, Taylor's sys-

This case was prepared by Dr. Sudhir Kakar. The material for this case is taken from his book: *Frederick Winslow Taylor: A Study in Personality and Innovation*, initiated and completed as part of the program in applied psychoanalysis at the Harvard Business School under the direction of Professor Abraham Zaleznik.

tem was taking on the trappings of an international movement, independent of particular economic systems or political ideologies. In France, a circular of the Ministry of War, dated February 26, 1918, and signed by George Clemenceau, pointed out the imperative necessity of the study and application of the methods of work according to the principles of "Taylorism" and ordered the establishment in each plant of planning departments, a central feature of the Taylor system. At the opposite end of the ideological spectrum, *Pravda,* in its issue of April 28, 1918, published an article by Lenin exhorting the Soviets to study and master the Taylor system.

The fact that both a conservative bourgeois regime in France and a revolutionary regime in Russia propagated Taylor's system should not be a surprising one. To them, Taylor's work was a part of *technology* with its implications of *universality* and *neutrality.* What Taylor had done was to enlarge the concept of technology which had hitherto been restricted to mechanical and chemical processes. His effort was to bring human work and the organization of work into the realm of technology. The principal moral "commandment" of his system was to increase productivity.

Taylor's system was directed to the following ends:

(a) the *standardization* of work, which meant the determination of the "one best way" of working; and

(b) a *control* so extensive and intensive as to provide for the maintenance of all these standards.

The time and motion studies, the introduction of planning departments, the charts for routing and scheduling, the standardization of tools as well as working conditions, the incentive schemes, the new methods of cost accounting. . . all of these innovations were parts of a system which took the control of production out of the workers' hands, as had hitherto been the case, and placed it firmly with the management. He was thus a prophet of modern work, revolutionizing industrial work to a degree which is hard to visualize without an extensive knowledge of the work patterns of the eighteenth and nineteenth centuries.

Exhibit 1

FREDERICK WINSLOW TAYLOR

Important Dates

1856	Born in Germantown, Philadelphia
1869–1872	Trip to Europe with parents, brother, and sister
1872–1874	Exeter
1874–1878	Apprenticeship in Enterprise Hydraulic Works
1878	Joined Midvale
1884	Marriage
1890	Left Midvale
1890–1893	General Manager of Manufacturing Investment Company
1893–1898	Independent consulting work
1896	Mother's stroke
1898–1901	Bethlehem Steel Company
1901	Dismissal from Bethlehem
	Adoption of children
	Giving up of paid work
1906	Elected president of A.S.M.E.
1909	Death of father
1911	Publishing of *Principles of Scientific Management*
1915	Died in Philadelphia

CHILDHOOD AND EARLY YOUTH

Frederick Taylor was born in 1856 in Philadelphia. He was the fifth generation of his family to be born in America, descending from an English Quaker who had settled in the region of the lower Delaware River in 1677. The family had steadily prospered and Taylor's grandfather, Anthony Taylor, had been a leading merchant who had amassed a fortune in trade with the East Indies. This had enabled him to retire at the age of 38 to a country estate. He was also a banker and a financier and one of the original organizers of the Farmer's National Bank of Bristol. Taylor's father, Franklin Taylor, was the youngest of Anthony Taylor's 11 children. To describe him in a sentence, one would say that Franklin Taylor was a gentleman of leisure, the Philadelphia counterpart of the English "squire," a pillar of the Philadelphia Quaker community which was concentrated around Rittenhouse Square and in Germantown.

Though the Quaker elite had lost political control of Pennsylvania after their refusal to support the Indian Wars of the 1750s, they formed a "solid" upper class parallel to the "fancy" Episcopalian upper class which lived on the Main Line. The dominant characteristics of this Quaker upper class were seclusiveness, simplicity, moral fervor, and clannishness. The Quaker aristocracy was more intellectual and introspective than its Episcopalian counterpart, and had a strong sense of family tradition and of caste. Franklin Taylor was a member of this caste. He shared and accepted its norms and it may not be, in fact, unreasonable to describe him as a gentleman of leisure, with the present connotations of the term. Of course, one did not work in the sense of holding a job to make money, or to get ahead. On the other hand, the Quaker ideal frowned on "one-who-did-not-work," or the wastrel. This resulted in a few of the professions being considered worthy of a gentleman . . . medicine, law, banking, and running the family firm. A lawyer in Philadelphia, using Esq. after his name, while everyone else had a Mr. before his, was accorded the same reverence as a Divine in Puritan Massachusetts or as a Herr Professor in Germany. The dilemma of how to get around the "job aspect" of the profession was resolved by not being a practicing lawyer for any great length of time. Though there were non-practicing doctors, much more common were the non-practicing lawyers.

In keeping with his position and the values of his times, Franklin Taylor was graduated from Princeton in 1840, took his M.A. from the same university, settled down in Philadelphia and was admitted to the bar in 1844. His practice of law, perfunctory at best, was soon given up and the only work which took up any amount of his time was his position as a secretary to a charitable organization. He thus fulfilled the Quaker ideal of combining "work" with "good works." Franklin Taylor was a cultivated man who loved poetry, history, and languages, especially the classical ones, and spoke highly of Cicero's *Orations*. Taylor's recollection of his father was "of his soft, mild manner and a gentleness which is almost that of a woman."[1]

Emily Winslow Taylor, Frederick's mother, had the stronger character. The women in the Winslow family were reputed to have been strong, self-reliant, and willful, believing in the power of private inspiration. Emily Taylor's grandmother, Thankful Hussey, had acquired some fame as a Quaker female preacher who often travelled unattended and on horseback from Maine to Rhode Island, preaching en route. Emily Taylor herself was a strong energetic woman, one of the leaders of the suffragette movement, who believed in the English ideal of keeping all one's emotions properly and decently suppressed. Her system of child-training was all "work, drill and discipline" while her household "truly was a thing, ruled, regular..."

> To one member of the family was assigned the duty of seeing that all the match receptacles were kept filled; and when after two years, she one day found a receptacle that had not been filled, the important thing with her was, not that all receptacles had been kept filled for two years, but that on this day there had been a lapse.[2]

Birge Harrison, who knew Taylor almost all his life writes in his recollections:

> Fred was always a bit of a crank in the opinion of our boyhood band, and we were inclined to rebel sometimes from the strict rules and exact formulas to which he insisted that all of our games must be subjected. To the future artist [Harrison] for example, it did not seem absolutely necessary that the rectangle of our rounders court should be scientifically accurate, and that the whole of a fine, sunny morning should be wasted in measuring it off by feet and by inches.[3]

Taylor suffered from insomnia all through his life. At the age of 12, being troubled by nightmares, he constructed for himself a harness of straps and wooden points, the latter so arranged that whenever in his sleep he turned over upon his back the wooden points would press the dorsal muscle and at once awaken him. Before going to a dance he would consciously and systematically list the attractive and unattractive girls with the object of dividing his time equally between them. In the diary of his trip to Europe, the only curious feature is the occasional listing of all stations that the train passed through with the exact times of arrival and departure.

It is also noteworthy that Taylor never was at ease in witnessing hostile scenes. Time after time he would play the role of the peacemaker. Throughout his adult life, Taylor would insist that scientific management was the only system that would make for peace and harmony between management and workers and that this was its only *raison d'etre*. As one of the workers who worked under Taylor during his early years at Midvale Steel perceptively put it:

.... His work, under the new Taylor System, seemed to be of the most contradictive character, that is he was working hard and quarrelling with many people to establish a system . . . the aim of which was to make permanent peace between employer and employee.[4]

In 1872, at age 16, Taylor entered Exeter along with his brother to prepare for Harvard. It was intended that the brothers follow the two sacred professions; Edward was to become a doctor and Frederick a lawyer, his father's profession. At Exeter, in his senior year, he led his class and diligently studied the classics, Virgil's *Bucolics, Georgic* and *Aeneid, Plato* and *Herodotus* in Greek. However, Taylor would write in a school essay:

In practical life a knowledge of the classics is of no benefit to any but professional men . . . when there are so many other studies which are equally good training for the mind, and which would be of use to us in our business and our professions in after life I do not think that time is well spent in studying Latin and Greek.[5]

He suffered from frequent headaches and restless sleep which he later attributed to the hard work of this period. He experimented with the harness and a variety of pillows, one made of tufted hair cloth and another made from a board covered with canvas. He also tried stretching strings across the bed uprights, and would then wake up with marks of the strings covering his face. In spite of the troubled sleep, he passed his entrance examination for Harvard with honors. He thus seemed to be well set for a career in law when he complained of failing eyesight, and went back to his parents' home in Germantown.

It must be mentioned that his father had complained in one of his letters to Taylor of "a great weakness of my eyes . . . indeed I cannot read or write for any length of time without pain in my eyes and headache, but I think with time and care I shall entirely recover."[6] After returning home and having abandoned his plans to attend Harvard and pursue a career in law he is reputed to have been a very disappointed young man.

Taylor spent a few months at home, restless, roaming about the house, unable to study and avid for the smallest jobs, such as carrying stones for his mother's hotbeds. If there were any reproaches made for his "failure" it was not by his parents but by his own conscience.

In late 1876, he joined a small firm, Enterprise Hydraulic Works, as an apprentice pattern maker and machinist. In the small, dark machine shop, the hours were long. Taylor would breakfast at 5:30 in the morning and then begin work by sweeping the floor. Although he hated manual labor and his eyesight was very early restored, he persisted in the weary duties of an apprenticeship, earning nothing in his first year, $1.50 a week in the second and third years and $3 per week in his fourth year. He was perhaps the only common laborer in America who was a member of the Philadelphia Cricket Club.

He sang tenor in a choral society and enthusiastically played in amateur theatricals, in which, besides being well known for his interpretation of the part of a German doctor who spoke broken English, he was famous for the fidelity and true to life quality of his performance of feminine roles.[7] In the four years of his apprenticeship, Taylor tried hard to identify with the workers. He imitated their dress and manners and always regretted that he could not learn to chew tobacco. More important, to the consternation of his family and friends, he learned to swear.

> . . .he would let loose a few good ones in the presence of the ultra respectable and the ultra staid. . .He did not swear when most men would and did swear when most men would not dream of it. . . . We may imagine that no feathered, non web-footed mother was more amazed and bewildered upon seeing her chicks take to water than was Emily Taylor when her offspring brought back from the shop a readiness to use words beginning with a big-big-D.[8]

Taylor later came to remember the apprenticeship period as the best training he ever had. This period, he said, taught him a profound respect for the American workman. In a lecture to Harvard students in 1910, he elaborated on this theme.

> Now, I assume that most of you gentlemen are not the sons of working men, and that you have not yourselves worked during any period of time, at least, with working men, and on the same level with them. The fact is, that in all essential matters, they are just the same as you and I are. The working man and the college professor have fundamentally the same feelings, the same mo-

tives, the same ambitions, the same failings, the same virtues . . .
We are all of the same clay.[9]

Taylor started his career in industry in 1874 during the period of very rapid industrial expansion which, by the end of the century, had made the United States the greatest industrial power in the world. This period brought the Industrial Revolution to its full flowering; by its end the United States had overtaken Great Britain and outraced Germany in industrial manufacturing. This was also the factory age, with the number and size of factories steadily increasing, spelling the destruction of the old artisan handicrafts. Until the middle of the nineteenth century, America had been a nation of small and medium businesses, but in the second half of the century the situation changed radically. As late as 1850, one of the biggest plants in the country was an ironworks that employed about 1,000 workers. The average New England textile mill employed two to three hundred operatives. No shop was so large that the manager did not know the older workers, and in most cases the manager was the owner or the active partner. The management style was a *personal* one, problems being solved *ad hoc,* empirically for each establishment. Knowledge about the solution was transmitted by observation or word of mouth and in most new firms had to be again rediscovered. Management was a kind of personal autocracy, depending completely upon the personality of the owner. With increasing factory size and increasing separation of ownership and management, the stresses on personal, autocratic management became correspondingly acute.

The problem was further complicated by the social upheavals in the aftermath of the Civil War and by the increasing labor unrest. Frequent depressions, lightning changes in technology that led to job insecurity and urban overcrowding, increased the labor unrest and gave impetus to the trade union movement. The stage was thus set for Taylor's work and Philadelphia, his hometown, was very much in the center of these changes and the strain they effected on social and industrial life.

YOUNG ADULTHOOD

In 1878, at age 22, Frederick Taylor finished his apprenticeship as a pattern maker and machinist. In the same year he joined the Midvale Steel Works as a common, unskilled laborer. In the year Taylor joined

Midvale, there were perhaps 400 men employed there. In a way, it was a microcosm of the industrial world in the period of transition between relatively small and large scale production, bigger than the typical factory before the start of industrial expansion and much smaller than the steel works of the early twentieth century. It was owned jointly by two friends of the Taylor family, E.W. Clark and William Sellers. There is much evidence to suggest that Taylor selected Midvale because of Sellers' personality.

Sellers was one of the most noted engineers in the country. He had an impressive physical presence—powerful build, bushy eyebrows, curving mustache and an imperial beard. Extremely self-confident, he had the reputation among his employees of being able to "growl like a lion, kick like a steer, and bawl like a bull."[10] Taylor, and there is no other word for it, absolutely adored Sellers. Sellers gave him "character," which Taylor defined as the ability to control oneself, body and mind, the ability to do things which are disagreeable along with unquestioning obedience to one's superior. There were many incidents with Sellers that demonstrated these lessons in character. Once Sellers gave him some drawings that he wished to see developed further. In a day or two Taylor returned with an entirely new set of drawings of his own preparation. "What are these?" asked Sellers as he started to look them over.

Enthusiastically Taylor informed him that he had become convinced that his (Sellers') ideas were impracticable and so he had worked up some of his own. In Sellers' office a fire was burning in the grate, and Sellers promptly threw the drawings into the fire.

"The next time," said Sellers, "perhaps you won't abandon any of my ideas as impracticable till you have first tried them out."[11]

There were other incidents of this kind, and later in his life while lecturing to young men in college, Taylor spoke of the important lessons they contained.

> For success, then, let me give one simple piece of advice beyond all others. Every day, year in and year out, each man should ask himself, over and over again, two questions. First, "What is the name of the man I am now working for?" and having answered this definitely, then "what does this man want me to do, right now?" Not, "What ought I do in the interest of the company that I am working for?" Not, "What are duties of the position that I am filling?" Not, "What should I do for my own best interest?" but plainly and simply, "What does this man want me to

do?" . . . . the most important idea should be that of serving the man over you his way, not yours; and that this lies, generally speaking in giving him not only what he wants but also giving him a little extra present of some kind.[12]

Taylor came to work directly under Sellers only in 1881. For the first three years, his superior was Charles Brinley, a "scholar and a gentleman," whom Taylor cordially hated for his "aloof," aristocratic ways. Taylor's private chamber of horrors consisted of bankers, scholars, theologians, and Germans and he never lost an opportunity to express his disdain of classical education or gentlemanly ways. If he had really wanted to, after his entry into the company, with his Exeter education and his social connections, there would have been no difficulty in getting a white collar job, at least as a clerk. Taylor had to substitute as clerk for a short time but his comment on that experience was:

I did the work all right, although it was distasteful to me, and after having trained another clerk to do the work of the shop I asked permission of the foreman to work as machinist.[13]

Shortly after this the management wanted a gang boss to take charge of the lathes and Taylor was appointed to this position. Previously the workmen in the shop, including Taylor, had an agreement to limit output. This limit was about one-third of the possible output and was a good example of restriction of output found in all industrial countries.

As soon as Taylor became the gang boss some of the workers came up to him and the following conversation (in Taylor's words) followed:

Now, Fred, you are not going to be a damn piecework hog, are you?

If you fellows mean you are afraid I am going to try to get a larger output from these lathes then, yes, I do propose to get more work out. You must remember I have been square with you fellows up to now and worked with you. I have not broken a single rate; I have been on your side of the fence. But now I have accepted a job under the management of this company and I am on the other side of the fence, and I will tell you perfectly frankly that I am going to try to get a bigger output from these lathes.

Then, you are going to be a damned hog.

Well, if you fellows put it that way, all right.

We warn you, Fred, if you try to bust any of these rates we will have you over the fence in six weeks.

That is all right. I will tell you fellows again frankly that I propose to try to get a bigger output off these machines.[14]

This was the beginning of a piecework fight which lasted nearly three years. Taylor fought with the usual management methods of time, fines, and dismissals while the workers, even the new ones, persisted in refusing to increase the output. The fight generated increasing bitterness. Taylor, who had set such great store on his good relationship and camaraderie with the workers, became increasingly anxious as this relationship steadily deteriorated.

Some of the workers even threatened him with physical violence and in one case actually threatened to shoot him. In spite of this evidence Taylor, in his testimony at the Congressional hearings in 1912, maintained that his relationship with the workers was one of mutual friendliness and that any strains existed only inside the factory and were forgotten by him, and presumably by the workers, immediately after working hours.

Later on he would say:

> I was a young man in years, but I give you my word I was a great deal older than I am now with worry, meanness, and contempt-ibleness of the whole damn thing. It is a horrid life for any man to live, not to be able to look any workman in the face all day long without seeing hostility there and feeling that every man around is his virtual enemy. This life was a miserable one and I made up my mind either to get out of the business entirely and go into some other line of work, or to find some remedy for this unbearable condition.[15]

In these three years, Taylor worked in the shops of Midvale from 6:30 in the morning to 5:10 in the evening and then walked the two miles back to his home. He often volunteered to work on Sundays as well as overtime on weekdays. After work he studied at home, taking courses in science and engineering. After walking home from work and eating dinner he would set his alarm clock for 2:00 a.m. when he would rise, bathe, and dress in his working clothes to study until 5:00 a.m. He would then lie down for half an hour's sleep before eating breakfast and catching the six o'clock train at the Reading railway station which would bring him to work. As the fight with the workers progressed his study habits were to change. After finishing studying he would not go to sleep immediately but take a midnight run through the deserted streets of Germantown.

In 1881 the fight with the workers came to an end. The "aloof" Brinley had retired and Taylor came in close contact with Sellers. Taylor now tried to analyze the causes for the fights with the workers and came to the conclusion that no one really knew what a fair day's work was. Realizing this, he asked permission from Sellers to make a series of experiments to find out how quickly various kinds of work ought to be done. One of the types of investigations which was started at that time came to be later known as the "time study."

The years between 1881 and 1890, when Taylor left Midvale, may also be called the "years of achievement." Freed from personal anxiety, he was now able to direct his tremendous energy toward revising and incorporating a theoretical solution into a practical system. By 1883, at the age of 27, Taylor had received his master's degree in mechanical engineering, through home study, from the Stevens Institute of Technology. By 1884, in a period of six years, he had advanced from the position of unskilled laborer to that of chief engineer of Midvale. This was also the year in which he married Louise Spooner, a young woman he had known since childhood. In this period the foundations of scientific management were laid; the standardization of tools, the establishment of a repair shop with standardized procedures for the inspection and repair of machine tools and belting; the setting up of a central planning room which scheduled the route of each assembly and subassembly in advance, the introduction of a refined cost-accounting system, the systematization of purchase and inventory control, the use of printed job and instruction cards, the time study, the incentive system, and others.

He was slowly winning a grudging respect from his fellow executives who eventually began to concede:

> that in the madness of a man who gets two forgings turned where only one had been turned before, there must be a gleam of method and that it might be a good thing for the works in general to go crazy to this extent.[16]

By 1890, Taylor, then 34 years old, seemed to be well set for a highly successful and brilliant career in industry. In this year, however, an even more glittering opportunity came his way. Some members of President Cleveland's inner circle, financiers linked with

Standard Oil interests, were organizing a company known as the Manufacturing Investment Company for the conversion of forest products into fiber suitable for the making of paper. Taylor was offered the job of general manager which he accepted. The company was, however, not too successful. His difficulties with the workers were foreseeable. They resented the "city man" with his newfangled notions of running a mill, mistrusting even the improvements he made for their benefit. For example, "barkers" who stripped the bark from logs with revolving steel discs were put inside cages in order to prevent serious accidents should passersby knock against them. The men resented this and thought it amounted to "making a monkey out of a man."

By far the most serious source of disappointment, however, was his inability to get on well with his employers—the financiers who had organized the company. Taylor said:

> Personally my experience has been so unsatisfactory with financiers that I never want to work for any of them. If there is a manufacturer at the head of any enterprise, such as shipbuilding or construction work of any kind, and he is a large minded man, that is the man whom I want to be under. As a rule financiers are looking merely for a turnover. It is all a question of making money quickly, and whether the company is built up so as to be the finest of its kind and permanently successful is a matter of complete indifference to almost all of them.[17]

Taylor's antipathy became so intense that he resigned in 1893 and had a breakdown, the symptoms of which were insomnia and stomach trouble.

He now decided that it was unwise to carry on the double burden of executive and proselytizer for his ideas—of running a factory and introducing his system of management. He chose to concentrate on the latter, and set himself up as a consulting engineer. His consulting work was not too successful for he constantly got into fights with his employers. His increasing inability to control his hostility towards "those financiers" undoubtedly played a major role; forever anticipating their opposition, he antagonized them with his belligerence and impatience.

One of the more noteworthy events of this period is that he spent the winter months of 1895 working at a lathe in Sellers' company in Philadelphia and Sellers agreed to share the expenses of experimentation with cutting tools. Taylor's work eventually led to the publication of a book entitled *On the Art of Cutting Metals*. Taylor made the statement that "it was the easiest and happiest year I have had since I got out of my apprenticeship."[18]

In 1898, Davenport, an old associate from Midvale days, who was then a vice president of Bethlehem Steel Company, offered Taylor a long-term job to reorganize Bethlehem. This offer gave him not only another chance to repair his confidence in himself and his methods, but an undreamed of opportunity to work on a much larger scale than had hitherto been his lot.

Bethlehem Iron Company (renamed Bethlehem Steel Company in 1899) had been started around 1860 in Bethlehem, Pennsylvania by two brothers who simply bought a farm and established a blast furnace on it. When Taylor went to Bethlehem, although a scion of the original owners was still the company's president, effective power had passed into the hands of Philadelphia financier Joseph Wharton. After his talk with Davenport, Taylor met briefly with the president, Linderman, and then went to see Wharton, to assure himself of the backing of the most powerful man in the company. The meeting was a satisfactory one and Taylor, buoyed with hope and confidence, went in to tackle his greatest challenge.

MIDDLE AGE

Next to Midvale, the three years at Bethlehem were Taylor's most productive years. It was during this period that high speed steel was discovered, and much of his work took its final form. His work at Bethlehem was twofold: the introduction of his management principles first in the yard, and second in the machine shop. The description of the first part of this task, known as the "Story of Schmidt" (Exhibit 2) became a classical example of scientific management, and was frequently used by Taylor as an illustration in his writings and speeches. The "Story of Schmidt" also shows the authoritarian streak in Taylor, at complete variance with his assertion that scientific management was a means of harmony and cooperation between the management and the worker. Taylor insisted repeatedly that scientific management was not an efficiency system for increasing productivity, though it was that too, but a "mental revolution" which made the management and the workers partners.

Despite the unusual financial prosperity and productivity of these years, the Bethlehem episode was also Taylor's greatest setback. The cause lay in his running battles with the great majority of Bethlehem's executives and owners whom he damned openly as "those financiers." Though the trouble with the president, Linderman, (whom he considered a typical aristocrat and financier) started soon after his arrival, he could afford to ignore him as long as Davenport and Wharton supported him. There is the story that some of the directors assembled one day and tried to heckle Taylor into submitting his resignation. Taylor, however, still backed by Wharton, let them know in no uncertain terms that he was aware of their purpose but that if they wanted to get rid of him they would have to fire him, and "What was more, they one and all could go to blue blazes."[19] The violence of his responses was steadily mounting, and Taylor's written communications with Linderman did not excel in tactfulness:

> . . . Today Mr. Davenport called my attention, for the first time to a drawing of the foundation for your new steam hammer which is being put up . . . I have not been consulted about this by anyone, and therefore, will not assume the slightest responsibility either direct or indirect, regarding it.[20]
>
> . . . It is a curious psychological fact, and one for which the writer can find no explanation, that of all the parties who have visited the works and who are acquainted with what has been done here the only ones who have failed to congratulate the writer upon the results accomplished are with one or two exceptions the leading officers of the company.[21]

Men in his own little group were shocked by some of his outbursts. Clearly a crisis, psychological and professional, was in the offing, and finally did occur in 1901. Taylor complained of poor health and nervous strain. The old symptoms of a breakdown— stomach trouble, sleepless nights—appeared once again. At Bethlehem, Wharton, tired of the squabbling, withdrew his support and Taylor, along with all his associates, was summarily dismissed. The greatest application of the new management system was brought to an abrupt halt and for the moment, in his own eyes, Frederick Taylor was a failure.

After his dismissal, Taylor did not look for a new job. He and his wife had no children and they now decided to adopt two boys and a girl and move back to Philadelphia. In Germantown, Taylor rented a house very near to "Cedron" where he spent the first 11 years of his boyhood. Every evening he would walk down to Ross Street to visit his invalid mother. He also saw a lot of his old chief of Midvale days, William Sellers, and made plans to continue his metal cutting investigations in the Sellers shop. He now decided that he could "no longer afford to work for money" and would spend the rest of his life in the propagation of his system.

The period between 1902 and 1910, if not the happiest, was at least the calmest period of Taylor's adult years. Although he had given up working for money, he had by no means lost the habit of work. Relatively freed from personal attacks, which had intruded upon his middle years, and settled into family life, he found a measure of serenity in what had been until then such a turbulent life.

The mornings were set apart for work, which now consisted of writing, keeping up with his correspondence, and counselling a growing number of followers engaged in introducing his system into different factories throughout the country. In the afternoons he played golf; while the evenings belonged to the family. Soon after he had moved back from Bethlehem to Germantown, he started writing his first paper which was to give a complete outline of his system. "Shop Management" was read before the Saratoga meeting of the American Society of Mechanical Engineers in 1903, although limited notice was taken of it at the time.

Meanwhile, Taylor's reputation as an engineer, based partly on his discovery of high speed steel, had been steadily growing. In December 1905 he was elected president of the A.S.M.E. for the following year. This drew attention to his earlier paper on management and interest in his ideas steadily grew. There was now a small but steady stream of men who came to meet Taylor and hear about scientific management. Taylor set aside certain days on which he arranged to speak to these groups at home and then to take them to see scientific management in action in the demonstration shops. The movement was gaining in credibility and respectability, attracting attention and followers in government and academic circles. Although Taylor's ideas had spread steadily among professionals, they had not yet caught the attention or imagination of the lay public. The situation changed abruptly with the publicity provided in 1910 by Louis D. Brandeis and the Eastern Railroad Case. In this case Brandeis, arguing against the railroad's proposal to increase freight rates, attacked their inefficiency, mentioning that they could save a million dollars a day by adopting the methods of scientific management.

The "million dollars a day savings" idea immediately caught the fancy of the press. Though Taylor had not appeared as a witness in the rate hearings, his name had constantly been mentioned as the "father" of the movement responsible for such "miracles." The public spotlight now shifted to the 54-year-old prophet. In the following years, hundreds of articles on scientific management appeared in newspapers and magazines. In 1911, *Principles of Scientific Management,* probably the single most important book in the history of management, was published, and by 1915 had been translated into eight European languages and Japanese.

This flood of notice and praise was marred, however, by the increasingly disparaging criticism that began to appear in editorial articles and correspondence columns in the national press. For a while Taylor, in his role as a reformer, was able to meet the criticism philosophically. "I have found that any improvement of any kind is not only opposed, but aggressively and bitterly opposed, by the majority of men, and the reformer must usually tread a thorny path."[22] But the sniping continued, in spite of the efforts of his disciples to reassure him "the reformer is always misunderstood and misrepresented."[23] Taylor had, as we have seen, a low tolerance for sustained hostility. The situation steadily worsened, the attacks on him multiplied, as organized labor now entered the fray and scattered sniping developed into a broad fusillade. Samuel Gompers, the president of the A.F.L., sarcastically held forth against Taylorism:

> So, there you are, wage-workers in general, mere machines— considered industrially, of course. Hence, why should you not be standardized and your motion power brought up to the highest possible perfection in all respects, including speeds? Not only your length, breadth and thickness as a machine, but your grade of hardness, malleability, tractability and general serviceability can be ascertained, registered, and then employed as desirable. Science would thus get the most out of you before you are sent to the junk pile.[24]

Taylor became more and more upset and in his last years was reputedly a disappointed and disheartened man. He withdrew more and more from the hub of the movement he had created. Fearing old age and looking back on his life he apparently experienced nagging despair and doubt about the worth of his work. On March 10, 1915, he entered a hospital with pneumonia. He was there for nine days before he died. His biographer recorded Taylor's manner in death as follows:

> Every morning in the hospital, he would get up and systematically wind his Swiss watch at the same hour. On the ninth day he was heard to wind his watch at half-past four in the morning, an unusual hour. When the nurse entered his room half an hour later she found that he was dead.[25]

Exhibit 2
THE STORY OF SCHMIDT

One of the first pieces of work undertaken by us, when the writer started to introduce scientific management into the Bethlehem Steel Company, was to handle pig iron on task work. The opening of the Spanish War found some 80,000 tons of pig iron placed in small piles in an open field adjoining the works. Prices for pig iron had been so low that it could not be sold out of profit, and it therefore had been stored. With the opening of the Spanish War the price of pig iron rose, and this large accumulation of iron was sold. This gave us a good opportunity to show the workmen, as well as the owners and managers of the works, on a fairly large scale the advantages of task work over the old-fashioned day work and piece work, in doing a very elementary class of work.

The Bethlehem Steel Company had five blast furnaces, the product of which had been handled by a pig iron gang for many years. This gang, at this time, consisted of about 75 men. They were good, average pig iron handlers, under an excellent foreman who himself had been a pig iron handler, and the work was done, on the whole, about as fast and as cheaply as it was anywhere else at that time.

A railroad switch was run out into the field, right along the edge of the piles of pig iron. An inclined plank was placed against the side of a car, and each man picked up from his pile a pig of iron weighing about 92 pounds, walked up the inclined plank and dropped it on the end of the car.

We found that this gang were loading on the average about 12-1/2 long tons per man per day. We were surprised to find, after studying the matter (time study), that a first class pig iron handler ought to handle between 47 and 48 long tons per day, instead of 12-1/2 tons. This task seemed to us so very large that we were obliged to go over our work several times before we were absolutely sure that we were right. Once we were sure, however, that 47 tons was a proper day's work for a first-class pig iron handler, the task which faced us as managers under the modern scientific plan was clearly before us. It was our duty to see that the 47 tons per man per day, in place of 12-1/2 tons, at which rate the work was then being done. And it was further our duty to see that this work was done without being on a strike among the men, without any quarrel with the men, and to see that the men were happier and better contented when loading at the new rate of 47 tons than they were when loading at the old rate of 12-1/2 tons.

Our first step was the scientific selection of the workman. In dealing with workmen under this type of management, it is an inflexible rule to talk to and deal with only one man at a time, since each workman has his own special abilities and limitations, and since we are not dealing with men in masses, but are trying to develop each individual man to his highest state of efficiency and prosperity. Our first step was to find the proper workman to begin with. We therefore carefully watched and studied these 75 men who appeared to be physically able to handle pig iron at the rate of 47 tons per day. A careful study was the made of each of these men. We looked up their history as far back as practicable and thorough inquiries were made as to the character, habits, and the ambition of each of them. Finally we selected one from among the four as the most likely man to start with. He was a little Pennsylvania Dutchman who had been observed to trot back home for a mile or so after his work in the morning. We found that upon wages of $1.15 a day he had succeeded in buying a small plot of ground, and that he was engaged in putting up the walls of a little house for himself in the morning before starting to work and at night after leaving. He also had the reputation of being exceedingly "close," that is, of placing a high value on a dollar. As one man whom we talked to about him said, "A penny looks about the size of a cart wheel to him." This man we will call Schmidt.

The task before us, then, narrowed itself down to getting Schmidt to handle 47 tons of pig iron per day and making him glad to do it. This was done as follows. Schmidt was called out from among the gang of pig iron handlers and talked to somewhat in this way:

Schmidt, are you a high-priced man?

Vell, I don't know vat you mean.

Oh, yes, you do. What I want to know is whether you are a high-priced man or not.

Vell, I don't know vat you mean.

Oh, come now, you answer my questions. What I want to find out is whether you are a high-priced man or one of these cheap fellows here. What I want to find out is whether you want to earn $1.85 a day or you are satisfied with $1.15, just the same as all these cheap fellows are getting.

Did I vant $1.85 a day? Vas dot a high-priced man? Vell, Yes I vas a high-priced man.

Oh, you're aggravating me. Of course you want $1.85 a day—everyone wants it! You know perfectly well that that has very little to do with your being a high-priced man. For goodness sake answer my questions, and don't waste any more of my time. Now come over here. You see that pile of pig iron?

Yes.

You see that car?

Yes.

Well, if you are a high-priced man, you will load that pig iron on that car tomorrow for $1.85. Now do wake up and answer my question. Tell me whether you are a high-priced man or not.

Vell—did I got $1.85 for loading dot pig iron on dot car to-morrow?

Yes, of course you do, and you get $1.85 for loading a pile like that every day right through the year. That is what a high-priced man does, and you know it just as well as I do.

Vell, dot's all right. I could load dot pig iron on the car to-morrow for $1.85, and I get it every day, don't I?

Certainly you do—certainly you do.

Vell, den, I vas a high-priced man.

Now, hold on, hold on. You know just as well as I do that a high-priced man has to do exactly as he's told from morning till night. You have seen this man here before, haven't you?

No, I never saw him.

Well, if you are a high-priced man, you will do exactly as this man tells you tomorrow, from morning till night. When he tells you to pick up a pig and walk, you pick it up and you walk, and when he tells you to sit down and rest, you sit down, and you don't talk back at him. Now you come on to work here to-morrow morning and I'll know before night whether you are re-ally a high-priced man or not.

This seems to be rather rough talk. And indeed it would be if applied to an educated mechanic or even an intelligent laborer. With a man of the mentally sluggish type of Schmidt it is appropriate and not unkind, since it is effective in fix-ing his attention on the high wages which he wants and away from what, if it were called to his attention, he probably would consider impossibly hard work.

What would Schmidt's answer be if he were talked to in a manner which is usual under the management of "initiative and incentive?" Say, as follows:

Now, Schmidt, you are a first class pig iron handler and know your business well. You have been handling at the rate of 12-1/2 tons per day. I have given considerable study to handling pig iron, and feel sure that you could do a much larger day's work than you have been doing. Don't you think that if you really tried you could handle 47 tons of pig iron per day, instead of 12-1/2 tons?

What do you think Schmidt's answer would be to this?

Schmidt started to work, and all day long, and at regular intervals, was told by the man who stood over him with a watch, "Now pick up a pig and walk. Now sit down and rest. Now walk, now rest," etc. He worked when he was told to work, and rested when he was told to rest, and at half-past five in the afternoon had his 47 1/2 tons loaded on the car. And he practically never failed to work at this pace and do the task that was set him during the three years that the writer was at Bethlehem. And throughout this time he averaged at little more than $1.85 per day, whereas before he had never received over $1.15 per day, which was the ruling rate of wages at that time in Bethlehem. That is, he received 60 per cent higher wages than were paid to other men who were not working on task work. One man after another was picked out and trained to handle pig iron at the rate of 47-1/2 tons per day until all of the pig iron was handled at this rate, and the men were receiving 60 per cent more wages than other workmen around them.

COMMENTARY

We can delineate with reasonable clarity from Taylor's history the psychological symptoms that caused him considerable suffering for a large part of his childhood and adulthood. Prominent among these symptoms is insomnia. It is not clear whether he suffered from nightmares, although his use of a rig that he designed to control his sleeping posture suggests that the sleeplessness may have been associated with enuresis. Again, there is no direct evidence that Taylor as a child was a bed wetter. We have merely speculated that his problem of control, related to insomnia, was connected to bed wetting. During adolescence, he may also have been affected by sexual fantasies and masturbatory urges. But these speculations stand in position with some hard facts, such as his insomnia and his use of a self-designed rig to control his position in bed. It is not likely that he went to the lengths he had to prevent himself from sleeping if the fears of nightmares, and some disturbing fantasies, were not involved in the causes of his insomnia. The disturbance in sleeping and indications of significant depressive reactions, along with somatic symptoms in the form of stomach distress, pursued Taylor through his adult life.

We should note in this connection that Taylor had periodic breakdowns. Beginning with his reluctance to enter Harvard, his decision to return to his parents' home in Philadelphia after completing preparatory school at Exeter was the first experience with retreat from expectations alongside marked depression. At the conclusion of his program at Exeter, Taylor was slated to enter Harvard and pursue a career in law. Frederick's father, Franklin Taylor, was a lawyer, perhaps more accurately, a gentleman lawyer who substantially retired from the active practice of law while in his forties. You will recall that Franklin Taylor complained in a letter to Frederick about problems he was having with his eyesight. It is not accidental that Frederick complained of vision problems as part of his disability, leading to his withdrawal from studies and a career in law.

The combination of circumstances suggests that part of Frederick's psychological problems was based on an ambivalent identification with his father. He consciously rejected what his father represented, his gentleness, his cultural refinement, and his propensity for leisure. Frederick Taylor consciously rejected men who appeared gentle and tender in their character and disposition. He consciously admired men, such as his mentor, William Sellers, to whom he was to return as he encountered impasses in his life and suffered breakdowns as a consequence. The overtly aggressive, manly, gruff, and even crude men appealed to his ideas about masculinity. But beneath the conscious rejection of the softness of his father and the attraction to men of the opposite type, Taylor may well have had to face an unconscious attraction to a gentle male, perhaps more accurately, a maternal male, who in many ways evoked the longing one might easily associate with a warm and giving mother. Taylor's mother appeared neither warm nor overly giving, although she strongly looked out for the interests of her children, particularly their education.

Frederick Taylor clearly had no taste for formal education, although he performed brilliantly at Exeter in his classical studies. As he commented in his essay on the study of the classics, he could find no practical value in Latin and Greek, and evidently his mind had already turned away from books to the practical world of business, which for him meant the factory. As part of his twisting and turning in attempting to find comfortable identifications, financiers were anathema along with scholars. In his experience in business, he blamed his troubles on the financiers, while looking for support from his ideal type of man, a "bull-in-the-woods" factory manager along the lines of a William Sellers.

Taylor found his way to Sellers through his father. Although Frederick Taylor had consciously rejected his father and what he represented, Franklin Taylor did not reject his son. For the times and circumstances of Taylor's formative years, becoming an apprentice in a machine shop hardly suited the family's socioeconomic status. Yet Taylor's parents seemed to have developed an acute and sympathetic understanding of their son's search for work, and encouraged his deviant status as an apprentice in a machine shop. This was the place Taylor wanted to be, and Sellers was the father surrogate Taylor needed to help him tame the impulses in back of his substantial psychological conflicts.

It is important for our understanding of Taylor's creativity to pin down, if possible, the nature of his symptoms and some of the underlying desires that caused him so much trouble as he sought to ward off these desires. In plain language, Frederick Taylor had to work hard to contain these troublesome impulses and their derivative fantasies. Work was his therapy, because the attention to detail provided the buffer he needed to control his inner world.

Taylor suffered from an obsessional neurosis. Features of such a disturbance are low tolerance for one's own desires, faulty and ambivalent identifications, the sense of guilt surrounding one's own emotional experience, and a dominant effort to control emotions and desires. Isolating thinking from feeling, doubting, and the need to do and undo decisions frequently accompany obsessional neuroses. As with Hamlet's doubting, the underlying cause of the doubting is the attempt to control hostile impulses, usually directed at one or both parents. The sense of guilt is a derivative of these hostile impulses, and therefore compulsive behavior becomes characteristic of the search for control. Working on repetitive tasks and checking and rechecking what one has done enter into this picture of being afraid of losing control.

Frederick Taylor had a predilection for compulsive behavior as evidenced by his practice, on and off, of recording exact arrival and departure times during his rail rides in Europe. This attraction to exactness, to minutiae, while entailing considerable costs as a young boy and adult, Taylor later turned to good use in his development of methods analysis, time study, and work flows.

Taylor's neurosis reached a climax of sorts when he declared his intent to reverse the life course set for him by his parents. That he could not bear to follow in his father's footsteps is clear, but we should ask ourselves why it took the workings of a nervous breakdown, with complaints of vision problems much like his father's to effectuate a significant change in his life.

What were the alternatives? Looking back on his life, it seems so easy to suggest that instead of falling ill, he could have, or should have, sat with his father and, speaking from the heart, explain to him why scholarly pursuits and the law were not for him. He could have (or should have) explained the appeal factory work held for him, and why he wanted to become an apprentice machinist. Maybe Frederick did have this "heart-to-heart" talk with his father, because he did venture into a life of work far different from what his parents had expected of him and from what his membership in the Philadelphia Quaker elite had predicted for him. But if this intimate and heartfelt discussion did take place, it could only have come after the onset of his breakdown, depression, and abandonment of his social status and the definition of himself implied in this status.

The presumption of frank discussion is in the background of his life history. The foreground is occupied by the nervous breakdown. The explanation of the breakdown begins with the presence of unconscious conflict. Young Taylor probably had no idea of what he wanted to do with his life. More likely, he was propelled by the messages of his illness, which were to rebel, turn against his father, and find some mechanism to keep at bay the frightening fantasies (both sexual and aggressive and probably a morbid admixture of the two) that lay at the core of the illness.

Give the devil its due! In retrospect the compromise inherent in the illness allowed Frederick Taylor to have his cake and eat it too. He needed to rebel, but could not afford to lose his parents', and particularly his father's, love and support. To allow an illness to proclaim itself produces sympathy rather than scorn. Furthermore, in seeking compulsive hard work as his form of therapy, Taylor was anything but a malingerer. An accounting of his routine—his day beginning at the crack of dawn, a run to his job, a day filled with attention to detail, a night of study—defines only a rigorous, dedicated laborer for the world to see. For himself alone, these outward acts of self-definition had a healing purpose: to erect impenetrable barriers to the pathways to consciousness of the impulses, and their consequences, which Taylor had not yet, and probably never, learned to accept as a genuine part of his nature.

If compulsive hard work was Taylor's path to health, William Sellers was his doctor. It was to Sellers that Taylor returned time and time again, when the displacements of his conflicts onto others embroiled him in devastating stressful situations. Each such malevolent experience produced its equivalent of a nervous breakdown. Like a pigeon returning to its home, Taylor reverted to his position with Sellers, seeking once again the tenuous route to the restoration of his health. Finally, Taylor learned that he could not live in an ordinary working relationship with authority figures he fundamentally despised, and with peers who could not easily share the vision of industrial peace through the rationality of scientific management. They responded not to its vision of peace, nor to its demand for a willful subordination to its rationality. They responded to the shift in the locus of power that was a direct consequence of removing the power to determine the way work was performed from management and labor, and transferring this power to a group of experts called more generously industrial engineers, and pejoratively efficiency experts. Instead of a peaceful world resulting from his vision, Taylor discovered the meaning of power conflicts, which became too stressful for his fragile psyche.

In his retreat to the therapy Sellers' shop provided, Taylor only intensified his focus on his vision of scientific management. It seems as if he learned little about the cause of industrial conflict. Social or psychological empiricism had no attraction for Taylor. He only intensified his drive to reform the industrial world through the application of scientific management. He became a prophet.

The difference between a prophet and a pragmatist is that for the prophet, situations and people as they are make little difference, while for the pragmatist, they make all the difference in the world. To sacrifice the best for the good, as is the wont of a pragmatist, is to engage in compromise, give and take, and negotiation. You are either right or wrong, says the prophet. Integrity is in the ideal, which should not be sacrificed to what will work now. Once on the road of compromise and negotiation, the ideal falls victim to the immediacy of trade-offs. Following this path will only vitiate the vision in back of the prophecy. In the case of scientific management, work is either subject to total rational control, or it is left to the vicissitudes of power relations. Here, he who is strongest prevails, an everyday version of might makes right. Yet where is the justice in such negotiated solutions to industrial relations and productivity? One day's settlement of conflict becomes the basis of tomorrow's haggling, bringing out the meanest side of human nature. One person seeks to best another in the endless conflict for control of the workplace and the rewards of factory production. For the prophet in Frederick Taylor, there is a sickness in this niggling and jousting for position. Better to subordinate one's power interests to an ideal system based on rationality than to continually search for incremental advantage over someone else's interests. Manager and laborer alike should seek harmony through rational control. This was the message of the prophet as embodied in the system called scientific management.

Of great advantage to Taylor in his shift from factory management to prophecy was the withdrawal from battle and the stabilization of his psyche. It was left for his disciples to do battle. The prophet himself could detach himself, and devote his energies to teaching his students and to improving his brainchild. Fighting with others brought him closer to problematic aggression and the closer he came to the sources of his aggression, the more his psychological conflicts intensified.

Learning to fight is no mean task. It requires access to one's aggressive impulses, which then can be transformed from primitive and destructive aims into a constructive force for accomplishing work. Sublimation of aggression permits one to look after individual and group interests without the interference of exaggerated notions of the damage that can be done to others with the release of aggressive energies. Engaging others in conflict for constructive goals is an art. Without access to this art, commonly learned in childhood, individuals become passive, unable to work interactively with others, and sometimes so inhibited as to make themselves disabled for productive work.

If a gifted person, such as Frederick Taylor, finds it impossible to engage in constructive conflict, the alternative is to reach for a more abstract level of work and less interaction. It was exactly this compromise that Taylor sought as he became a prophet for industrial peace with productivity.

Productivity has at least three faces. The first is the face of technological improvement. When Taylor did his experiments in metal cutting and wrote his book, *The Art of Cutting Metal,* he was confronting this first face of productivity. With this confrontation, without intention he allowed other people to try something for themselves, without the intervention of experts and without the alterations in the power structure required when someone is telling another person what to do in order to reach a certain goal.

The second face of productivity engages people in altering their work ethic. It is this second face of productivity that becomes revealed as economically backward nations encounter the problem of improving their standard of living. All the technology in the world will help little without the cultural and psychological change that induces people to work hard.

The third face of productivity appears in the guise of the managerial mystique. The ideals of modern management have been expressed in various ways, but the form and content evolved in the most fundamental sense from Frederick Taylor's work. As Taylor discovered, if it were possible to introduce new technologies without engaging the culture and psychological underpinnings of work, and without affecting the power structure in the ways modern management does, there would be little difficulty in improving levels of productivity. But the truth seems to point to the interaction of all of the faces of productivity. In Taylor's metaphor, the art of cutting metals is not simply the optimization of speed, feed, and depth of cut. It is how in getting to this optimization human motives become entangled, including especially the desire to consolidate and maximize power.

Frederick Winslow Taylor achieved an uncertain and tenuous truce in his battle with his obsessional neurosis. His work in the organization of work played a large part in achieving this truce. As for industrial society, the contribution of scientific management is but another step, not to be minimized, in the effort to better the way men and women earn their daily bread.

Endnotes—Chapter 13

1. Taylor to Morris W. Cooke, December 3, 1910, Taylor Collection, Stevens Institute of Technology, Hoboken, NJ.

2. Frank B. Copley, *Frederick W. Taylor, Father of Scientific Management* (New York: Harper Bros., 1923), vol. I, p. 53.

3. Birge Harrison, *Recollections*, August 25, 1915, Taylor Collection.

4. William Fannon, *Recollections*, Taylor Collection.

5. Frederick W. Taylor, "The Study of Classics," Taylor Collection.

6. Letter from Franklin Taylor, February 22, 1874, Taylor Collection.

7. Copley, *Father of Scientific Management*, p. 88.

8. Ibid., p. 90.

9. Frederick W. Taylor, "Workmen and their Management," (unpublished lecture manuscript, Harvard Business School, 1909), pp. 13, 14.

10. Copley, *Father of Scientific Management*, p. 108.

11. Ibid., p. 135.

12. F. W. Taylor, lecture on "Success."

13. House Special Committee, *Hearings to Investigate the Taylor and Other Systems of Shop Management*, 1912, vol. III, p. 1413.

14. Ibid., p. 1411ff.

15. Ibid., p. 1414.

16. Copley, *Father of Scientific Management*, p. 334.

17. F. W. Taylor, *On the Art of Cutting Metals* (New York: A.S.M.E., 1907).

18. Hearings, Wheeler testimony, vol. I, p. 76.

19. Copley, *Father of Scientific Management*, p. 47.

20. Taylor to Linderman, March 15, 1899, Taylor Collection.

21. Taylor to Linderman, March 1901, Taylor Collection.

22. Taylor to Gilbreth, November 9, 1909, Taylor Collection.

23. Barth to Taylor, January 3, 1910, Taylor Collection.

24. Milton I. Nadworny, *Scientific Management and the Unions* (Cambridge: Harvard University Press, 1955), p. 51.

25. Copley, *Father of Scientific Management*, p. 452.

THE ABSENCE OF RESTRAINT—JIMMY HOFFA AND THE TEAMSTERS

Jimmy Hoffa's life story reads like a tragedy. To qualify as a true tragedy, a life has to go beyond misfortune. The life has to read as a series of misunderstandings. The grossest of misunderstandings is not to know one's own talents, how to use them, how to hone them, how to recognize limits in them, and perhaps most importantly, how to create abstractions that enable one to see beyond today and tomorrow into a future that can alter permanently, and for the good, people's lives. In this definition, Jimmy Hoffa's life assumes the proportions of great tragedy.

Like Henry Ford and Frederick Winslow Taylor, Jimmy Hoffa brought substantial talent to his life's work, which was heading the International Brotherhood of Teamsters. But unlike Ford and Taylor, Hoffa's talents lay outside the range of designing manufacturing processes, or designing and making products and selling them to consumers. Hoffa's talents were political. Consequently, the examination of his life requires in the first instance some grasp of what power is objectively, and what power meant to Hoffa.

Hoffa's subjective experience with power began in his relationship with his mother, and in coming to terms with the early death of his father. Later, when he went to work for the Kroger grocery company, Hoffa expanded the scope of his experience with power into conflict between management and labor and conflict within the politics of his union. As his experience with power broadened, Hoffa became expert in the tactics of power in the labor movement. Hoffa moved up the power structure of the union. Beginning with leading his co-workers in a wildcat strike at the Kroger warehouse dock, Hoffa moved into the higher realms of power, ultimately taking on as adversaries the Kennedy clan, especially Robert Kennedy, and finally the criminal justice system.

In the end, Hoffa landed in jail, a bitter irony for someone who fought passivity, who sought control and ended up being controlled in prison, at the hands of wardens, guards, and the tedium of involuntary confinement. When Hoffa and his lieutenants made their deal with the Nixon administration and Hoffa was released from prison, he took his release to mean the opportunity to regain power. Instead, Hoffa mysteriously disappeared and is presumed dead. Thus ended a life dedicated to power and control. A violent man by temperament, Hoffa succumbed to violence in the shadow of intrigue in the criminal world.

Some would assert that Hoffa had more than a trace of paranoid thinking in his personality. In looking at the vendetta between Hoffa and Robert Kennedy, it appears as though Hoffa altered the struggle with Congress and later the Department of Justice from a concern for law and order into a personal struggle between himself, as the representative of the oppressed, and Robert Kennedy, the representative of the privileged. This failure to understand in a more abstract way what was at issue in his fight with the government suggested a fatal flaw in Hoffa's character. Whether afflicted with paranoid thinking or not, Hoffa missed the point. He failed to recognize the limits of power and the restraints necessary in exercising power.

Those who argue for the theory that Hoffa's mistrust and sense of persecution were paranoid in nature have to take account of the subtleties of power. Hoffa may indeed have been afflicted with paranoid thinking, if not paranoia itself, but on the stage in which he played out his life story, he had many reasons to be suspicious. In the end, he may not have been suspicious enough to save his life. He went on a rendezvous, presumably to work out his return to power.

Instead he met his death, a violent death only befitting a man who saw himself engaged in a struggle in which survival was at stake.

Hoffa's leadership of the Teamsters, his voice for the working man, was for him a life and death battle. His inability to see the Teamsters, the government, and American society in terms other than this primitive conception of the power struggle, led to his demise. In reading Hoffa's story, you may begin to wonder about the fine line that distinguishes a leader who is prisoner of his own history from a leader who breaks out of the constraints of his history to accomplish great work. Hoffa is an instance of the leader who is a prisoner of his personal history. As you read his story, you may find yourself asking, "What was missing in this man's life? What kept him from greatness?"

JAMES HOFFA AND THE PRESIDENCY OF THE INTERNATIONAL BROTHERHOOD OF TEAMSTERS

The story that James R. Hoffa had been shot in the head, encased in concrete, and sunk off the shore of Key West, Florida proved to be an ex-convict's spoof which cost CBS considerable embarrassment and $10,000 in advance payments.[1] But the theory of Hoffa's disappearance which the FBI had come to accept by 1978 was no less gothic. Hoffa, FBI officials had tentatively concluded, was knocked out, strangled, and then shipped off to a sanitation company in Hamtramck, Michigan where his body was disposed of in a shredder, a compactor, and/or an incinerator.[2]

The FBI's tentative version of the events behind Hoffa's disappearance from a suburban Detroit restaurant parking lot on July 30, 1975 was based on what an FBI spokesman called the "largest investigation ever conducted by the bureau for someone believed to be dead." When in July 1977 the FBI declared the investigation had collapsed, it had lasted for two years and cost the government over a million dollars.[3] Although the FBI lacked the corroborating evidence that would enable its case to stand up in court, it possessed a massive dossier of information on what probably happened to Hoffa.

This case was prepared originally by Andrew Silver and revised by Elizabeth C. Altman, research assistant, both under the direction of Professor A. Zaleznik. Copyright © 1979 by the president and fellows of Harvard College.

Evidence indicated that when Hoffa left his home at 1:15 p.m. on July 30, telling his wife he had an appointment at the Machus Red Fox Restaurant, he was expecting to meet Anthony "Tony Jack" Giacalone and Anthony "Tony Pro" Provenzano in order to bring about a reconciliation between himself and Provenzano, a former dedicated supporter and friend of Hoffa. Provenzano and Hoffa had had a violent disagreement in 1967 when both men were serving sentences in Lewisburg Prison. Reports differed as to the origin of the dispute. Hoffa claimed that Provenzano was angered because he had refused to help Provenzano obtain a Teamsters' pension payment because of his conviction on an extortion charge. A prison witness said that the two men argued over how they would divide the Teamsters' turf when they got out of prison. Several people had approached Hoffa about a possible peace meeting before that July afternoon.[4]

Sometime after 2:00 p.m. Hoffa called both his wife and Louis Linteau, a man he had seen earlier that day, whom the FBI reports called "a notorious con man,"[5] to tell them that the men he was to meet were late. Hoffa was never heard from again.

Provenzano was at first the prime suspect, but as the investigation continued, the circle of suspects widened. Frank Fitzsimmons and Russell Bufalino were soon believed to have played a role in the murder and disappearance.

In Hoffa's own account of his career with the Teamsters he wrote that he made "two disastrous mistakes in his life": his blood feud with Robert F. Kennedy and his appointment of Fitzsimmons to stand in for him as president of the International Brotherhood of Teamsters (IBT) while Hoffa served his time in prison.[6]

Hoffa reportedly chose Fitzsimmons because he felt he could control this seemingly pliable, loyal, and incompetent man whom he had raised to his present position. For three months Fitzsimmons appeared content to act on behalf of Hoffa, but in July 1967 he publicly asserted that he was in charge and was no longer taking orders from Hoffa.[7] By 1975, Hoffa was convinced that Fitzsimmons was hoping to become the permanent president of the IBT and that he had conspired with John Dean and Charles Colson in order to get Nixon to add a condition to Hoffa's 1971 commutation that would prohibit him from engaging in any union activities before 1980.

Other informants claimed that it was Bufalino, one of the top leaders of organized crime in New York City, who, with the help of Provenzano, bribed Nixon forces to attach the condition to Hoffa's commutation. In either case Hoffa's efforts in the spring of 1975 to obtain a release from the condition constituted a potential threat to the existing power structure of the IBT. Bufalino, according to several sources, preferred to keep Fitzsimmons in power rather than have to deal with Hoffa who might either carry out his announced plan to clean up the Teamsters or, contrarily, demand a cut in the share of existing rackets. According to Steven Brill in his study of the Teamsters, evidence collected by the FBI and himself suggests that either Bufalino urged Provenzano to carry out his intention to murder Hoffa or else he himself used the feud between Provenzano and Hoffa as a smoke screen for his own plan to get rid of Hoffa.[8]

The FBI made it known that it was disappointed in the results of its massive investigation, but it was still hoping that witnesses might come forward to give corroborating evidence for its suppositions about Hoffa's supposed death, either because they needed government protection from mob violence against likely informers or because they hoped to receive a lighter sentence for another crime in exchange for information about the Hoffa case. One such potential witness had already been gunned down on a street in New York's Little Italy.

Eleven years earlier, Hoffa, even though he was about to go to prison, had seemed to hold a position of unassailable power as president of the IBT, an organization that Robert Kennedy once called "the most powerful institution in the country, next to the government itself."[9]

THE IBT

In 1967 the Teamsters was the nation's largest union with 1.9 million members, governed in a highly centralized organization. It was less the vast membership than a strategic position in the national economy that gave the Teamsters Union its power. Of the 1,200 largest trucking companies, fewer than six operated without a contract with the Teamsters.

The microeconomics of the trucking industry magnified Teamster power, since the industry was fragmented into many extremely competitive small carriers. A selective strike against one carrier was usually disastrous because of low profit margins, high debt/equity ratios, financial weakness, and severe competition.

Despite this competition, however, the truckers were highly dependent on one another, since no single carrier served every city, and a shipment usually passed through two or three truckers before final delivery. The three broad categories of operation—local cartage, short-haul carriers, and over-the-road long-haul carriers (more than 200 miles)—served and serviced each other. Work stoppage in any one company instantaneously affected the tonnage of other truckers. For example, a shipment originating in Portland, Maine, and destined for Chicago, had to pass through Boston. A strike in key truck terminals in Boston immobilized freight to and from Maine.

HOFFA'S POSITION OF POWER

Through personal, constitutional, and contractual devices—paradoxically supported by many employers—James R. Hoffa grasped almost complete control of the Teamsters and he was loath to share it with anyone. He dominated labor relations of over-the-road trucking and, largely through his strategy and tactics, brought immense power to the Teamster presidency.

Hoffa had exerted control in the Teamsters for over a decade, first as key assistant to a rather disinterested General President Beck between 1952 and 1957, and since 1957 as general president himself. However, official leadership within the international organization and practical authority over the Teamsters' locals were not synonymous before the 1950s. Hoffa gave the general presidency its control by widening the scope of the Teamster trucking bargaining units and placing the IBT general president at the head of the union's new bargaining mechanism.

Hoffa's detractors stigmatized his refusal to delegate authority and responsibility as an outgrowth of an insatiable appetite for personal power. As one of them said:

> Hoffa himself would deny that a desire for personal power had motivated these structural changes. He would assert that he has desired only such goals as greater economic effectiveness for the union, Teamster compliance with new labor legislation, and the stabilization of the trucking industry in his widening efforts. There is, however, ample evidence that the creation of the broader units has allowed the general president to convert the

traditionally strong IBT local autonomists into his local subordinates.[10]

Another critic commented:

At least Beck just stole money. Hoffa has usurped everybody's authority and now all the decisions in contract negotiation and administration are made solely by him.[11]

Hoffa changed the organization of the Teamsters Union by building another tier in the organization level, the area conference, which, in one sense a smaller replica of the International Union, consisted of all the locals within its geographic region. This "organic body," the area conference, was financed equally by the International and its own locals, but Hoffa, while replacing the authority of the locals with the authority of the area conference, made certain the conference itself was subordinated to the International Union. The constitution, in fact, insisted that conference activities "shall at all times, be subject to the unqualified direction and control of the General President." The International Union president (Hoffa) chose the conference director (usually an International vice president) and approved the conference's bylaws. Even after approval, however, the president of the International Union had the unqualified right to make any amendments or changes in the bylaws "as he deems to be in the best interests of the International Union."

Bargaining

Hoffa bargained in a carefully planned sequence of steps. He formulated his bargaining demands far in advance of formal negotiations, and presented ethical justifications for his goals, e.g., men performing the same job in other places received higher pay. By stressing such arguments at mass membership meetings, he whipped up an emotional crusade to eliminate social inequity and economic inequality. In negotiating with employers, Hoffa sternly and indignantly lectured on the ethical implications of his demands, stressing his conservatism, his deep desire to avoid a strike, and his reputation that Jimmy's word was his bond. For Hoffa, achieving his goals in negotiations seemed a personal concern and a matter of winning or losing in a struggle to which he was committed. That the West Coast employers recognized his generalship as well could be seen in such remarks as: "Jimmy knows what he is doing; if we just leave everything to Jimmy, things will turn out all right," and, "I used to be afraid of him—now I know it's all important that he be in control."[12]

As the showdown neared in negotiations, Hoffa typically urged employers to think "realistically" and meet his demands. If they did not submit, he exploded angrily, seemingly out of control, tearing up the written offer and flinging it at the negotiators. He used cries of class warfare and personal vengeance, threats of a massive strike, and sometimes walked out of the conference room.

In his bargaining skirmishes on the West Coast, Hoffa constructed and consulted room-sized maps of routes and freight interchanges, pinpointing a few strategic terminals that, if struck, would cripple western trucking. He amazed Teamster officials and horrified employers with the estimated low cost to the union of such a massive shutdown. The majority of nonstriking members who would be thrown out of work by the stoppage could collect state unemployment benefits, rather than money from union funds.

Hoffa often split the employer negotiating group by playing off one interest against the other. To this end he used a combination of three weapons: (1) his professed desire to respect the letter of the law by bargaining separately with independent employer groups in the absence of multigroup bargaining; (2) threats of "selectively" striking unnamed, but predetermined, carriers; and (3) the assertions to the employer negotiators that their policy committees were depriving them of freedom of action.

Hoffa was also expert at applying secondary pressures. Large intercity trucking lines, which Hoffa most closely controlled, induced smaller highway or local cartage carriers with whom they interchanged freight to capitulate. Even shippers urged their carriers to avoid a strike harmful to everyone.

Organizing Strategy

In 1948 Hoffa made a major innovation in organizing strategy. Called the "hot cargo" clause, it was of supreme tactical importance in the most crucial period of Hoffa's expansionary drive during the late forties and early fifties. Union members, backed by the clause, could refuse to cross picket lines or handle "unfair" goods. Ordinarily this would have constituted a secondary boycott, but in 1949 the National Labor Relations Board ruled that employers agreeing to honor the clause had been "induced"—which was still lawful —and not coerced. Hoffa applied it by sending notice of intention to invoke the clause to an employer; if the employer did not comply with Hoffa's wish, Hoffa then had legal grounds for an immediate work stoppage.

Gradually the "hot cargo" clause developed in complexity and detail. In 1952, Hoffa expanded the definition of "unfair goods" and in 1953, included in his contracts the following paragraph:

> The union and its members, individually and collectively, reserve the right to refuse to handle goods from or to any firm or truck which is engaged or involved in any controversy with this or any other union.[13]

Hoffa could thus order employers to abide by the hot cargo clause and cease dealing with any company he designated. Employers complied, as ceasing to do business with another trucker seemed preferable to a strike. Subsequently, the Landrum-Griffin Act outlawed Hoffa's hot cargo clause.

In 1960, Hoffa insisted on common contract expiration dates for all area pacts in any one industry. With this weapon he would refuse to sign a contract in one area until employers in another area agreed to sign, thus forcing the employers themselves to apply the pressure to accept contract terms.

Long an advocate of area-wide agreements, Hoffa described them as "major pillars in the [union's] collective bargaining structure."[14] His proposal for a national master freight agreement, however, aroused great furor because of its implications for a potential national truck strike, but Hoffa steadfastly denied that he ever planned to enforce his contract demands through a national shutdown, "At no time, and I make this as a flat statement, will there ever be a nationwide strike of over-the-road [local] cartage and dock. It just isn't good business for the union."[15]

Hoffa stood virtually unique among American labor leaders in opposing the formal closed grievance proceeding, one of two possible procedures. Under a closed grievance procedure, when a worker felt wronged by management, he complained to his local union official. If the local official concluded the contract had been violated, he began a formal "grievance procedure," of which the first stage was negotiation between low-level union and management representatives, generally the shop steward and the terminal manager. If the issue could not be settled there, the grievance would move successively to higher and higher union and management representatives. The final step in a closed procedure was arbitration by an impartial third party. With arbitration the union agreed not to strike to enforce its point of view. Most labor leaders strongly favored arbitration, as it helped ensure settlements and also because it did not oblige leaders to stop work over a grievance involving only one man. Hoffa, however, said, "I think everyone here realizes that in an arbitration award it is more or less a 50-50 proposition—you get a kick and a pat on the back."[16] He preferred, instead, what he called an "open-end grievance procedure," without arbitration, and with the union retaining the right to strike without exposure to damage suits.

Hoffa used the open-end grievance procedure as a major control mechanism between negotiations since it permitted him to threaten a strike any time or anywhere he wished. His regulation of grievance decisions also buttressed his domination of the union and helped explain why many local officials went along with his drive toward centralized bargaining despite the resultant lessening of their own status and authority.

In the absence of fixed rules and standards, the union wielded the upper hand at grievance meetings, for most trucking operators dreaded strikes. Hoffa set the line for all other union representatives. The extreme complexity of the contract and industry further enhanced his power, since the intricacies were beyond the comprehension of many union and management officials, and they gratefully relied on "Jimmy."[17]

Before every decision Hoffa clarified his position. As a result, almost every vote was unanimous. To insure goodwill on both sides of the table, Hoffa granted or withheld favors through the grievance procedure. For example, employers might be induced to break ranks with other carriers in Hoffa's divide-and-conquer bargaining technique by the implicit promise of grievance procedure benefits. When a carrier incurred Hoffa's wrath, locals were instructed to "dig up grievances—bring them to me, and we'll deadlock them and strike."[18] With several cases deadlocked, Hoffa held the constant threat of work stoppage over the offending employer. Indeed, some western Teamsters and truckers thought the general president had personally inherited—on an informal basis—all the authority formerly reserved for the permanent umpire. Sam Kagel, arbitrator for the western Teamsters from 1958 until displaced by Hoffa in 1961, declared: "Hoffa's system is not a grievance procedure of the union at all. Rather it is control of the employer and political manipulation of the union."[19]

At meetings of the main grievance committee it was Hoffa

who called up the grievances, questioned the union and company representatives to ferret out facts and clarify the issues, and decided when the parties should be excused. Invariably in the executive sessions it was the Teamster leader who suggested the course of action for the joint committee to take, together with a statement of his reasons for this, often including a detailed recitation of relevant precedents.

Augmenting the controlling feature of the grievance procedure was the contractual change-of-operations procedure, which required permission before employers could change their terminal cities, routes, intermediate stopping points, or equipment. Here again Hoffa's discretionary judgment could come into full play, as there was always a "reasonable" reason to refuse a change, and an employer had no contractual criteria to invoke in his defense. Hoffa thus had tremendous power to block changes.

Popularity

Hoffa appealed to the rank and file of the IBT because he delivered the goods in the form of higher pay and better working conditions. He consistently delivered attractive wage and fringe packages, but there were other significant elements to his success.

First, he capitalized on his great popularity, stemming from his accessibility to the Teamster rank and file. Virtually nobody familiar with the Teamster organization shared the belief that Hoffa maintained his leadership only through "rigged" elections. Except for a very few anti-Hoffa Teamsters, Hoffa was extremely popular with his followers.

His office was open to anyone and he received phone calls at all hours. He insisted that no problem was too small for his personal attention. One reason suggested for his attention to detail was his almost obsessive fear that he might lose contact with the ordinary members. Hoffa once explained to his Teamsters,

> I have had experience with general presidents who have lost touch with the members...I have no desire to forget where I came from. I am not ashamed of my background. I am proud of it.[20]

A second reason for his success was that Hoffa had extremely impressive constitutional power within the union and unparalleled control over local unions and power of purse and patronage.

Third, Hoffa was willing to compromise with local union leadership in the terms of the labor contracts. And fourth, the plausibility of his economic and legal arguments for widened bargaining scopes carried weight with most Teamsters.

Money Management

For a number of years Hoffa preferred the high liquidity on noninterest-bearing bank accounts for the reserves of his Detroit Local 299, but he dropped this practice as the treasury expanded, and in the 1940s felt he should be getting something in return.

Several things distinguished the Central States Pension Fund (CSPF) from pension funds in other industries. First, in no other industry did labor dominate decision making as it did under Hoffa. Second, the CSPF specialized in speculative mortgages on ventures which other lenders were reluctant to finance. Third, the fund offered large loans, based on favorable loan to value ratios. Fourth, the fund charged low interest rates. The CSPF objective seemed to be to keep its borrowers happy, even if the fund did not maximize yield (through high interest rates), protect its principal (by more conservative loan to value ratios), or make a social contribution (lending to schools or hospitals). There was no full-time staff to advise, evaluate, or administer the investments until 1961, when a man was hired to check the mortgage investments periodically.

Hoffa controlled and dominated the pension fund trustees, half of whom were employers, through the open-end grievance procedure and his subsequent ability to strike the trustees selectively, which left Hoffa with sole responsibility for the fund's success or failure.

Hoffa denied that he ever took bribes from employers, but he frequently had on hand enormous amounts of cash. He explained simply that he "accumulated it." He dealt only in cash, maintained no bank account, and probably wrote only one personal check in his life. He certainly did not spend his annual salary of $100,000 on himself, as he consistently led a modest life.

The AFL-CIO condemned and expelled Hoffa's Teamsters for corruption following the McClelland Committee investigations of undemocratic procedures, racketeering, and violence in the IBT. The AFL-CIO's drastic expulsion became necessary because of "Hoffa's refusal to use his constitutional powers as union president to clean up the mess uncovered by the committee investigators."[21] When confronted with allegations that he and his Teamsters Union tolerated the presence of racketeers, Hoffa said: "All this hocus-pocus about racketeers and crooks is a smoke screen to carry you back to the days when they could drop you in the scrap heap like they do a worn-out truck."[22]

Personal Style

Hoffa had flashes of uncontrollable rage, and although he learned to keep his feelings under control in public, he occasionally resorted to bare fists when aroused. Flaring up viciously at his associates, he undermined the self-respect of those he admired most. In a rage he inflicted his vivid profanity on subordinates and adversaries alike.

Hoffa selectively directed his temper, most often abusing his closest subordinates, especially IBT Vice President Harold Gibbons, and Gibbons' close associates. After a bad outburst he would often say, in semi-apology, "If I can't get mad at my friends, who can I get mad at?"[23] Once, in full view of several employer and union negotiators, he broke chairs and repeatedly hurled the same few words of extreme vulgarity at the employers in the room. According to one witness: "He quivered and shook like a man out of his mind, as he was for that length of time. It was frightening. But he ultimately regained his composure and was obviously chagrined at what had happened."[24]

Although some observers interpreted Hoffa's flares of temper as sometimes designed to impress spectators with his complete dominance and control, others felt the opposite was often true. On one occasion, Kennedy aides wanted to examine Teamster records without any Teamster officials looking over their shoulders. Hoffa, seated at his desk on a raised platform and surrounded by his lieutenants, told the investigators (Carmine Bellino and Pierre Salinger) that they would have to look at the records in a room at union headquarters and that his accountant and one of his lawyers must be present at all times. Bellino plainly told Hoffa, "We don't work that way." Furious at being crossed in front of his men, Hoffa flew into a tantrum. He jumped up and shouted, "Go to hell! Take the records to Washington. The hell with you!" The invective lasted several minutes. Later, Bellino and George Fitzgerald, Hoffa's lawyer, worked out what they thought to be a fair arrangement and Bellino told Hoffa about it that afternoon. Again, Hoffa broke out in a rage, but this time at Fitzgerald. Bellino, standing in the hall outside the office, said he could hear Hoffa screaming at Fitzgerald, cursing in the foulest possible language, and finally threatening to fire him. It became so bad that Bellino, embarrassed for Fitzgerald, interrupted and offered to give way on certain points.[25]

Hoffa was seldom good-tempered when confronted with opposition or a suggestion that he made a mistake. Apparently sincere, he maintained he had never made a mistake: "Dammit, I may have faults, but being wrong ain't one of them."[26]

In Hoffa's Washington office the following quotation hung on a wall:

> If I were to try to read, much less answer, all the attacks made on me, this shop might as well be closed for any other business. I do the very best I know how—the very best I can; and I mean to keep doing so until the end. If the end brings me out all right, what is said against me won't amount to anything. If the end brings me out wrong, ten angels swearing I was right would make no difference. (A. Lincoln)[27]

Hoffa would shrug off apparent mistakes by saying, "It's not the battle that counts, but the war." He felt opposition would never make him budge, and never took the blame when something went wrong. If a pension fund loan went bad, it was the result of poor management, not the bad judgment of either Hoffa or his thoroughly dominated trustees who had approved the investment. Instead Hoffa would find a scapegoat, usually one of his lieutenants.[29]

Much to his wife's disappointment, Hoffa held no religious beliefs, viewing religion as an opiate of the masses. He also rejected another institutionalized system of right and wrong: the law. He governed his own conduct, he felt, by an alternative, highly personalized sense of ethics. Yet he was fascinated by Judaism and particularly the Passover Seder, which has to do with the Hebrews' flight from slavery in Egypt and their success against great odds in reaching their goal.[30]

His personal "code of ethics" was simple and pragmatic: behavior which improved performance was sanctioned, actions that impaired effectiveness were self-prohibited. Loyalty to family and friends and honoring his word were also part of the code. Before giving his word, however, he permitted himself leeway on the grounds that it increased his effectiveness. He felt that "life is a jungle."[31]

That Hoffa had a keen, agile mind could be seen in his ingenuity in negotiating contract clauses, destroying the popular notion that he was all brawn and no brain. He conceived of his mental capacities as a major resource to be trained and controlled. Hoffa carefully avoided taking notes, determined to keep his file cabinet in his mind, which he perceived as being highly compartmented. When deep in thought, he cupped his hands over his nose, fingers pointing toward his forehead, which, as he explained, was his way of telling his mind to organize its various compartments and to separate emotional from rational considerations.[31]

He disliked abstract thinking and discounted theoretical notions and conversation. He had a reputation for quick decision making and stamina. John English, Teamster secretary-treasurer, said, "When it comes to work, Jimmy Hoffa surpasses them all."[32] His day as Teamster president generally began at 6:30 a.m. with push-ups, and business started with breakfast. After that it was one long succession of meetings which ended with Hoffa's clearing his desk of the day's work to begin afresh the following morning.

Communists and anarchists in the 1930s—the radical left —influenced Hoffa's conception of the function and destiny of American political economy. The business cycle theory taught by his Trotskyite acquaintances from Minneapolis, at a time when the millions of jobless seemed to validate their ideas, significantly affected Hoffa's later thinking.

He had a Marxist view of capitalism: automation— overproduction—unemployment—more automation—more overproduction—more unemployment, and so on. Monopoly would hasten the forthcoming disaster, he thought, and he predicted that General Motors and Ford would swallow up the automobile industry and that five major railroads, four major airlines, and eight supermarket chains would control and dominate their respective industries. Similarly, Hoffa believed there would be consolidation and merger in the motor carrier industry, diminishing from the many thousands extant in 1967 to a few hundred, with a handful of transcontinental lines dominating long-distance hauling. Intrigued by the increased efficiency he felt was inherent in larger business units, Hoffa favored this movement toward "industrial concentration," although he believed it would lead to a glut of unused commodities and layoffs of workers.[33]

The depression that Hoffa—and many others—foresaw as coming at the end of World War II was, he felt, only temporarily delayed. Government measures against unemployment, including monetary and fiscal policy or legislative cuts in the work week, were, he felt, too temporary, too superficial and ineffective to counter the fundamental instability of the economy. The net result, as he frequently asserted in private conversation, was the radicalization of the American labor force and the flowering of left-wing political movements. He believed capitalism doomed, as Dobbs had taught him in the 1930s, despite his attraction to a vigorous free enterprise economy, advocacy of business experience for union leaders, and support of many Republican candidates. He professed to favor the present system, but did not believe in it.[34]

To Hoffa, the law represented a set of principles designed to perpetuate those already in power, rather than those aspiring to power. He held strong convictions about those in power, the Establishment.

> You had the great Senate of the United States with subpoena powers to reach out anywhere in the United States, pluck out an individual, insist that he grab an airplane, go to Washington, and appear in front of this committee. He had to come without any knowledge of the questions he might be asked, without any right of having counsel cross-examine the witness against him, without any right of research to present a proper case, without any rules of law.[35]

The Senate Committee hearings involving Hoffa lasted over two years and were a continual source of frustration and anger. In a 1962 speech, Hoffa gave vent to some of his feelings of oppression and persecution:

> Once and for all, we will determine whether we are first, second, or third class citizens. It is their desire to tear down individuals once they are indicted to make them crawl and squirm, to make them live in fear prior to their trial. They want to crush us morally, mentally, and financially. I was brought up on the street and nobody is going to make me squirm, wiggle, twist, or turn—to hell with them.[36]

HOFFA'S PERSONAL LIFE AND BACKGROUND

In Detroit, Hoffa had the reputation of a warm, attentive family man. He often flew home to spend weekends with his wife and children. His daughter, a Phi Beta Kappa student at college, taught school before she married; his son, an all-state football star in high school, studied law. His pride in his family came through in his acceptance speech at the 1961 convention:

> My daughter finished college. It is the first generation for either a Hoffa or Poszywak, my wife's family on her mother's, her father's, my mother's, and my father's side to have had an opportunity to complete college. It is a great American institution that permits men like myself to move from a warehouse to here, my wife from a laundry to where she stands here today.[37]

Hoffa's children had warm memories of their childhood:

> He never spanked us. He would laugh at it—whatever Mother scolded or spanked us for. He would say you should spank the child immediately after the incident or not at all. But he disciplined us. Oh! Did he ever. He always wanted to see our grades; and, if anything didn't please him he'd point that finger . . . he helped with our lessons when we were little kids.[38]

A Spartan in his personal life, Hoffa rejected whiskey and tobacco, despising the weakness and lack of self-discipline which indulgence in either represented to him. They consumed time and impaired effectiveness. Puritanical about sex, he was embarrassed by a striptease show or a sexy joke, berating those who enjoyed "such things." This puritanism even went so far as to prohibit him from enjoying coffee and tea.

He continually fretted about his diet. The ten pounds he added during the 1961 negotiations seemed of more concern to him than reports of a membership revolt in Cincinnati. Indeed, one of the few changes he made in the impressive Teamster headquarters Dave Beck built in Washington was to install a steam room, complete with masseur, parallel bars, and calisthenics equipment.

Hoffa's origins were lower-class. Born on Valentine's Day, 1913, in the small midwestern town of Brazil, Indiana, he was the son of a German-Dutch coal driller. His father was often absent from home and died in 1920 of coal poisoning, leaving a wife, two sons, and two daughters. Jimmy was the third child; the others were Jeannette, two years older, Billy, one year older, and Nancy, a year younger than Jimmy.

Hoffa's mother, a strong and demanding Irish woman, moved the family to nearby Clinton, Indiana, the third move since Jimmy's birth. To support her family, Mrs. Hoffa took in washing until, in 1925, she found a factory job and settled down with her children on Detroit's west side.

Her children learned the meaning of the word discipline long before they could pronounce it. She was, Hoffa recalled, "a pretty tough woman." He liked to think of her as the "frontier type." All the children had vivid memories of frequent punishment by razor strop and castor oil.

After school, Jimmy cleaned basements, carried in coal and wood, dumped out ashes, and bagged potatoes (which also occupied Saturdays). He gave his mother all the money he earned doing odd jobs for a number of retail stores in the neighborhood: delivering groceries, passing out handbills, loading and unloading trucks, sweeping and cleaning. He told his biographer that no one who has not experienced it can imagine the feeling of sheer goodness that engulfs a child of a poor family when he hands to his mother money that he has earned completely on his own and without her suggestion or insistence.[39]

Hoffa remembered his mother as very demanding. Every evening she cleared the table and made the children study, though she never examined their assignments or homework. At the end of term she looked at the results on the report cards and penalized poor performance with the razor strop and castor oil.[40]

Though Jimmy earned a good reputation in school for retentive reading, he hated reciting and having to stand up and deliver in front of the class, and would sometimes feign ignorance even when he knew the subject well. Not surprisingly, he never appeared in a school play.[41]

On finishing the ninth grade, Jimmy left school and took a job, lasting 18 months, as a stock boy in a dry-goods store. Although the hours were long and pay was meager, without a second thought he turned over to his mother all the money he earned. He was frugal and hitched rides to and from work on the rear of the trolley, crouching to avoid the conductor's eye. Rarely did he participate in recreations that cost money; he never had dates and seldom went to the movies. He liked sports, but as a participant, rather than spectator.

Singularly conformist and seldom visible, young Jimmy was a quiet, obedient, and submissive child. He did his chores regularly, rarely misbehaved, and showed very little sign of the rebelliousness which marked his later life.[42]

At 17 he took a job in Kroger's grocery warehouse unloading incoming produce from railroad cars and loading trucks that delivered to retail stores. There was no remuneration for waiting time. He enjoyed describing those early days: "We would report in at 4:30 a.m., stay around as long as they wanted us to. When a boxcar came in, they would call a few of us to unload. For that we got paid 32 cents an hour—but only for the time we actually worked."[43] At Kroger's he had an opportunity to socialize during the long, irksome waiting periods. These first associations with his fellow workers were far more congenial than those with authority. The workers became lifelong friends; one married Hoffa's older sister, and others held office in the Teamsters. But his memories of the relationship with the foreman, Al Hastings, were extremely bitter.

> What made our situation completely unbearable was that we had a foreman who was a solid gold son of a bitch. Actually he was called "the Little Bastard " by all the men. This guy was a real sadist. He thoroughly enjoyed screaming out commands and then cursing a man and threatening to fire him if he didn't move quick enough. He was a little tin Jesus in the warehouse and the only time he smiled was when he had fired somebody. Nor, at that time, was there any appeal, any form of job security.[44]

In 1931, Hoffa and five other men led their fellow workers out on strike just as a load of strawberries arrived. Confronted with the possible loss of its perishable fruit, the company capitulated. The workers received a labor contract containing a small pay increase, improved working conditions, and an insurance plan. The little local soon picked up a charter from the AFL and in 1932 was incorporated into the Teamsters as Local 299. Later, on being fired by the warehouse, Hoffa became a paid representative of the local, mainly concerned with organizing employees. During this period in Detroit, the automobile industry was the scene of sitdown strikes, and labor-management violence. They were tough, brawling days in Detroit and as Hoffa remembered them:

Our cars were bombed out. Three different times someone broke into our office and destroyed our furniture. They hired thugs who were out to get us. The police would beat your brains in for even talking union. If you went on strike, you got your head broken . . . but I can hit back. Guys who tried to break me got broken up. It was no picnic, but I gave as good as I got.[45]

Hoffa considered his background a definite asset. He had a self-image of toughness, as suggested in this comment following a fistfight over the ratification of a contract: "The other guys got the worst of it. They got a few knots on their heads. I can get along."[46]

Unlike many labor leaders in the twenties and thirties, Hoffa boasted that he never needed to hire professional thugs, a practice he thought both weak and dangerous, as the professionals might end up in control. He was proud of his muscle and that of his lieutenants.

Toughness was important to him as a way of life. He once told his associates how he had put his son, then six years old, alone in a duck blind for six hours with a gun and a bottle of pop. Proudly he proclaimed, "If I were an employer, I'd be the meanest bastard that God ever created."[47]

Both Hoffa's background and his relationships with the Senate and the law struck chords of empathy and sympathy in his union members, and Hoffa was not loath to capitalize on it. He shouted, "To hell with all our enemies!" as he presented the image of himself in the role of the persecuted. As with contract negotiations and grievance procedures, Hoffa loved to squeeze the maximum drama out of any inherently explosive situation.

Robert Kennedy, commenting on his first encounter with Hoffa, remarked:

Hoffa, I was to discover, can be personable, polite, and friendly. But that evening, though friendly enough, he maintained one steady theme. . . . "I do to others what they do to me, only worse". . . . It seemed to me he wanted to impress upon me that Jimmy Hoffa is a tough, rugged man.

. . . .

On my way home I thought of how often Hoffa had said that he was tough; that he destroyed employers, hated policemen, and broke those who stood in his way.[48]

In his early twenties James Hoffa met Farrell Dobbs, who

proved to be a significant person in his life. From Dobbs he received an ideology as well as ideas, tactics as well as strategy, office as well as inspiration. It was Dobbs' teachings Hoffa applied when he became president of his small local in 1937. It was the successful application of Dobbs' principles that laid the groundwork for Hoffa's rise to power as well as the foundation for Teamster strength.

Farrell Dobbs was an early labor leader from Minneapolis who organized the Central States Drivers Council, of which he was chairman. He was a convinced Trotskyite and in 1940 left the field of labor unions to pursue his socialist ideology as the Socialist Workers Party candidate for United States president. He lost, and despite his leadership of the Socialist Workers Party, disappeared from public view after his campaign for the presidency.

Dobbs' key concept was that the trucking industry was a group of extremely independent carriers who were at the same time locked in intricate interdependencies. He hypothesized the instant effect on operators in other cities of a work stoppage in a key city, and used Chicago as the first "pressure point" in a "test case." Mere realization of the effects of the work stoppage by the large truckers was all the pressure needed to make them capitulate. The area conference was born from this successful strategy.

The conference idea, all-important in the union's development, went through several metamorphoses. The Trotskyites had designed the Drivers Council to implement their Marxist belief that unions were instruments of the class struggle. Beck, devoted to the ideology of the business community, merely used the same structure to increase the size and power of the union, and at the same time extend his own influence within it. Capitalizing on the spread of industrial unionism, Beck set up locals whose membership ranged far outside the traditional Teamster jurisdiction. The new locals were then grouped into separate trade divisions established on an industry-wide basis, and all these diverse groups were then brought together in the area conference.

Hoffa carried this process a significant step further. Where Beck's contracts were limited to city-wide negotiations, Hoffa insisted on uniform area-wide agreements. These he negotiated himself, fixing terms for all employers within the area. It took Hoffa years to persuade local unions to give up their local autonomy for these area-wide agreements with uniform contract provisions, and years and an occasional strike to persuade some employers. The multistate area pacts were obviously only a step toward Hoffa's ultimate goal of a national pact with uniform nation-wide conditions.

It was also Dobbs who recognized how the threat of work stoppage could be used for organizing purposes. The large carriers had already signed up with the Teamsters; it now remained to organize the smaller companies. The South and states like Nebraska, where strong anti-union legislation had been enacted, were especially troublesome. Dobbs made a test case of Omaha. He had pinpointed Kansas City as the key. Pressuring already organized carriers in that city would force the surrender of employers in Omaha because of the motor carriers' route structure and the flow of commerce between the two cities.

Dobbs saw the over-the-road driver as a potentially extremely effective communication medium—both cheap and selective. Though not so revolutionary as the printing press or the radio, it was an innovation in communication, and spread Teamster ideology throughout the country. Dobbs taught Hoffa these strategies, but it remained for Hoffa to refine and apply them with expertise. Dobbs bowed out of the labor movement in 1940 and Hoffa filled his vacated office of chairman of the Central States Drivers Council. Dobbs had not taken much note of Hoffa, who was still in his early twenties, but Jimmy paid close attention to him. Hoffa quickly perceived the potential power of a network of vigorous Teamster locals connected, both figuratively and literally, by the over-the-road drivers, and saw as well the unlimited strategic advantage of Dobbs' pressure and leverage techniques. To apply these successfully depended, he realized, on a thorough knowledge of the trucking industry, which observing Dobbs' master stroke in starting with Chicago and choosing Kansas City as the pressure point for Omaha impressed fully upon him.[49]

In March 1937, while picketing a laundry, Hoffa met Josephine (Jo) Poszywak, a laundry worker, and married her in September. When she asked him why he picked her over far prettier girls on the picket line, he enjoyed telling her, "You looked like you needed a good meal."[50] The Hoffas had a daughter in 1938 and a son in 1941.

In 1937, Local 299 elected 24-year-old Hoffa president. In his first major objective, organizing car-hauling drivers, he put to use Dobbs' ideas in establishing one of the first national trade conferences in the union, the autotransport section of the industry, which he later used as a model for similar groups throughout the Teamster structure. His outstanding abilities as negotiator brought him the chairmanship of the Central States Drivers Council (CSDC) bargaining team by 1940. Two years later, a seasoned Hoffa of 29 formed the Michigan Conference of Teamsters.

Recognition of Hoffa's growing influence came in 1948 when IBT President Daniel Tobin named the 35-year-old Hoffa to a vacant trusteeship in the International Union. Four years later Hoffa brought to the 1952 convention a bloc of votes big enough to force his election as vice president. Dave Beck, IBT president from 1953 to 1957, fell under government fire in 1956-57. Presumably on Hoffa's orders, he announced his retirement and Hoffa took the presidential reins in October 1957. After that Hoffa continued to tighten his control and forward his strategy: one national master contract, common contract expiration dates, equality in wages, and improvements in all negotiable areas (wages, hours, work rules, conditions, fringes).

Hoffa expanded the use of the over-the-road driver into a new technology for gaining membership. Called the "leapfrog technique," Hoffa used it to broaden his personal power as well as LET and CSDC jurisdiction. He developed strong over-the-road locals and used these as a base for organizing other industries. As Hoffa said and proved, "Once you have the road men, you can get the local cartage, and once you have the local cartage, you can get anyone you want."[51]

Warehousing was a prime Hoffa target. In a speech before the CSDC in 1948, he said:

> Now, I know that certain warehouses where highway trucks back into all day long are not organized, and you know it is true. I know that certain wholesale groceries that, if it wasn't for the highway trucks, couldn't exist, yet are not organized in certain territories of people sitting right here in this room and it's absolutely inexcusable for that to exist any longer.[52]

HOFFA AND KENNEDY

Some observers felt that Kennedy's prosecution of Hoffa took on the character of a personal vendetta. Certainly Hoffa felt so. His behavior was significantly influenced by "that little monster" Robert Kennedy. He believed that under Kennedy's direction FBI agents followed him wherever he went, tapped his phone, opened his mail, and beamed electronic listening devices on him from half a mile away—aided by invisible powder they had rubbed onto his clothes.

During the 1961 Miami convention, Hoffa warned the delegates that Kennedy had sent female spies to pry secrets out of them and ordered them to avoid strangers.[53] His conviction that Kennedy would try to stop the convention never materialized, but he claimed that dozens of FBI agents, disguised as bellhops, desk clerks, doormen, maids, and waiters, swarmed about the hotels where his executive board met, to spy on him. Hoffa was "sure" that officers in his own organization, including two vice presidents, reported to the FBI, so he had listening devices installed in his Detroit and Washington headquarters, with a control box in his office. From his desk Hoffa could flip a switch and hear either a recording or an amplified reproduction—monitor—of any conversation on telephones or of any conversation in any major room in the building. The system was installed at night so employees would be unaware of it.[54]

Hoffa's sense of persecution was apparent in many of his statements.

> I've been investigated on a continuous basis over half my life. I can look over my shoulder any time and spot someone shadowing me. They watch me every minute. When I went to Israel to dedicate a hospital, they sent them along. They keep my telephone tapped so they can hear everything I say, too. They keep three or four guys busy year-round checking my taxes, trying to find a two-bit mistake to pin on me![55]

But he also said, "Don't get the idea that I feel like I'm being picked on. Hoffa can take care of Hoffa."[56]

Hoffa was correct in believing that he was the prime target of Kennedy's attack on organized crime, but his ideas about Kennedy's single-minded pursuit of him and the types of surveillance techniques Kennedy ordered to be used against him were seemingly exaggerated.[57] Whatever the truth of the matter, Hoffa and his entourage were convinced that all possible forms of spying were permissible where he was concerned. They took elaborate precautions in their communications and left a trail of false clues about their activities.[58]

The Kennedy-Hoffa feud received widespread publicity, and both sides provided the media with good copy. The following were some of Hoffa's statements about Kennedy:

> Now, I regard Bobby Kennedy as a spoiled brat. He never had to

work, wouldn't know how to make a living. He's just a brat that believes that everybody is supposed to surrender and give in to whatever he wants, right or wrong. In my opinion, he prostitutes his oath of office, and he's violated the Constitution of the United States and is subject to go to jail. He used government funds when he was out campaigning for legislation which is a violation of the law.

I was reading a story about Bobby Kennedy which talked about he was born to the silk and I was born to the burlap and what the difference would have been if I had been born to the silk and Kennedy to the burlap. Well, you can't change life very easily and you can't go back. But, I would venture to say that, knowing what I did to get where I am now and what it took me to be part of building this union, that Bobby Kennedy would have found out that it is one thing to make people do things and another thing to get people to do things without making them. When you are rich everybody wants to do things, favors, everything for you. When you are poor, nobody wants to do a damn thing for you. That's the difference in my life, the way I came along and where I am, and his life. I know because I've had it both ways. He can't know because he never had it but one way—the rich way.

I'm willing to debate with Bobby Kennedy on radio or TV at my own personal expense, anywhere in the country, on any issue he desires to debate, and then let the American people vote on whether or not they believe that the image created by Kennedy is the actual Jimmy Hoffa who is president of the International Brotherhood of Teamsters, or whether he has not used every underhanded tactic he could use, and the greatest public relations campaign in the world, to try to distort, deceive, and destroy, if possible, James Hoffa. It's hard to conceive that the American people are willing to accept the theory that a young millionaire who never worked in his life, never had to face up to meeting a budget, would be able to understand to determine, what is good or bad for the working people.[59]

After nine years of unsuccessful efforts to get Hoffa convicted, Kennedy's team finally succeeded in March 1964 in having Hoffa sentenced to eight years of prison and a fine of $10,000 on a charge of jury tampering during a previous trial. Shortly afterwards Hoffa was convicted on a second charge of fraud in connection with loans made from the Teamsters' pension fund. Hoffa fought the first decision for almost two years, but on February 28, 1967 the Supreme

Court upheld the conviction after twice reviewing the evidence and affirming that no illegal methods were used in the prosecution of Hoffa. In March, Hoffa entered Lewisburg Federal Penitentiary.

COMMENTARY

Little evidence disputes the conclusion that the harshness of young Jimmy's early childhood fixed for life his naked aggression and taste for power. But what is not so easily understood is the mechanism underlying the drastic change that occurred in Jimmy's transition from a child to an adult.

As a child, Jimmy was compliant, obedient, and respectful of the rules authority established. There was little if any evidence to project an image of how Jimmy Hoffa was to become as an adult and as the leader of the Teamsters' union. What brought about the change, and did the way the change occur fix Hoffa's orientation to power into a rigid, authoritarian world view populated with enemies and persecutory figures?

The change from compliance and passivity to rebellion and aggressivity is evident enough. Why the change and the route the change took is far less clear. A leading hypothesis suggests that Hoffa's underlying rage was always present and, presumably, exacerbated by the death of his father and the absence of a male figure with whom he could identify in his assertiveness and striving for independence. Instead, as a child Jimmy's identifications tracked toward his mother. Unfortunately for her, she had to act as both the nurturant and the disciplinary figure, with little room for overt nurturance and maternal warmth, given the harshness of her life. She worked to support her children and was solely responsible for raising them to become responsible adults. She punished swiftly and harshly, using the strop and castor oil as her agents.

The invasiveness of her means of punishment, which resulted in physical loss of control in the most humiliating sense, brought about the results she sought, but my conjecture is that the forms her punishment took resulted in identifications that made it difficult for Hoffa later as an adult to play with the idea of power. This playfulness as a thought mechanism permits a range of possibilities for the uses of power which on the one hand keeps the power holder in check, and on the other hand provides him with satisfactions as the power achieves flexibility in its aims.

Exhibit 1
THE HOFFA CHRONOLOGY

The Beginning of the Road

1913	Born in Brazil, Indiana
1914	The last of four Hoffa children, Nancy, is born early this year
1920	The frequently absent father dies, Jimmy does odd jobs, mother starts a home laundry
1923	The family moves to Clinton, Indiana—the fourth move in ten years
1925	The family moves to Detroit
	Jimmy quits school and takes a job as a stock boy, works at odd jobs

Finding the Road

1930	Jimmy takes job moving produce at Kroger's Food Warehouse
1931	April—The Strawberry Strike—Local 299 formed
	Later—fired from Kroger's, he becomes organizer for Local 299, a small and weak local
1934	Appointed business agent of debt-ridden Local 299
1936-1937	Meets Farrell Dobbs—is influenced by his teachings
	Meets Josephine Poszywak in March—marries her in September and leaves home for the first time
	Becomes president of Local 299

The Road to Power

1940	Dobbs resigns as chairman of CSDC to go into politics—Hoffa takes his place and uses this as a vehicle to propel him to national prominence
1942	Hoffa forms the Michigan Conference of Teamsters
1946	Hoffa becomes president, Detroit Council of Teamsters
1951	Hoffa is charged with improper relations with employers under contract (with a truck leasing firm)
1952	He is elected an international vice president of the Teamsters

The Road from Power

1957	Elected Teamster president
	Indicted for bribery, acquitted
1962	May—indicted for accepting payment from an employer (same as 1951 charge)
1963	May—indicted for jury tampering in connection with 1962 indictment
1964	Tried and convicted for jury tampering
	Indicted for misuse of union funds
1967	March—Hoffa enters jail for jury tampering

Hoffa's identifications were with the aggressor. The formula behind identification with the aggressor is to repeat in the active mode what one endured in the passive mode. As he was punished as a child, leading to his compliance and obedience, so he punished as the leader, seeking compliance and obedience from the objects of his power.

He was intolerant of anyone who questioned his power or the means he used to display it. In negotiations with truckers, in dealing with his lieutenants, he expected and received total compliance. He expected the same from government authorities. When he encountered Robert Kennedy, the balance between his expectations and actuality tipped against him. The rigidity of this thinking, which grew out of his identification with the aggressor, did not permit an understanding of the government's role in the labor scene, and of Kennedy's power through the legitimacy of the U. S. Senate and its committees.

Hoffa understood very well rivals for power. Because he could read rivalry through the screens of his own psyche, as well as his own ambitions, he could take on rivals with the confidence that he could dish out more naked aggression than he incurred and that he would endure, a set of beliefs he was to maintain throughout his prison years and following his release. Kennedy was another story. A man born to the silk lived in a special realm, leagues removed from what Hoffa understood. He could hate a man born to the silk, he could demean his manliness, but in the end he feared such a man because the means employed for the uses of power were not discrete, bound into a short time cycle, and concrete. They were subtle, legalistic, and slow moving. These processes of power seemed mysterious to Hoffa. Willing to confront Robert Kennedy face-to-face symbolically was a way of shifting the conflict into an arena Hoffa understood, and on terms that fit his conceptions of manliness and control. It would have been for Hoffa the equivalent of bare fists. Instead, Hoffa had to deal with agents, legal proceedings, representation through counsel, and the slow motion of investigative processes. Already short-tempered, this loss of control put Hoffa at a serious disadvantage in this higher order of conflict between his union and the government, between Robert Kennedy and himself.

Just as Hoffa misunderstood power in his dealings with the government, he misunderstood power as a personal instrument and as a means for institutional leadership. Power was personal. He had grasped it through the application of the principles that Farrell

Dobbs had taught him in his early days with the union. These principles directed Hoffa's attention to contract negotiations as a means for maximizing his control over the employers and his union. He centralized contract negotiations in the area conferences, which resulted in the loss of power at the local level as he gained personal power at the executive level of the international. He learned from Dobbs the significance of pressure points in the geography of over-the-road transport. By applying only modest pressure at these sensitive points, he could get his way in the contract negotiations that he conducted personally. Not only did Hoffa accumulate power at the expense of the local union hierarchy, he also gained power at the expense of the international hierarchy. He delegated to no one in his effective control of the union's contract negotiations and grievance procedure.

While Hoffa's tactical acuity assured him control over his adversaries in the employer-owner group, the same tactics of control assured that he would make enemies among the middle and upper levels of management in the Teamster hierarchy. The loss of power at these levels assured Hoffa's control of the Teamsters union, but it also assured him of the loneliness of his power position. He had no trusted allies, few if any with whom he could consult. His trusted ally was his wife, and while this assured Hoffa of warmth and support in the home, it is questionable what his wife could do to help him see power in its many different perspectives.

Another side to Hoffa's identifications was his empathic concern for the masses, the union rank and file. His attachment to the rank and file (no issue of concern to them did he treat indifferently) was almost mystical. To Hoffa, the rank and file was himself. These people were the deprived, the oppressed, the victims of a harsh fate and a cruel and ungiving authority. Their enemies, like Al Hastings, the Kroger foreman, were his enemies. Just as Hoffa vowed never to be dominated by another, he vowed (and acted out) dominance. He wanted higher wages and improved working conditions for the rank and file, but of equal importance he wanted their lives free of the tyranny of control.

Hoffa was a mass leader. His positive identifications were with the masses. His alliance was with the rank and file. These identifications were the closest Hoffa came to an abstraction in his life. To feel empathy with the masses is to feel no attachment to particular people. The masses as embodied in the rank and file of the Teamsters provided a link between Hoffa's world view of the oppressed and the oppressors, and the tactics of conflict in the struggle for power, dominance, and control. The masses provided his legitimacy, his self-esteem, and the feeling that he was redeeming his past, particularly his beleaguered mother and his destroyed father. What was missing was the self-assurance that comes from cognitive awareness of who one is, what the basis of power is, and the multiple ways power can be used to accomplish socially valuable goals. There was no end to the meanness and hostility implicit in Hoffa's world view. Constant vigilance was necessary to maintain control. In this world view, life was a battlefield where today's victories provided no assurance for tomorrow's battles.

Hoffa's mentor, Farrell Dobbs, was a self-styled radical. As a socialist who followed Leon Trotsky, Dobbs was an ideologue, more interested in fostering his precepts than in securing his power base. He left the Teamsters Union to run for the presidency of the United States under the banner of the Socialist Workers Party. He lost the election but never returned to the union. As far as we can discern he disappeared from public view and from Hoffa's life. The lasting impression he left on Hoffa concerned the tactics of power in the over-the-road trucking industry. While Hoffa professed some allegiance to the Trotskyite views he learned from Dobbs, Hoffa was far more the practitioner of power than the ideologue. Ideas interested him little, and consistency less. He could feel sympathy for the class struggle, but just as easily support the Republican Party, Richard Nixon, and other conservative politicians who lost little sleep over the plight of the working man. Even here, Hoffa's support of the Republicans were means to ends and not identification or sympathy with the politics and ideas of the Republicans he helped. It is difficult to understand Hoffa's management of the pension funds (mismanagement is perhaps more to the point) given his positive identification with the rank and file. The purpose of the pension fund was to protect the economic security of the membership and to provide for their comfort in retirement. To follow the logic of this purpose, as well as to enhance Hoffa's identification with the rank and file, Hoffa should have been inclined to perfect the management of the pension funds. With the aggregate of the monies involved, Hoffa could have secured the best investment advice available. He could have established an impeccable group of trustees whose only interest would have been to gain the maximum returns at the level of conservative management consistent with the objectives of a pension program.

Hoffa took none of the steps one might have expected from a leader so clearly in sympathy with the needs and aspirations of the working man. One explanation for this lapse that ultimately became implicated in his loss of power in the Teamsters is that Hoffa stole money from the pension funds. While it is true he had large amounts of cash at his disposal, I am skeptical of this explanation. Hoffa lived a simple life. Unlike his predecessors, material things meant little to Hoffa. The more likely explanation is Hoffa's need for control and unwillingness to share power persuaded him to personalize the management of the funds and to use this management as a lever in his power base.

Unfortunately, the lever was connected with mobsters. The investments with these mobsters were dreadful and implicated Hoffa in dealings far removed from what was in the best interests of the rank and file.

Early in this chapter I asked you to consider what kept Hoffa from greatness and what was missing in his life. The answer to these questions does not direct us to the possibilities of a childhood different from what he had. The misfortunes of life are irreversible. The significance of these misfortunes is subject to change and can become a force for ambition, achievement, and personal growth.

Hoffa achieved a great deal in his life. He did accumulate power and his influence affected the lives of his constituencies. His personal reputation, while favorable among the rank and file, was negative to the American public at large, and to its legitimate leadership structure. What was missing in Hoffa's psychology, as with Henry Ford and other powerful figures with limited education, was the ability to think abstractly. This limitation is a disability, a form of deprivation that ultimately accounts for the leader's demise. It is a fatal flaw, seemingly irreversible, not because of lack of formal education. We are considering here the educated mind capable of allowing ideas to play on one's imagination and to project the product of this play into one's spheres of influence.

From the vantage point of psychopathology, perhaps the inability to engage in abstract thinking is a product of a mind built along the lines of the rigid obsessive, even the obsessive with the tendency to bifurcate the world into the good and the bad, to create a hostile environment and to perpetuate this hostility by making enemies instead of allies.

One could argue that Hoffa lacked a teacher, an extension of a good father. While he had a teacher in Dobbs, it was short-lived in duration and of narrow purpose: how to get control of the union as an apparatus for wielding power. But to say he lacked a teacher is indeed a misfortune, but not such a simple misfortune attributable to an unkind fate. To find a teacher is itself a creative act that results directly from intellectual curiosity, the need to know and understand the world as it is and not as it is concretely formed in one's mind out of a base of hostility and mistrust. For James Hoffa, the quest for power was too personal, too engrossed in the fruitlessness of remaking the past.

Endnotes—Chapter 14

1. *New York Times*, 9 Dec. 1975.
2. Steven Brill, *The Teamsters* (New York: Simon and Schuster, 1978), p. 56.
3. *New York Times*, 7 July 1977.
4. Brill, *The Teamsters*, pp. 45-49.
5. Ibid., p. 50.
6. James R. Hoffa, *Hoffa, the Real Story*, as told to Oscar Fraley (New York: Stein and Day, 1975), p. 13.
7. Brill, *The Teamsters*, p. 86.
8. Ibid., p. 65.
9. Ibid., p. 12.
10. Arthur Allen Stone, *Union-Employer Relations in the Over-the-Road Trucking Industry* (Ph.D. diss., Harvard University Graduate School of Business Administration), p. 373.
11. *Wall Street Journal*.
12. Ralph James and Estelle James, *Hoffa and the Teamsters: A Study of Union Power* (Princeton: D. Van Nostrand and Company, Inc., 1965), p. 27.
13. From the 1953 International Brotherhood of Teamsters contract with the trucking industry in the Midwest.
14. James Hoffa, 1955 speech to the Teamsters Union.
15. James, *Union Power*, p. 161.
16. Ibid., p. 168.
17. Ibid., p. 171.
18. Ibid., p. 173.
19. Ibid., p. 183.
20. James Clay, *Hoffa! Ten Angels Swearing* (Beaverdam, VA: Beaverdam Books, 1965), p. 142. The following account of Hoffa's life relies heavily on this "authorized biography."

21. Sam Romer, *The International Brotherhood of Teamsters* (New York: John Wiley and Sons, 1962), p. 29.

22. Bernard Nossiter, *The Teamsters*, (New York: Harpers, 1959).

23. James, *Union Power*, p. 60.

24. Ibid.

25. Clark Mollenhoff, *Tentacles of Power: The Story of Jimmy Hoffa* (New York: The World Publishing Company, 1965), p. 243.

26. *Wall Street Journal.*

27. Clay, *Hoffa!* p. 10.

28. Ibid., p. 61.

29. James, *Union Power*, p. 49.

30. Ibid., p. 68.

31. Ibid., pp. 49-50.

32. Clay, *Hoffa!*

33. James, *Union Power*, p. 115.

34. Ibid., p. 116.

35. Clay, *Hoffa!* p. 166.

36. Ibid., p. 167.

37. Clay, *Hoffa!* p. 163.

38. Ibid., p. 80.

39. Ibid., p. 45.

40. Ibid., p. 46.

41. Ibid.

42. Ibid., pp. 47-48. James, *Union Power*, p. 69 says Hoffa only completed the seventh grade.

43. James, *Union Power*, p. 69.

44. Hoffa, *Real Story*, p. 31.

45. Nossiter, *The Teamsters*, p. 37.

46. James, *Union Power*.

47. Ibid., p. 53.

48. Robert Kennedy, *The Enemy Within* (New York: Paperback Books, 1963), pp. 41, 43.

49. Clay, *Hoffa!* p. 72.

50. Ibid., p. 78.

51. Ibid., p. 73.

52. Reprinted from a speech in the Teamsters' *Newsletter.* Quoted in James, *Union Power*.

53. James, *Union Power*, p. 62.

54. Rudolph L. Doeliche, a witness at the Hoffa wiretapping trial, testified that he helped install the system in Hoffa's office in the Detroit Teamsters' headquarters. He also testified that he instructed Hoffa as to its use for listening to conversations in other rooms as well as on the telephones. Hoffa admitted such a system was installed, but denied

knowing that it could be used for wiretapping. He also denied that he had ever received instructions from Doeliche, and insisted that he believed it was a legal device for simply listening to conversations in other rooms. In *U.S. vs. James R. Hoffa* in the U.S. District Court for the Southern District of New York.

55. Clay, Hoffa! p. 84.

56. Ibid., p. 172.

57. See Arthur M. Schlesinger, Jr., *Robert Kennedy and His Times* (Boston: Houghton Mifflin, 1978), for a review of these issues.

58. James, *Union Power*, p. 63.

59. Clay, *Hoffa!* pp. 172-173.

THE INVENTION OF A
LIFE—COCO CHANEL

History is pervasive. It permeates a life and is inescapable. Yet, as case studies of leaders demonstrate, history is transformable. It does not disappear, like chalk from a blackboard, so that what once existed is no more. It is omnipresent, but subject to transformation.

The events in one's history still exist in memory. But the meanings attached to these events can be changed. The events themselves rarely cause problems, but rather the meanings create mischief. A child loses a parent. Did the parent abandon the child? Was it intentional, meant to inflict harm? Was the child unlovable and therefore intolerable? Did the child commit a grievous sin and need to be punished? Was the child voracious, greedy, and consuming, and therefore dangerous?

This sample of questions suggests how one can personalize events until one is implicated beyond any reasonable connection between cause and effect. Yet these questions can be changed, leading to different answers and different outcomes in work, love, and personal relationships.

In reading Coco Chanel's story, you will be struck by the

CHAPTER

15

pervasiveness of history in her life. You will also be struck by Coco's adroitness (is compulsive need too strong?) in altering her history. She wanted to talk about her past, yet she wanted to evade her past as both a public and personal issue.

Coco Chanel was busily engaged in inventing her life and her past. There was little separation between Coco's public and private self. What she did in fashion she did as a businesswoman, but also as a woman singularly dedicated to changing women's perception of themselves as a prelude to changing men's perception of women. The most superficial glimpse at the fashion photographs preceding and following Coco Chanel's impact on the world of couture will demonstrate the remarkable change that resulted from Coco's work. Women were liberated, their body image changed, and their freedom of movement significantly increased.

While Chanel did not originate the short hair style she adopted, the fact that she cut her hair made an impact on women as well as men. We could well ask ourselves whether Coco's aim (unconscious of course) was to masculinize the feminine image, or whether economy, function, and simplicity were pure fashion expressions, an idea whose time had come, quite apart from personal history.

Coco Chanel's life also raises interesting questions about sexuality and its uses in a career. Coco was provocative. She never married, but apparently was never without male lovers, and many male admirers. She kept this side of her life no secret. In fact it appears she was a clever marketer and understood intuitively, if not intellectually, the product she was making and selling. The seductiveness of her personality became a tool of her craft and a device to promote her brand.

The reliable facts about Chanel indicate she had a horrible childhood, abandoned by father and mother, turned over to an orphanage, and left as a young adult to fend for herself. She did not escape into the safety of a conventional marriage. Evidently, her ambition and ideals did not permit such a seemingly facile solution to the problems of an insecure person seeking security in a harsh world. Burning ambition comes to nothing without a talent. It will be interesting for you to wonder about the talent Coco had. As a designer, she worked unconventionally. She did not (or is it could not?) draw. She worked with clothing on her mannequins, using scissors to rip and cut, and then sent the garment back to the workrooms.

The iterations of this procedure ultimately produced a garment and a collection.

Chanel was also a businesswoman who attacked a competitive industry in which men had been dominant. She became the major presence in her industry and a figure of international renown. Her collaboration with the Wertheimers in the perfume business is noteworthy. Partners they were, but also antagonists in the distribution of the riches that flowed from Chanel No. 5.

You may find it almost too obvious to consider why Chanel abandoned her business in 1939, making her last collection in 1938. It was not until 1953 that she reactivated the House of Chanel. The obvious explanation of her decision to terminate her business is that she saw the war coming and knew that couture had no place in a world at war. But there is also a hint that Coco faced competition from an Italian designer, Elsa Schiaparelli, and the war gave Coco an easy way to withdraw from competition. Does Coco's withdrawal, in the context of her life history, suggest that she characteristically put expediency before ideals? If so, one must then inquire into the nature of her conscience and ego ideal. What was her self-image? What was the source of the entitlement that permitted her to be an entrepreneur, a leader in fashion, and a force for change in the relationship between the sexes and women's images of themselves in the twentieth century?

COCO CHANEL (1883-1971)

> Chanel a dress designer? Come now! A captain of industry, one of the last great industrial barons and creators of this country."
>
> **—Francoise Giroud, L'Express**

Who was Coco Chanel? A callous, egotistical businesswoman, satisfied only when disparaging employees? Or a driven designer, desperate to reshape her image and rectify the humiliation of her impoverished, neglected childhood?

She was born into an age when French women could not vote or drive automobiles. But by 1935 Gabrielle "Coco" Chanel was

This case was prepared by Anthony W. Artuso, MBA 1987, under the supervision of Professor Abraham Zaleznik. Copyright © 1987 by the president and fellows of Harvard College.

the founder, owner, manager, and creative force behind a Paris fashion house that employed 4,000 women and had sold 28,000 dresses in Europe, the Near East, and the Americas. Additionally, she was president of Parfums Chanel, makers of Chanel No. 5. Her business was described as "the biggest empire ever built by any woman with her own hands."[1]

Even though she did not receive the Fashion Oscar from Stanley Marcus until 1958, Coco revolutionized women's fashion 40 years earlier during World War I. "Her objective was to give new 'forms' to women—to furnish her rich customers with first-rate work, with clothes so perfectly made that they would not see them all over the place . . . 'Fashion should not come from the street, but it must reach down into it,' she said."[2]

Motivated by this creative philosophy, Coco simplified women's clothing, designing it for an active lifestyle, which in the fashion world launched a new type of emancipated woman. Some would call her creativity subversive, for it lacked the ceremonial splendor of prevailing fashion. Indeed, Coco considered "ceremony" in fashion oppressive. Others would link Coco's taste in fashion to her psychology: "With her, encumbrance was an obsession. (Said Coco) 'Sometimes I can't even bear a blanket over me.'"[3]

Yet, in 1939, without any warning or explanation, Coco closed the fantastically successful House of Chanel and disappeared from public view into the obscurity of retirement. Still more surprising, in 1953, after a 14-year absence from the fashion world, Coco at the age of 70 staged a comeback because she was bored. Even after her comeback, she complained of boredom. By 1958, however, she again was employing 400 people and selling 7,000 suits per year. Yet, Coco was not satisfied with her success. She claimed that every collection was her last. Late in life she described herself as a failure, feeling imprisoned by her work environment even though designing dresses and coats provided a secure refuge. To an observer, her "failure," her concept of "imprisonment" by her own good fortune may seem self-inflicted. To Coco, nevertheless, her lifestyle was an encumbrance, not allowing her the freedom to " . . . go out to buy things I need."[4]

By the time she died in 1971, Coco had become one of the richest women in the world. She left a fortune estimated in excess of $10 million to a trust that distributed it to charity. Among these charities was a fund established to help craftsmen who had lost use of their hands through an accident. She set up the charity after she experienced a paralysis of her right hand in 1966.

EARLY LIFE (1883-1908)

Gabrielle Chanel was born August 19, 1883, in a poorhouse hospital in Saumar, France. Her father, Albert Chanel, an itinerant merchant, was absent at her birth. At the time, he and her mother, Jeanne, were unmarried, but they did marry in 1884. She was the second daughter in a family that would eventually include three daughters and two sons.

Coco grew up in grinding poverty. Her father was away most of the time; her mother, despite fragile health, was obsessed with following him, carrying Coco and her older sister along. Coco's mother, who suffered chronic asthma attacks, returned to her family's home in Courpiere only long enough to recover. During one recovery period, when the children were still very young, Coco's mother left Coco and her sister with farmer relatives before again seeking Albert. Thereafter she would return to Courpiere long enough to bear another child, recover her health, and go on the road again. In 1893, over her family's objections, she again took Coco and her older sister on the road. By 1895, Jeanne's health had seriously deteriorated, and she died on February 16 at the age of 33. Characteristically, her husband was absent at the time of her death.

Shortly after Jeanne's death, Albert turned the boys over to public welfare, gave the girls to his family, and disappeared, never to be heard from again by Coco. Her grandparents, in turn, sent 12-year-old Coco to an orphanage run by an order of Catholic sisters, where she continued to endure the personal indignities that inevitably engulf someone born in poverty and acutely aware of its stigma. These indignities were accentuated when, sometime before her twentieth birthday, Coco was sent as a charity student to a boarding school in Moulins. There the disparity between charity students and paying students was made painfully clear in clothing and accommodations. Obvious and exposing poverty prevented Coco from controlling her appearance where the boarding school girls had the wealth and power to display whatever appearance they chose (most likely that of wealth and power).

In 1903 Coco left boarding school to work as a seamstress in Moulins. She also began singing in a cafe. Although she dreamed of a future as a singer, Coco's attempts in the theater in Vichy in 1905 proved unsuccessful. She returned to Moulins for a short time before running off to Paris with an aunt her own age. After returning to Moulins, she met her first lover, Etienne Balsan, and lived with him on his estate in Royallieu—a "kept" woman.

Coco's Story

Although factual accounts of her early life differ, the preceding account is reliable. It, however, vastly differs from Coco's self-report. As if determined to suppress a past she despised, perhaps even fearful that it might reappear, Coco ". . . seldom told the truth when asked about her early life."[5] Though her lying seemed only pathetic attempts to conceal, it could also be interpreted as her grasp for self-empowerment—her wish to define herself, her appearance, and her story.

Her Father's Influence

Coco told a variety of conflicting stories, for example, about her father. At one time she told Truman Capote that her father had been a blacksmith in the Basque country. At other times, she claimed that her father was a wine merchant. She also insisted that he had not abandoned his family but had gone to America to seek his fortune and was planning to come back to get them.

One thing she did say consistently was that her father loved her and she loved him. For Coco, remembering an age when the meager trappings of intense poverty began to bear on her child's mind, his perceived love and her adoration of him gave her support. But competition would soon change Coco's world. This competition would hone the jealousy and singular possessiveness of her personality and eventually spawn the drive that would carry her to the top of the business world.

What triggered this personality development? Was it lack of love from her parents, or maybe typical sibling jealousy? Coco, herself, admitted that her rivalry with her younger sister for her father's affection was intense. Coco remembered the time before her sister's birth as idyllic. In her mind's eye, Coco represented these times as "good days, fun, happiness"; she even assumed that she was born into an ideal situation.[6] But after her sister's birth, Coco's "dream" stumbled against reality. Her father's temperament changed; he became meaner and apparently less loving toward Coco. She responded by grasping for his love, while at the same time blaming her sister for the loss of love from their father.

Coco believed her father loved her more than her sister. This assertion conflicted with her feeling that he was disappointed in her—disappointed that she had not been born a boy. Nevertheless, in her own way, she returned her father's love—conditional love to be sure for she " . . . couldn't have borne for him to feel the same about us both."[7]

Equally confusing was Coco's story about her father's extramarital affair with a servant. Her father, she asserted, kept a mistress, who Coco said bore him a son. Coco also claimed to have power over this woman, but seemed confused about what was actually happening and what "power" really meant: "I knew she slept with my father—that is I didn't know. I didn't understand anything of that sort of thing, but I guessed and I used to frighten her by saying I'd tell my mother."[8] Of course, since the Chanels were incredibly poor, it is unlikely that her father ever employed a servant with whom he could have had a dalliance.

Remembering a turbulent, often mentally suppressed, time, especially in early childhood, was difficult for Coco. As time went by, the desire to create a favorable image about someone she was "supposed" to have loved often overcame the negative realities. Coco's remembrances did swing back and forth, and thus reality became rather elusive. In a moment of reflection, perhaps when her defenses were not being assailed, Coco said: "You have a father and you love him very much, and you think he's perfectly all right. He wasn't perfectly all right, that's all."[9] Although some characterized him as a man who "lived only to seduce, procreate, run away, and begin again," and even though he had abandoned her, Coco would not accept criticism of her father.[10]

Her Mother's Influence

As with her father, Coco had unfocused memories of her mother. According to Coco, her mother came from an affluent family, a status Coco assumed for herself in outright denial of her humble origins. "I'd have liked to come from peasants," she once said in a fiction that was the parody of truth, "I always get on well with them."[11] Coco also said that all she remembered of her mother was that she died of TB. Jeanne actually died of asthma; the symptoms probably appeared similar.

That Coco seldom talked about her mother leads to speculation about her relationship with her and how deeply Jeanne's death affected Coco. Did Coco again feel a lack of love, a lack of attention? Did she suffer the same sibling rivalries for her mother's love? And were the feelings manifested, even in later years, by Coco being unable to accept her childhood void of parental attention?

Adolescence and Adulthood

During her adult life, but probably starting earlier, Coco submerged the pain of her childhood and adolescence from consciousness. Instead, Coco said she was raised by a pair of aunts, who "had promised to bring me up but not to love me."[12] These aunts were probably purely fictional; their occupations varied from story to story.

Coco was consistent in portraying her childhood as extremely unhappy. The theme of death, including her own thoughts of suicide, also dominated her recollections. She seemed infatuated with death. "We lived near a cemetery. For me a cemetery was not a sad place. I loved it and went there as often as possible. . . . I brought them [the dead] flowers as often as I could, and forks, spoons, or anything I could steal at home."[13]

Even after she had become successful, Coco never acknowledged how the consequences of this early life influenced her.

Because Chanel also never mentioned her brief career as a singer, even the origin of her nickname, "Coco," is shrouded in mystery. She may have acquired the name as a cafe singer in Moulins, where her favorite song was "Who's Seen Coco in the Trocadero?" and her audience would call for her by chanting "Coco! Coco!" Instead, Chanel claimed that her father didn't like the name Gabrielle and called her Little Coco until he thought of something better. According to Chanel, the name stuck. "It was awful, and I'd have loved to get rid of it, but I never will."[14]

Whatever the particulars of her early life, they left Coco with a burning desire for independence and control. Thus, even though she was well provided for as the mistress of Etienne Balsan, she dreamed of a business for herself: money and independence. The stage career having failed, she looked for something else. Whether she consciously recognized the opportunity or not, the fashion business provided an excellent starting point.

BUSINESS CAREER

Couture: The Industry

The typical Paris fashion house of 1900 catered to an exclusive clientele. Only the wealthiest women—wives of royalty, government bureaucrats, and rising bourgeois—could afford to have their clothes custom-made by a couturier, or designer. Generally, a couturier would present a collection of dresses each season, and a customer could order a dress from the collection to be made for her. Accordingly, the couturier's workshops would turn out the dress for one particular customer, and this is how money would be made. With the spread of department stores later in the century, store buyers replaced individual customers. Eventually, with the development of mass merchandisers and ready-to-wear, particularly in America, the high fashion designs of the coutures would be imitated and sold off the rack to thousands of women. Thus, coutures were more than the dressmakers for the well-to-do. They were trend setters for all women's fashions.

By 1900, the production of collections, as well as the economics of them, was well defined. Generally, after selecting the fabrics to be used in the approaching season's dresses, the designer sketched the dresses to be included in a particular collection. The fashion house's cutters and seamstresses would make the dresses, fitting them on a living model or mannequin. The designer would then examine the clothes as they looked on a real woman and would alter the design accordingly, sending the dress back to the seamstresses once or twice until it was right.

At the turn of the century, Paris couture was dominated by three men: Charles Worth, Paul Poiret, and Jacques Doucet. To say that their designs tended toward the extravagant is an understatement; one Poiret dress even included electric light bulbs. A contemporary described a well-dressed woman in these words: "A veritable arsenal of spangles, jewels, corsets, whalebone stays, steel clinchers, flowers and feathers was girded onto this splendid armored car of pleasure."[15] Modern authors take a dimmer view: "Long skirts, cumbersome hats, tight shoes, high heels, everything that fettered a woman's movements and made it necessary for a man to assist her. . . ."[16] Coco the businessperson sensed an opportunity to change all this. Her fashions would be elegantly simple: designs that would not confine but instead allow her to express her own need for an unencumbered existence.

The Start-Up (1908-1918)

In 1908, at her insistence, Balsan with Arthur (Boy) Capel set Coco up in Paris as a milliner. Although Balsan first resisted the idea of his mistress running a business, he acquiesced when his friend Capel started showing interest in Coco and her idea for a hat shop. The two of them helped her financially. Eventually a romantic struggle for Coco ensued between Capel and Balsan, and Capel won. For both men, the idea was amusing, like watching a child at play for their own entertainment. This condescending attitude was not lost on Coco. She recalled: "I was able to create my house because two men did battle over my little self."[17] Balsan and Capel's infatuation with Coco, in its own curious way, created a new life not only for her but for the world of women's fashion. In an understatement, Coco later recalled: "They didn't understand how important this was to me."[18]

Coco's plain hats, many of them simple straw boaters, stood out in sharp contrast to the feather- and fruit-laden creations of the day. They were instantly popular and profitable. Even though she had grown up in poverty, Coco had learned a great deal about the ways of the rich when she lived with her wealthy lover, Balsan. "The rich had introduced her to money, and this had helped her to work things out when she was setting prices. She knew that they would pinch pennies over necessities and bankrupt themselves for frivolities."[19] She put this knowledge to good use when marketing her hats: "[Hat] blocks bought at the Galeries Lafayette [a Paris department store] for pennies, touched up with a gimmick, a touch of something on top, and there you are, madame, just for you . . . . Meanwhile thinking to herself: idiot, if you're too stupid to make it for yourself, then pay, pay!"[20] Coco's mark-up on these slightly modified store-bought hats was probably four or five times the price she paid for the hat block.

Now funded solely by her new lover Boy Capel, Chanel's business expanded steadily. In 1910, she moved her store to a larger site on rue Cambon. In 1912, she opened a second shop in the summer resort of Deauville. In 1915, Coco officially went into couture, making dresses of a kind of wool never before used in women's clothing. She also opened a shop in Biarritz, thus entering the Spanish market. By 1916 Coco employed 300 people and was able to reimburse Boy Capel. By the end of World War I, Chanel's fashion house was firmly established.

Maturity (1918-1939)

During the 1920s and 1930s the House of Chanel continued to flourish. Chanel's style matched the times perfectly. World
War I had shattered a staid Victorian culture, and women began to
lead more active lives. Coco's simple clothes, stripped of encumber-
ing finery, gave the emancipated women of the twenties the freedom
they sought. The very simplicity of the clothes also made them more
profitable; where Poiret needed ten yards of material to make trou-
sers, Coco needed only one yard and charged Poiret's prices.

While Coco certainly did not invent all the trends of the
flapper era, she helped accelerate them. For example, she popularized short hair by cutting her own and her model's hair. She also
popularized sunbathing—heretofore inconceivable. She feminized
masculine attire; she said some of her first dresses were inspired by a
man's polo sweater.[21]

She also made profitable line extensions. In 1924, she entered into a partnership with perfume industrialists Pierre and Paul
Wertheimer, and formed Parfums Chanel to produce Chanel No. 5
and other fragrances. Around 1934, Coco designed costume jewelry
on a large scale.

Coco realized that the United States represented a large,
unexploited market. "Chanel is as American as hamburger," she declared on a visit to New York in 1929.[22] A few years later she was in
Hollywood designing dresses for Sam Goldwyn's stars. She was even
willing to embellish her ideal of simplicity in order to gain market
entry. "In the United States, where she felt lay the future and survival
of couture, Coco. . . was ready to make concessions."[23]

In 1939, however, Coco closed the House of Chanel. The
closing may have stemmed from an employee strike in 1936, where
Coco compromised only after long and bitter negotiations. In typical
benevolent despot fashion, however, Coco remained generous with
her employees; she even left a vacation home in Mimizan at their disposal. But one biographer says Coco never forgave her employees for
the strike—for daring to stand up to her. Her conception of laborers
obeying passively and showing gratitude to their benefactor—
perhaps acquired from her own hard lessons in a poor family—was
shattered. Her unexpected closing in 1939 may have been her revenge.

The start of World War II in 1939 might also have affected
her decision, although the war had little effect on France until the
Germans invaded in 1940. Besides, World War I hadn't stopped

Coco; her fashion business thrived despite threats to Paris from German zeppelins and long-range artillery.

A more plausible influence on Coco's decision to close shop was that, in 1939, for the first time in 20 years, the House of Chanel faced stiff competition from a new designer: Elsa Schiaparelli. Chanel styles had become classics that varied little from season to season; this new Italian designer threatened Coco with fresh styles.

Schiaparelli first made a splash in the Paris fashion scene in 1927 when one of her designs was named "sweater of the year" by *Vogue*, but Coco proceeded largely unchallenged. By 1936, however, Schiaparelli and Chanel designs shared space in *Vogue*. Although at least one biographer said this rivalry did not hurt Coco's business at all, by 1938—Chanel's last collection before retirement—she was matching Schiaparelli point-for-point. When Schiaparelli launched the color shocking pink with great fanfare, for example, Coco countered with gypsy-style dresses. Although her taste was directly opposed to Coco's, Schiaparelli's mode of operation paralleled Coco's in many ways. Like Coco, she had a fashion nickname, "Schiap"; like Coco, she had many friends among the period's great artists; and she sought Coco's clientele. In the fickle world of fashion, Coco had ceased to be an iconoclast and had instead become the target of iconoclasts like Schiaparelli.

Retirement (1939-1953)

The most significant historical event during Coco's retirement was France's occupation by Nazi Germany. It is not clear what effect this event had on Coco, if any; one biographer says that Coco's egocentricity left her untouched by the occupation. Nevertheless, Coco was suspected of German collaboration. In September 1944, shortly after Paris's liberation, French freedom fighters arrested Coco as a suspected collaborator. Although they released her after a few hours of questioning, she was furious and never forgave Charles de Gaulle or the Resistance: "Those Parisians of the Liberation with their shirt sleeves rolled up. Four days earlier, when they were with the Germans, they didn't have their sleeves rolled up," she snorted.[24] Another biographer, however, claimed that Coco herself was part of the French Resistance because of her connections with the English and her friendship with Winston Churchill.

Accusations of her collaboration stem from Coco's wartime affair in Paris with a German baron with the nickname Spatz

(Sparrow) whom Coco claimed to have met before the war. Although Spatz definitely worked for the Nazis, his dedication to the Reich is questionable. Thirteen years Coco's junior, the well-bred Spatz was not known for commitment to causes or women. His independence may have been ideal for Coco, who never married but instead maintained singular control of her life.

Spatz's principal concern during the occupation was to lie low and remain unnoticed by German high command who might assign him away from Paris and his comfortable lifestyle with Coco. After three years, however, the liberation of Paris forced Spatz to leave Paris and Coco.

While a cloud hung over Coco after the liberation, her fate was not as hard as that of some suspected collaborators. Most women who were romantically involved with Germans faced innumerable humiliations, including having their heads shaven, a swastika marked on their foreheads, and being forced to parade nude through the streets. Chanel managed to escape punishment and reach Switzerland without difficulty. She remained there eight years, an exile who returned to France only for brief visits. Later, she even was allowed a visa to the United States.

Comeback (1953-1971)

Claiming that she was bored and felt the need to work again, Coco reopened the House of Chanel in 1953. Even though her workrooms had stood practically empty, she had continued to lease them throughout her retirement; therefore she reopened at the same rue Cambon location where she had started before World War I. She must have felt that memories of the occupation had faded enough to allow her safe return to Paris. Or maybe she judged that the French economy had sufficiently recovered from the war to support a luxury industry such as fashion. Certainly after 14 years the memories of Coco's style had faded somewhat, and she found herself an iconoclast again—this time in the age of the miniskirt rather than the corset. Parfums Chanel paid half of her start-up costs, and Coco presented her comeback collection in February 1954.

Although the British and French press reacted quite negatively (labeling her comeback collection a "melancholy retrospective" and "a fiasco"), American reaction was considerably more enthusiastic. Seventh Avenue buyers—who bought Coco's collection sight unseen—found it sold well. The American issue of *Vogue* declared " . . . if the simplicity of her line was not new . . . its influence is unmistakable." *Life* said, "She is already influencing everything. At 71, Gabrielle Chanel is creating more than a fashion: a revolution."[25] One reason that her fashions were so revolutionary in America was that they fit America's mass-produced, ready-to-wear industry but still appealed to the ultra-elite.

Still, Chanel remained unregarded in Europe. The 1960s were the era of the miniskirt, but Coco railed against suggestions that she shorten her skirts, asserting that knees simply weren't attractive. She bitterly attacked designers such as Dior and Cardin, asserting that a man could not properly make women's dresses. She went to great lengths to separate herself from competitors, never showing her line publicly as they did. One of these more commercial designers, Pierre Cardin, incurred much of her criticism, probably because of his romance with her own customer and friend Jeanne Moreau. Coco never forgave either of them.

When presenting a collection of dresses, Coco appeared to feel apprehensive. She complained to a biographer: "If you knew the awful stage-fright I'm in. The day the collection opens I have lunch at the rue Cambon [the House of Chanel], take a Nopirin, and then sit on the stairs [in the showroom to watch the fashion show]. After that I don't know where I am, my nerves give way."[26]

Another perceptive biographer who knew Coco in her later years said that Coco perpetually was preparing her 'last' collection. It was a ritual that kept her intact. Coco herself said, "For me, fashion's not amusing—it's something on the edge of suicide."[27]

Although universal acclaim was slow in coming, Coco nevertheless affected 90 per cent of ready-to-wear. Her persistence paid off; by 1971, her Paris sales were up 30 per cent. As one biographer concluded, "Mademoiselle Chanel is coming out victorious in the war that has been declared against her style."[28] Unfortunately, Coco could not enjoy the fruits of her victory. She died January 10, 1971.

THE BUSINESSWOMAN

Coco as Employer

Although Coco sought in her business the power to control her personal definition, she also fought bitterly to control others. She lacked the technical knowledge to give her the necessary quiet confidence in her ability, and therefore often disparaged knowledge-able employees. She also revealed her insecurity by becoming in-creasingly inflexible and authoritarian as she aged. She said, "I'm not going to let myself be trampled on in the very firm I created. . . . Peo-ple want you to be gentle. Gentleness doesn't get work done. . . . It's anger that gets work done."[29] Once, when speaking to her workers about a holiday, Coco said, "All right, if you don't want to work, we won't work, but I'll treat you all as loafers."[30] Her relationships with employees were always stormy. For example, she fired and rehired her secretary Lilou so many times she lost count. She demanded that her workers use the respectful "Mademoiselle" when speaking to her; and sometimes Coco's anger became paranoid, suspecting most everyone of stealing from her.

One employee said that Coco never gave compliments but was able to keep employees only because of their individual devo-tion to fashion, not to her. She never mingled with employees in the work rooms, but rather would call workers to her to tell them what she wanted. Then, despite her authoritative tone and her natural flair for fashion, she had trouble expressing her wishes because she lacked the necessary craftsmanship. Therefore, when the results were not what she envisioned, she belittled her employees.

An observer during a work session heard Coco tell a fore-woman: "I told you yesterday. You've got to take that pleat out. Why don't you obey me?"[31] Whether or not Coco had actually ordered it yesterday, said the observer, was irrelevant. Arguing would only pro-long the session.

One former employee said of Coco's imperiousness: "When a fitting did not go well, she flew into terrible rages. She loved to enrage people. Believe me, I often cried in those days."[32]

Coco could also be hard on mannequins, the models on whom she altered dresses. For example, she insisted that all her models wear their hair short; once, Coco dismissed a mannequin be-cause she'd cut her hair—on Coco's orders—and she looked unattrac-tive. Being a mannequin could be difficult, humiliating work. In describing what Coco did to a mannequin's clothes when altering them, one observer concluded: "Hardly anything is left except a few unrelated pieces of material, stuck rag-like on the mannequin who, but a few moments ago, had seemed elegant. Finally the mannequin is sent off with an almost-kind word, meant to make up for every-thing."[33] Being a mannequin for Chanel also meant ignoring personal comments, as one observer discovered. Coco "ran her hand over the model's bosom. 'This design is supposed to be flat, and look at it! She has no bosom and yet this gives her one!'"[34]

Yet, Coco could inspire her workers. Forewomen, who otherwise may have felt apprehensive working for a woman, found that Coco's charm overcame many difficulties. A model, who later worked for other designers, also expressed satisfaction in working for Coco: "The dress was created on us, was *modeled* after our reflexes and the movements of our body. We almost felt the fusion of our skin with that of the fabric. . .I have never again had this impression."[35] Coco herself said she felt very close to her models. She saw herself in them. They were described as her daughters, her court, her possible successors—even, it was rumored, her lovers, but Coco denied this.

COCO AS DESIGNER

Because Coco lacked formal training in fashion design, she managed the creative process unconventionally. While most designers started with sketches, Coco merely described what she wanted to the cutters. When the proposed dress was put together, Coco would see it for the first time on a mannequin modeling it for her. Then she would go to work on the dress—cutting, tearing, pinning—while the dress was still on the mannequin. Afterwards, she would send the dress back to be redone. She might repeat this process 20 or 30 times before she was satisfied. Coco took her own advice in this regard: "Keep working 'till you hate the sight of it."[36]

Coco realized her process was unusual. She said that dressmakers who didn't take her seriously in the beginning were right. For example, at one point her milliners made all her dresses because Coco did not realize she could hire specialized workers.

A Chanel director from 1956-1957 once described Coco the designer:

> She wasn't the creative genius she was cracked up to be. She always repeated the same designs, changing only details. She wasn't really a dressmaker. She had a great knack for ripping everything apart and sending it back to the workrooms to be put back together again. The most precious assets of the Chanel firm were the forewomen, who were real professionals.[37]

However true that may have been, Coco loved her work. When working: "Something inexpressible in [Coco] took over and carried her away, plunged in her true element. . . Her desperate alter ego, the lonely child, was always in danger. . .[because] Coco Chanel couldn't sew. She cut."[38] Coco best expressed why she felt most fulfilled by her work: ". . . when I had to choose between the men I loved and dresses, I always chose the dresses. . . work has always been a sort of drug for me. . . ."[39]

Coco as Partner

As a young woman in a male-dominated society and profession, Coco had to be careful in business partnerships. Businesswomen in that period were rare and considered easy targets. Coco, nevertheless, was quite capable of taking care of herself, as her lawyer later testified:

> Mademoiselle Chanel had a series of eminent "advisors," but really they were. . . pawns that she moved around with an astonishing intuitive understanding of psychology. . . And we all fell into the trap, even when we knew we were being manipulated. Her grasp of detail and ability to execute ideas were remarkable. But she allowed none of this to show.[40]

Her relations with the Wertheimer brothers, Paul and Pierre, were particularly litigious and stormy, ending with lawsuits that lasted until Coco's death. Pierre, who was something of a playboy, apparently had amorous ambitions regarding Coco; she, however, was not interested. Instead, she undermined both brothers at every turn, and they did the same to her.

For instance, during the occupation, Coco took advantage of the fact that the Wertheimers, Jews, had fled the Nazi invasion, leaving the perfume company with a trustee. Taking advantage of a Nazi law allowing the seizure of Jewish-owned property, Coco attempted to acquire the property. Fortunately for the Wertheimers, their Aryan trustee and some well-placed bribes among the Germans kept the company out of Coco's hands.

The Wertheimers, for their part, also used the war to try to take advantage of Coco. Under the agreement, Coco released to the Wertheimers rights to all brands she had marketed under the name Chanel. In exchange, she received 10 per cent of the French Parfums Chanel stock, plus 10 per cent of each new office opened around the world. Chanel's share was cut to almost nothing during the war when the Wertheimers sold Parfums Chanel to their new corporation in the United States: Chanel, Inc., New York.

Thus, peace in Europe did not bring peace between Coco and her perfume partners. In 1946 Coco sent "presents" of her original No. 5 perfume to New York buyers. Since the No. 5 formula the Wertheimers sold was modified, they were duly threatened. In 1947 she won from them the right to produce perfumes, including 180,000 U.S. dollars, 20,000 British pounds, and 5 million French francs in damages. Chanel also won a two per cent royalty on all gross sales of Chanel perfumes throughout the world plus a personal monopoly on Chanel sales in Switzerland.

Despite these legal battles, the Wertheimers were supportive of Coco during her arduous comeback, and paid, through Parfums Chanel, 50 per cent of Coco's start-up costs. The Wertheimers became even more supportive of Coco when she threatened to mass merchandise her dresses. After all, Chanel No. 5 would lose its valuable exclusive image if Chanel dresses could be bought from mass merchandisers! Although the Wertheimers later bought Coco's fashion house, she still ran it.

Later, the prospect of a successor for herself made Coco indignant. In fact, she broke with her favorite model, Marie Helene Arnaud, because, as her heir-apparent, she threatened Coco. Commenting on this episode, one biographer concluded that Coco was "perpetually on trial before her own tribunal—not for conviction and sentence but for self-justification."[41]

Coco as Myth Maker

Coco was a talented and in some ways compulsive myth maker, as the disparity between the facts of her childhood and her fantastic stories about her youth indicate. On one level she clearly realized what it took to build a reputation, yet she also denied the fact that she invented stories, telling one biographer, "I never tell a lie. I don't like living in ambiguities."[42]

Certainly her fantastic stories were important in marketing the House of Chanel—"Prestige is my business," she once said when describing her product.[43] Acquiring her own celebrity status was another key to her successful business: "She was much more like the founder of an order than a personality of Parisian life. One could very well have said about her: 'Mademoiselle Chanel founded the order of the Sisters of Beauty.'"[44]

Coco wanted her exclusive customers to feel they were buying fame, so she made sure the popular press noticed Chanel. She gained this notoriety by giving away dresses to society women temporarily out of money, staffing with Russian royalty (escapees to Paris from the Russian Revolution), and employing a number of princesses as mannequins.

Coco also realized that to be a celebrity, one must behave like a celebrity. One employee recalled how well Coco acted the part: "You should have seen her, getting out of her Rolls-Royce in front of the firm on the stroke of noon. . . .She was a queen! She would stay until two or three o'clock, even later if she had famous customers. Then she retired to her drawing room, where she entertained a great deal."[45]

Coco knew the value of personal identifying symbols. When she worked on mannequins, for example, she always hung a pair of scissors around her neck, ready to cut away superfluous details. For her, these scissors were such a powerful symbol that at the 1937 Exposition des Arts et Techniques in Paris, Coco's display included an engraved crystal plate of a pair of scissors cutting fabric. Below the scissors was inscribed: "I used these scissors to cut all that was superfluous in the creations of others. Coco Chanel."[46]

Coco also told stories to explain her fashion statements that made her fashions seem more the result of accident than design. For example, Coco claimed to have started the short or bobbed hair style for women, and to have started it by accident. She said that a gas ring exploded in her apartment one night as she prepared for the opera, singeing her hair. To hide the damage Coco cut off her long locks. Because long hair was conventional at that time, Coco's bobbed style created quite a stir among the first-night crowd at the opera. While it is true that Coco's appearance may have drawn attention, her coiffeur was by no means accidental. In fact, she copied the idea of short hair from the popular dancer Caryathis, who had appeared with bobbed hair in a Stravinsky ballet three years earlier in 1913. One biographer concluded about Coco's story: "Rather than an accident, we should imagine a deliberate act, a calculated decision worthy of the cool-headed businesswoman she had, in the meantime, become."[47]

Despite her publicity-seeking words and deeds, Coco seemed to resent public attention. "I'm exploited," Coco complained near the end of her life, "I've been turned into an object."[48] Given her desire for publicity, Coco should have been eager to attend the 1966

Broadway opening of the musical comedy, *Coco*, based loosely on her life. Before the performance, however, *Coco's* right hand became paralyzed so that she had to be hospitalized. Although *Coco* was still playing three months later when she recovered, she never saw it. Perhaps she found the theme distressing. As *Coco's* script writer, Alan Jay Lerner, said: "Coco is a woman who has sacrificed everything for her independence and who, having gained it, pays the exorbitant price of loneliness for it."[49] Coco's only comment about the script was, "I don't do very much—I just sit there and everything marches past me. They come and sing me the songs that I liked."[50]

HER LAST YEARS

Near the end of her life, Coco became a vituperative critic. She delivered her withering witticisms in gnomic maxims, with a kind of imperial detachment, planning one day to publish a book of pithy sayings. One biographer said that, at the end of Coco's life, "Once and for all she condemned everything she saw or heard about."[51] Another biographer said the reason for her scathing wit was her deep-seated insecurity. "Her need to hurt in order to make sure she was loved, her constant denunciation—both were forms of retaliation."[52]

For example, Coco often entertained celebrities at dinner, but, as soon as they had left for the evening, she would malign them to anyone who remained. "People with tiny talents bore me to death," she once told a biographer.[53] Coco did not spare her friends from her criticism. According to Jean Cocteau, "She looks at you fondly, then slaughters you."[54]

In the end, Coco was left with only servants and a few close friends for companionship. Yet, however turbulent her personal and business relationships, when Coco Chanel died in 1971, the fashion world paid her homage.

COMMENTARY

Coco Chanel was a great innovator as well as entrepreneur. Her accomplishments suggest that she had found within herself the permission to perform. Permission in this deeply personal sense goes far beyond the issue of legitimacy in the accumulation and use of power. The idea of legitimacy suggests that an outside agency confers power, such as voters electing public officials, or boards of directors appointing a chief executive officer. In a sense, Coco secured legitimacy in the overwhelming acceptance she received from fashion makers, such as *Vogue* magazine. In the same sense, she received confirmation most importantly from the consumer, who adopted her styles as well as her collections' overwhelming messages of simplicity, if not masculinization, and freedom. Beyond legitimacy, the idea of permission suggests an entitlement deeply rooted in her entire being. She experienced an entitlement, in a way suggesting a "calling" and a vocation: "This I must do!" The act of assertion was for Coco an end point, a culmination as it were, in which she simultaneously negated the conventional position of marriage and its hints of subservience, and forged a new position as entrepreneur and force for change. When she opened a millinery shop with the financial support of her lovers, her intention must have gone beyond what still could have been a conventional role: the mistress who seeks economic security by opening a shop. Without marriage, Coco would have faced an objective threat. As she grew older, it would not have been easy for her to exist simply as mistress to a wealthy man. She probably understood this economic insecurity. But the millinery shop was far from the plaything or amusing pastime that the two men competing for her affection perceived it to be. It was the activation of her deep commitment to independence. Her first hat designs expressed the simplicity she sought in women's dress, and the new aggression that evidently grew out of her unique sense of entitlement.

The uniqueness of her sense of entitlement needs careful assessment. Entitlement is a strange phenomenon. It has a regressive side. To think, "I am entitled" leads to a passive-aggressive position, much like the one taken by hypochondriacs. "I am entitled, therefore you must take care of me, and minister to my wishes and needs." This passivity becomes punishing to the objects upon whom this position is cast.

Another type of entitlement, exemplified in the life and work of Coco Chanel, is to take completely the active stance. "I desire and need, therefore I must do." The "doing" in her case was to take her ideas about women, men, fashion, and clothing and become an entrepreneur. She started a business and developed it into a formidable competitor in the world of couture.

Coco had plenty of opportunity to observe the futility of

the passive form of entitlement. Her mother was the victim of her own dependence (also hopeless love affair) with an irresponsible man. Rather than bemoan her fate, and engage in repetitions of the masochistic position—to suffer as an expression of love and dependence—Coco took the opposite position of the aggressor. She maneuvered two intelligent and wealthy men to compete for her love. While she became lover to Boy Capel, abandoning Balsan, she enacted the one who accepts and rejects, the active mode, rather than the one who is being accepted or rejected. She became the aggressor in her personal as well as public life as an entrepreneur.

To argue that Coco unconsciously sought revenge against her father and the redemption of her poor and beleaguered mother sounds too reductionistic. But we should not be surprised to find a link between her burning ambition and her identifications with her mother and father. The fact that she recreated her past to make her father into someone who cared about her simply masks the negativity that she may well have projected upon all men. Her tendency to feel beset and put upon may also have been a mild expression of her identification with woman as sufferer, which she consciously rejected in the enactment of her entrepreneurial career. Yet, in these cross-currents of identification, Coco seldom sustained herself without a man, a lover, in her presence. During World War II, she took as her lover a German officer and later had to pay the price. France rejected her as a Nazi collaborator, and she sought asylum in Switzerland.

As a counter to this search for deeper explanations of Coco's career, one could easily argue that taking up with a German officer in defeated France was simply an extension of her pragmatism. She did what was expedient. She adapted to circumstances.

This counter argument has a great deal of validity. To be expedient and infinitely adaptable suggests a very loose construction of conscience and ego ideal. Evidently, Coco felt little guilt about consorting with a Nazi officer, nor did she seem to experience shame in failing to measure up to standards. She had few standards, and her conscience became subordinated to her drive for independence.

These aspects of her superego (to use the technical term) were not fortuitous. They were outgrowths of her identifications with parents scarcely suited to help a young person grow and develop with a conscience and ideals reflective of a mature relationship with one's society.

A number of years ago, I was called upon to reflect on the psychology of the entrepreneur. It occurred to me that the super-ego of the entrepreneur probably had a great deal to do with the capacity to innovate and start new businesses. The analog I discovered was between the entrepreneur and the juvenile delinquent.

In this analog, I was scarcely suggesting that entrepreneurs break the law. What I was suggesting is that like the juvenile delinquent, the entrepreneur does not experience anticipatory anxiety that ordinarily inhibits action. For example, I want to do something. I feel anxiety stemming possibly from guilt. I respond to this anxiety by delaying action and in its place begin to think about what I want to do. The end point of this substitution of thought for action may very well result in my failure to carry out my intentions.

In my view, the juvenile delinquent and the entrepreneur are short on anticipatory anxiety. We have to reckon with the fact that most entrepreneurs are unsuccessful. It is the rare one who succeeds, as venture capitalists like to remind us, justifying the high payouts they seek for their invested capital. Perhaps more entrepreneurs would succeed if a measure of thought replaced action.

Another line of inquiry concerning the entrepreneur takes us into the related issue of risk and its management. A real estate developer I know who practices entrepreneurism to the hilt informed me that venturesome businesspeople are sensitive to risk, responding to my analogy between the entrepreneur and the juvenile delinquent. He argued that good entrepreneurs don't take big risks. In his field, the real estate developer takes on partners to the extent, if possible, that he has little, if any, of his own money invested in a project. He also isolates projects so that if one should fail, it will not undermine the capital stability of other projects.

My response was that he was perhaps describing his way of working and not that of the majority of entrepreneurs, who typically go forward undercapitalized on the faith that they can demonstrate the potential pay-out of their ideas and get more capital as they need it.

Coco Chanel showed little fear of failure and sensitivity to risk. At first, her money was not at stake. She also expanded her business in a sound way by utilizing internally generated cash to finance expansion, first by adding new shops, and then going international in her quest for markets. By the time she was venturing into the U.S. market, her source of cash had expanded to include the payments she received from the Wertheimers in their joint venture in the perfume business.

All of this discussion leads to an overwhelming conclusion: Coco Chanel was an exceptional businessman (the feminine version scarcely captures the environment in which she operated). She did not perform on a high wire despite the fickleness of her business and the world of haute couture in general. She sensed the readiness of the market for her ideas about how women should appear, and with the initial confirmation, moved forward deliberately and aggressively, using her marketing acuity to personalize her business. The House of Chanel was Coco. All the aura of her sexuality was designed to seduce women to follow her lead. Follow they did, dragging her competition along.

You may have wondered whether Coco's basic sexuality ran along masculine lines and whether she was homosexually oriented despite her succession of male lovers. Unfortunately, we have little evidence that would permit us to settle these questions. At the same time, I have little desire to trivialize these important questions by pointing to the rather superficial evidence of the masculine character of her designs and even the short hair style she made popular.

The significance of her sexual orientation lies in understanding more fully her sense of entitlement, which I have argued is at the root of her motivation to achieve. I cannot settle the question with the evidence at hand. But I can conclude this inquiry into the life of a great entrepreneur by suggesting, rather speculatively, how her sexual orientation might have related to her identifications with her parents and supported her active version of entitlement.

First, she might have identified with her highly unreliable father to overcome her sense of loss and rejection, and possibly a deep conviction that she was unlovable. Second is the possibility of an identification with an ideal father, who is successful in his life and work. Third, with the incorporation of this image of the successful father comes a mechanism for redeeming her poor and beleaguered mother. In other words, Coco Chanel might have established a masculine identification to revise her traumatic history and faulty experience with her parents. With these identifications, Coco Chanel became a successful entrepreneur and a force for altering perceptions of women.

Endnotes—Chapter 15

1. Marcel Haedrich, *Coco Chanel: Her Life, Her Secrets* (Boston: Little, Brown and Company, 1971), p. 247-48.

2. Edmonde Charles-Roux, *Chanel* (New York: Alfred A. Knopf, 1975), p. 6.

3. Claude Baillen, *Chanel Solitaire* (New York: Quadrangle/The New York Times Book Co., 1971), p. 108.

4. Ibid., p. 70.

5. Pierre Galante, *Mademoiselle Chanel* (Henry Regnery Co., 1978), p. 7.

6. Haedrich, *Coco Chanel,* p. 29.

7. Baillen, *Chanel Solitaire,* p. 169.

8. Ibid., p. 70.

9. Haedrich, *Coco Chanel,* p. 23.

10. Charles-Roux, *Chanel,* p. 14.

11. Baillen, *Chanel Solitaire,* p. 73.

12. Galante, *Mademoiselle Chanel,* p. 13.

13. Ibid., p. 12.

14. Haedrich, *Coco Chanel,* p. 23.

15. Ibid., p. 93.

16. Charles-Roux, *Chanel,* p. 96.

17. Haedrich, *Coco Chanel,* p. 72.

18. Ibid., p. 81.

19. Ibid., p. 93.

20. Ibid., p. 84.

21. Haedrich, *Coco Chanel,* p. 91.

22. Baillen, *Chanel Solitaire,* p. 99.

23. Galante, *Mademoiselle Chanel,* p. 162.

24. Haedrich, *Coco Chanel,* p. 148.

25. Charles-Roux, *Chanel,* p. 366.

26. Baillen, *Chanel Solitaire,* p. 149.

27. Ibid., p. 68.

28. Haedrich, *Coco Chanel,* p. 267.

29. Ibid., p 80.

30. Ibid., p. 226.

31. Galante, *Mademoiselle Chanel,* p. 239.

32. Ibid., p. 239.

33. Haedrich, *Coco Chanel,* p. 247-8.

34. Galante, *Mademoiselle Chanel,* p. 213.

35. Baillen, *Chanel Solitaire,* p. 66.

36. Galante, *Mademoiselle Chanel,* p. 213.

37. Baillen, *Chanel Solitaire,* p. 66.

38. Galante, *Mademoiselle Chanel,* p. 111.
39. Ibid., p. 88.
40. Haedrich, *Coco Chanel,* p. 200.
41. Baillen, *Chanel Solitaire,* p. 117.
42. Ibid., p. 76.
43. Galante, *Mademoiselle Chanel,* p. 7.
44. Ibid., p. 39.
45. Charles-Roux, *Chanel,* p. 300.
46. Ibid., p. 126.
47. Haedrich, *Coco Chanel,* p. 199.
48. Ibid., p. 208.
49. Ibid., p. 209.
50. Galante, *Mademoiselle Chanel,* p. 264.
51. Baillen, *Chanel Solitaire,* p. 186.
52. Ibid., p. 122.
53. Ibid., p. 15.
54. Galante, *Mademoiselle Chanel,* p. 60.

ORGANIZATIONS IN CRISIS

PART

IV

VIOLATION OF THE CODE— GENERAL PATTON IN SICILY

In its public manifestations, life is a waiting game. We lie in wait for the moments when narrative takes over and we become audience to the events that explain our national purpose, define our collective character, and that permit us to reaffirm who we are and what we stand for in our relationship to authority.

World War II was an overwhelming narrative. But it too contained chapters that allowed the nation to focus its attention on questions of morality and purpose in the uses of power. In the 1960s and early 1970s, Vietnam served this purpose, punctuated as it was with Richard Nixon's disgrace of the presidency. In the 1980s the Iran-Contra scandal served a similar purpose, with the renewed questions of who knew what, and who is covering up for whom. The reach of Iran-Contra goes beyond Robert Gates and his successful attempt to be named the head of the Central Intelligence Agency. It continues to pursue Ronald Reagan, and with him President George Bush.

Going back in time, the McCarthy hearings of the 1950s in a serious way defined Dwight David Eisenhower and his relation to American politics. As a presidential candidate, General Eisenhower refused to take on McCarthy even though McCarthy attacked General George C. Marshall, Eisenhower's superior officer. Eisenhower owed a considerable debt to General Marshall and later publicly expressed his respect for him. Was Eisenhower a wily politician who knew how to wait and to use the moment for his purposes, or was he a true example of the consensus politician constantly in a rush to get ahead of the parade and appear as its leader?

Going back another decade, Eisenhower figures massively in a story that gripped the nation. Drew Pearson leaked to the American people that one of the Army's most colorful and seemingly courageous generals had violated the code of conduct expected of superior officers in the military (and anyone else who happens to wield considerable power). On two separate occasions, but closely spaced in time, General Patton slapped two soldiers during his visit to field hospitals in the midst of vicious battles against the German armies in Sicily. Eisenhower was Patton's superior officer, and it did not take long before Patton's behavior reached Eisenhower's attention. What was he to do? There were immediate military, political, and moral issues confronting General Eisenhower, including the moral question of dealing with a friend in the context of a formal organization, with well-defined structures of superior and subordinate relations.

While we find ourselves engrossed in Eisenhower's dilemmas, we are also attracted to the intriguing questions of the circumstances that would lead a powerful figure to lose control of himself. In discussions of this case over many years, with executives and MBA candidates, with American, Japanese, British, Malaysian, and Israeli executives, I have noticed a strong inclination to accept at face value Patton's justification of his actions. You will soon see for yourself that Patton rationalized his behavior by saying that he slapped the soldiers for their own good, quickly recounting a story of a friend who lost courage and killed himself. I never let these discussants off the hook without going beneath the rationalization into some consideration of the psychology of control and its loss in a rageful moment. The moment is revealing, and we must consider questions about the nature of courage, of bravery, of fear, and of the phenomenon called battle fatigue, or "shell shock." I would usually force my discussants to face an issue they would rather ignore: that courage and bravery carry many disguises, just as cowardice can hide behind the masks of bravura. In the end the question revolved around Patton's fitness for command. General Eisenhower answered this question for himself when he decided to protect General Patton. But questions remain that will help us explore the dimensions of command and an individual's fitness for command.

For this case study, the events in Sicily bring into relief questions about charismatic and consensus leadership. Can one be both a consensus and a charismatic leader? Could anyone function in Eisenhower's position as a charismatic leader, or the type of leader that Patton seemed to portray? In the end, is a leader a victim of circumstance, defined by his constituencies and the stated purposes surrounding his selection for command?

General Eisenhower did have complicated constituency problems, not the least among them being his relations with the press and in turn the American people and public opinion. Eisenhower might have solved his constituency problems, at least as far as the American people were involved, by firing Patton and doing it quickly upon hearing of the incidents in Sicily. He felt he could not take this action. Indeed, he cleverly drew the press into his problem, and had it not been for Drew Pearson, a populist rather than a regular member of the journalistic profession, the issues in this case might never have appeared.

These and many other questions surface for our consideration. I believe you will become as fascinated as I have been with this story, because it is truly an example of how an event becomes a narrative by condensing the emotional currents surrounding our attachments to authority.

GENERAL PATTON AND THE SICILIAN SLAPPING INCIDENTS

The central figure in this case is General George Smith Patton, Jr. On two separate occasions in early August 1943, General Patton, while in command of the U.S. Seventh Army, slapped two soldiers who were in evacuation hospitals with diagnoses of anxiety states. The incidents became public knowledge and resulted in a furor involving the press, the Congress, the Secretary of War, as well as General Eisenhower, who was Supreme Commander and Patton's superior officer. The narrative in this case, taken from a biography of Patton, details the circumstances surrounding the incidents and their aftermath.

BIOGRAPHICAL SKETCH

George Patton was born November 11, 1885, in California, and died December 21, 1945, in Germany, following an automobile crash which paralyzed him from the neck down for the two months preceding his death.

Patton and his younger sister grew up on a huge ranch in Southern California, indulged children of wealthy parents. His father was a successful lawyer, originally from a moneyed Virginia family, a learned man who had tried to break with the Patton family tradition of distinctive military service. He was at the top of his class at V.M.I., but went to California to take up law instead of going on to West Point. Patton's mother was the daughter of Ben Wilson, one of the leading California landowners, a pioneer who had been active in the state's fight against the Spanish, and the ranch on which the Pattons lived was part of Wilson's huge estate. Mrs. Patton was an expert horsewoman and very early taught her son to ride as expertly as she. Patton's father did not believe in formal education for the very young, so he taught his son at home. George could quote from memory long passages from the classics and knew the Bible by heart, but when he was sent to school at the age of 12, he could neither read nor write. Despite this, he quickly learned to read and became an accomplished writer.

When he was 17 he met Beatrice Ayer, daughter of a wealthy "old-guard" New England family. They met on Catalina Island where their families both had summer homes and by the end of the summer had fallen in love. Their courtship was carried on by letter for the next three years while Patton spent a year at V.M.I., then entered West Point. He told her of his decision to become a soldier and of his dread of what he termed "The Call."

"When my cousin Robbie Patton was a student at the University of Virginia," he said, "he had no intention of becoming a clergyman. But then all of a sudden he had 'the call' and he felt obliged to respond to it." Patton prayed every night that the call would pass him by, sparing him the passive fate of the ministry it would bring with it.

On his graduation in 1909 from West Point, he planned to

Dr. Anne Jardim wrote this case study under Professor Abraham Zaleznik's supervision. From *Patton: Ordeal or Triumph,* by Ladislas Farago. New York: Astor-Honor, Inc., 1964. Its use in this book by permission of its publisher.

marry Beatrice Ayer, but had first to explain to her father why he had chosen an Army career. Patton said in his letter,

> With reference to the profession of soldier, I think I appreciate most of its drawbacks. As you say, it is very narrowing, but don't you think that a man of only very ordinary capacity, in order to succeed against great competition, must be narrow? That is, have only one motive. I have no experience, but from what I have read of successful men, they seem to be of the one-idea sort.
>
> It is hard to answer intelligently the question: "Why I want to be a soldier?' For my own satisfaction I have tried to give myself reasons but have never found any logical ones. I only feel it inside. It is as natural for me to be a soldier as it is to breathe and would be as hard to give up all thought of it as it would be to stop breathing.
>
> But being a soldier and being a member of the Army in time of peace are two different things. I would only accept the latter as a means to the former.

Patton now continued to follow his family tradition of gentleman, soldier, and sportsman. He was captain of the Army polo team with his own string of horses, amassed innumerable cups and ribbons in horse shows across the country, went fox hunting and rode in steeplechases, and found time for skeet shooting, tennis, squash, handball, and flying lessons.

Although Patton and his wife lived in luxurious grandeur on their private income, Patton dedicated much time to writing papers on strategy and tactics which were published in military journals, attracting attention by their unorthodox views and style.

> History, he wrote, is replete with countless instances of military implements each in its day heralded as the last word— the key to victory—yet each in its turn subsiding to its useful but inconspicuous niche. New weapons are useful in that they add to the repertoire of killing, but, be they tank or tomahawk, weapons are only weapons after all. Wars may be fought with weapons, but they are won by men. It is the spirit of the men who follow and of the man who leads that gains the victory. In biblical times this spirit was ascribed, and probably with some justice, to the Lord. It was the spirit of the Lord, *courage,* that came mightly upon Samson at Lehi which gained the victory—not the jawbone of the ass.

Patton had won battlefield promotions to the rank of full colonel as pioneer of tank warfare during the last weeks of World War I, and for some time after the war, when he reverted to his permanent rank of captain, worked to keep alive Army interest in a Tank Corps. The Army was not responsive, and he abandoned the subject abruptly to join the cavalry where it took him 18 years to attain the rank of colonel again. In 1940 he was transferred to Fort Benning, arriving in customary regalia with his entourage of horses and servants, to take charge of a newly formed tank brigade.

Flamboyantly dressed in specially tailored uniforms with two pearl-handled pistols in his belt, he practiced what he called "spiritual leadership." He ordered an amphitheater built and harangued his men with a series of profanity-punctuated lectures. "War is a killing business," he told his men. "You've got to spill their blood or they'll spill yours. Rip 'em up the belly or shoot 'em in the guts." He wanted to install in them a masculine attitude toward war, and a fighting spirit. The brutality and crudeness of his language, delivered in a naturally high-pitched voice, was, he said, intended to shock them out of their ordinary ways of thinking. His men responded, after the usual bellyaching, by believing implicitly in his leadership. On October 23, 1942, he set sail with his men in a convoy from Norfolk for the European theater of the war.

THE SICILIAN CAMPAIGN

On August 3, 1943, General Patton, as Commander of the Seventh U.S. Army, left Palermo, Sicily, for Advance Headquarters on the road to Messina.

On July 22, Patton had captured Palermo in tacit violation of a plan of action devised by General Montgomery and agreed to by General Eisenhower and General Alexander, the British Commander-in-Chief of the invading Allied Forces.

Strategic planning for the invasion had centered from the start on the need to capture Messina, in the extreme northeast of the island. As Sicily's major port, two miles from the Italian mainland, Messina was the source of supply for the German and Italian garrisons, and its capture was imperative if the campaign were not to bog down in a protracted struggle for territorial control, mile by difficult mile. The original plan of operations had called for the capture of Palermo in the northwest by Patton's forces, while on the southeastern coast Montgomery's Eighth Army was to secure the city of Syracuse. This plan, due to Sicily's triangular shape, would have given to both Patton and Montgomery a similar chance of capturing Messina: the city lay at the apex of the triangle in the northeast, with the ports of Palermo and Syracuse roughly equidistant from it on the sides of the triangle which led northwest and south. Victory in the Sicilian campaign would have gone to the army capable of the most rapid advance on Messina.

Under intense pressure from Montgomery, General Alexander changed his mind. The original plan was discarded, and with Eisenhower's concurrence, Patton was ordered to land on the beaches of the southwest coast, some 60 miles across from Syracuse, which remained Montgomery's objective.

> "The risk," General Alexander wrote in his report of the operation, "was unevenly divided and *almost the whole of it would fall on the Seventh Army*....In other ways also it might well seem that *the American Troops were being given the tougher and less spectacular task:* their beaches were more exposed than the Eighth Army's and on some of them there were open sand bars, they would have only one small port for maintenance and the Eighth Army would have the glory of capturing the more obviously attractive objectives of Syracuse, Catania, and Messina, names which would bulk larger in press headlines than Gela or Licata or the obscure townships of central Sicily. Both I and my staff felt that this division of tasks might possibly, on this understandable ground, cause some feeling of resentment."

Patton accepted the change after an angry meeting with Alexander, and on July 10 his army landed on the beaches in what was essentially a flanking maneuver to permit a rapid British thrust northeast to Messina.

To Patton it must have seemed that the laurels of victory were already Montgomery's. Some months earlier in Tunisia, he had strongly opposed Alexander's plan to re-assign the Corps that he was then commanding. "As I see it," Patton wrote in protest to Alexander, "the question is neither one of command nor of signal communication, but of prestige. Should it eventuate that in the last scene of the opening act of our Allied effort, elements of the United States Army appear, however erroneously, to be acting in a minor role, the repercussions might be unfortunate." Still earlier in the Tunisian campaign, he had demanded the retraction of a statement made by Air Vice

Marshall Cunningham of the RAF questioning the battleworthiness of Patton's troops. In a General Order issued to his troops shortly after Cunningham expressed his regret over the incident, Patton said,

> "After 22 days of relentless combat in mountains whose ruggedness beggars description, you have won the battle of El Guettar. Each one of you in his sphere has done his duty magnificently. Not alone on the front line, where death never ended his gruesome harvest, but everywhere else all of you have demonstrated your valor and constancy. . . .Due to your united efforts and to the manifest assistance of almighty God, the splendid record of the American Army has attained added lustre."

But, as he fought his way off the Sicilian beachhead in command of an army relegated to the least glorious role in the campaign, Patton learned that Montgomery had secured Alexander's agreement to his appointment as Supreme Commander of the invasion, replacing Alexander himself, and with overall control of Patton's forces. The final decision was Eisenhower's. After an agonizing delay he rejected the British proposal, freeing Patton from the dismal prospect of control by a man whose rivalry was becoming more and more evident.

Within days of the landings it became clear that Montgomery's plan had broken down. The Eighth Army was blocked halfway up the coast to Messina and Patton, on Alexander's orders, surrendered roads along which its own forces were moving to permit a British advance. An entire U.S. division had to be pulled back to the beachhead and any real progress in the west was restricted by Alexander on the grounds that as guardian of the British flank, Patton should commit himself to no major engagements. Patton's interpretation of this order, however, was sufficiently elastic to permit "reconnaissances in force" by subordinate officers and in this way village after village on Alexander's list of prohibited "major engagements" was taken by Patton's troops. On July 17, Patton had advanced so deeply into the west that Alexander had little option but to agree to the capture of Palermo, and on July 22 the city fell. With strategy stretched to give him his original objective, Patton's army now lay 150 miles west of Messina, the original and overridingly important objective of the campaign. On the eastern coast, Montgomery had 50 to 60 miles still to cover to reach the city.

Interviewed in Palermo by J.P. Marquand, Patton heard that the general impression given in the newspapers was that the U.S. forces had cut through only nominal Italian resistance while the British had borne the brunt of the fighting against Catania (a town half-way up the eastern coast where Montgomery bogged down from July 23 to August 2).

> "By God," Patton shouted at Marquand, "Don't they know we took on the Hermann Goering Division? Don't they know about Troina? By God, we got moving instead of sitting down, and we had to keep moving every minute to keep them off balance, or we'd be fighting yet—and what were they doing in front of Catania? They don't even know how to run around end. All they can do is to make a frontal attack under the same barrage they used at Ypres."

On August 2 Patton, determined to outmaneuver Montgomery, toured the front with a timetable for what had become "the race to Messina." His attention was divided between the desperate resistance which now faced his troops from the Fifteenth Panzer Grenadiers, and Montgomery in the southeast accelerating his advance toward Catania.

For the first time things were going hard against him. Nearly all his divisions had suffered heavy casualties. Sergeants were commanding platoons for the lack of officers and while the number of dead and wounded spiralled, no replacements were in sight.

Only the day before, confronted with bad news from the front, Patton had visited a military hospital.

THE SLAPPING INCIDENTS

"Whenever Patton felt the need to bolster his own morale," his biographer writes, "he would visit the nearest hospital because he gained solace and inspiration from the sight of men whose badge of courage was their wounds."

As much as he needed these visits to reassure himself, he thought the men needed him even more to lighten their sufferings. Patton regarded these visits as the high points of his command and his noblest task. He was always gratified to see that he was a tonic for the maimed men.

To take his mind off the bad news, he had called on Colonel Daniel Franklin, the Seventh Army's Surgeon, on August 2, and—with a load of 40 Purple Hearts—visited the patients at the Base Hospital. He walked from bed to bed and talked with easy familiarity with the men.

"Where did you get it, boy?" he asked a soldier whose bandage was concealed under the cover.

"In the chest, sir."

"Well," Patton said, raising his voice, for he wanted the whole ward to hear his pep talk, "it may interest you to know that the last German I saw had no chest and no head either. To date you have captured or killed over 80,000 s.o.b.'s—that's the official figure, but as I travel around, my nose tells me that the figures are much bigger and before the end they will double that. Get well quickly, boy—you want to be in on that final kill." He made a different speech at each ward, another to the nurses, still another to the doctors.

Just before leaving, he walked up to a bed in which a soldier was breathing heavily under an oxygen mask. When Patton realized that the man was unconscious, he took off his helmet, knelt down, pinned a Purple Heart on the pillow, whispered something into the ear of the dying man, then stood up at attention. If it was a corny performance, it did not seem so to the nurses on the ward. "I swear there wasn't a dry eye in the house," wrote his aide, Colonel Codman, who witnessed the impromptu drama.

Patton was so overcome by the experience that he went straight to a chapel to pray before he returned to his quarters.

On August 3, the military situation showed no improvement and Patton spent his first day at the front encouraging and exhorting the men—doing the job he reserved for himself and which he thought he was best qualified to perform. This was what he meant when he wrote in his diary on the eve of the landing in Morocco, "I feel that my claim to greatness hangs on an ability to lead and inspire." Now, in the pressure-cooker of Sicily, he put it more plainly. "I am the best damn butt-kicker in the whole United States Army," he told General Bradley, who, under the circumstances, was not so enthusiastic about this aspect of Patton's technique of command.

"In the unhappy part of his career," Bradley later wrote, "George's theatrics brought him much contempt, and his impetuousness outraged his commanders . . . In Sicily, Patton, the man, bore little resemblance to Patton, the legend."

In front of Troina, as he mingled with the men, even his

most inspired butt-kicking did not seem to work. He was appalled by what he found in the First Division. Having borne the brunt of two campaigns, the division had become temperamental, and even insubordinate. Discipline was lax, rules were disregarded, superiors were disobeyed. The commander, General Allen, "too much of an individualist to submerge himself without friction in the group undertakings of war," appeared to be either unable or disinclined to do anything about it. Discouraged by the hard going and left to brood about their fate in Allen's *laisser-aller* regime, his men developed too much pride in their past achievements and too much self-pity in their present plight.

Casualties had left gaping holes in the line, and Patton saw a tangible connection between them and his difficulties. Morever, he was told that an increasing number of men had gone to the hospital with nothing but combat fatigue, a form of neurosis for which he had neither understanding nor sympathy. The departure of these men from the tough battle for Troina was felt seriously by the hard-pressed regiments, which were in any case becoming substantially reduced by *bona fide* casualties. Since no replacements could be obtained, every man was indispensable.

It was with the fresh memories of his visit to the First Division boiling in him, on this August 3, that Patton spied signs on the road to Mistretta showing directions to the Fifteenth Evacuation Hospital. He told Sergeant George Mims, his driver, "Take me to that Evac," not so much to seek solace this time but to see for himself how crowded it was with those combat-neurosis cases.

The Fifteenth Evac, a typical forward hospital under canvas, was headed by Lieutenant Colonel Frank Y. Leaver. Leaver and his staff respected Patton's obviously sincere concern for the wounded, and appreciated his profound interest in the medical facilities of his Army. Nonetheless they viewed him with somewhat jaundiced eyes because of lingering memories of his strict disciplinarian regime in Tunisia.

In Tunisia Patton had no sooner taken command than an order of his appeared on the bulletin board of the hospital threatening fines of up to $25 for not wearing a steel helmet at all times, or going without leggings. "Since it was impossible for a doctor to get a stethoscope in his ears while wearing a helmet," wrote Major Max S. Allen with tongue in cheek, "and still worse to attempt to operate while wearing a helmet, the order had to be ignored inside the tents, but everyone wore his helmet on going from one tent to another."

Though Patton's visit was unexpected, the Fifteenth Evac was up to Patton's strictest standards when Mims drove him through its improvised gate to the tent where Colonel Leaver had his office. The colonel escorted the general to the receiving tent, where they were greeted by Lieutenant Colonel Charles N. Wasden, the receiving officer.

The grand round inside the tent cheered Patton, because the men appeared to be legitimate casualties so far as he could judge from the abundance of bandages evident. He talked effusively with the patients, and was particularly pleased to meet the first sergeant of the Thirty-ninth Infantry Regiment because its commander, Colonel Harry Albert "Paddy" Flint, was one of his best friends. Flint was an eccentric soldier in Patton's own mold. With helmet, a black silk scarf and rifle in hand, he led his men on Troina stripped to the waist "so that he might be more easily identified." Patton spent some time at the bedside of the sergeant, talking about "Paddy," and telling the noncom how proud he ought to be to serve under such a valiant leader.

He was about to leave the tent when his eyes fell on a boy in his mid-twenties who was squatting on a box near the dressing station with no bandage on him to indicate that he had been wounded. He was Private Charles Herman Kuhl, ASN 35536908, of Mishawaka, Indiana, a bright-faced, good-looking young soldier eyeing the general with what Patton thought was a truculent look.

"I just get sick inside myself," Patton later told his friend, Henry J. Taylor, a millionaire businessman who doubled as a war correspondent in Sicily, "when I see a fellow torn apart, and some of the wounded were in terrible, ghastly shape. Then I came to this man and asked him what was the matter.

"The soldier replied: 'I guess I can't take it.'

"Looking at the others in the tent, so many of them badly beaten up, I simply flew off the handle."

What happened next was described the day after by Kuhl himself in a letter to his father. "General Patton slapped my face yesterday," he wrote, "and kicked me in the pants and cussed me. This probably won't get through, but I don't know. Just forget about it in your letter."

The letter passed the censor, but the Kuhls in Mishawaka—his parents and his wife Loretta—did exactly as Charley advised. They "forgot" about "it," probably because they were inclined to give the general the benefit of the doubt.

A carpetlayer in civilian life, Kuhl had been in the Army eight months, with the First Division about 30 days, serving in L Company of the Twenty-sixth Infantry Regiment. He had been admitted to the aid station of the Third Battalion at 2:10 p.m. on August 2, with a diagnosis of "exhaustion" made by Lieutenant H.L. Sanger of the Medical Corps. He was then evacuated to the First Medical Battalion, well to the rear, where a note was made on his emergency medical tag that he "had been admitted to this place three times during the Sicilian campaign."

Kuhl then was sent on to the clearing company by Captain J.D. Broom, was put in "quarters" there and given sodium amytal on a prescription signed by Captain Ralph S. Nedell.

On August 3, he was examined by Captain T. P. Covington, who wrote on Kuhl's medical tag: "Psychoneurosis anxiety state, moderately severe. Soldier has been twice before in hospital within 20 days. He can't take it at the front evidently. He is repeatedly returned."

As Taylor reconstructed the incident on the basis of his first-hand information, "Patton squared off in front of the soldier. He called the man every kind of a loathsome coward and then slapped him across the face with his gloves. The soldier fell back. Patton grabbed him by the scruff of the neck and kicked him out of the tent."

When Patton was through, he turned to Colonel Wasden.

"Don't admit this sonuvabitch," he yelled. "I don't want yellow-bellied bastards like him hiding their lousy cowardice around here, stinking up this place of honor." Then turning to Colonel Leaver and still shouting at the top of his high-pitched voice, he ordered:

"Check up on this man, Colonel. And I don't give a damn whether he can take it or not! You send him back to his unit at once—you hear me, you gutless bastard," he was now shrieking at Kuhl again, "you're going back to the front, *at once*!"

Kuhl was picked up by a group of corpsmen attracted to the scene by the noise. They took him to a ward, where he was found to have a temperature of 102.2 degrees. It also developed that he had been suffering from chronic diarrhea ever since he joined the First Division at the front. A blood test then showed that he had malaria.

Neither the medical staff, nor Kuhl nor his family in Mishawaka followed up the incident, and that seemed to close the case. Patton himself dismissed it from his mind after issuing the following General Order:

"To: Corps, division and separate unit commanders.

"It has come to my attention that a very small number of soldiers are going to the hospital on the pretext that they are nervously incapable of combat. Such men are cowards and bring discredit on the army and disgrace to their commanders, whom they heartlessly leave to endure the dangers of battle while they, themselves, use the hospitals as a means of escape. You will take measures to see that such cases are not sent to the hospital but are dealt with in their units. Those who are not willing to fight will be tried by court-martial for cowardice in the face of the enemy."

There was still nothing on the front to lift Patton from his depression.

On August 4, 72 fighters of General House, each loaded with 500-pound bombs, plastered Troina, leaving it wreathed in grey dust. Next day, General Allen's units stormed a number of high positions overlooking the city, established themselves in several of them, and made things so hot for the Germans that they decided to do something about it. When day broke on August 6, scouts of the First Division found the city deserted. The Germans had sneaked out under cover of darkness.

But when Allen pushed east from Troina, he could advance only about a mile when he was halted again by the determined *Landser* family established in their new positions. And the Third Division was making little or no headway with its attack on San Fratello Ridge.

Patton continued to tour the front, looking for "tricks" to speed the advance. "We are trying to win the horse race to the last big town," he wrote to his wife, referring to Messina. "I hope we do . . . ."

On August 6, he moved his camp to a new command post in an olive grove up the coast. Now he was very close to the front, within range of enemy artillery. No sooner had he settled down at the CP than the Germans began to shell it—gropingly at first, getting only "overs," then coming in with "shorts." When the shells exploded on the ridge, their fragments passed directly over the CP. Patton was disgusted, but not because he was under fire. He had timed his pulse with his watch and found to his dismay that it had gone up.

Patton's chief reason for moving to the coast was to get as close as he could to an operation he had devised to speed General

Truscott's advance along the seashore. The Second Battalion of the Thirtieth Infantry Regiment had been reorganized into a small amphibious force to make a landing on the coast about two miles east of Sant' Agata. The battalion—reinforced with two batteries of the Fifty-eighth Field Artillery, a platoon of tanks and a platoon of engineers—jumped off the night of August 7 and caught the Germans asleep. By 4:00 a.m. the Second Battalion was firmly established 12 miles nearer to Messina.

Patton was overjoyed with the success of the operation. He called Bradley to his olive grove to arrange for another amphibious envelopment, this one at Brolo to outflank the next coastal roadblock the Germans had put up at the Zapulla River. Patton was in a hurry. He scheduled the landing for August 11, by which time he expected Truscott to be close enough to link up with the battalion at Brolo, 12 miles behind the Germans.

Bradley checked with General Truscott, but Truscott objected vigorously. He was encountering difficulties with this advance. The Seventh Infantry Regiment had run into increasing German resistance. It was under heavy artillery fire, some of it coming from the long-range guns the Germans had on Capo d'Orlando. Enemy observation posts were spread too wide to enable Truscott to screen with smoke, and he was running low on smoke shells anyway. His Fifteenth Infantry needed a mule train to gain the ridge south of Naso.

Patton himself was astounded by the terrain. On August 7, for example, he went to an observation post about 300 yards from a place his men had under attack. He could see the 60-mm mortars and hear the machine guns and rifles—but it took seven hours for the troops to march from where he stood to the battle he was watching. "It is the Goddamnedest country I have ever seen," he complained.

Yet he refused to listen to Truscott's objections and insisted that the landing be staged on August 11 as he had originally scheduled it. Bradley interfered and asked Patton to give Truscott another day. "The amphibious attack means nothing," he argued, "unless we tie in with Truscott's forces by land." Patton remained adamant. When Bradley left the olive grove he had in his pocket Patton's final directive.

On August 8, things looked up a bit in both areas on which Patton's eager attention was riveted. Truscott took Sant'Agata. The Forty-seventh Infantry of the Ninth Division reached Cesaro on the road to Randazzo. The Sixtieth Infantry captured Monte Camolato, six miles northwest of Cesaro. And in the east, Montgomery was not doing too well. The Germans were delaying his advance on Messina by the direct route through Randazzo. He had to waste time on regrouping his forces for what he called "a greater effort" along the east coast.

August 9 was sheer hell again. Patton spent the entire day fretting and fussing in his olive grove, writing letters, trying hard to keep from bursting at the seams.

On August 10, Truscott's Third Division moved closer to Brolo, where it was to rendezvous with the seaborne force. But the advance was not fast enough, and Bradley called Patton again, pleading with him to postpone the landing a day. Patton remained hard.

"No," he shouted. "And I don't want any more arguments."

"I was more exasperated than I have ever been," Bradley wrote.

And so was Patton.

Bradley's call left him fuming. He was not immune from once in a while suspecting his commanders of sabotaging his decisions which they disliked and now he feared that Bradley and Truscott might pull something to delay the landing after all. He dropped everything, sent for Mims and drove to II Corps command post for a showdown with Bradley.

Patton was highly agitated on the drive and eager to get to Bradley as quickly as possible. But when he saw signs of the Ninety-third Evacuation Hospital in the valley near Sant'Agata di Militello, he ordered Sergeant Mims to take him there. He walked unannounced to the admission tent, where Colonel Donald E. Currier, commanding officer of the hospital, hastily advised of the general's arrival, caught up with him. Patton greeted Currier amicably. The surgeon was from Boston and was a friend of his family. The visit thus started out auspiciously.

Waiting at the entrance to the admission tent was Major Charles Barton Etter, the receiving officer. Then the familiar grand round began. Accompanied by Currier and Etter, General Patton moved down the aisle, going from litter to litter. He had the usual small talk with the soldiers and congratulated them on the performance of their divisions. But those who had seen him on previous such inspection trips now noticed that he was quite tense and was not acting with his customary jocular ease and friendliness. He turned almost grim when he stopped at the litter of a soldier without splints or dressing, the obvious indication of a malingerer in his eyes.

"What brought you here, boy?" he asked.

"I'm running a fever, sir," the soldier answered, and the doctor chimed in: "Yes, sir, a little over 102 degrees."

Patton raised his eyebrow, obviously not convinced that the man's temperature was high enough to justify hospitalization. He seemed to be getting ready to say it when he noticed a young soldier squatting near the exit holding a cigarette in trembling fingers.

"And what's the matter with you?" Patton snapped at the boy, his unspent irritation over the fever case turning into anger.

What followed was described most graphically by Major Etter in the report he prepared for "Surgeon, II Corps, A.P.O. 302, U.S. Army (Att'n: Colonel Richard T. Arnest)." It read in full:

1. On Monday afternoon, August 10, 1943, at approximately 1330, General Patton entered the Receiving Ward of the 93rd Evacuation Hospital and started interviewing and visiting the patients who were there. There were some 10 or 15 casualties in the tent at the time. The first five or six whom he talked to were battle casualties. He asked each what his trouble was, commended them for their excellent fighting; told them they were doing a good job, and wished them a speedy recovery.

   He came to one patient who, upon inquiry, stated that he was sick with a high fever. The general dismissed him without comment. The next patient was sitting huddled up and shivering. When asked what his trouble was, the man replied, "It's my nerves," and began to sob. The General them screamed at him, "What did you say?" He replied, "It's my nerves. I can't stand the shelling any more." He was still sobbing.

   The General then yelled at him. "Your nerves Hell, you are just a Goddamn coward, you yellow son of a bitch." He them slapped the man and said, "Shut up that Goddamned crying. I won't have these brave men here who have been shot seeing a yellow bastard sitting here crying." He then struck at the man again, knocking his helmet liner off and into the next tent. He then turned to the Receiving Officer and yelled, "Don't you admit this yellow bastard, there's nothing the matter with him. I won't have the hospitals cluttered up with these sons of bitches who haven't the guts to fight."

   He turned to the man again, who was managing to "sit at attention" though shaking all over, and said, "You're going back to the front lines and you may get shot and killed, but you're going to fight. If you don't, I'll stand you up against a wall and have a firing squad kill you on purpose. In fact," he said, reaching for his pistol, "I ought to shoot you myself, you Goddamned whimpering coward." As he went out of the ward he was still yelling back at the Receiving Officer to send that yellow son of a bitch to the front lines.

2. All this was in such a loud voice that nurses and patients in adjoining wards had come outside to see what the disturbance was.

Had General Patton been able to control his nervous temper after the first incident in the admission tent of the Fifteenth Evacuation Hospital, his slapping of an apparently sick soldier would probably never have become public knowledge. The slapping created no hysterics in the tent. It was discussed only in passing at the hospital and the story never got beyond it. It was not reported to higher echelons by the medical staff.

Private Kuhl mentioned the first incident in a letter to his family but advised them "to forget it." His parents and wife kept silent or, as the older Kuhl put it, "I am willing to let the case rest as is and drop the whole thing, and get on with the war. I have no personal feelings against General Patton. If he is a good man, let's keep him. We need good men."

But the second incident was different. The boy Patton slapped was no Sunday soldier. Private Paul G. Bennett, ASN 70000001, a simple 21-year-old farm boy from South Carolina, had enlisted in the regular Army before Pearl Harbor and served with impersonal distinction with the 105th Field Artillery Battalion in North Africa and Sicily. When his wife gave birth to their first baby he became restless, and when she sent him a picture of herself with the infant he began to show symptoms of acute nervous tension. A front-line psychiatrist diagnosed his condition as a case of anxiety neurosis—"a passing disturbance of his mind regarding some uncertain event"—probably caused by "fear that he would not be able to see his newborn baby before he died."

Bennett's condition became aggravated on August 6 when his best buddy in C Battery was wounded in action at his side. He could not sleep that night because, as he put it, the shells going over had "bothered" him. "I keep thinking they're going to land on me," he kept saying. On August 7 he became increasingly tense and showed morbid concern for his wounded friend. An aid man then sent him to the rear echelon, where he was given some sedative. But it did not seem to do him any good. He remained badly disturbed.

On the morning of this fateful August 10, a medical officer ordered him to the Ninety-third Evac, even though "Bennett begged not to be evacuated because he did not want to leave his unit." It was a tragic coincidence, then, that General Patton happened to pay an impromptu visit to the hospital, virtually minutes after Bennett's own arrival in the admission tent.

At the height of the brief but violent encounter, Patton appeared to have been shaken by his own conduct. He began to sob, wheeled around, and told Colonel Currier, "I can't help it. It makes me break down to see brave boys and to think of a yellow bastard being babied."

But whatever he himself thought of the incident, he did not think it necessary to make a report of it either to General Alexander, his immediate superior, or General Eisenhower, the commander in chief.

"I felt ashamed of myself," he later told Henry J. Taylor, "and I hoped the whole thing would die out."

The Aftermath

But the incident could not be filed and forgotten with his departure. He had attracted far too much attention. It thoroughly shocked the doctors and nurses, and became the topic of conversation in the Seventh Army.

Colonel Arnest's detailed report of the incident was handed to General Bradley who ordered it placed in his safe in a sealed envelope. As Patton's subordinate he did not consider it necessary to report to Eisenhower.

When Arnest realized, however, that Bradley would not forward his report, he opened another channel and sent it to Brigadier General Blesse, Eisenhower's Surgeon General. Blesse took the report to Eisenhower.

It was 10:30 a.m. on August 17, the very moment when General Patton was entering Messina as a conquering hero. General Truscott had made a U.S. victory official at 8:25 a.m. on August 17, when he reached the center of the city and took formal possession at the town hall a few minutes before a breathless British lieutenant colonel rolled up in a dust-covered tank in an unsuccessful attempt to stake Montgomery's claim.

In Algiers, Eisenhower was not unduly alarmed. He told Blesse, "I guess I'll have to give General Patton a jacking up." He kept the Surgeon General in his office for some small talk. Ike praised Patton for the "swell job" he had done in Sicily but disputed his contention that there were any laggards in the Seventh Army or in any part of the United States Army, for that matter. General Blesse was inclined to agree with the Supreme Commander. His medics reported, he told Eisenhower, that on the contrary, many American soldiers had marched over rough terrain until they had literally worn the skin off their feet. When the meeting broke up, Eisenhower instructed Blesse to go to Sicily, investigate the incident on the spot, then report his findings directly to him.

In this way he started the ball rolling—to clear up the case in all its details, punish Patton if need be, but keep the matter strictly in the family. He clamped a tight lid on the incident because, as he said to General Blesse, "If this thing ever gets out, they'll be howling for Patton's scalp, and that will be the end of Georgie's service in this war. I simply cannot let that happen. Patton is *indispensable* to the war effort—one of the guarantors of our victory."

After Blesse left, Eisenhower called in Dr. Long, a prominent and distinguished surgeon from Massachusetts, who was serving as his theater medical consultant with the rank of lieutenant colonel. He instructed Colonel Long to make a separate investigation—"for my eyes only," as he put it— without fear or favor, brutally to the facts.

Then he sat down and wrote in his own hand a personal letter to Patton. It was a blistering epistle in which Eisenhower expressed all his disgust with the incident. He characterized Patton's conduct as "despicable." And he ordered him—in a historic and unprecedented move—to apologize to the soldier he had slapped, to all the doctors and nurses who were present in the tent at the time, to every patient in the tent who could be reached, and last, to the Seventh Army as a whole through individual units, one at a time. It was a savage punishment for so proud and arrogant a general as Patton, and Eisenhower realized that he was running a serious risk. Patton might resign his commission rather than go through with it. But he took the risk, sealed his letter, and gave it to General Blesse, who was leaving that afternoon, for delivery into Patton's hands.

Colonel Long's initial report left no doubt about the seriousness of the incident. After describing the event on the basis of Major Etter's report, he wrote:

> The deleterious effects of such incidents upon the well-being of patients, upon the professional morale of hospital staffs and upon the relationship of patient to physician are incalculable. It is imperative that immediate steps be taken to prevent recurrence of such incidents.

General Eisenhower now sent for General Lucas, who was both his and George Patton's friend, and ordered him to Sicily to undertake yet another investigation, this one strictly from the soldiers' point of view.

He hoped that he would be able to close the case with that. But then the situation changed abruptly, and the incident began to cause the deepest concern to Eisenhower because he now feared that he would not be able to "keep it in the family" after all. The correspondents accredited to the Seventh Army had gotten hold of the story, and they took a very dim view of an American general slapping a sick American boy in a hospital at the front. The Supreme Commander turned from his optimism and grimly told General Walter Smith, his friend and Chief of Staff, "I might have to send Georgie Patton home in disgrace after all."

It had taken less than 24 hours for the story to reach the press camp. It was broken by a young captain in Public Relations who happened to be in love with a nurse in the Ninety-third Evac. On the night of the incident he visited her while she was on duty in a tent adjoining the receiving tent where the helmet Patton had knocked from Private Bennett's head had landed. When told of the incident, the captain felt, as did everybody else at the hospital, that the incident should be reported. However, he realized that this could not be accomplished through "channels," as it seemed certain that his report would be pigeonholed at Bradley's headquarters. So he decided to tell some of the reporters whose stories he was censoring daily. The first three correspondents the anonymous captain reached in his righteous indignation were Al Newman, with *Newsweek,* Merrill Mueller of the National Broadcasting Company, and Damaree Bess of the *Saturday Evening Post.*

The day after the incident, Major Etter was interviewed, with Colonel Currier's permission, by Newman, Mueller, and Bess;

and again the next day by Newman and Mueller, who were now joined by John Charles Daly of the Columbia Broadcasting System. "The idea of the interviews, as we understood it," Etter recalled, "was that they could take the story directly to General Eisenhower for action without it having to go through 'channels.'"

Other reporters poured into the hospital in their wake. The press camp was ablaze with the story and its implications. They viewed Patton with jaundiced eyes anyway, violently opposed to his undemocratic methods and the childish bluster, as they saw it, in his character. They now recalled how he had ordered the mules of a poor Sicilian farmer shot because they obstructed his passage over a bridge. They remembered, too, that he had fined a soldier $25 for not wearing his leggings and never gave the boy a chance to explain that his legs were swollen with a mysterious ailment.

The correspondents discussed the case, then decided to take it up directly with General Eisenhower before breaking the story. Bess, Mueller, and Quentin Reynolds of *Collier's* left for Algiers. On August 19 they handed Bedell Smith a complaint against Patton, with an accurate description of the incident at the Ninety-third Evac. "If I am correctly informed," Bess wrote, "General Patton has subjected himself to general court-martial by striking an enlisted man under his command." Bess told Smith that he and his colleagues, who had looked into the case in Sicily, had refrained from filing stories about it. He ventured the opinion that it would be difficult, if not impossible, to keep such "a colorful scene," as he called the incident, out of the press for any length of time.

Reynolds asserted that there were "at least 50,000 American soldiers in Sicily who would shoot Patton if they had a chance." Daly mentioned as an extenuating circumstance that "probably Patton had gone temporarily crazy." But he was most outspoken in his demand that Patton be punished, even suggesting that he be removed from command because "he was obviously unfit to lead troops."

"All the press," Eisenhower's aide noted in his diary on August 21, "while not printing the story, are incensed."

Under this hammering, Eisenhower began to take a grim view of the incident. He called Bess, Mueller, Reynolds, and Daly into his office and told them that he was trying to do everything at his command to keep Patton in his job.

"His emotional tenseness and his impulsiveness are the very

qualities that make him, in open situations, such a remarkable leader of an Army," he explained. "In pursuit and exploitation there is need for a commander who sees nothing but the necessity of getting ahead. The more he drives his men the more he will save their lives. He must be indifferent to fatigue and ruthless in demanding that last atom of physical energy. Patton is such a commander. I feel, therefore, that Patton should be saved for the great battles facing us in Europe."

He pleaded with the correspondents to keep the story in the family. A similar plea was made to the correspondents accredited to Eisenhower's headquarters in Algiers by General Smith. The newspapermen and radio reporters—impressed with Eisenhower's sincerity—agreed to "forget" the incident. They entered into a gentleman's agreement with the Supreme Commander to refrain from breaking the story either in their papers or on the radio.

By then Patton also realized that his impetuous conduct was having repercussions. Eisenhower's letters and General Blesse's arrival had brought home to him the seriousness of the situation—and yet although he was sincerely penitent and castigated himself for his thoughtless conduct, he consoled himself that he had been right and had acted properly, even though "with little tact."

Thus on August 20, he wrote in his diary:

> After lunch General Blesse, Chief Surgeon AFGH, brought me a very nasty letter from Ike with reference to two soldiers I cussed out for what I considered cowardice. Evidently I acted precipitately and on insufficient knowledge. My motive was correct, because one cannot permit skulking to exist. It is just like any communicable disease. I admit freely that my method was wrong and I shall make what amends I can. I regret the incident as I hate to make Ike mad when it is my earnest desire to please him. General Lucas came at 1800 to further explain Ike's attitude. I feel very low.

No matter how peeved Patton was by Eisenhower's "very nasty letter," he answered it on August 29, offering his abject apologies in his most humble language. It was a formal letter, written on the official stationery of Headquarters Seventh Army:

My dear General Eisenhower:

Replying to your letter of August 17, 1943, I want to commence by thanking you for this additional illustration of your fairness and generous consideration in making the communication personal.

I am at a loss to find words with which to express my chagrin and grief at having given you, a man to whom I owe everything and for whom I would gladly lay down my life, cause for displeasure with me.

I assure you that I had no intention of being either harsh or cruel in my treatment of the two soldiers in question. My sole purpose was to try to restore in them a just appreciation of their obligation as men and soldiers.

In World War I, I had a dear friend and former schoolmate who lost his nerve in an exactly analogous manner, and who, after years of mental anguish, committed suicide.

Both my friend and the medical men with whom I discussed his case assured me that had he been roundly checked at the time of his first misbehavior, he would have been restored to a normal state.

Naturally, this memory actuated me when I ineptly tried to supply the remedies suggested. After each incident I stated to officers with me that I felt I had probably saved an immortal soul.

He closed the letter with "Very respectfully" and signed it "G.S. Patton, Jr., Lieut. General, U.S. Army."

Even so, the case was drawing rapidly to its close and it seemed that it would be filed with the pathetic gesture Patton was compelled to make. In his letter, General Eisenhower explicitly directed him to apologize *en masse* to the soldier he had insulted and also to the medical staff who happened to be present. Orders were issued to the II Corps Surgeon to round up this audience and send them to the Royal Palace in Palermo for a ceremony to take place at 11:00 a.m. on August 22.

It was a Sunday. At 10:00 a.m., dressed magnificently for the occasion and wearing his most formidable frown, Patton retired to the Cappella Palatina, the royal chapel of the palace, a magnificent edifice with incomparable mosaic decorations and frescoes built in A.D. 1132. Kneeling in the nave in front of the huge Byzantine marble candle holder, Patton prayed for almost an hour. Then he moved ceremoniously into the magnificent Spanzadi Ruggero on the second floor, where his audience was waiting for him.

Of the various eyewitness accounts of the humiliating event, Major Etter's description is the most dramatic:

> The "apology" went like this. We were ordered to the General's office in the palace of the former King of Italy one Sunday morning. We were not informed why we were there, so we were quite startled when we were ushered before General Patton's desk in a very large room. His aide, then Brigadier General Gay, took us [groups from both hospitals] up before General Patton.
>
> We stood at attention while he told us that a good friend of his, in a fit of depression, had committed suicide during World War I. He felt that if someone had been "rough with him" and "slapped some sense into him," his life might have been saved. He explained he considered his action for the soldiers' own good. He felt that we should understand his, the General's, motives, that we must realize our responsibilities as officers and watch over personnel who were in trouble.
>
> With that as an explanation for his conduct, we were advised to forget the incident and were dismissed.

Dr. Etter (now a prominent pediatrician in Memphis, Tennessee) concluded this recollection of what he called "an old and unpleasant subject," by saying, "All of our personnel admired General Patton and thought him a great general. We felt that the incident was unfortunate, unnecessary, and certainly, regrettable. My own hapless part was that I happened to be in the right place, to be sure, but at the wrong time."

The memories of the odious incident were receding. For a few weeks following the ceremonial apologies, Patton kept to his palatial residence in Palermo, resting on his laurels behind the marvelous Norman gates of his palazzo.

Early in September, Patton received a visit from Norman H. Davis, chairman of the American Red Cross. To give the soldiers an opportunity to express their gratitude for the services of the Red Cross, Patton assembled a large contingent of them at a theater. He escorted Mr. Davis to the stage. This was his first public appearance since the scandal and he was somewhat self-conscious, since he had been told of the comments which were supposedly circulating about him among the GIs.

When Davis finished his speech, he introduced Patton. The general stepped to the front of the platform, pulled himself up to his full height, then said with a grim face, "I thought I'd stand up here and let you fellows see if I am as big a son-of-a-bitch as you think I am."

The GIs went wild. They practically raised the roof of the theater with their cheers.

Then something else occurred which suggested to General Patton that the case had been filed and forgotten. He received word from Algiers that he was soon slated to get his new command. The Allies had landed on the Italian mainland at Salerno. But on September 14 a signal from Admiral Hewitt, who commanded the Navy in the landings, informed Eisenhower that General Clark, commander of the Fifth Army on the Salerno beachhead, was in trouble. Eisenhower moved heaven and earth to aid his friend, with whom he grew into his present high command and who had rendered invaluable service to him in North Africa. But it was becoming obvious that Clark was not quite able to cope with the situation. It was doubtful whether he could hold the beachhead pending the arrival of Montgomery's Eighth Army, coming up from the toe of the Italian boot.

General Alexander suggested to Eisenhower that Patton be given comand of the Fifth Army. It now seemed definite that he would be given this command, certainly before the Fifth Army began its march on Rome, scheduled for later in the year, probably around November.

And back in Washington—on October 1, barely seven weeks after the slapping incident—Patton was nominated for the permanent rank of a major general. Though he had been made a temporary lieutenant general the previous March, the promotion was long overdue, for he was still only a Colonel of Cavalry on the regular Army's permanent list.

But on November 21, 1943, the scandal burst into the open despite Eisenhower's best efforts to keep it quiet. Drew Pearson—who was not bound by the gentleman's agreement— "exposed" one of the incidents on his regular Sunday radio program on the American Broadcasting Company network. It was not a scoop by any means, for the story was fully known to hundreds of newspapermen who had agreed to withhold it in the national interest; and Pearson could give only a garbled, third-hand account, adding his own interpretation in his ponderous, sonorous, and ominous delivery. But his airing of the stale story hit the nation with the force of a blockbuster, especially because of Eisenhower's apparent attempt to hush up the incident.

Congressmen immediately began to receive the usual

mail, written mostly by irate correspondents like Mrs. Nattie Hodge of Pacolet Mills, South Carolina, for example. "I request," she wrote, "that an investigation be made in the conduct of General George S. Patton in his actions toward the shell-shocked soldier of the Seventh Army."

Mr. B.B. Waters of Greer, South Carolina, wrote: "Patton . . . should be thrown out of the Army. An officer that can't control himself any better than that is not fit to command a company, much less an army."

One of the largest American Legion posts in Iowa wired Representative Charles B. Hoeven: "Respectfully request that you demand a full investigation of the General Patton incident with A.E.F. These are American soldiers and not Germans. If our boys are to be mistreated, let's import Hitler and do it up right." Congressman Hoeven added words of his own indignation: "Perhaps we have too much 'blood and guts' now."

Another congressman, Joseph R. Bryson, in whose South Carolina district Bennett, the slapped soldier, lived, invoked the Bible against the general: "He that is slow to anger is better than the mighty; and he that ruleth his spirit, than he that taketh a city." Other legislators chimed in, one of them demanding that Patton be moved from command of the Seventh Army to that of the Japanese Evacuation Centers on the west coast. He could apparently think of no lower assignment than this for the disgraced general, and did not seem to care how much Patton would slap the faces of "those Japs."

The case soon became a burning national controversy handled by Secretary Stimson himself in the War Department and causing concern even inside the White House. Pressed by Senator Robert R. Reynolds, chairman of the Military Affairs Committee, the Secretary asked General Marshall to order a complete report directly from Eisenhower.

On November 24, General Eisenhower sent a telegraphic report to Washington "in regard to the conduct of Lieutenant General George S. Patton, Jr., U.S.A. Commanding General Seventh Army." It was a summary of the case extracted from the files of the incident and is here reprinted in full:

> During the Sicilian campaign General Patton was the mainspring of the effort during the sustained drive of the Seventh Army from Gela all the way to Messina. He absolutely refused to accept procrastination or any excuse for delay, with a resulting

rapid advance of that Army which had much to do with the early collapse of resistance in Sicily. He drove himself as hard as he did the members of his Army throughout the campaign and consequently became almost ruthless in his demands upon individual men.

While visiting wounded in hospitals in two instances he encountered unwounded patients who had been evacuated for what is commonly known as "battle anxiety," specifically nerve difficulty. Also, one man had a temperature. He momentarily lost his temper in these two instances and in an unseemly and indefensible manner upbraided the individuals, and in one of the cases cuffed the individual involved so that the man's helmet rolled off his head.

These incidents were first reported officially to me by a medical officer, this report being followed by reports from three reputable newspapermen. Prior to receiving the report from the pressmen I took the following action:

First, to General Patton, I wrote a letter advising him of the allegations, expressing my extreme displeasure, and informing him that any repetition would result in his instant relief. Further, I told him that he would necessarily make, on his own initiative to the individuals involved, amends, and, if necessary, take the necessary steps to make proper amends before his whole Army. I also told him that I would reserve decision affecting his relief from command of the Army until I could determine the effect of his own corrective action.

Second, the problem before me was whether the incidents as reported were sufficiently damaging to Patton and to his standing in his Army to compel me to relieve him, thus losing to the United States his unquestioned value as commander of an assault force, or whether less drastic measures would be appropriate. I sent General Lucas to make a complete investigation of the affair. I also sent another general officer to Sicily and made a short visit there myself for the purpose of determining whether or not any resentment existed in the Seventh Army against General Patton.

The following action was taken by Patton: He personally sought out the individuals involved and the persons who were present at the time the incidents took place. In addition, he visited each and every division of the Seventh Army and called together all officers, to whom he registered his regret that he should have been guilty of any conduct which could be considered unfair and un-American. The officers of these divisions in turn relayed this message to the enlisted men.

The measures taken by Patton were discussed by me with the three newspapermen who have reported the incident, and apparently they were convinced that the measures taken were adequate in the circumstances. On the top of all this I sent the Theater Inspector General to make a thorough investigation of the Seventh Army with the particular mission of determining whether or not there existed in that force any general resentment against Patton. The Inspector General reported to me that, while there was more or less general knowledge that incidents of the character described had taken place, the men themselves felt that General Patton had done a splendid overall job and no great harm had been done.

In this connection it must be remembered that, while the conduct of Patton in these specific cases was indefensible and resented by every officer who knew of it, Patton has in thousands of cases personally supported, encouraged, and sustained individuals. The net result was that throughout the Sicilian campaign the Seventh Army had a high morale. I personally supervised this investigation throughout and took those steps that seemed applicable in the circumstances because I believe that General Patton had a great field of usefulness in any assault where loyalty, drive, and gallantry on the part of the Army commander will be essential.

General Smith had a press conference yesterday with all of the entire story as given above. This was done because of reports of the publication in the United States of exaggerated versions of the story. In this connection I commend the great body of American newspapermen in this theater because all of them knew something of the facts involved and some of them knew all, including the corrective action taken and the circumstances that tended to ameliorate the obvious injustice of Patton's acts. These men chose to regard the matter as one in which the High Command acted for the best interests of the war effort and let the matter rest there. To them I am grateful.

Summing the matter up: It is true that General Patton was guilty of reprehensible conduct with respect to two enlisted men. They were both suffering from a nervous disorder and one man in the case had a temperature. Following an exhaustive investigation including a personal visit to Sicily, I decided that the corrective action as described above was suitable in the circumstances and adequate. I still believe that this decision was sound. Finally it has been reported many times to me that in every recent public appearance of Patton before any crowd composed of his own soldiers he is greeted by thunderous applause.

On December 3, Secretary Stimson sent Chairman Reynolds a report dealing with both slapping incidents. Stimson hinted
that serious military considerations were behind the handling of the
case and bluntly stated that Patton's retention in high command was
of the utmost interest to the war effort. The secretary wrote:

> General Eisenhower was obliged to consider this matter from a
> military viewpoint rather than that of what is termed "public re-
> lations." In his last report he has again reported that these in-
> stances [of violence] have not affected General Patton's standing
> as a tactical leader, one who successfully concluded, in record
> time, a complicated and important military campaign, and one
> whom his officers and men would again be willing to follow
> into battle. He reports that the serious aspect of this case is the
> danger that the Army will lose the services of a battle-tested
> Army commander, and also afford aid and comfort to the enemy.

By this the irate secretary meant to slap down Pearson for
his intemperate and inopportune exposé of the slapping incidents.
The high military considerations of which the secretary spoke involved Patton's transfer to the Fifth Army, which General Alexander
was urging with increasing vigor. Ambitious plans were in the making for an acceleration of the campaign and a move northward in Italy, and they needed a bold and dashing leader like Patton. Now it
became abundantly evident to Secretary Stimson and General Marshall in Washington, as well as General Eisenhower in Algiers, that
Patton would not be available for this assignment. Although his competence fully qualified him for the job, his new reputation in the public eye had sorely disqualified him.

It was a major tragedy, for Patton personally, and for the
nation and the war effort. There are ample reasons to believe that
with Patton commanding in Italy, it would not have taken until June
4, 1944, to reach Rome.

COMMENTARY

It is difficult to pin down the state of Eisenhower's mind when he
first caught wind of Patton's behavior in the field hospitals. Reflecting on the events in his book, *Crusade in Europe*, Eisenhower displayed awareness of the many sides to the issues involved. For

example, he found the act reprehensible, unbecoming to an officer of Patton's rank. On one hand, he explained the behavior as a result of the tensions Patton was under in the difficult Sicilian campaign. On the other hand, Eisenhower felt that Patton's "emotional tenseness and his impulsiveness were the very qualities that made him, in an open situation, such a remarkable leader of an army."

Eisenhower sent no less than three officers to inquire into the situation, suggesting there were substantive concerns on his mind. Two of the officers were physicians. While it would appear as though the medical officers were sent to represent the medical corps, which had inadvertently become involved since the slappings took place in hospitals, perhaps another reason lay in back of Eisenhower's decision to bring physicians into the investigation.

Eisenhower recognized that Patton's impulsiveness had gone beyond the accepted boundaries for field commander. He also recognized that Patton was in a highly emotional state, under stress. Was Patton in the midst of a nervous breakdown? Eisenhower never mentions this concern in his memoir. But he straddled the issue by referring more than once to Patton's highly emotional state, and almost in the same breath to the qualities required of a field commander. Eisenhower did not indicate that he had issued explicit instructions to the medical officers he sent on the trail of the investigation. But implicit in their mission was the need for an answer to this question: Was Patton breaking down, and in losing control undergoing a major psychological regression? Of course, implicit in this question is the possibility that what Patton was undergoing mentally was the phenomenon that goes under the rubric of "battle fatigue." In his view battle fatigue did not exist, and if it did, needed to be stamped out quickly because he believed battle fatigue was nothing more, nor less, than cowardice. The issue really was one near and dear to leadership in the military: Fitness for command! The fact that Eisenhower did not raise this question explicitly when assigning three officers to conduct an informal investigation is not to say the issue was not uppermost in his mind. The manner in which Eisenhower dealt with this situation was entirely consistent with his style of working all of the issues simultaneously, keeping his options open as to what action he would ultimately take. For Eisenhower was dealing not only with a potential crisis in his structure of command; he was also concerned about a man whom he called George and whom he considered "my old friend."

To be relieved of command at the height of the war would

have been a personal disaster of incalculable magnitude for General Patton. As he wrote to his father-in-law to be, "It is as natural for me to be a soldier as it is to breathe and would be as hard to give up all thought of it as it would to stop breathing." But being a soldier for Patton meant testing his manliness. As Patton continued in his letter to his soon to be father-in-law, "But being a soldier and being a member of the Army in time of peace are two different things. I would only accept the latter as a means to the former."

General Omar N. Bradley conveyed some interesting insights into Patton's mentality. Bradley and Patton were contemporaries in the officer corps and as fate would have it, Bradley served as a subordinate commander to Patton in the Sicilian campaign and later as his superior officer in the European campaign, reflecting perhaps on the differing natures of the two men. Patton exemplified the impulsive and Bradley the reflective type of commander. Bradley wrote about Patton, "To George the war was not so much an ordeal as it was the fulfillment of a destiny to which he shaped his life. He believed war to be a chronic ailment of mankind, destined to pursue civilization to its grave." Bradley continued, "Since conflict was to be the inevitable lot of all mankind, George reasoned that man should resign himself to it and indeed welcome it as a manly challenge. Exhilarated as he was by conflict, he found it inconceivable that men, other than cowards, should want no part of war. At the same time, he could not believe that men could break under intense mental strain as a result of the hardships endured in war. To him it was axiomatic that those who did not wish to fight were cowards. If one could shame a coward, George said, one might help him to regain his self respect."

Exactly what is a coward? I suspect that George Patton was obsessed with this question. Surely cowardice cannot be defined as the opposite of heroic behavior. Experiencing anxiety and fear for one's life is ubiquitous in war and likewise does not define cowardice. General Patton reacted in disgust to his elevated pulse rate under fire, yet there may be instances in which being the coward and the heroic warrior are not too far apart.

Such might be the case with General Patton. His preoccupation with cowardice, his fear of passivity, the scorn with which he held people of gentle character (including his own father?) seem to portray a man for whom manliness had to be proved and constantly reaffirmed, in order to quiet doubts as to one's identity.

The psychological phenomenon of projection is familiar

enough. It works almost as an automatic response. "What I observe in and hate about myself I will discover in others. In savagely destroying those characteristics in others I will be destroying them in myself. Thus, my fears will be quieted, my integrity maintained." This maneuver is not especially calculated. People, the heroes and the cowards alike, have to do what for them has been a lifelong necessity.

As General Eisenhower commented, Patton was under severe stress. The stress resulted not only from the objective and harsh conditions of war, but also from Patton's encounter with destiny during the war: his need to prove to himself his superiority during warfare, which meant vanquishing the enemy, being the clear-cut victor, and overcoming internal anxieties. The hapless soldiers in the field hospitals were minor characters in a narrative in which circumstance and personal history met to resolve the familiar dichotomies of the weak and the strong, the manly and the effeminate, the victor and the vanquished.

As a result of this encounter between circumstance and personal history, General Dwight David Eisenhower once again had the opportunity to display his talent for the middle course. Among his multiple constituencies were the press, their representatives in the Congress, the hierarchy of, as it was then called, the War Department, leading from Secretary Henry Stimson to the president of the United States. Eisenhower also had to take account of the military hierarchy, including his superior officer and the Chief of Staff, General George C. Marshall, his peers in the allied command, and his subordinates from the high reaches of authority to the lowliest foot soldiers. Finally, Eisenhower desperately wanted to save the career of his old friend and preserve for future service a man whom he considered a first-rate field commander and ground gainer.

To ignore the event, hoping it would die a natural death in the surfeit of news from the battlefield, would have run the risk of later exposure. A public uproar, which occurred despite Eisenhower's efforts to "keep it in the family" (a family in which Eisenhower included the reporters assigned to the Mediterranean Theater) would make his superiors, both military and civilian, highly vulnerable.

Eisenhower's course of action assured that he was complying with the necessities of the case. He had assurance from the medical observers that Patton was not so severely regressed psychologically as to be a hazard, rather than a source of strength, in the field. He kept the trail of paperwork, but always in an informal vein. His letter to Patton served as a reprimand, but its informality did not cause higher powers to enter the scene. His confidential talk with the reporters allayed their concerns that he was indifferent, while its tone and implication invited the reporters to become members of the family serving a higher purpose than the immediate need to report the news.

"Measure the response while covering all bases" seems to describe how Eisenhower thought and the consistent logic that lay in back of his actions. When the news leaked through Drew Pearson, who was anything but an insider in the profession of journalism, Eisenhower was prepared. He was able to make a report to General Marshall presenting in considerable detail his involvement and control in dealing with a general who had broken the code of the military in an egregious loss of personal control.

It is easy to conclude from this narrative that situations determine how leaders behave, and perhaps, how they *should* behave. But seasoned students of both situations and leadership know there is more than one correct answer to the enigmas that narratives present to the head man. Eisenhower's measured responses to the constituencies' claims on him, his ability to address more than one constituency's need with a single action, appears impressive from this distance in history. But this was the man. Eisenhower the general was not too different from Eisenhower the campaigner for the highest office in the land, or Eisenhower the president, whose boldest action took place upon leaving office rather than entering it. In his farewell address to the nation, he warned of the ominous and growing influence of "the military-industrial complex." Was this concern a new insight he decided to reveal to the American people? Why wait for the moment he was relinquishing power? Perhaps Eisenhower and Patton were alike in one respect: two great men held hostage by their own characters.

WHEN AUTHORITY FAILS—THE *SATURDAY EVENING POST*

Cary Bok, the grandson of Cyrus Curtis, founder of the Curtis Publishing Company, suggested, "The real history [of the company's failure] is going to have to be written by a psychiatrist." Had a group of psychiatrists tested the mental state of the actors involved in this drama of corporate abuse, each individual probably would have been declared sane. The pathology of the *Saturday Evening Post* and its corporate parent would not be found in the mental deficiency of its individual executives and board members. Yet the story of the *Post* rings throughout with pathology. Something went awry in the Curtis Publishing Company, yet the cause had to be found elsewhere than lack of sanity in the upper echelons of power.

Looked at from another perspective, it would not take you or me very long to detail where the company and its star producer went wrong in its business strategy. In fact, I will state my analysis now, even before you have had a chance to read the case, to show you how easy it is to detail what is right and wrong about this strategy. Here goes!

The company did not know the business it was in. As a col-

CHAPTER

17

lective, it acted as though it was in the business of manufacturing—in this case, manufacturing a magazine. When you are a manufacturer, you work on the principle of economy of scale. The management operated on this principle, so they integrated backwards and invested in fixed assets such as printing plants, presses, paper mills, and forests to feed the mills. But the management misunderstood the business it was in. It was in the communications business. It produced a product supposed to inform, entertain, and as a result of the pleasure produced for its readers, collect large amounts of advertising revenues. Instead of doing all this for its readers and keeping Madison Avenue interested, the *Post* lost touch. Its audience turned to the new journalism of Henry Luce, and to the new medium of television. Declining revenue on top of high fixed costs spelled the end of the Post and of Curtis. In sum, Curtis and its flagship the *Saturday Evening Post* failed to change.

Now maybe what Cary Bok had in mind in advising that the history should be written by a psychiatrist is the following. One definition of insanity is the failure to keep in touch with reality. So far as the record reveals, no one was hallucinating, so the way people lost touch with reality is not all that clear. Astute readers might at this point begin to believe that while reality is there to behold, sometimes people don't want to see reality for what it is. Besides, isn't reality subject to a number of interpretations?

Another way of looking at the question of reality is that sometimes it is clear what is going on, but it is difficult to decide what to do about it. Interestingly enough, a high-powered self-appointed task force worked up an alternate strategy for the company, but it died aborning. This plan was strikingly similar to one proposed in a report entitled, "Tomorrow Morning Plan." A highly placed Curtis Publishing executive, Clay Blair, Jr., offered this plan in response to an inquiry from an important director. The two plans, similar in design, fell flat. They both were prepared rapidly (and for free) and perhaps died in childbirth because of the absence of proper theater to gain the attention of the audience. This question of what goes into strategy suggests that politics often overrides substance in the councils of the mighty.

I have long held the belief that psychopathology in business and other organizations falls into a category totally different from ordinary considerations in psychiatry and psychoanalysis. Individuals who are sane as individuals are capable of regressing under the influence of group psychology. The possible lesson to be learned from this theory of mine is how to keep your head intact in the face of the most debilitating psychological forces present in groups.

The *Saturday Evening Post* narrative holds considerable promise in instructing us on the problems of keeping or losing one's head when authority fails.

THE *SATURDAY EVENING POST*

The real history is going to have to be written by a psychiatrist.

Cary Bok, grandson of the founder of Curtis Publishing Company

On the afternoon of January 9, 1969, standing before the glaring television lights at the Overseas Press Club in New York City, Martin Ackerman, Curtis Publishing Company's fourth president in six years, calmly read, "This is one of the saddest days of my life, a sad one for me, for our employees, officers, and directors; indeed, it is sad for the American public. Apparently there is just not the need for our product in today's scheme of living."[1] With Ackerman's announcement, Curtis officially ceased publication of the *Saturday Evening Post*.

The *Post*, which had been suffering from increasing costs and decreasing revenues for the past decade, had once been the most profitable magazine in the United States, considered both the pulse and maker of American opinion. The death of the *Post* had been predicted by denizens of Wall Street and Madison Avenue since its first financial troubles in the early 1960s. It is impossible, though, to isolate the plight of the *Post* from the plight of the Curtis Publishing Company, a company whose assets included not only such national magazines as the *Post, Ladies' Home Journal,* and *Holiday,* but also paper mills in Pennsylvania, a sprawling printing plant outside Philadelphia (where every copy of every Curtis publication was printed), a circulation company, and extensive timberlands. During the years 1960-1968 inclusive, Curtis's operating revenues (net of

Audrey Sproat revised this case from the original © 1971 by the president and fellows of Harvard College, prepared by Research Associate John M. Wynne, under the supervision of Profession Abraham Zaleznik.

commissions) declined from $192.8 million to $98.7 million, and the company sustained a cumulative loss of $67.6 million.

HISTORY: 1897-1962

In 1897, Cyrus Curtis, the founder of Curtis Publishing Company, purchased a struggling journal put together for $10 a week by a newspaperman in his spare time. The journal, which Curtis bought for $1,000, consisted of a mailing list of 2,231 names, a wagonload of battered type fonts, and a name, the *Saturday Evening Post*. At the time, Curtis was the publisher of the leading women's magazine in the nation, the *Ladies' Home Journal,* which he and his wife had built from scratch to a circulation of 446,000 during the six-year period between 1883 and 1889. Referring to the *Post, Printers' Ink,* the printing trade journal, commented that the *Ladies' Home Journal* was a "wonderful property" but that Curtis was "blowing his profits on an impossible venture" with the purchase of this latest magazine.[2]

Curtis was undaunted, for he felt that just as the *Journal* had become a success by dealing with what was most important to the American woman, her home, the *Post* would become a success by dealing with what was important to men, "their fight for livelihood in the business world."[3]

THE LORIMER POST: 1899-1936

For the first year under Curtis, the *Post* was edited by William Jordan, but Curtis soon became dissatisfied, and the editorship passed to George Horace Lorimer. The son of a famous Boston minister, Lorimer was considered one of the best newspapermen in Boston.

Lorimer immediately proceeded to alter the *Post,* changing it from a weekly newspaper into a magazine and cutting the price from 10 cents to 5 cents, thus making it less expensive than any competitive periodical. He also instituted a new procedure in American publishing, that of paying authors at the time their material was accepted for publication rather than when it was actually published.

> Lorimer knew exactly what he wanted to make out of the *Post*. It was to be a magazine without class, clique, or sectional editing,

but intended for every adult in America's 75 million population. He meant to edit it for the whole United States. He set out to interpret America to itself, always readably, but constructively.

As he settled into the job of interpretation, Lorimer sensed accurately the mood of the country at the beginning of the new century. People were weary of reading about problems, politics, radicalism, war, and even uplift. They wanted to read historical novels and dwell in the past, and Lorimer gave them covers showing Ben Franklin, Washington, and Independence Hall in appropriate poses, while inside he displayed the romances of the Rev. Cyrus Townsend Brady and Robert W. Chambers.

Always the accent was heaviest on business. Charles R. Flint praised the benefits of the business combination; the mayors of San Francisco and Baltimore wrote jointly on the need for better business methods in civic administration; and Harvard's director of physical culture advised the businessman on home gymnastics.[4]

Lorimer himself contributed several articles related to business, which appeared in the *Post* as an unsigned serial entitled "Letters from a Selfmade Merchant to His Son." An immediate success, this series was later published in book form and translated into a dozen foreign languages.

Lorimer must have hit a chord in the heart of the country, for the *Post*'s circulation increased from 33,000 in 1898 to 97,000 in 1899, and then to 182,000 in 1900. By 1927, circulation was 3,000,000.

A propitious environment

During the early 1900s fundamental changes were occurring in America. Mass production, transportation, and distribution were making America a nation rather than a collection of geographically contiguous regions. Curtis anticipated the need for a national magazine and adroitly applied the evolving principles of mass production and distribution to his publications.

Advertising revenue for the *Post* increased from $8,000 in 1898 to $160,000 in 1899 and then to more than $1 million in 1905; by 1910 it was $5 million. By the end of the 1920s, advertising revenue was over $50 million and the *Post* collected almost 30 cents of every advertising dollar spent in magazines in the United States. "The vehicle that the *Post* rode to tremendous financial success was the automobile. The *Post* carried its first auto ad, about a W.E. Roach horseless buggy, in an issue in March 1900. For the next two decades auto advertising expanded as rapidly as the industry; at one point it made up 25 per cent of the total volume."[5]

The zenith of this period of the *Post*'s history was the December 1929 issue, a virtual paper monument to Curtis and Lorimer.

> It contained 272 pages and weighed almost two pounds. Sixty 45-ton presses rolled around the clock for three weeks to produce it, consuming 6,000,000 pounds of paper and 120,000 pounds of ink. The reading fare was enough to keep the average adult busy for more than 20 hours, *Post* editors estimated. And the issue—largest of any magazine in Curtis' history—put $1,512,000 from 214 national advertisers into Cyrus Curtis' money box. This grandiose effort was so mammoth in bulk that scrap dealers eagerly paid five cents to newsstands for the paper alone.[6]

A series of blows

With the end of the prosperity of the 1920s, *Post* advertising revenues decreased substantially. By 1932, issues of only 60 pages, a quarter of them filled with advertising, were commonplace.

Cyrus Curtis died in 1933 at age 83, leaving his daughter and two grandsons effective control of the company with 32 per cent of the stock. Lorimer, retaining his position as editor of the *Post,* assumed the presidency. During the period from 1933 to 1936, the year of his retirement, Lorimer increased advertising revenue from an $18 million low in 1933 to $26 million in 1936, in spite of the severe economic conditions and increased competition from Henry Luce's *Time* and *Life*. During this period, Lorimer placed the editorial power of the *Post* behind an attempt to defeat Franklin D. Roosevelt in his 1936 re-election bid.

Lorimer called the New Deal "a discredited European ideology"; he railed against "undesirable and inassimilable aliens," and the *Post* declared: "We might just as well say that the world failed as the American business leadership failed."[7] The election landslide for Roosevelt and his New Deal in 1936 was a humiliating blow to Lorimer and indicated "a fundamental, distinct shift of the *Post*'s role in American life. It would be accepted as entertainment, but not as a guide to life."[8]

HANDPICKED SUCCESSORS: 1936-1962

Following Lorimer's retirement in 1936, Walter D. Fuller, Lorimer's choice, was named chief executive officer of Curtis. Fuller, a man more conservative politically than Lorimer, had worked his way up from the accounting department as successively controller, corporate secretary, first vice president, and president, all under the guidance of Curtis and Lorimer.

Fuller was chairman of the board from 1950 to 1957, and his protégé Robert MacNeal became president and chief executive officer. MacNeal had first attracted management attention during the 1920s by designing a folding machine that enabled the *Post* to print more than 200 pages, the previous limit.

> Even when he became president he would go into the machine shops and, at the risk of soiled white cuffs, talk about and help solve mechanical problems. In his coat pocket was a little leather-bound black notebook crammed with facts and statistics about Curtis and its multitude of subsidiary companies. The information—even including the names and addresses of directors—was typed on a "miniature Gothic" typewriter so more characters would fit onto a page. Why the notebook? Mac-Neal's superior in the scheduling division had carried a similar book way back in the 1920s. "He was the fount of all knowledge, so we had to have one, too," MacNeal explained.[9]

Corporate strategy

Fuller and MacNeal's strategy was to build Curtis into a fully integrated magazine publishing company that grew its own trees, made its own paper, printed every issue of every magazine, and distributed the magazines through a circulation subsidiary. This was an arrangement that other publishers looked upon unfavorably, since it accentuated corporate losses in periods of economic decline, served as a drain on funds available for diversification, and increased the size and complexity of corporate management.

Otto Friedrich, in *Decline and Fall*, discussed the Fuller and MacNeal years as follows:

> Fuller's presidency began during the difficult days of the Depression, when Curtis and many other companies tottered near bankruptcy, and the value of ideas may well have seemed less obvious than it does today. And then, during World War II, the

shortage of supplies convinced many an executive of the value of hoarding and stockpiling. Whatever his reasons, Fuller held to his empire-building philosophy with an exceptional singleness of purpose. He could have bought the entire Columbia Broadcasting System for $3 million, but he declined the offer; a few years later, he declined a similar opportunity to buy the American Broadcasting Corporation. Television, radio, the growth in book publishing, the so-called "paperback revolution," the rise of suburban newspapers, the increasing need for school texts— Walter Deane Fuller had not been blessed with a gift for prophesying such developments. Instead, just after World War II, he bought a 108-acre site on the outskirts of Philadelphia, shipped in 20 new printing presses, and constructed the gigantic Sharon Hill printing plant. It was, in its day, the largest and best-equipped printing plant in the world. And as late as 1950, when Fuller finally passed on the presidency to his protégé Robert A. MacNeal, Curtis reaffirmed its dedication to machinery by investing $20 million to become full owner of a paper company in which it already held a controlling interest.

By 1960 the number of individuals actually employed in creating the Curtis magazines was minuscule compared with the number engaged in its manufacture:

The editorial staff of the *Post* numbered about 125 people; the employees in the printing division numbered 2,600; the employees of the whole corporation numbered about 11,000. And in surveying the corporate assets, Curtis executives liked to boast that the company owned not just a few magazines but a $40 million printing plant, three large paper mills, 262,000 acres of timberland, and a circulation company that distributed 50-odd magazines through 100,000 outlets.[10]

Editorial strategy

In 1936, Lorimer's successor as editor of the *Post* was Wesley W. Stout. Like Fuller and MacNeal, Stout was handpicked by Lorimer and was politically conservative:

In editorial outlook, Stout was every bit as conservative as Lorimer; the popular support given the New Deal by voters in 1936 goaded the *Post* into increasingly vicious attacks on the Administration. President Roosevelt never answered directly, but he showed several visitors a large envelope containing what he termed the "dirtiest" attacks published against the government. The bulk of them were from the *Post*. The magazine's editorials were a cacophony of ridicule directed against organized labor, social reform programs, social security, the Tennessee Valley Administration—in sum, just about anything attempted by FDR.[11]

Advertising revenue dropped $4 million during Stout's first year as editor, and at a stockholders' meeting in 1941 minority stockholders "denounced management's isolationism and called for the opening of *Post* pages to opposing points of view."[12] Stout's editorship of the *Post* came to an end in 1942 with what has been called "the biggest misunderstanding in Curtis editorial history."[13] Stout had published a three-article series on the American Jew, the last article of which was entitled "The Case Against the Jew." A furor erupted, with cancellations of subscriptions and advertising, threats of a boycott, and destruction of *Posts* at newsstands. In May 1942 the *Post* ran an editorial apologizing for the article, saying that Stout had believed "a frank airing of the whole question would serve to clear the atmosphere in this country and perhaps help prevent anti-Semitism from gaining a foothold here. The *Post* expressed regret that the article had been 'misunderstood.' "[14]

Discord between Stout and Fuller had been rumored for some time, and the controversy over the article and the *Post*'s operating loss for the first quarter of 1942 precipitated Stout's resignation. The editorship of the *Post* then went to Ben Hibbs, a native of Kansas, who had been the editor of another Curtis magazine, *Country Gentleman*. Hibbs immediately began making major changes in the *Post*. He found the *Post*'s editorial content resting on the same "glamour of business" product that Lorimer had developed decades earlier. Feeling that this product was dated, Hibbs broadened the *Post* by stressing what he considered to be the more enduring part of America—namely, life in country towns. But Hibbs also looked beyond middle America and recognized World War II as "the greatest news story of our time."

Hibbs and his lanky young managing editor, Bob Fuoss, reduced the emphasis on fiction and set out to cover World War II. The *Post* then had only one war correspondent, who was home on leave in New York. Hibbs recruited MacKinlay Kantor, Samuel Lubell, Edgar Snow, Richard Tregaskis, Damaree Bess. C.S. Forester wrote about the sinking of the *Scharnhorst*, Ambassador Joseph E. Davies wrote from Moscow about the Russian front, and Norman Rockwell painted his version of Roosevelt's slogan, the Four Freedoms. In this silver age, the money came and went at an unprecedented rate. Hibbs spent $175,000, a record for extravagance at that time, for *My Three Years with Eisenhower,* by the general's naval aide, Captain Harry C. Butcher. He spent another $125,000 for the memoirs of Casey Stengel, and $100,000 for a biography of General Douglas MacArthur. At the same time, Hibbs willingly led the *Post* into a circulation war against *Life* and *Look,* and the *Post* bought its way up from 3.3 million to more than 6.5 million during his 20-year regime. Advertising revenue rose just as spectacularly, from $23 million to $104 million a year.[15]

Losing the postwar race with competition

Under the continued guidance of Fuller as chairman, MacNeal as president, and Hibbs as editor of the *Post,* the 1950s proved to be difficult years. Although *Post* advertising revenue increased over the decade, the number of advertising pages per issue decreased. The circulation battles of the late 1950s between the *Post, Life,* and *Look* were a mixed blessing for Curtis. A two-year subscription to the *Post* cost the subscriber $7.95 and represented a liability to the *Post* of $20 (the production and delivery costs). The larger circulation figures led to increased advertising rates, but these made it impossible for many of the small manufacturers, on whom the *Post* had depended for a substantial amount of its advertising revenue, to continue advertising in the magazine. At the same time, the *Post* was losing large corporation advertising to television, which in the years following World War II had built up advertising revenues twice those of magazines.

Market research studies continually eroded the effectiveness of the *Post* as an advertising medium. For example, *Life* underwrote a study that showed each of its issues had a readership of 5.2 persons; that readership, multiplied by circulation, brought *Life* equal to radio and television in the numbers game of media reach—a claim the *Post* could not equal. *Life* then underwrote another study that indicated the *Post* was a magazine bought for reading and not for looking; *Life* immediately turned this fact to its advantage by stressing to advertisers that the busy young housewife would not have time to read *Post* articles, so advertising in the *Post* would be less effective than in a magazine bought for looking, such as *Life.*

Madison Avenue wanted to cover the younger segment of the consumer market (base age of 35), which had extra dollars for discretionary buying. In the late 1950s, *Life's* circulation included twice as many families in this category as the *Post's*.

Life was also active during the 1950s building a power base with merchants. *Life* persuaded merchants to tag goods "as advertised in *Life*" with the implication that *Life* put its editorial integrity behind the product.

The business recession of 1961 caused the number of advertising pages per *Post* issue to plummet even more. As the advertising pages decreased, the *Post* became thinner and thinner, and the professionals on Madison Avenue started placing even fewer ads in the *Post* as a result.

Curtis's profits declined from $6.2 million in 1950 to only $1.6 million in 1960. Although gross advertising revenue (including commissions) increased from $98.6 million to $151.8 million during the 10-year period, advertising pages decreased. Production and distribution expenses rose substantially over the same time, and selling and administrative expenses more than doubled, going from $27.7 million to $61.2 million.

The new *Post*

Late in 1960, an administrative decision was made under President MacNeal that a new *Post* should be created with a fashionable look that would appeal to Madison Avenue, increase *Post* advertising revenue, and thus increase corporate profits. Editor Hibbs, on the other hand, felt that the *Post* was already hitting the American market:

> The *Post* was widely considered to be old and stodgy, edited by the old and stodgy to be read by the old and stodgy, and Ben Hibbs couldn't accept it. "The ad people were always hollering in my last year about the Norman Rockwell covers, that they were old-fashioned," he protested. "Heck, those were the *Post's* most popular feature." And the books he kept buying kept becoming best sellers. "Dammit. We were hitting the American market," said Hibbs. "We had to be with that kind of record." And did someone say that *Post* fiction was unreal? "After all, the world is not entirely composed of hydrogen bombs, juvenile delinquency, race riots, mental institutions, heart disease and cancer," said Hibbs. "I can remember the time when people thought it was fun to read."[16]

The new *Post* was developed during 1961 and first appeared in September of that year. Six million dollars in advertising was sold for this issue, and its 148 pages created the thickest *Post* in years. Described as a "peculiar mixture of new and old,"[17] it featured a Norman Rockwell cover depicting the artist puzzling out a new *Post* cover, a new column entitled "Speaking Out," different print and layout styles, and articles ranging from the memoirs of Casey Stengel to an account of an American doctor in the jungles of Haiti. The response to the new *Post* was immediate.

> The look of the "new" *Post* infuriated its readers, and they wrote in to protest at a rate of ten thousand letters a week. "Idiotic . . . please change it back . . . Cancel my subscription . . . I have been betrayed—and many others with me." As for Madison Avenue, for which the "new *Post*" had been created, it responded as it usually does to such efforts—with a shrug. "The mistake was," in the words of one cynical old *Post* editor, "that you forced them to read the magazine." Basically, the *Post* had announced change and then attempted to counterfeit change, and the increased advertising didn't last a month. Over the whole year, in fact, advertising plummeted from $104 million to $86 million. The *Post* consequently went into the red by $3 million, and Curtis by $4 million.[18]

CHALLENGE AND CHANGE: 1962

On March 29, 1962, President MacNeal announced Curtis's $4 million loss for the previous fiscal year, the first corporate loss since the company's inception in 1891. Apparently the loss would have been nearly $9 million except for a tax credit of $1 million and a nonrecurring profit of $3.5 million from the sale of securities.

Ten days earlier, the *Gallagher Report,* a Madison Avenue newsletter, had suggested that a major shake-up in Curtis's corporate leadership might be in the cards: "The Curtis Crisis. Major changes in Curtis Publishing management and ownership expected shortly. Financier Peter G. Treves has been quietly buying Curtis stock for more than a year, and has acquired sizable holdings."

Apparently Curtis was an attractive target for corporate raiders. For one thing, the corporate assets were understated: Two hundred fifty thousand acres of timberland, for example, were valued at $10-$15 per acre, although they were carried on the books at $3 per acre. Moreover, the company's stock was underpriced by the market, with the two issues of Curtis preferred selling well below their liquidation values.

In 1962, when Treves was buying into the company, effective operating control was in the hands of Curtis's heirs. A trust, to continue through the life of Curtis's daughter and her two sons, controlled 17.3 per cent of the outstanding stock, and the Curtis heirs themselves owned 14.6 per cent. With 32 per cent of the Curtis stock, the heirs over the years had placed family friends and management sympathetic to the wishes of the family on the board of directors.

A minor change, however, had occurred in the late 1950s, when minority stockholders complained that common stock dividends were too low ($.00 from 1933 to 1950 and $.20 from 1951 to 1956) and threatened a stockholder suit. As a result, President Mac-Neal had increased the size of the board and had dropped from it those Curtis executives who held ex officio seats. The newly opened board seats went to investment and insurance interests. At the same time, however, effective working control of the company became vested in a newly created executive committee that included the same editors and executives who had been removed from the board. Moreover, the men filling the newly opened board seats were sympathetic to the wishes of the heirs and thus were considered "family members" of the board.

In April 1962, Treves and Co. and J. R. Williston and Beane, the firms that had been purchasing Curtis stock, sent an emissary, Milton Gould, to the Curtis Building. Gould was a Philadelphia lawyer who was to play a major role in Curtis's subsequent history. On this occasion, Gould requested an immediate appointment with MacNeal and stated that the interests he represented wanted two seats on the Curtis board. Not knowing the extent of Treves's and Williston and Beane's ownership, the board agreed to enlarge the number of seats from eleven to thirteen, with the two new seats going to Gould and R. McLean Stewart, an investment banker. Asked why the directors did not fight the intrusion, Cary Bok, grandson of Cyrus Curtis and member of the board, replied:

> "There are many reasons," Bok said one winter morning in
> 1964, during a rambling interview at his seaside home in Maine.
> "First of all, you never are assured of absolute con-

trol unless you have 51 per cent. We have only 32 per cent; we were unsure of what other people had.

"Second, the Curtis board is elected with cumulative voting. The others could have pooled their votes and elected one director for sure; probably two, and possibly three."

Third, Bok said, the company didn't relish the idea of a public proxy fight during a time of internal stress. First-quarter losses that year had already touched $4 million—more red ink than went on the books during all of 1961. Curtis management had more important things to do than scurry around the countryside soliciting proxies from widows and small-time investors. The Wall Street groups, on the other hand, specialized in just this type of scurrying. Had Curtis chosen to fight, there was at least a 50-50 chance that Curtis would have been licked. Management and the heirs feared this, because they didn't know any more about the investors' long-range intentions than they did of the investors' holdings.

Additionally, Curtis by this time was so desperate for cash that it was ready to befriend anyone who came along and offered new ideas and fresh leadership. That spring it was forced to peddle two of its strongest sidelines to raise operating cash. Curtis sold part of its holdings in Bantam Books, Inc., and Treasure Books, Inc., to Grosset & Dunlap, Inc., for a $4.8 million profit. Both companies were returning a profit. But the need for immediate cash was overpowering and the book subsidiaries were something that could be conveniently cut from the empire.[19]

In an interview given shortly after he joined the Curtis board Gould said that he had sought a directorship because the brokerage houses that had taken a substantial financial position in Curtis had become alarmed by the accelerated operating losses and by Curtis's inability to adapt to changing markets.

UNDER NEW MANAGEMENT: 1962-1969

In the early summer of 1962, MacNeal left for a trip to Europe, and during his absence, spurred by Gould, the board voted him out as president. Although it was decided to withhold the news from the press until his return, the news was leaked to the *Wall Street Journal* three hours after the meeting ended. An executive committee was formed to run the company until a new president could be found. Gould was named legal counsel to the executive committee.

THE CULLIGAN YEARS: 1962-1968

Gould's personal choice for the presidency of Curtis was Matthew J. Culligan, an executive at Interpublic, an advertising conglomerate headed by Marion Harper. Previous to his employment at Interpublic, Culligan had been an executive vice president at NBC, where he had been credited with turning around the failing NBC radio network. Gould arranged a meeting between Culligan and the Curtis executive committee, which Culligan later described as follows: "Gould conditioned the executive committee on my behalf, warning them that I was just about the final hope and softening them up for my salary demands and fringe benefits. He actually assigned one of his associates to write my contract for me!"[20]

Shortly after meeting with Culligan, the executive committee named him president. Culligan described his first week at the company as frantic. He raced between the editorial and sales offices in New York City and the corporate offices and the circulation, manufacturing, and paper companies in Pennsylvania. Marion Harper, Culligan's boss at Interpublic, got together the best "media brains" in his organization "to contribute the best cerebration and intuition to the problems at Curtis"[21] in order to help Culligan in his new position. Culligan described the resulting suggestions as follows:

> When the report was finished, Harper invited me to his office and gave me the benefit of the accumulated experience and judgment of a dozen of his best people. The report was fascinating. In essence, it said that Curtis could not survive in the form in which I had inherited it—with the same magazines, same circulations, same frequencies—under the economic conditions then prevailing at Curtis. The task force recommended that the *Post* go biweekly; that *Holiday* be sold to generate working capital; that *American Home* be folded into the *Ladies' Home Journal*, saving millions in subscription costs. The final recommendation was to get Curtis out of the paper and manufacturing business. I accepted the Harper report with overflowing gratitude and rushed back to Curtis as though I'd found the Holy Grail. Calling in my inherited key men—Bob Gibbon, secretary of the executive board; Ford Robinson, head of operations; Leon Marks, head of manufacturing; G.B. McCombs, number two man in circulation—I discussed the report with them. My soaring spirits plummeted as each of the Harper recommendations was shot down in flames, not because the ideas

were faulty, but because of artificial, legal, or financial strictures that appeared to block every turn.[22]

Immediate tasks

After assuming the presidency of Curtis, Culligan was faced with Curtis's $22 million debt to four creditor banks that were expressing concern over Curtis's financial position. Culligan promised an extensive cost-reduction program, and the banks agreed to a 12-month extension of the loan with a commitment for an additional $4 million in working capital. One additional stipulation was that Culligan would attempt to remove a debt restriction from the Curtis bylaws that required a two-thirds vote of the preferred stockholders before management could pledge any collateral for loans. This provision protected the preferred stockholders in the case of liquidation, but it also barred long-term loans. Up to this point, all Curtis debt had been short term at higher interest rates. Culligan proposed the removal of the restriction to the preferred stockholders, who eventually voted down the change.

During the period he was negotiating with the banks, Culligan also busied himself with two other major problems: the need for cost reductions, and the increasing loss of advertising. In a move that was to have serious repercussions, Culligan called in a former colleague, J.M. Clifford, who was suffering from political infighting at NBC, and made him executive vice president of finance and operations. Clifford ordered an immediate 20 per cent cut throughout the entire Curtis structure:

> By mid-1963 enough rank and file deadwood was chopped out of Curtis—3,500 jobs in all—to lower the annual payroll by $13 million... Fixed expenses dropped by $15 to $18 million annually, meaning the *Post* and the other magazines had a lower break-even per issue. According to Curtis annual reports, selling, general, and administrative expenses in 1961 were $62.6 million; this was down to $58.2 million in 1962 and $44.9 million in 1963. Production and delivery expenses dropped from $116.3 million to $106.5 and $103.2 million in the same stages.[23]

With the internal organization left to Clifford, Culligan set out to do what he knew best—selling.

> Curtis was bleeding to death. Too much unnecessary expense and not enough advertising income would bury Curtis by Janu-

ary 1963, unless. . . . I was the "unless"; no one else was in a position to deliver. This statement is not intended to be boastful—the burden was actually on my shoulders. No amount of promotion, advertising, or sales calls by others would suffice. So I followed my instinct and decided on an unprecedented personal sales effort. I determined to do what no other executive in United States business had ever done—call personally on the heads of America's two hundred leading corporations within six months.[24]

Culligan, described as a rambunctious figure, began selling the presidents of the nation's largest companies on the *Post:*

The new president set out on an orgy of salesmanship, with press agents keeping track of every move. It was said that he traveled 3,500 miles a week to sell ads. It was said that he flew to Detroit and made presentations to General Motors, Chrysler, and Lincoln-Mercury all in one day. It was said that he signed $30 million in new ads within his first month. "From late fall of 1962 through the spring of 1963," said Culligan, "I ran Curtis almost entirely by telephone, memo and crash personal meetings at airports, in cars roaring along turnpikes, in the Curtis plane, . . . and even a helicopter, which I leased, to cut down the time wasted getting from New York to Philadelphia." He expressed his philosophy by saying, "I had two choices. I could have stayed in Philadelphia and listened to everybody's problems, or I could go out and start selling, and let the problems take care of themselves."[25]

Despite Culligan's selling efforts, advertising revenue of the *Post* continued to decrease, from $86 million in 1961 to $66 million in 1962 to $60 million in 1963. Curtis's losses, which had been $4 million in 1961, soared to $18.9 million in 1962, then decreased to $3.4 million in 1963, the first year for which Culligan was fully responsible. But part of the improvement was of an accounting nature. At the time of Culligan's takeover, Price Waterhouse, attempting to get Curtis's business, had suggested that Curtis change its accounting policies and handle subscription liabilities in the same manner as most other publishing firms. Following this advice, Curtis spread its subscription liabilities over the life of the subscriptions and thus decreased its losses for 1963 from $10 million to $3.4 million.

By mid-1963, Culligan was again faced with the problem of the short-term bank loans coming due. Assistance came in the form of Serge Semenenko, vice president of the First National Bank of Boston. Russian-born Semenenko was considered a mystery man of U.S. finance. His loans from the First National for the period 1920-1950 "practically supported the United States film industry,"[26] and his list of corporate saves included Fairbanks, Whitney; the International Paper Company; the Hearst publishing empire; and the Kindall Company.

By August 17, which was the deadline on the short-term loans to Curtis in 1963, Culligan and Semenenko had agreed on a $35 million loan from six banks.

> Semenenko doesn't sign blank checks, however, and especially when they are for $35 million. From Curtis he elicited a pledge that all management decisions be "reasonably satisfactory" to him, as the designated agent of the banking syndicate. As a service fee Semenenko's bank got one fourth of one per cent of the loan ($87,500)—plus, of course, its interest, one per cent above the prime rate of its share of the total loan.
>
> There is conflicting testimony on just how active a role Semenenko took for himself in the day-to-day conduct of Curtis' affairs. One former executive maintains that Culligan "wouldn't push the elevator button without calling Serge." This is disputed, however, by Cary W. Bok. "All he asks is that he be kept informed of what's going on," Bok said recently. "So long as he is given complete information on what management is doing, he's satisfied." Bok had unconcealed admiration for Semenenko.
>
> "Were it not for Semenenko," he said, "Curtis would have been dead. . . . He is a quiet little genius who inspires confidence in everything he touches."[27]

Corporate infighting

Although it appeared in early 1964, with the bank loans refinanced and a modest first quarter profit for Curtis, that Culligan's major problems were over, internal problems were about to erupt that he had not anticipated. These problems were precipitated by Clay Blair, Jr., a Curtis executive who had aspired to Culligan's or Clifford's job.

Blair had come to Curtis in 1959 as assistant managing editor of the *Post* under managing editor Robert Sherrod, Blair's one-time supervisor at the Pentagon when both had worked for *Time-Life*.

When Fuoss, who had replaced Hibbs as editor in December 1961, resigned after four months, Sherrod became editor of the *Post,* with Blair moving up to managing editor. In 1962, Blair had been aware that Curtis was in financial trouble, that MacNeal would go, and that there would be a void which he might be able to fill. In bidding for the presidency, Blair had hoped to gain some leverage from his friendship with Admiral Lewis Strauss, at the time a member of the brokerage firm that was providing the stimulus behind Curtis and Doubleday & Company (book publishers) merger talks. What made the friendship relevant to Blair's ambitions was its implied ability to influence Doubleday.

At the same board meeting during which MacNeal had been fired, Blair had been elected vice president with unspecified responsibilities in the editorial offices of Curtis magazines. Asked by Gould what he would do if elected president of Curtis, Blair had responded with a written report entitled Tomorrow Morning Plan.

> Blair's recommendations were Draconian. For one, he recommended the liquidation of the *Ladies' Home Journal* and *American Home* which were losing several million dollars a year. He recommended selling the Curtis Building in Philadelphia, getting rid of the paper mills, tightening the Curtis Circulation Company, moving everything except printing and distribution to New York. For the *Post* he recommended a deliberate reduction in circulation from 6.5 to 5 million.[28]

Blair recounted that his Tomorrow Morning Plan had upset ex-president Fuller, who was still a power at Curtis as a board member and an executive committee member. Blair attributed his inability to attain the presidency of Curtis to Fuller's opposition. "It was Fuller who had integrated Curtis, bought the paper companies, built the Sharon Hill printing plant. Now he seemed disturbed that I wanted to divest them," Blair recalled.[29]

After Culligan was chosen as president, Blair was placed in the newly created position of editorial director of all Curtis magazines, a position above that of his old boss and mentor, Sherrod. Blair related a conversation between Gould, Culligan, and himself on the day of Culligan's takeover:

> "Culligan," Gould said, "you're Mr. Outside." Then turning to me: "Blair," he said, "you're Mr. Inside." He paced the floor and

puffed on a huge cigar. "Culligan, you bring in the advertising and straighten out the image of this company. Blair, you keep the books, fix the products, and deal with manufacturing and the rest of it." It was an eloquent proposition, and when he finished, Culligan and I took the deal, with Culligan pledging then that "no one will ever come between us." We shook hands all around.[30]

If Blair had believed that he would be Mr. Inside, he was quickly disappointed, for Culligan in effect turned this position over to Clifford.

The conflict between Clifford and Blair came quickly and inevitably. They fought over every one of the technical and financial problems that lie at the heart of corporate power. "During 1963, Clifford got a throttle hold on the company," Blair said later. "He took over circulation, manufacturing, and paper mills, then accounting, personnel, and legal. He brought in three obnoxious lieutenants: Maurice Poppei, controller; Gloria Swett, legal; Sidney Natkin, personnel. By summer, Clifford's control of money and people was so complete that nobody, including me, could hire or fire or give a raise or sign a check without his specific approval."[31]

By January 1964, Blair was refusing to permit any of Clifford's staff on the editorial floors of the Curtis Building in New York. Clifford retaliated by refusing any cooperation of the corporate operations and finance areas that he controlled. The conflict grew to include not only Blair but most of the Curtis editors. Recognizing that action had to be taken, Culligan gave Clifford a $20,000 raise and removed him from his position as executive vice president of finance and operations. Culligan temporarily took over the duties of operations, which consisted mainly of manufacturing, and gave the financial responsibilities to Maurice Poppei, then treasurer.

Changing editorial policy
At the same time he was fighting Clifford, Blair was also solidifying his control over the editorial pages of the Curtis magazines. Two months after becoming editorial director, Blair announced that he was taking over the editorship of the *Post* and that Sherrod would go to India with Norman Rockwell, the *Post* cover artist, to produce a story on Nehru. Blair asserted his control over the

other magazines by immediately firing the editor of the *Ladies' Home Journal* and three members of the *Journal's* art department.

As editor of the *Post,* Blair set out to change the magazine:

> Blair really needed only a few weeks, all in all, to change the entire magazine—not just what it published, photographic covers, investigations and exposés, fiction by celebrities, and raucous editorials, but the way it operated. Instead of letting editors putter along in their departmental specialties, he insisted on getting everyone involved in the continuous uproar. And at the end of these first few weeks, in January of 1963, he sent us all a memorandum: " . . . You are putting out one hell of a fine magazine. The articles are timely, full of significance and exclusivity. The . . . visual aspects have improved tremendously . . . .; [Fiction] could be one of the great breakthroughs in magazine publishing. The final yardstick: We have about six lawsuits pending, meaning we are hitting them where it hurts, with solid, meaningful journalism."[32]

One of the lawsuits was to cost the Curtis Publishing Company over one million dollars. The *Post* had published an exposé of an alleged football fix between coaches Butts of Georgia and Bryant of Alabama. Even though Georgia's attorney general concluded that the evidence "indicates that vital and important information was given about the Georgia team, and that it could have affected the outcome of the game and the margin of points scored,"[33] Butts won his libel suit, and the *Post* settled with Bryant out of court.

Building coalitions against Culligan

During the days of corporate infighting and changing editorial policy, Blair was busy building coalitions against Culligan. He formed an editorial board consisting of the editors of the major Curtis magazines, with the idea "that it might serve as a political tool to offset the tremendous corporate political drives of Culligan and Clifford."[34] Blair also formed an alliance with Marvin Kantor, a former member of Williston and Beane, the brokerage firm that had helped to put Gould and Stewart on the Curtis board in 1962. Kantor joined Curtis early in 1963 as a member of the board of directors and had become chief executive assistant to Culligan in January 1964. Kantor stepped into the power vacuum created by the fight between Blair and Clifford:

Within three months of his arrival at Curtis, Kantor had taken charge of editorial, advertising sales, manufacturing, and just about everything else that interested him. At this point, Culligan was doing his best to portray Curtis as a company that had been saved, a company that had already moved from paralyzing losses into a state of profit by the end of 1963. Once Kantor got access to the ledgers, however, he began expressing suspicions of Culligan's optimistic predictions. In March, Curtis neared the limits of its bank credit, and Kantor brought in some new cash by selling Curtis' one, halfhearted venture in book publishing, a one-third interest in Bantam Books, for $1.9 million. Culligan got the board to agree to new investments in Curtis' printing and paper plants, but Kantor, after looking into the plants, began arguing that they should be sold, just as Blair's group had said two years earlier. And when Kantor checked Culligan's advertising forecasts for the *Post,* he decided that they were going not up but down (in actual fact, *Post* ad revenues for the first six months of 1964 eventually proved to be 17 per cent lower than similar revenues for 1963). All in all, Kantor told Blair, Joe Culligan was leading Curtis not to salvation but to ruin. The company would again lose heavily during 1964, Kantor said—perhaps another $10 million. Blair was appalled.[35]

Blair and Kantor joined forces early in 1964 in an attempt to gain the presidency and control of Curtis. They presented findings of mismanagement to individual members of the board, rallied the editorial departments behind their bid, and even met with a dozen of the company's leading editors and publishing executives to plot Culligan's overthrow. Largely at Kantor's insistence, Blair was elevated to the Curtis board in February 1964, replacing Stewart.

Culligan received a temporary reprieve from the Blair and Kantor onslaught in April 1964, when it was announced that Texas Gulf Sulphur had discovered major deposits of copper, zinc, and silver, valued at up to $2 billion, just 300 feet from 110,000 acres owned by a Canadian subsidiary of Curtis, the T. S. Woolings Company. Immediately Curtis stock rose from $6 to $19.25 per share.

Although the ore find promised a degree of financial solvency for Curtis, by Labor Day 1964 Curtis's losses for the year were predicted to be $7 million and eventually would reach $14 million. The company's working capital position was also dangerously close to the $27.5 million minimum level set by the banks. Given the discrepancy between Culligan's "turn around" predictions earlier in the year and the company's actual financial position, Blair and Kantor made their move, armed with a proposal for saving the company and with a letter signed by most of the editors asking that Culligan be stripped of his executive power.

Confrontation—an "ancient tribunal"

A confrontation took place between Blair, Kantor, and Culligan at an ensuing board meeting. Otto Friedrich, in *Decline and Fall,* discussed the composition of this tribunal:

> Who, then, controlled the Curtis board of directors? Unlike many boards, which are acquiescent allies of the reigning management, the Curtis directors were divided into a number of factions, which not only were hostile to one another but scarcely even comprehended one another. The chairman was Joe Culligan, who counted on the support of his own appointees—Clifford and Poppei—but their loyalties were less than certain. Clifford, having been demoted from the Number Two position by Culligan, apparently believed that he himself would be a more efficient president than Culligan. Poppei's loyalties seemed to belong partly to Culligan, partly to Clifford, partly to the discipline of the accountant's profession. On the insurgent side, Blair spoke only for himself and the editors. Kantor had made himself an ally of Blair's but still had ties to the stock interests that brought him to the board in the first place. The most ambiguous of all these new directors was Milton Gould, once the attorney for Kantor, once the discoverer of Culligan. Gould was also a partner in the law firm of Gallop, Climenko & Gould, and since the *Post* alone paid him more than $600,000 a year for legal expenses, Gould had a natural interest in this aspect of Curtis.
>
> Since none of the main antagonists could create a majority, their conflicts served as a kind of ballet staged for the amusement of the old board members, who represented a plurality of the stock, and who retained a veto over any attempts to save the corporation. Of these old board members, the basic group was known as "the family," which owned 32 per cent of all common stock and officially consisted of two people: Mary Louise Curtis Bok Zimbalist, then aged eighty-eight, the daughter of Cyrus H.K. Curtis, who occasionally was wheeled into critical board meetings by her Negro servants; and her son, Cary W. Bok, aged fifty-nine, who was in rather poor health but periodically came to Philadelphia, dressed in the old khakis that he liked to wear at

his country place in Maine. (There was another son, Curtis Bok, who might have helped to save the company, but that was not to be. Lorimer had denounced him a generation earlier as "that damned Bolshevik," and things were arranged so that Curtis Bok would never have a voice in the operation of the Curtis magazines. He went on to become a distinguished judge, and his son became dean of Harvard Law School). As for Mrs. Zimbalist, let us remember her by a story told by a retired executive. Once a year, according to this chronicler, Mrs. Zimbalist would engage in exactly the same colloquy with Walter Deane Fuller, who was then president of the corporation. "She would very respectfully ask Mr. Fuller that her salary as a director be doubled. Very gravely he would reply that economic conditions were such that this could not be done. She would thank him and sit down. Of course, her salary was only one dollar. But she and Mr. Fuller seemed to enjoy the byplay."

The rest of the old directors tended to support "the family," to the extent that they could determine what the family wanted, but Mrs. Zimbalist and her son rarely attended board meetings during these declining years—refusing either to sell the stock they had held all their lives or to exercise the authority that these stocks gave them. The old directors were thus left to decide matters for themselves, and for this, they were of an age and distinction that would have done credit to the United States Senate. The most senior of them, of course, was Walter Deane Fuller, the tiny, bald gentleman of 82, who had joined the accounting department of Curtis in 1908 and worked his way up to be president and board chairman for more than 25 years. Next came Albert Linton, 77, retired president of the Provident Life Insurance Company of Philadelphia and now chairman of the board's executive committee, assigned to deal with the accusations. Then there was Walter S. Franklin, aged 80, retired president of the Pennsylvania Railroad; and Ellsworth Bunker, aged 70, former president of the United Sugar Company, former U.S. ambassador to India, former president of the American Red Cross; Moreau D. Brown, aged 61, partner in the private banking firm of Brown Brothers, Harriman; Harry C. Mills, aged 63, retired vice president of J.C. Penney; and Curtis Barkes, aged 58, executive vice president of United Air Lines.

Once the managerial civil war had broken out, it soon became apparent that this board, this ultimate court of appeals, knew relatively little about the Curtis Publishing Company and was quite bewildered by the problems that were being placed before it. More than half of the directors were over 60—"Why," someone asked Clemenceau, "are the presidents of France always octogenarians?"—and most of them, except for the actual combatants, were weary of combat. Thus, when Blair and Culligan wanted to accuse each other of guilt for Curtis' condition, they had to carry their case before this ancient tribunal, which, in consenting to hear the arguments, denied that the ultimate guilt was its own.

The result of the confrontation was the immediate dismissal of Blair and Kantor on October 30, 1964, and the eventual removal of Culligan from the presidency. Culligan's removal was announced after a meeting of several of the directors at Bok's apartment in Philadelphia. Culligan, not allowed to attend, found out a year later that Clifford and Poppei had threatened to resign if Culligan remained as president.

Rumors began to circulate as to whom the next president of Curtis would be. Reportedly the job had been offered to Newton Minow, chairman of the FCC under Kennedy, and to Ed Miller, publisher of *McCall's;* both turned the position down.

THE CLIFFORD PRESIDENCY: *1964-1968*

Apparently the board's difficulty in finding a new chief executive and the banks' increasing concern over Curtis's financial position created a situation Clifford could move into. Clifford, supported by the second most senior board member, Linton, made a bid for the presidency and was accepted in December 1964.

Once in power, Clifford fired several editors, demanded that the magazines cut their budgets by 40 per cent, appointed acting editor William Emerson editor of the *Post,* and changed the *Post* into a biweekly publication.

Worried about the $37.3 million that Curtis owed the banks, Clifford sold a paper mill in Pennsylvania for $10.3 million and used $8 million for debt reduction. He also negotiated $24 million in cash from Texas Gulf Sulphur for mining rights on Curtis's Canadian timberlands and utilized the money to pay off bank debts. During 1965, Curtis's assets decreased from $112.6 million to $86.9 million with liabilities decreasing from $103 million to $68.4 million. Curtis lost $3.4 million in 1965 and showed an operating profit of $347,000 in 1966, the first profit of the decade. Otto Friedrich described the method by which Clifford produced this profit:

> The technique was simple. The conscientious employees worked hard at their jobs, because that was their nature, and then the supreme command ordered everyone to cut costs until the year's activities came out even on the balance sheets. This was not simply a matter of operating expenses. It was a philosophy of life. It was a perfect example, however, of the cost accountants' system of doing business—to cut, shrink, tighten, until we reached the theoretical goal of not producing anything at all. Or, as Emerson put it, "It's like being nibbled to death by ducks."[36]

The nibbling apparently would not save Curtis. The company recorded a loss of $4.8 million for 1967, which Clifford blamed on an advertising decline "due primarily to softened national economic conditions and costly strikes in key industries.[37] The company's cash position during this period became dangerously low: "As of the end of the year, current assets had declined by more than $6 million, liabilities had increased by more than $1 million, and actual cash in hand had dropped from $10,102,000 at the start of 1967 to $425,000 at the start of 1968. Obviously, for a company that was operating on a budget of almost $130 million a year, a cash supply of $425,000 was virtually no cash at all."[38]

The low cash position necessitated a quick cash inflow. Clifford attempted to sell the old Curtis Building in Philadelphia and offered CBS Curtis's magazines for $15 million, provided CBS gave Curtis a printing and distribution contract. CBS reportedly was amazed, since they had just done a study on Curtis that indicated the magazines alone would earn $10 million a year without the other Curtis overhead.

ACKERMAN TAKES OVER

Into this precarious financial position, with the banks reportedly pushing for a management change, stepped Martin Ackerman, who was quickly pressed into service as Curtis's next president. Ackerman, age 36 and a former lawyer, was currently head of Perfect Film & Chemical Corporation, a conglomerate he had pushed from sales of $20 million in 1962 to $100 million in 1964 through a series of acquisitions.

Ackerman related the origin of his interest in Curtis and also the events of a special meeting of the board in April 1968 that led to his entry into Curtis management:

> J.M. Clifford, then president of Curtis, reported a proposal which I had made under which Perfect Film & Chemical Corporation, which I headed, would arrange for a $5 million loan to Curtis. This loan was to be secured and guaranteed, and would give Perfect Film a chance to see whether the combinations of the activities of the two corporations made any sense. The proposal was discussed at length, along with a number of alternate proposals for obtaining the immediate capital needed by the company. Later in the afternoon, Milton Gould, a director, told the Board that I had informed him that the Perfect proposal was subject to withdrawal if not accepted then and there at the meeting. Accompanied by former governor Alfred Driscoll, another director, I was invited to attend the board meeting for about twenty minutes.
>
> After further discussion, my proposal was approved and I was elected a regular director, along with Eugene Mason, Perfect's attorney. Clifford was voted out of the presidency of Curtis and elected chairman of the Board of Directors. I was made president in his place.[39]

Ackerman began his presidency in April 1968 by arranging a two-month extension of all overdue bank loans and outlining a plan to save the *Post*. Ackerman announced that the *Post*'s circulation would be cut from 6.8 million to 3 million and that the *Post* would be promoted "as a magazine of class, not mass."[40]

In August 1968, Ackerman issued a report on the financial position at Curtis for the first half of 1968. A loss of $7 million on revenues of $58 million was reported, compared with a loss of $370,000 on revenues of $63 million for the first half of the previous year. He also disclosed that Curtis's bank loans of $13.2 million had been taken over by Perfect Film from the Semenenko group at an interest rate of 1 per cent above the prime rate with maturity on demand.

During his first six months at Curtis, while liquidating part of the Curtis empire, Ackerman also worked incessantly at the *Post* offices in New York, developing schemes to save the magazine, and attempting to write editorials and a column (much to the dismay of the editors). But with increased losses for 1968 becoming more evident, Ackerman moved out of the Curtis offices into a townhouse he had purchased. Friedrich describes the changes that ensued:

> An environment not only expresses a man's ambitions; it also changes his perspectives. The Ackerman who sat enthroned in the townhouse was not the same man who bustled in and out of offices on our editorial floor. Now, he received us only by appointment, negotiated through one of his two secretaries, and we appeared not as the managers of our own domain but as emissaries to his castle. And in the act of physical withdrawal from the Curtis Building, he inevitably withdrew, to some extent, from his intense physical involvement in the day-to-day problems of the *Post*. This was quite understandable, too, for in six months of hard labor, his involvement had really accomplished relatively little. And so, as all executives like to fall back on the specialties that originally brought them their success, Ackerman in his townhouse began to revert to what he had been before he ever came to Curtis, a financier, a maneuverer of stocks and corporations, an expert at mergers and acquisitions, a banker and millionaire.

As a financier and maneuverer of stocks and corporations, Ackerman reportedly was a master. For example, ostensibly to raise cash for Curtis, he sold the *Ladies' Home Journal* and *American Home* to Downe Communications, Inc., for 100,000 shares of Downe stock valued at $5.4 million, a price low enough to "evoke the image of a fire sale."[41] He later had Curtis turn the Downe stock over to Perfect Film for a $4.5 million reduction in the Curtis loans and then sold the stock privately through a Wall Street firm for $5 million.

> The same day that his sale of the Downe shares was disclosed, it was announced that Perfect Film was spending $9 million to buy from Gulf & Western two Desilu film studios in Culver City, California, the 14-acre Culver Studio and the 29-acre Culver Backlot, both of which were being used by Paramount and various television producers.[42]

But for all Ackerman's financial wizardry, by early 1969 he apparently had neither the ability nor the desire to save the *Post*. The predicted losses for the *Post* for 1969 were between $3.7 million and $7 million, based on the trend of decreasing advertising revenue.

Utilizing this financial data as justification, Ackerman, who six months before had stated that as long as he was at Curtis "there would not be a last issue of the *Post*,"[43] announced the end:

> No other decision is possible in view of the sizable predicted losses which continued publication would have generated. Quite simply, this is an example of a new management which could not reduce expenses nor generate sales and income fast enough to halt mounting losses. . . . Having refinanced the Saturday Evening Post Company with $15 million in new capital, I assured directors and stockholders of the company that regardless of my own personal feelings, if we could not return a profit we would have to shut down the *Post*.[44]

The reaction from the stockholders was immediate. Philip Kalodner, a young Philadelphia lawyer and representative of minority stockholders, filed suit against Ackerman for alleged illegal, oppressive, and fraudulent action that had wasted and misapplied more than $45 million of Curtis assets. The trustees of the Cyrus Curtis estate also began an assault against Ackerman:

> They, too, accused Ackerman of dissipating the Curtis assets, and they publicly demanded that he resign from the presidency by noon on the coming Saturday, February 8. They also demanded the resignations of his closest allies on the board of directors. The trustees were vague in their accusations, citing only "conflict of interest," but Cary Bok told a reporter who telephoned his home in Camden, Maine: "That company is in such a damn mess that it's time we got into it—don't you think?"[45]

POSTSCRIPT

In March 1969, at the next board meeting, Ackerman resigned as president in favor of G.B. McCombs, who had recently been promoted to senior vice president, after being with Curtis since 1930. Kalodner, who held only 100 shares of stock, was named vice president, director, and a member of the executive committee "in return for agreement not to press his lawsuit against the company."[46]

McCombs lasted five weeks as president; the position then went to Kalodner after some stormy board meetings:

> The board itself, depleted by the latest resignations of Ackerman, Gould, and McCombs, now consisted of only six members (one of whom was serving as U. S. ambassador to Saigon). Three of these had been allies of the departed Milton Gould, and they all favored a petition of bankruptcy. "But I spoke up against them," Kalodner said. "In fact, I filibustered against them." The board meeting went on for five hours, and then ended inconclusively. And the day after the crisis, Kalodner simply decreed himself to be, if not the president of Curtis, then "chief executive officer." Once again, Curtis was without a president.
>
> The deadlock lasted through most of April, and then, on April 24, it was broken long enough for Kalodner, like yet another Roman emperor, to become president. In that capacity, he offered repeated invitations to unhappy trustees to "join" him in salvaging the wreckage of the company, but the trustees had no intention of collaborating in Kalodner's presidency. Kalodner alone, therefore, had the responsibility of announcing that the Curtis operating loss during the Ackerman year of 1968 had been $18.3 million. He also had to admit that the Curtis contract to print the *Ladies' Home Journal* and *American Home* for Downe Communications would run out at the end of June. "The contract," said the *Wall Street Journal*, "is practically the only ongoing venture Curtis has left."[47]

Kalodner and the trustees spent the early weeks of May 1969 mailing rival proxy statements to the stockholders in anticipation of the May 21 stockholders' meeting. At the meeting, the trustees won nine seats on the board of directors, and a representative of the trustees, Arthur Murphy, past president of *McCall's*, became president and chairman of the board. A short time later, Murphy dropped the presidency, and W.J. MacIntosh, a lawyer for the board, took over as acting chief executive officer.

In May 1970, the trustees sold the 700,000 shares of Curtis stock they had controlled since 1933 to Beurt SerVaas, a self-made millionaire from the Midwest, who took over control as president and principal stockholder of Curtis. "I came into this company to preside over its death, but instead I decided I could save it," he said. "I'm the first person since Cyrus Curtis himself who's been both the chief executive and the chief stockholder, and so I've had the kind of authority you have to have in order to make vital decisions." Throughout the summer and fall SerVaas sold all the manufacturing companies that Curtis owned, including a printing plant and a paper mill, decreased the overall size of its staff from 9,000 people to 100, and "reduced its voluminous debts to zero."

It was the burden of these financial responsibilities that prevented the company from reaping profits, SerVaas explained.

> "Now we're no longer in manufacturing and real estate," he added, "we're just a little publishing company that puts out magazines, and for the first time in years we're no longer in the red."
>
> SerVaas has decided that the *Post* will return to publication as a "200-page quarterly directed toward the 'middle American.'"
>
> "Toward the end the *Post* became worldly and sophisticated and hard-nosed in an attempt to rejuvenate itself," Mr. SerVaas said, "but it failed, and what we intend to do now should make everyone happy. We're not going to print any more exposé or muckraking articles; we're going to concentrate on writing about those institutions and mores in contemporary America that are good for America."[48]

COMMENTARY

In the introduction to this case, I suggested it did not require the mental acuity of a genius to understand the problems of the *Saturday Evening Post*. Changes in strategy were needed to overcome the debilitating effects of loss of advertising revenue combined with an increase in costs, many of which were attributable to the policy of vertical integration. Marion Harper of Interpublic, a leading advertising conglomerate, assembled a task force that expeditiously arrived at a new strategic plan to offer Matthew J. Culligan, the new president. The Harper task force's plan resembled in many respects the plan that Clay Blair, Jr. had proposed as "Tomorrow Morning Plan." Blair's plan was his campaign platform, prepared at the invitation of Milton Gould, a director, who asked Blair what he would do if he were named president.

Both plans would have cut back circulation, divested some of the magazine properties to raise cash, and sold off printing plants and other fixed assets. Essentially, it was a call to return to the magazine business without the overload of vertical integration. The assumption of the new strategy, implicit in the summaries shown in the case study, was the reconceptualization of the business. This reconceptualization was much more than a sound economic analysis of the *Post*'s failing strategy. It was also a dramatic alteration in the system of beliefs that had taken control of the self-image as well as the corporate image of the Curtis Publishing Company. It was undoubtedly this alteration that infuriated Walter Fuller and led him to veto Blair's election to the presidency.

There are at least two ways of looking at this "resistance to change" that fairly characterized Curtis's leadership since the onset of the depression in the 1930s. First is the question of how individuals acquire self-esteem in the power structure of corporations. The second is the deeper psychological issue of how ideals become fixed in the minds of successions of leadership, and become totally insensitive to reality and the dictates of good business sense.

Self-esteem is to the psyche what oxygen is to the bloodstream. Without it there is no life. Therefore, it should not surprise us to learn that threats to self-esteem will produce various protective reactions.

When a individual accrues self-esteem through his own talents and hard work, the threats result in a protective reaction that is really quite useful. For example, suppose a talented individual begins to observe that what he had customarily done is no longer working for him. Does he keep repeating the formerly successful acts, or does he stop and begin to appraise the causes of unsatisfactory results? The tendency to repeat is powerful, but the wise person stops, looks, listens, and thinks. The protective reaction in this case is to turn inward and take a passive instead of an active stance. If the thought process during this passive mode is creative, some experiments will become clear and a return to activity will yield results. New questions will be asked, new data will appear, and new insights will result.

To repeat strategies that have worked in the past without adequate reflection suggests protective measures that deny the facts of experience: old strategies no longer work. This denial becomes deadly because as time goes on, the costs associated with change increase and the potential returns diminish.

This analysis of self-esteem and resistance to change will not satisfactorily explain why authority failed in the Curtis Publishing Company. The missing ingredient in this case is the absence of individuals who relied on their own talents and resources for the accrual of self-esteem. It appears as though self-esteem in Curtis grew as a result of belonging to the organization, gaining power in it, and managing to hold the power by perpetuating the beliefs and ideals that inherently defined the Curtis Publishing Company and its flagship publication, the *Saturday Evening Post*. I suggest that this syndrome, which I shall call the pathology of membership in large corporations, is a malaise found in many large organizations that once were great and suffered decline. In the United States, General Motors comes to mind, along with once stellar corporations in the steel, railroad, electronics, and other large industries. Indeed, IBM, affectionately known as the "big blue," may well be in the midst of this syndrome of pathology of membership. AT&T may well have been saved from this fate by the intervention of Judge Harold Green, who forced the Bell System to dissolve into independent operating companies, regionally defined, leaving AT&T with its long distance business, Bell Labs, and Western Electric. The recent raid on NCR demonstrates the change that occurred in AT&T. Whether you approve or disapprove of hostile takeovers as a matter of principle, you surely will agree that for AT&T to engage in that maneuver to strengthen its position in the computer and communication businesses was a change of considerable magnitude in a once staid organization known ambivalently as "Ma Bell."

The accrual of self-esteem through membership depends upon the success of the organization and its capacity to distribute rewards to its members. The success and the rewards induce individuals to stay in the organization and to compete for higher status, which in turn mean greater self-esteem and higher rewards. Underneath this continuing attraction is an indoctrination into the beliefs and ideals that once accounted for the success of the business.

The *Saturday Evening Post* as conceived by Cyrus Curtis and his editor, George Horace Lorimer, was a product for a rural America, steeped in the values of the Protestant Ethic, conservative in its outlook, and implicitly rejecting new immigrants and the pluralistic culture America had grown into. The *Post* was more than a product, a vehicle of communication. It symbolized a dominant view of America, even to the designation of boys who carried and delivered the *Post* as youngsters who believed in America and the opportunities it afforded to those who worked and saved. It was a true descendant of Ben Franklin, who was the prototype for sociologist Max Weber's treatise on the Protestant work ethic. Curtis prospered as the representative, spokesman, and symbol of this New World, just as the *Post* served as the reinforcer of the values deep in the psyche of the dominant culture of America. So long as it was the dominant culture, the *Post* was the favored medium for advertisers to reach their market with the message, particularly of the automobile, heralding the continuing prosperity of the nation. But America was undergoing change.

The depression of the 1930s raised a new challenge to the political body. As the promise of infinite prosperity faded into the despair of unemployment, Americans questioned the old values of unfettered free enterprise in business and laissez-faire in government. Lorimer's attacks on President Franklin Delano Roosevelt culminated in the debacle of the 1936 presidential election, which led to Lorimer's retirement.

It would appear as though this debacle would have jolted Curtis's management to examine itself, leading to a reconceptualization of its keystone product. From a purely objective point of view, the *Post* was a product, nothing more nor less, just as the Model T in Henry Ford's time was a product capable of performing functions in a variety of guises. But as with Henry Ford, the *Post* management could not alter their conception of the product. It was more than a product. It had come to symbolize their membership and their source of self-esteem.

There were superficial changes in the *Post*. But these changes did not alter the basic conception of the *Post* as a carrier and indoctrinator into the values of a conservative, dominantly Republican nation that would tolerate, but hardly call its own, the new immigrants.

The 1936 decision to appoint Walter D. Fuller to succeed Lorimer as chief executive officer, and the succession that followed in 1950 when Fuller became chairman and his protégé, Robert Mac-Neal, became president and chief executive officer, demonstrated clearly how deeply the board of directors and top management had incorporated the dominant and traditional image of the *Post*. The product had achieved a permanence reflected in the decision to integrate backwards with the construction of the *Post*'s own printing plant, and the purchase of paper mills and forest land. The appointment of MacNeal, the designer of a new folding machine, indicated the track along which the power structure pursued its collective self-image.

Why not pay attention to environment, objectify the product, and reconceptualize the business one is in? To say that people protect their source of self-esteem, while valid, is only a partial insight into the important question of resistance to change. Pure rationality dictates that to preserve power and self-esteem one *should* pay careful attention to markets and anticipate trends in order to preserve, if not enhance, competitive position. There must be more to the problem of resistance to change than the preservation of power and self-esteem would suggest.

Let us put aside for the moment the possibility that individuals selected to head corporations from within may be too narrow in their perspective and simply lack the intellectual reach to look at the world around them and draw conclusions. In the same vein, we should put aside the distinct possibility that managers become risk averse as they stay in an organization and move up the hierarchy. It appears too easy to encounter the error of omission rather than the error of commission. To act is to risk being proved wrong. In the case of failure to act, chances are that the one responsible for failing to act will have long been out of office. Who is to know, and how will accountability be reckoned? Furthermore, as one achieves office in an organization such as Curtis, a sense of rectitude takes over, as though the organization and its products have been designated as the preserver of values and ideals. It takes remarkable objectivity to alter course and embark on new strategies.

The key to change is objectivity—the ability to look at the world as it is, to apply imagination in reaching conclusions, and to gain insight into where the world is heading. This objectivity is not simply a function of intellect. It is a state of mind in which a fair degree of narcissism is an essential quality. This narcissism is not borrowed from the organization and from membership. It is a quality generated within the individual. It belongs to him or her and to no one else.

The Curtis Publishing Company was organization enmeshed in ideals. These ideals became transformed into the politics of the organization. Simply put, the likelihood of anyone who was not a true believer ever achieving power was, as they say on the street, slim to none. Lorimer chose Fuller and Fuller chose Mac-Lean, all true believers, although the last two named came up via the operations route, unlike Lorimer, the editor. Yet Lorimer understood they were believers. Ask yourself what chance this organization had to change after 1936, with this combination of strong believers in the ideals of the organization, and little affinity, given their experience, with the abstract worlds of communication, ideas, and entertainment? Of course using hindsight we can say that passing up the chance to buy CBS and ABC was the height of stupidity. But the systematic quality of these errors indicates that the judgment is not too harsh. What the power holders actually did in building printing plants and buying paper mills testifies to the strength of their ties to the ideals of Curtis. It was as though Fuller and Mac-Lean in turn testified to the belief that America was the *Saturday Evening Post,* and that the *Post* was the guardian of an America that no longer existed, if indeed it existed at all.

Curtis needed new leadership and the new leadership needed objectivity. To transform this individual objectivity into a collective culture required an act of symbolic patricide. In killing the father, metaphorically speaking, the hold of these antiquated images of the corporation, its products and markets, its goals and aspirations, would have been expunged. The killing of the father, or fathers in the form of the collective memories and myths of Cyrus Curtis and his original son, George Horace Lorimer, was the central function of new leadership. The story of the *Post* following the selection of Matthew Culligan as its leader is a story of missed opportunity. There was new blood on the board, and despite its unwieldy size and attachment to the "family," the shareholders along with their representatives on the board were awaiting leadership while remaining mired in their habituated passivity.

Why did Culligan miss the opportunity? With an immobilized board of directors, he could have seized the initiative, dominated the board and his organization, and used this consolidation of power to implement the strategy that Marion Harper and his Interpublic brain trust had designed for his accession to the chief executive's job. When Matthew Culligan permitted his inherited bureaucracy to shoot down the Harper plan with traditional objections, he made it known that he had little understanding of and taste for power. He then became the victim of his own misperceived position, and took flight in the superficially heroic effort to bring in advertising revenue. We shall return presently to this flight into activity.

Culligan's misconception of his position offers some interesting insights into the play of power in corporate life. Had he realized the stalemate that existed in Curtis's management, including the board of directors, had he understood their abject dependency upon him as their new CEO, he would have been free to implement the program Marion Harper provided. He seemed to display little realization of the power that was his for the taking. Furthermore, he had little conviction to establish himself as the CEO. For example, if he seriously believed Harper's program offered the correct strategy, it would have been impossible for his holdover subordinates to shoot the program down with such feeble efforts. Culligan lacked conviction. It appears he had little taste for power and little capacity to internalize his power and project it in a dramatic, and effective, parting from the past. His new strategy, indeed it should have become *his* despite the authorship of Marion Harper, was the weapon he needed to expunge the stultifying hold that the images of Cyrus Curtis and George Horace Lorimer maintained over the minds of corporate executives and Curtis's habitual way of doing business.

To have been assertive would have required considerable aggression, available to Culligan free of guilt and attached to a rational program designed to set the corporation on a fruitful path. The strategy was there, but the aggression was absent. Perhaps another way of putting the issue is to consider the nature of assertiveness and "the will to power." These inner qualities of leaders usually accrue under the guidance of parents, teachers, and later authority figures. To gain personal comfort with responsibility and the willingness to use power, the superego must be tamed so extraneous and guilt-laden concerns do not intrude on the exercise of legitimate authority. Another quality that facilitates the willingness to use power in the service of a valid strategy is the relative independence of the power holder. Put another way, neediness destroys effectiveness. The ability to walk away from a position when offered is the best test of this quality of independence.

The case provides two interesting examples of independence. Ed Miller, the publisher of *McCall's*, turned down the job of succeeding Culligan as CEO when the conditions he laid down were not met. Upon learning that the bankers would not cooperate in a moratorium on debt servicing and bringing John Kluge of Metromedia to take charge of finances, Miller said, "To hell with it," and walked away from the job. Earlier, Newton Minnow, former chairman of the Federal Communications Commission, also refused the job, but for undeclared reasons. To need a power position to feed one's ego is hardly a propitious reason to undertake a demanding job.

Throughout the story of the demise of the Curtis Publishing Company runs a discouraging current of passivity and irresponsibility on the part of the board of directors. Superficially, there was never any doubt, objectively, of the board's power. The unwillingness of the board to coalesce suggests an absence of leadership. We have already considered the position of executive board members, who were so tied psychologically to the past. But what of the nonexecutive board members, including the heirs of Cyrus Curtis? What is the explanation of their passivity and seeming confusion? Unlike the executive directors, the board members received little narcissistic gratification from their position. Furthermore, the family members were aware that their stake in the corporation was disappearing, slowly at first, but then precipitously. They had everything to gain in stepping forward aggressively to demand effective leadership. Perhaps they, too, were irrevocably bound to the images of the past in the legacies of Curtis and Lorimer. Perhaps, too, they were unable to muster the aggression it would have taken to provide forceful leadership. It is all too common for generations born to wealth to become passive and lacking in the drive to achieve.

Another possible explanation comes to mind. I would speculate that the failure of the enterprise might have been foretold in the family's latent hostilities to the generations that preceded them. While we have no evidence to hold on to, the clue offered us in Curtis Bok's break with the family is highly suggestive of a potential for rebellion and the need to separate from the family's ultra-conservative position. Curtis Bok was Cyrus Curtis's grandson, who became an outstanding judge. The undercurrents in families and in family businesses are difficult to exaggerate.

Individuals who inherit wealth often carry peculiar ideas about where their riches came from, the permanence of what they own, and ambivalent attitudes toward their forebears as well as themselves. They often become suspicious of others, and more frequently than not, develop compulsions to protect themselves against hidden dangers. They will go to absurd lengths to make sure that the government takes as little as possible from their storehouse of wealth. They hate paying taxes, leading them to make foolish investments, not for economic value, but for the prospect of sheltering their income and wealth against taxation.

Little evidence is available in the *Post* case to instruct us in the family's attitudes toward their inherited wealth, and whether these attitudes, mostly unconscious, played a part in their passivity and near wish to see the enterprise go down. Yet the content of power relations in this story is more than suggestive of magical thinking, from the seemingly harmless ritual in which Mrs. Zimbalist would request an increase in her fees, from one dollar to two dollars, only to be told ritualistically that the company could not afford the increase, to the belief in the invulnerability of the *Post* as the symbol of America, and, finally, to the rush to magic in Matthew Culligan's barnstorming to sell advertising. The presence of magical thinking holds the potential for causing great harm to corporations. The lesson the *Post* story teaches is the vulnerability of power holders, individually and collectively, to the destructive force of magical thinking. The antidote, of course, is the presence of one or more leaders with the personal confidence and courage to look at the world as it is and to act according to the opportunities reality presents. This state of mind requires, above all, objectivity in positioning oneself as a leader and in examining the state of the corporation, unfettered by wishful attachments to symbols of past greatness.

Endnotes—Chapter 17

1. Otto Friedrich, *Decline and Fall* (New York: Harper and Row, 1970), p. 449.

2. Joseph Goulden, *The Curtis Caper* (New York: G.P. Putnam's Sons, 1965), p. 22.

3. Ibid.

4. John Tebbel, *George Horace Lorimer and the Saturday Evening Post*. (New York: Doubleday and Company, Inc., 1948), pp. 23-36.

5. Goulden, *Curtis Caper,* pp. 25-26.

6. Ibid., p. 32.

7. Friedrich, *Decline and Fall,* p. 10.

8. Goulden, *Curtis Caper,* p. 45.

9. Ibid., p. 71.

10. Ibid., p. 15.

11. Goulden, *Curtis Caper,* p. 48.

12. Ibid., p. 49.

13. Ibid., p. 51.

14. Ibid.

15. Friedrich, *Decline and Fall,* p. 12.

16. Ibid., p. 13.

17. Ibid., p. 17.

18. Ibid., pp. 17-18.

19. Goulden, *Curtis Caper,* pp. 123-124.

20. Culligan, *Curtis Culligan Story,* p. 35.

21. Ibid., p. 60.

22. Ibid., pp. 60-61.

23. Friedrich, *Decline and Fall,* p. 64.

24. Culligan, *Curtis Culligan Story*, pp. 78-79.

25. Ibid., p. 64.

26. Goulden, *Curtis Caper,* p. 157.

27. Ibid., p. 163.

28. Friedrich, *Decline and Fall,* p. 32.

29. Ibid., p. 33.

30. Ibid., pp. 33-34.

31. Ibid., p. 50.

32. Ibid., p. 40.

33. Ibid., p. 461.

34. Ibid., p. 50.

35. Ibid., p. 76.

36. Ibid., p. 270.

37. Ibid., p. 307.

38. Ibid., pp. 307-308.

39. Martin Ackerman, *The Curtis Affair* (Los Angeles: Nash Publishing, 1970), pp. 8-9.

40. Friedrich, *Decline and Fall,* p. 328.

41. Ibid., p. 417.

42. Ibid.

43. *Newsweek* (May 20, 1968): 70.

44. Friedrich, *Decline and Fall,* p. 449.

45. Ibid., p. 466.

46. Ibid., p. 469.

47. Ibid., pp. 472-473.

48. *New York Times,* 6 Nov. 1970.

CONTROL THROUGH PSYCHODRAMA— WATERFORD COLLEGE

The case of Waterford College is indeed a study of an organization in crisis. The crisis revolved around a simple fact: Waterford was in financial trouble. It generally spent all of its income, sometimes even going into debt. The college relied on tuition for its income, and about 80 per cent of its expenditures were paid with tuition revenues, while the balance came from grants of one sort or another.

In an age of inflation the higher nominal costs needed to run the college meant that Waterford had to increase tuition to meet its budget. As tuition rose, Waterford moved closer to pricing itself out of its market. In short, the organizational crisis at Waterford really questioned its ability to survive. The issue of survival was not distant. It was immediate and omnipresent in the consciousness of its faculty, administration, students, trustees, and alumnae.

The story of Waterford's crisis centered on its chief executive officer, Rupert Harrison. Dr. Harrison came to Waterford College in 1960, at age 42. Eighteen years later, as Harrison neared age 60, he yet another time called attention to himself in his renewed definition of Waterford as an organization in crisis. The problems of the sixties and seventies had remained unresolved in the eighties: Waterford needed money. How Harrison faced the money issue tells us a great deal about him as a leader and as a man.

A good question to keep in the back of your mind as you read the Waterford College case is this: How effective was Dr. Harrison in his job as president of Waterford College?

In reflecting on this question, bear in mind that many students of organizations believe that the question of leadership is one of situational analysis. Indeed, you will discover that Rupert Harrison himself believed that the situation determined the "style" of leadership. He called this belief "contingency theory," and went to great lengths to praise contingency theory to his colleagues, as well as the casewriter.

While the situation has a bearing on results, my conviction is the man or woman makes the job. They try to make the situation work for them, but in the end character will tell the story. While the case tells us little about Dr. Harrison's personal history (or how his character had evolved), the narrative makes clear what Harrison was like as a man, even though we don't know how he became the man he portrayed to himself, to his work associates, and ultimately to us as readers of his story.

Without intending to be patronizing, I should make it clear that I believe Harrison was a decent as well as a highly intelligent man. So don't go looking for lapses in ethical standards, at least as these standards are conventionally understood. He had a tough job in a changing social and economic scene. For his entire tenure as president of Waterford College, there were serious doubts as to whether the world needed his institution. In earlier times, the world very much needed a place like Waterford College (and there were many like it in the United States) to enroll intelligent young women of immigrant parents, and to prepare them for teaching in elementary schools. Young women today have far more alternatives to consider than waiting out their prospects for marriage in a teacher's college, a normal school as teachers' colleges were once called. But these newer and seemingly more glamorous career opportunities for women have not diminished the need for gifted teachers to enlist young students in the public schools of America to study, become literate, understand arithmetic and later mathematics, and to launch themselves into a productive life. The dismal statistics of declining test scores, high dropout rates, and low motivation, particularly in the urban schools, warn us that maybe we need Waterfords after all. And perhaps instead of funding them with increasingly costly tuitions, we should figure out how to finance and carry out the important missions assigned to these dying and beleaguered institutions.

Against this background of issues facing the president of Waterford College, evaluate his performance. After you have taken a stab at that piece of work, you will be in a reasonably good position to deepen the argument about person and situation, and the relevance of contingency theory to the understanding of what makes organizations run.

WATERFORD COLLEGE

In 1977 the administrators and faculty of Waterford College, an independent teacher's college in the northeast, took time for an intensive reassessment of the college's chances for survival.

The president of the college, Dr. Rupert Harrison, prepared a report for the trustees in which he reviewed his 18 years of tenure as president and presented them with his current thinking as to what Waterford's mission and goals should be for the next five years. His report followed a model prepared by a university administrator and drew on working papers prepared by himself, the deans of the undergraduate and graduate schools, and task force reports drawn up by six teams of faculty and administrators. These dealt with "Networking," "Cost Effectiveness," "Facilities Planning," "Funding," "Sexism and Sexual Stereotyping," and "Laboratory for Learning." The reports were based on a format provided by the College Planning Team, composed of the college's top eight administrators. The suggested format was divided into four parts: 1) a statement of goals with direct reference to an earlier working paper called, "The President's Goals"; 2) a statement of "objectives in terms of outcomes," which was to cover strategy for achieving the goals, the responsibilities of people involved, and a description of the means for evaluating success in goal achievement; 3) a strategy for overall evaluation; and 4) presentation of any materials which might help the trustees to understand the issues.

This case was made possible by an institution which chooses to remain anonymous. It was prepared by Dr. Elizabeth C. Altman, research associate, under the direction of Professor Abraham Zaleznik.

THE 1970 CRISIS AND ITS BACKGROUND

The problem of survival was not new. A precipitous drop in enrollment figures in 1970 had first shocked the college into awareness of its uncertain future. At that time Dr. Harrison had been president for ten years. They had been, as he said, "halcyon years," a time when he functioned merely as a "change agent" in an unperturbed and collaborative atmosphere.

Harrison, at the age of 42, accepted the position as president of Waterford because he felt it offered him an opportunity to change those traditionally accepted methods of teacher education which he felt were no longer effective. He had tried to introduce innovations into the programs of the large state university where he had been dean of the school of education for eight years, but had found that the bureaucratic processes of such a large institution worked as a force against change and that his programs were either significantly altered or aborted before they were put into operation.

Waterford College, which was founded at the turn of the century by a kindergarten teacher who used her home as a school for young ladies wishing to follow her own profession, had become, by 1960, an incorporated and accredited four year college for training women to become elementary school teachers. Its undergraduate enrollment was 363; there was a fledgling graduate school which as yet had no full-time students; and there were 23 full-time faculty and an administrative staff of 12. The college was housed in a dozen buildings clustered around Miss Waterford's spacious but economically inefficient home near the center of a culturally rich, multiuniversity city.

Waterford at that time had 11 trustees and 17 corporators whose goal was to create a small college of high excellence, and they agreed that Harrison was well suited to accomplish their purpose. He envisioned a college of 500 to 600 women, who would be taught by exceptional teachers using experiential methods of teaching.

Harrison's management policy

Harrison's administrative philosophy and style at the time were molded by his experiences with the National Training Laboratory. The NTL grew out of experiments in group development and group dynamics carried on at MIT and the University of Michigan. Its originators believed that advances in the social sciences were lagging woefully behind those being made in the physical sciences, and this had created a dangerous disequilibrium between progress in technology and science and in the social sciences. They felt that only by making advances in the social sciences could society deal with the rapid changes brought about by science and technology, but that progress could not be made until the existing psychological barriers against using the methods of the physical sciences for the understanding of human affairs could be broken down. In addition, they believed that objectivity and collaboration, which they thought were characteristic of the scientific method, were morally valuable in themselves. Thus, they deliberately chose the term "laboratory" to emphasize the scientific nature of their enterprise. They were also concerned because they believed that contemporary personal relationships had become sterile as a result of the growth of large, complex, inhumane bureaucracies.

In order to accomplish the twin goals of breaking down barriers to progress in the social sciences and the rehumanization of relationships, NTL leaders arranged small group meetings where people involved in education could come into close contact with each other without formal leadership or an agenda in order to generate ideas. On the basis of their own experiences in such groups, they believed that participants would form spontaneous leadership-follower patterns and, through close personal interactions ("transactions"), involving verbal or nonverbal exchanges ("feedback"), discover their own blind spots and uncover their emotional responses to each other's ideas and behavior, thus creating an exciting and stimulating setting for an exchange of ideas. They would then come to an understanding of themselves and their environment, learn how to diagnose problems, achieve "resocialization" or "renewal," and prepare themselves to become "change agents" or "facilitators" of the "change process" in other such small groups in the outside world.[1]

T-(training)-group was the name coined for such small group interactions. Initially the purpose of the T-groups was to seek solutions to particular problems, but the intimacy of the setting and a growing emphasis on the importance of psychological rather than sociological aspects of the experience changed their character. Many of the originators of the T-group as well as participants in early group sessions were disturbed by this development. Some tried to recapture the original character and purpose of the NTL; others disassociated themselves from the movement.

Using NTL methods, Harrison wanted to create a "laboratory for learning" at Waterford. These methods included using a "transactional model" which would involve all the major constituencies of the college (trustees, corporators, students, faculty, administrators, and alumni) in decision-making, valuing behaviors such as risk-taking and experimentation, integrating effective responses and working procedures, using feedback and model setting, and creating an "open system" receptive to changes in the environment. The success of these methods required that there be intellectual and emotional confrontations. And there were.

To achieve his purpose Harrison brought several other NTL followers to join him at Waterford; he turned over tenure and hiring decisions to the faculty; he encouraged collaborative problem solving; he invited faculty and administrators to participate in a week-long "human relations laboratory" on the campus; and he initiated voluntary group sessions for faculty, administrators, and students. As for turning the college into an open system, sensitive to changes in the environment, Harrison had no choice, for changes originating outside of Waterford forced their way into the life of the college.

During the sixties, politicization of educational issues, which had its origins in the immediate postwar years, gathered momentum. An increasingly large number of critics of the American educational system claimed that the belief that all Americans had equal access to educational opportunities was merely a myth. They insisted that opportunities for educational advancement should be made more open and accessible, especially to minority groups and the poor. Many spokesmen for this group argued that the traditional exclusiveness and elitism of private universities and colleges and their rapidly rising tuition rates precluded them from being acceptable institutions for achieving the goal of egalitarian education and that it could be successfully accomplished only in large, public educational institutions.

Less ideologically oriented educators and a concerned public also wondered at what point the high cost of tuition and room and board would put private institutions beyond the budget of most families and individuals. A 1973 report by the Carnegie Commission on Higher Education stated that liberal arts colleges with enrollments under 1,000 were at a "peril point," and a reported decline in the percentage of students who attended private institutions from 61 per cent in 1900 to 26 per cent in 1972 seemed to support its claim.[2]

The feminist movement of the sixties raised related issues

about separate education for women, and most private colleges responded by becoming coeducational.

The private teacher training colleges seemed to be especially threatened since most of their students were women who came from families belonging to the lower or middle classes, and such families were particularly affected by inflation and the rising costs of private education. Indeed, out of some 150 such colleges that were in operation in 1940, only five were still in existence in 1977. Waterford, as a private teacher training college which had decided to remain a women's college at the undergraduate level, seemed to be especially vulnerable.

In the late sixties, the importance of these pressures momentarily paled beside the more immediate and disturbing crisis which was precipitated by the reaction of students and educators to the United States' involvement in the Vietnam war. Although protests against the war at Waterford College appeared bland to a faculty member who had just arrived from a New York City campus, the effects were nonetheless grave. The academic year of 1970- 71 was a troubled and turbulent one at Waterford. Students and faculty members protested when Harrison dismissed the dean of the graduate school; they demanded representation on committees making decisions regarding parietal and personnel policies and on trustee committees; they insisted that workers from minority groups be hired for contracted maintenance and building work. The enrollment figures for September 1971 were evidence of the seriousness of the crisis brought on by these events. Freshman enrollment in September 1970 was 202; in September 1971 it fell to 125. Even more distressing to the administration was the fact that instead of the usual attrition rate of 8 to 9 per cent for freshmen, 34 per cent of the students who entered the undergraduate school in 1970-71 failed to return for their sophomore year.

Management policy changes

Dr. Harrison decided that these circumstances required that he change his management style and he turned from the NTL model to a "power" model of administrative behavior. In describing what he meant by this, Harrison said:

> The name of the survival game was power. No longer the covert tugging and hauling for influence, but the immediate and overt

exercise of power—power suddenly generated and tested through the deliberate provoking of conflict.

To pilot Waterford College past its "peril point," Harrison drew on "contingency theory." The term "contingency theory" was coined by Paul Lawrence and Jay Lorsch[3] to describe the theory they developed on the basis of evidence gathered by themselves, Burns and Stalker, and others (many of whom had been involved in human relations training groups) while studying organizations. They found that the organizations that functioned most effectively did not follow a single model of organization but rather adopted a design that was "fitted" to the external environment in which the organization was operating. They concluded that there is "no one best way to organize," since highly structured organizations with formalized rules and specific role descriptions "fit" a stable, certain environment while less formal organizations with less clearly defined roles are suited to an unstable, changing environment.

In explaining the applicability of contingency theory to his colleagues in education, Harrison began by describing Waterford's interaction with its environment:

> Thus, the college has taken an environmental input (student), been influenced by it and in turn processed it. If successful, it has returned that original input to the environment as a product which will find a useful place in society. The college best able to adapt to environmental demands and attract high-quality inputs as well as produce attractive outputs, is most likely to be successful as an institution.

He went on to say that the small, private college was facing a rapidly changing, uncertain environment and therefore should rely less on formal rules and structures and more on "decentralized decision making and influence processes." Liberal arts faculties (in contrast to professional school faculties) have tended, he continued, to be inflexible and to maintain the status quo, and not to be knowledgeable about, or readily influenced by, the most critical institutional (environmental) issues. Therefore "their conservative behavior becomes a focus of much of the energy which the institution must expend, thereby diverting energy from environmental requirements. Because of these attitudes," Harrison concluded, "the small private college, on the brink of disaster, can no longer continue a style of governance that affords relatively complete autonomy to its faculty." To ensure the survival of the institution, administrators would have to be more readily accepted as viable leaders on campus and "strive as quickly as possible to include and educate the lagging faculty."

Having made this decision to change his form of governance, Harrison called his chief administrators together for a series of intensive conferences to discuss the issues and to find ways of implementing his new administrative policy. The administrators agreed that there was a need to take a more proactive stance, but expressed some differences of opinion on the best way to do so. The dean of the undergraduate school, a committed NTL follower, was initially reluctant to accept the power model, but was persuaded to do so by the weight of the evidence presented to him.

Curriculum changes

Out of this planning session came the decision to impose from above a new program for freshmen, called the "January Program." According to the plan, four weeks in January would be set aside for independent contracted study under the voluntary supervision of faculty members and administrators. The "contract" feature was designed to ensure student commitment and allow for budget allocations of faculty time. Except in cases where special supplies were needed, students were to make no additional payments for these courses. Regular faculty were encouraged to offer programs or act as supervisors; administrators and part-time faculty would be encouraged to offer courses. Adjunct faculty would be recruited to teach additional courses.

The administrators decided to impose this curriculum change on the faculty (which traditionally considered such changes to be its inviolate responsibility) because 1) they believed it was essential that the existing unsatisfying freshman year be made more attractive and valuable to the students in order to stop attrition, and 2) they wanted deliberately to provoke conflict and confrontation. This latter intention was grounded in the teachings of contingency theory which advocates the use of confrontation in order to force all parts of an organization to recognize and cope with new information and then move toward appropriate changes.

The Waterford College faculty was told that after a year's trial and a period of evaluation based on data gathered from interviews, the faculty would decide the future of the program. In the spring of the following year, the faculty voted to extend the program to all four years. In spite of their enthusiasm for the program, Harrison felt that some members of the faculty continued to resent the fact that it had been imposed from the top.

Tenure policy changes

In the same year Harrison decided he would have to freeze tenure appointments because of the low enrollments. During the period when tenure decisions had been made by the faculty they had been, he felt, unable to say "no" to colleagues up for tenure. By extrapolating tenure and enrollment statistics, Harrison found that within two years 90 per cent of the faculty might be tenured. Accordingly, with the approval of the trustees, he announced that tenure, salaries, and tuition rates would be frozen at their existing levels while a committee studied tenure and possible alternatives to tenure. He also decided that in order to improve the quality of teaching of the undergraduate school he would have to fire five teachers. His decision aroused a storm of protest from both students and faculty. Two of the cases involved hearings held before a five-member faculty committee. Lawyers representing both the faculty members affected and the administration examined, cross-examined, and challenged witnesses during what Harrison described as an "exhausting and alienating" trial. The faculty committee finally overturned Harrison's decision in one case and upheld it in another. Harrison felt that although the hearings left a residue of bitterness, they also laid the groundwork for the faculty's acceptance of new tenure policies in the undergraduate schools.

In 1973 the graduate school faculty voted unanimously to replace tenure with a system of multiple year, renewable contracts which would be based on performance reviews. The first performance review took place when a faculty member had completed six years of teaching followed by a year of sabbatical leave. A majority of the undergraduate school decided in 1976 that tenure should be limited to not more than 20 per cent of the total faculty in each division. Nontenured faculty would have contracts on a yearly basis. The administration included a clause in faculty contracts to the effect that if a faculty member were not reappointed, the reasons for this decision need not be made available to the individual concerned.

A grievance procedure involving representation before three mediators, one of whom was chosen by the faculty, one by the administration, and the third by agreement between those two was made available to faculty members who challenged an administrative decision. The decision of the mediators was binding.

While involved in trying to solve the immediate and most pressing crises, Harrison was also engaged in developing a long-term management policy and a new organizational structure. He decided that the graduate school would be run according to a contingency theory model since it faced uncertain, rapidly changing conditions, whereas the undergraduate school could be administered according to a model combining traditional and NTL methods of governance, since it still operated in more stable and predictable circumstances even though it too faced an uncertain future.

For himself Harrison chose a managerial style which followed either an NTL model or a power model according to the circumstances. One of his associates felt that this fitted Harrison's natural inclination to respond to problems at times as a capable problem solver with a flair for producing data and with sufficient charisma to make a persuasive presentation of his point of view, at other times with a gut level reaction which seemed to indicate that he was responding almost intuitively and according to a set of rock bottom principles. In the latter case, he said, Harrison acted in a more paternalistic manner and was less likely to change his views.

ORGANIZATIONAL STRUCTURE, LEADERSHIP, AND FINANCIAL ORGANIZATION AT WATERFORD

Harrison, as president of Waterford, held the highest administrative position in the college, but final authority resided in the board of trustees which was responsible to the legislature and governor of the state in which the college was chartered. (See Exhibits 1 and 2 for a full list of officers and a diagram of corporate hierarchy.) In Harrison's view the tasks of the president included securing outside support for improved facilities and salaries, managing existing fiscal resources, encouraging innovation, experimentation, and research, optimizing and utilizing available human resources, delegating responsibility, conducting performance reviews with his subordinates, managing conflict, and communicating the goals, needs, and mission of the college.

Because Harrison's time was increasingly taken up by activities related to seeking outside support for the college and plan-

Exhibit 1

Principal Officers

Name	Position	Age (1977)
Baker, Arthur	Vice President for Undergraduate Academic Programs; Dean of Teacher Education; Professor of Education	60
Bradford, John	Vice President for Development	39
Finch, Tom	Vice President for Financial Affairs	60
Fulton, Bob	Associate Dean of Graduate Studies; Director of Summer School; Professor of Education	52
Harrison, Rupert	President	59
Mason, Jeffrey	Vice President and Dean of Graduate Studies and Continuing Education; Professor of Education	50
Winston, Bill	Executive Vice President	46

ning for Waterford's future, he decided in 1976 to appoint Bill Winston to the position of executive vice president. Initially Winston's role was largely that of a stand-in for Harrison, but he had acquired more formal administrative functions by 1978. Harrison decided that those offices engaged in operations that crossed organizational lines would report directly to Winston. Winston also continued to stand in for the president at faculty meetings and in some negotiations with the faculty over personnel policies.

Harrison's appointment of Winston was criticized by several women who felt that the appointment of a fifth male vice president highlighted the ironic fact that women at Waterford dominated only in numbers. In addition to their own feelings of resentment, they felt that it was important for students to have women whom they could emulate in administrative roles as well as teaching roles. They also felt that Winston was an especially unfortunate choice since he had sometimes been sarcastic and hostile when women's concerns were being discussed.

Harrison answered their criticism by saying that he had always searched diligently for women for top administrative positions, but he had not been able to attract the kind of person the college

The Corporation of Waterford College
Board of Trustees

Director of Planning ———————— President ———————— Administrative Assistant

Executive Vice President	Vice President Finance	Director National Center of Economic Education for Children	Vice President Waterford Consulting Collaborative	Vice President Undergraduate School	Vice President Graduate School	Vice President Public Affairs	Director of Admissions (Undergraduate)

Director Graduate Admissions

Associate Dean

Assistant Dean Elementary Education	Assistant Dean Therapeutic Arts	Assistant Dean Counselling Services	Assistant Dean Special Education	Dean Summer School

Administrative Assistant	Controller	Director of Physical Plant

Dean of Student Affairs	Education Division	Humanities Division	Science Division

DIRECTOR OF

Alumni Affairs	Public Relations	Developments

Placement	Registrar	Financial	Library

needed, perhaps because such women were so much in demand. Winston defended his position by saying that he thought it was probably his tendency to mix humor and seriousness and to tease (traits which were a part of his Yankee upbringing) which caused some people to be offended by his remarks. He felt he should have been more careful in distinguishing between his humorous and serious comments as well as in reining in his tendency to "come on strong" when he felt important issues were at stake. Because he was a strong believer in the importance of administrators and he shared Harrison's ideas about management theory, he felt that most of the faculty saw him as lacking sympathy for faculty problems.

The college was divided into ten offices—the graduate and undergraduate schools and eight administrative and support services. Of these eight, the Office of Financial Affairs and the Office of Public Affairs were administered by vice presidents, the others by directors.

The vice president for financial affairs was Tom Finch. He described himself as having a close and informal working relationship with Harrison with whom he shared a "hard business approach when it comes to what is good for Waterford."

Waterford's first budgetary principle was summed up in the phrase "Each tub on its own bottom." Each November, Finch sent every office of the school a copy of its budget for the previous year and requested, in return, an estimated budget for the following year with a statement of any unusual expenses or other budgetary changes.

When these were returned, Finch coordinated them and prepared a rough budget for the entire college which he presented to a management team composed of four or five top administrators. If income and expenses were approximately balanced, the budget was then sent to the board of trustees for approval. If income was insufficient to cover expenses, cuts were made after consultation with the heads of the affected offices. A program was sometimes carried for one or two experimental years, but after that it had to pay its way.

Total income for the college rose from approximately $700,000 in 1960-61 to over $8 million by 1976-77. By that time it cost approximately $700,000 a month to run the college. Close to 80 per cent of that income came from tuition, with the remainder coming from government grants, miscellaneous sources, endowment, conferences, and student aid funds, in that order. Most other private colleges at that time received from 30-50 per cent of their income from sources other than tuition. Waterford's disproportionately heavy reliance on tuition was largely caused by the fact that although a large proportion of the alumni made gifts to the college, these gifts were apt to be small since the teaching profession paid relatively less than other professions, and married women graduates tended to give more money to their husbands' colleges than to their own.

The graduate school

A desire to reduce Waterford's heavy reliance on tuition as a source of income was one of Harrison's reasons for deciding in 1970 to expand the graduate school. He felt that a larger graduate program would bring needed revenues to the college as well as enhance its scholarly standing. Its budget at that time was $112,000. By 1977 it had grown to $2 million, but because its increased income was matched by increases in expenses, its surplus revenues in 1977 were only $5,000. Finch said that though the graduate school had not fulfilled its anticipated functions of bringing in additional capital, it contributed significantly to the financial well-being of the college by paying approximately 50 per cent of the cost of running the buildings and services it shared with the undergraduate school. Finch also said that budgeting for the graduate school was crystal ball gazing since its growth rate was so rapid and its market so unpredictable.

In 1970 Harrison appointed Dr. Mason, who was then 44 years old, to run the new graduate school. Harrison believed that although Mason firmly rejected the idea that he followed any school of management theory, he intuitively practiced contingency theory.

He described Mason as a charismatic father figure who cultivated a slow, easy-going "sleeper" exterior behind which he acted decisively and quickly. Harrison said that Mason's talents were best suited for initiating an organization on a grand scale, but in that process he was likely to produce chaos and confusion. Mason was, therefore, an appropriate administrator at a time of rapid changes or crises but not the right man for managing and organizing in stable conditions.

Other colleagues also used the words "entrepreneur" and "father figure" when they described Mason, as well as calling him a "genius," "charismatic leader" and a "magician." One of his colleagues said that while most of the time he seemed to be relaxing behind a haze of cigarette smoke with his eyes half closed, he managed to make things move and to bring about startling changes.

Another colleague told a story about Mason's moving into one of the old buildings of the college and transforming it within a few days by creating an elegant interior and an instant lawn. He had found Mason one morning carefully removing a leaf from a bright green lawn that had been rolled into place the preceding afternoon.

When his colleagues tried to analyze Mason's administrative style, most of them referred to his almost intuitive sense for choosing good people and making them work "a thousand hours a week" for the college. One person said that he combined impatience with authority; rules and meetings with deep concern for discipline and excellence. Another commented that behind Mason's seemingly relaxed manner lay an almost obsessive concern for growth, and that this sometimes caused him to be impatient and thoughtless, thus creating unnecessary petty problems for himself and those around him.

Before coming to Waterford, Mason worked for nine years in community colleges which were oriented toward responding to community needs and encouraging student participation in administrative matters. He also worked for five years with a scientific research organization and three years with Xerox where, he said, he learned how to run a business operation. He said that in running the graduate school he tried to combine what he learned from each of these past experiences.

When he hired Mason, Harrison gave him free rein to run the graduate school as he saw fit as long as the school was not in financial difficulties. If the vice president for financial affairs informed him that he foresaw financial problems ahead, Harrison then took action. For several years, Harrison emphasized his laissez-faire approach to the graduate school by only attending its faculty meetings on special occasions, but in 1977 he decided that either he or Winston would be present at all future meetings. When speaking of graduate school affairs, Harrison, Mason, and many of the program heads used the language of the business rather than the academic world, referring to students as "products," to potential employers of graduates as "consumers," and to some of the programs as "profit centers." They often talked about "entrepreneurship," "risk-taking," and the "bottom line." This approach and Mason's leadership had brought about an exuberant and vigorous growth of programs in the graduate school as well as some problems of overlapping "territoriality" and organizational confusion.

Directly beneath Mason in the graduate school organizational structure was Assistant Dean Bob Fulton. Fulton compared the structure of the graduate school to a clothesline onto which programs could be added or removed without disturbing the overall structure.

In 1977 six of the graduate school programs led to M.A. degrees in a variety of teaching or teaching-related fields; one program led to a certificate of advanced graduate study in a specialized area; one program prepared students for administrative careers; and three programs were special programs which were designed to provide on-campus as well as community-based courses to meet the needs of experienced practitioners seeking continuing education opportunities. Students attending special programs in order to improve their professional standing were often eligible for partial tuition remission from their unions or organizations for successfully completed courses.

The regular faculty at Waterford had unusually high qualifications, reflected in their possession of advanced degrees, richness of experience, or both. Many had left higher-paying positions at better known, larger universities in order to come to Waterford. In giving their reasons for doing so, they talked of the opportunities at Waterford for innovation and experimentation in courses and teaching methods, the small size of classes, the high quality of students, and the sense of growth and excitement the graduate school offered them.

Part-time faculty for some regular programs and especially for those special programs which had an unpredictable and fluctuating enrollment were recruited from the large pool of highly trained practicing, part-time, or retired academics and other professionals in the area. This resource made it possible for the college to attract highly trained people at short notice and relatively low cost.

Members of the graduate school faculty differed over the question of what effects the contract systems of appointment and the school's emphasis on entrepreneurship had on the quality of its offerings. Mason believed that since most students were professional practitioners who were practically oriented they wouldn't pay Waterford's rather high tuition rates for "gimmicky" courses, and therefore the quality of the courses offered had to be high to attract them. Many people agreed with him and felt that the businesslike approach of the school was a stimulus to imaginative and high-quality teaching. But others, some of whom taught more traditional courses, felt that they were unable to attract as many students as those teachers or program coordinators who offered more novel courses. Since numbers were an important consideration in contract performance reviews, this kind of competition, they felt, led to insecurity and reduced creativity. One faculty member said that the sudden cancellation of several contracts in 1975 after the treasurer's office alerted the dean to an impending financial deficit reinforced this sense of injustice and insecurity and caused people to become more cautious.

Students in the graduate school had a fairly wide range of ages, backgrounds, experience, and interests. Of those who were interviewed or responded to questionnaires in 1977, the majority expressed enthusiasm for the content of the courses and the quality of teaching. Some who attended on- or off-campus special courses complained that occasionally teachers were of poor quality and felt this was due to their having been recruited without sufficient screening. Other students, particularly those in outlying areas, were pleased with the opportunity of being taught by gifted people in their own communities, with whom they would otherwise not have had contact. Several students, who taught and lived in suburban towns and rarely, if ever, went to the city, were pleased that they could avoid facing urban problems by taking courses offered in their own communities.

The undergraduate school

Dr. Arthur Baker, who was 60 in 1977, was the dean of the undergraduate school. Harrison invited him to come to Waterford in the early sixties because they both shared a belief in NTL methods and Baker had worked under Harrison at a state university as director of the laboratory schools Harrison administered there. Before that he had been an elementary school principal. Baker was the first of several NTL educators Harrison invited to Waterford, and he remained the most faithful follower of such methods. One of the other NTL followers hired in the sixties, who then delighted in getting people to open up in their relationships with the people they worked with, found that by the late seventies he was urging people to be more closed. Another, after observing the dangers of psychologically oriented T-group sessions, became sharply critical of NTL methods in general.

Baker, although he disapproved of psychologically oriented T-groups, maintained that a small group of people (12 being optimal), meeting together under a leader who was more of a sociological commentator than a director, could work out its own way to solve the problems it had set itself. He believed that the dynamics of this process led to a breakdown in the participants' perceptual screens and thus opened their minds to new information, created respect for democratic processes, and generated enthusiasm, self-renewal, and growth.

In a memorandum addressing the question of Waterford's future, Baker wrote:

> Waterford, in 1982-83, will still be best characterized by its problem solving, inquiry action research process. Use of process here has also been known as "Waterford College, the Laboratory for Learning." It was introduced in 1960, reinforced in 1965 and has served the College very, very well up to this time. . . . The value of this process stance is that it greatly increases the odds that the institution will respond creatively and productively to emerging environmental conditions. It is, to a large extent, an effective substitute for contingency planning. Central to the process, but so frequently lacking in educational enterprises, is seeking and using feedback with respect to all aspects of the operation.

When Baker first came to Waterford he used NTL methods to break down the existing tradition of authoritarian leadership and to raise the morale, enthusiasm, and commitment of the faculty. He said that this required five years of effort and that it left some scars, notwithstanding its beneficial effects.

The planning for a new interdisciplinary, team-teaching program in 1970-71 was based on the use of such group meetings as well as detailed reports from involved faculty members. After the program was accepted at a faculty meeting and implemented on a provisional basis, Baker requested evaluation reports from participating faculty and sent an eleven-page, multiple choice, open-ended questionnaire to participating students. The results of their responses were tabulated and transferred to a wall-size chart. At the end of each succeeding year the program was reevaluated. The chart thus provided an easily-read, visual record of the degree of success of various aspects of the program.

As this program was a radically new development, Baker watched its progress more closely than most, but all programs in the undergraduate school were monitored to some degree by the use of questionnaires and evaluation forms. In addition, Baker often solicited verbal feedback from participants.

Baker believed deeply in the value of participation, but he also recognized limits to its usefulness. When he announced a new plan for changing the organizational structure of the undergraduate school, he made the point that the college was "not a democracy," because it was accountable to the larger society through the college governing body. Hence, he argued, there might be times, when because of unusual circumstances, the president would be justified in overruling a decision made by the majority of the faculty.

In contrasting his leadership style with Harrison's, Baker said that the president's strength lay in bringing creative people to the college and in hiring consultants who provided fresh perspectives, while his own strength lay in implementing programs and getting things done on a day-to-day basis.

Harrison expressed considerable respect for Baker's talents as an experienced and dedicated educator who was deeply committed to maintaining high standards. Many members of the faculty shared Harrison's respect for Baker and, in addition, admired his kindness and essential goodness. Several members spoke of the strong influence his ideas about NTL methods had had on them individually and on the faculty as a whole.

Both Baker and Harrison were interested in raising the quality of undergraduate teaching as much as possible, but, according to Baker, Harrison believed this could be accomplished most quickly through hiring and firing while Baker relied more on his own personal growth approach.

Undergraduate enrollment grew from 363 students in 1961 to 788 in 1977-78. The College Planning Team in 1977 decided that the upper limit for enrollments in the undergraduate school should be set at about 850, a figure it expected the school would reach by 1982-83. Similarities of social and economic backgrounds as well as a narrower age range made the undergraduate student body far more homogeneous than that in the graduate school. Most of the students came from middle-income families that were seeking to move upward in their economic and social position. For many such families, particularly those which were recent immigrants, the teaching profession provided their daughters with an opportunity for improving their status. The ethnic composition of this segment of American society had changed over the years as succeeding waves of immigrants moved upward on the social and economic scale. In 1977, Italian, Polish, and Armenian names appeared most frequently on the enrollment lists.

Because the high cost of tuition tended to exclude the daughters of lower-income families, the college was trying to increase its scholarship funds in order to secure a more heterogeneous student body.

Students said that they were attracted to Waterford because of its size, its programs, its location, and its exceptionally high rate of placement, which was usually above 90 per cent, at a time when the demand for teachers was declining.

In 1978 Baker commented that he believed Waterford could overcome the mounting pressures working against the survival of small, independent women's colleges if it continued to emphasize and develop the special advantages of the education it offered, such as the size of classes, the high caliber of faculty and students, the faculty-student ratio of about 20-1, and the quality of the programs.

Plans for Waterford's future

The reassessment of Waterford College's potential for survival in an uncertain future centered around the question of how the college could ensure a financial basis which would enable it to grow in size, expand its scholarship program, prevent its tuition rate from becoming prohibitive, and also maintain its standing in the field of education and its commitment to excellence.

By 1977, Harrison had already laid the groundwork for several programs designed to improve both the college's financial position and its leadership role. First and foremost was his design for a consulting collaborative. The collaborative's function would be to work with "educators, governmental agencies, industry and institutions in the field, assisting in innovation, policy research, assessment and consultation" as well as serving as a conference center. Harrison had asked Mason to become its director. In doing so, he hoped to make the most effective use of Mason's talents for innovation and, at the same time, remove him from the graduate school which was in need of an administrator who could organize and control its chaotic growth. Harrison projected a surplus of $75,000 for the first 18 months.

Harrison had also begun efforts to find funding for an endowed chair in economic education for children for a proposed National Center of Economic Education at Waterford. The center would prepare software and curricula for teaching children about the American economic system and would provide consulting services for

principals, teachers, school boards, parents, and other groups interested in instruction in economics for children.

In order to find initial funding for these programs and to
increase the building and scholarship funds, Harrison hired John
Bradford, a highly trained and experienced public relations expert
and fundraiser to be vice president for development. Bradford
launched an intensive drive for funds in 1977.

Harrison said that although the faculty grievances of the
early seventies had been settled and forgotten by 1977, new faculty
members were agitating for greater faculty control of college governance. Winston added that if the faculty succeeded in uniting on a
stand against the administration and tried unsuccessfully, as he put it,
"to force the administrators to emasculate their power," they might
turn to unionization.

COMMENTARY

It might interest you to learn how the Waterford College case came
to be written. I knew Dr. Harrison professionally. He and I had on
occasion collaborated on human relations training projects. I found
him to be an interesting man, but one difficult to get to know. He
was affable, even-tempered and easy to get along with, since he was
not argumentative, nor particularly confrontational. He had his
own reasons, which he never revealed to me directly, for placing confidence in my judgment.

He had been invited to present a paper on his theories of
academic administration at a conference on educational administration to be held in Sweden. Reflecting a degree of shyness not common to administrators, academic or otherwise, Dr. Harrison
approached me with a request that I write a case study on Waterford
College that he would use to discuss his experiences and views as an
academic administrator. By using the case study, he would generate
group discussion, since the case would appear in the narrative form
you have read, without his interpretations and comments. Harrison's approach to this conference perhaps reflected his beliefs as an
educator: that one promotes understanding more by discussion than
by lecture. Consistent with his beliefs as an educator, he had a personal predilection to sell and not tell, to assume a passive rather
than an active role along with an aversion to self display, or in my
language, exhibitionism.

I readily accepted both aspects of Dr. Harrison's desire to have a case study written, particularly since on the face of it there is merit in his views about how people learn. Also, I have no categorical position about how people align their defenses. We all do the best we can, and God knows it is difficult enough running an organization, let alone having to justify one's mode of transforming unconscious defenses into strategic stances and organizational rationalizations.

I assigned my research assistant, Dr. Elizabeth Altman, to this case and the result is what you have before you. Incidentally, it is also the case Dr. Harrison presented for discussion in Sweden and the case he released for use in my course at the Harvard Business School.

When I discussed Dr. Altman's research with her throughout the investigation and writing, I was surprised by how confrontational and hospitable to conflict Dr. Harrison wanted to appear, not only to Elizabeth and me, but especially to the people with whom he worked in the daily labors of a school such as Waterford. As I said, Dr. Harrison seemed the most unlikely person in the world to generate conflict and to place himself at its center. He was idealistic, remarkably gentle, and somewhat detached. It was puzzling, to say the least, to visualize Dr. Harrison as a man who relished power and who loved a fight. It just did not fit his character.

Now there is a striking fact about Harrison's propensity for conflict. He appeared compelled to encapsulate his aggression in a theory, just as he sought to surround his more gentle response as chief executive in a theory. In one case, he advanced contingency theory and in the other laboratory theory, or the "National Training Laboratory model" of democratic participation through "T" for training groups.

It is easy to argue that a leader in an academic institution surely would rely on intellect and theory to figure out how to use his office. While the argument is easy to make, it happens not to fit the facts. There is no more pragmatic class of people than academic administrators, who have a penchant for eschewing matters intellectual and theoretical when it comes to running their organizations. The truth is, like corporate CEO's, academic presidents like to get on with the job. They understand that to give faculties the opportunity to debate decisions, especially around theoretical models, is to invite paralysis. When academic administrators do invite such discussion, it is usually a manipulation to deflect attention from real issues. Thus faculties will debate the distribution of requirements in the curriculum, or the grading system, but these debates seldom matter either in what and how students learn, or in drawing together the finances that will keep the institution vital.

About a decade ago William Cyert, president of Carnegie Mellon University in Pittsburgh, Pennsylvania, wrote an article for the editorial pages of the Wall Street Journal. Before his incarnation as a university administrator, Dr. Cyert was an organizational theorist of high standing. After running Carnegie Mellon, Cyert came to a realization that he could not bear to keep to himself: that the organization theory he and others had espoused was really of little substance or practical value. While Cyert did not single out the NTL or contingency models, I would include both in the range of organizational theories that Cyert had concluded was worthless. What Cyert discovered as an administrator, and did not realize as a theorist, was that organizations are made up of people. They are the scarce resource (talent being the distinguishing scarcity) one must administer. Cyert concluded that you should bend the organization to fit the people and stop trying to bend people to fit the organization, which incidentally exists only as an abstraction in the minds of the executives who wield power. Organizations are not real in the same way that people are real.

Cyert reached another conclusion. He stated that one should administer by consolidating and directing power toward strategic advantage (or comparative advantage). Hence, by controlling the flow of money to departments, the administrator is able to capitalize on advantage that he or she perceives, defines, and ultimately articulates.

The rub here is that the administrator must raise the money to expand and capitalize on advantage that he creates or perceives. If he cannot, or will not, raise money, his power is empty. Another rub is there has to be a potential, latent or realized, for advantage. If there is no advantage, it becomes exceedingly difficult to raise money, and therefore almost impossible to direct actively the affairs of the organization.

We would be badly underestimating Dr. Harrison to suggest he was not aware of the practical considerations that every wise administrator, including William Cyert, come to recognize. Therefore, we must wonder why Dr. Harrison elected to deal with the fiscal crisis at Waterford with his new-found enthusiasm for contingency theory, with his elaborate process of task forces, committees, organization structure, executive positions and other trappings of formal organization. It appeared to be all process and no substance.

Let us take a few steps back and examine Harrison's presidency over his close to 20 year tenure. He took over a teachers' college for women at a time when doubts existed (and still do exist) concerning the place in our society for schools like Waterford. Women were set on destroying stereotypes of what women should do in life. Earlier in the century women could teach grade school while they awaited marriage, but to aspire to professional education in law and medicine, or to aspire to a career as a business executive was out of the question. Women of means went to the sheltered halls of elite colleges such as Smith, Wellesley, and Vassar. Women without means, from immigrant families, went to teachers' colleges, to Waterford and other schools that were soon to face extinction. All this stereotypical thinking began to dissolve with a vengeance in the 1960s, but the forces were at work well before the Vietnam crisis. When Dr. Harrison became president in 1960, there were five teachers colleges like Waterford. Twenty years earlier, there were 150 such colleges. The teachers college was a dying breed, an institution without a purpose, so to speak, let alone without a strategic advantage. In the face of this decline, Harrison took the job, a decision that lacks a sense of reality.

What comes as another surprise in this story is the fact that Waterford survived another couple of decades, and Dr. Harrison survived along with his college. He increased the enrollment from 360 women to 800 and the income from $700,000 to $8,000,000 over a span of 16 years, from 1960 to 1976. Even discounting inflation the numbers are impressive.

What were the sources of the income? Student tuitions still made up some 80 per cent of the income. The new enrollment and income came from new programs. A graduate school, extension programs, and the like opened some new markets for Waterford. These new markets existed based on the tendency in public education to grant salary increases upon the completion of additional studies, hence the support for the graduate and extension programs.

But the hard and unspoken reality of Waterford, and Harrison's survival, was the willingness of the faculty to do the work necessary to generate the income. While the data are not available, it is fair to suppose that overall student-faculty ratios worked in favor of the budget, although only marginally, since the school barely broke even over the years of expansion. In other words, programs expanded and income rose, but there was no money for development. This fragile balance meant Waterford had no money to explore and test for ways to create strategic advantage. Hence it relied on a thin market and a narrow purpose despite the expansion into graduate and extension programs. Harrison's focus was survival, which makes rather amusing, if not pathetic, the uses of theory to justify his forms of crisis management.

There is another, rather unpleasant fact to contemplate. The school's constituency was female. Yet its power structure was entirely masculine. There were no women in administrative posts.

Frankly, I have nothing more than conjecture to deal with this fact. Did Dr. Harrison dislike, mistrust, fear, or feel otherwise uncomfortable with women? Did he find it easier to contemplate manipulating women than men? Be assured that his survival strategy depended upon manipulation. His mechanism was to use theory or organizational models, along with process, to engage the attention of his various constituencies as he provided for survival on very narrow terms. I doubt Harrison was conscious of ambivalent or negative attitudes toward women. He believed men could deal with power more easily than women. At the same time, with the possible exception of his vice president for undergraduate education, Arthur Baker, the male executive officers seemed to have an intuitive grasp of Harrison's survival strategy. They were adept at manipulating the processes he set in place for engaging the faculty in meaningless meetings, the preparation of task force reports, and the other mechanisms that deflected attention from the real problems of this organization. These problems centered on deriving income in an outdated economic position. Dr. Harrison and his male executive group scrambled to find markets for which programs could be provided, perhaps only marginally, given the capabilities of his faculty. For example, the program on economic education for primary school students superficially appeared to have a base for raising funds from corporations and associations of conservatives fearful that "economic illiteracy" posed a threat to free enterprise. But Waterford offered weak resources for mounting a program on economic education at the elementary school level.

Another way of looking at Harrison's survival strategy is to examine his actions as though he were an entrepreneur, a risk taker. Harrison's record indicates he was less than successful as an entrepreneur. After 20 years on the job, the mission had not changed. Waterford still needed money and operated in an atmosphere of crisis. Harrison's reliance on "models" revealed his discomfort in the role of entrepreneur, since neither the language of contingency theory nor the NTL models were likely to mean much to the sources of funding. Clearly, this language was for his internal audience of faculty and administrators, who because of their limited alternatives, reacted passively to Harrison's approaches to crisis. Paradoxically the passive position of the faculty exacerbated the crisis since the academic staff was potentially a source of ideas for new initiatives in the basic mission of Waterford College: to advance elementary education.

There was no evidence that the faculty, administration, or Harrison himself grasped the potential of breaking through the morass of bureaucracy, the stasis that surrounded public education. The mission and the resolution of the crisis was in front of the noses of the administration of Waterford College. But in the frantic scrambling to find ways to bring in incremental funds, the true mission had become obfuscated in the internal psychodrama Harrison fostered, surrounded in meaningless theory that bordered on ideology on the one hand (NTL models) and vacuous generalizations on the other (contingency theory).

The NTL model is a subset of a distinct ideology involving the shifting of power from the upper to the lower echelons of organizations. Sometimes it is in the language of democratization, sometimes in the language of participation, and sometimes in the language of individual growth, creativity, and self-actualization. The astonishing finding surrounding these models of shifting power from the top to the lower levels of the hierarchy is they don't work. The literature is full of reports of noble experiments in factories and offices in the United States and abroad which ended in failure. The experience is one of a fact in desperate search of a convincing explanation. The fact is these experiments fail. Yet we refuse to examine and learn from these failures.

Perhaps many of the experiments are not meant to succeed. As in the case of Waterford College, perhaps power holders have latent aims. They may be covering up for their own inadequacies and anxieties by creating psychodrama to deflect attention from the basic issues, such as squarely defining a purpose and fulfilling it in the clearest and most direct way possible.

Contingency theory is an attempt to explain away the failures of the democratization and participation movements. It says, in brief, that with a clearly defined purpose and direction, it's best to lead from the top, with structure and routines in place. Conversely, in organizations whose purpose is unclear, ambiguous, shifting, and constantly changing, it is better to lead by *distributing* power from the top to lower levels. Leadership style is contingent on the situation. How do you suppose purposes become clear, ambiguity disappears and is replaced by a sense of direction? When leaders lead purposes become clear, because the power holders work at figuring out what an organization should be doing. This activity is "real work" in contrast to the psychodrama of organizational process. When power holders refuse to take responsibility for establishing direction, process overcomes substance, the organization is adrift, and leaders are not leading. Viewing the Waterford College story using the current language of the contingency theorists, we would probably hear the argument that Waterford is in the knowledge industry and should shift power to the faculty, the "knowledge workers" of its industry. Perhaps, but can the sense of direction Waterford needs spring newly born from faculty process, or does it depend on leadership, and leadership from the top?

Let's ask ourselves an entirely different question than the aims and directions of leadership. Shift to the question of whether the attempt to continue breathing life into an organization, hopping frantically from one fiscal crisis to another, is justified. If I were a trustee of Waterford College, I would wonder out loud whether the crisis management was in the end a misuse of human talents. Perhaps Waterford should die, or merge with another institution more likely to foster the mission of advancing elementary education than Waterford going it alone.

If Dr. Harrison would listen to my inquiries as to where it is written that Waterford has to survive, he would soon have to face the fact that his survival as an executive is linked to Waterford's survival. He would have to be willing to put his immediate needs in a subordinate position to the needs of the faculty, the students, and education in general. Here, the trustees have an important job, which is to force to the surface what in my perspective is the underlying agenda of Waterford College—keeping the place alive in the service of Dr. Harrison's personal concerns.

Perhaps you think that I am too harsh and accusatory in my interpretation of the Waterford and Harrison story. I shall leave that judgment to you. If you judge in the affirmative, remember that you become responsible for figuring out what makes Waterford and Dr. Harrison run.

Endnotes—Chapter 18

1. Leland P. Bradford, Jack R. Gibb, Kenneth D. Benne, *T-Group Therapy and Laboratory Method* (New York: John Wiley, 1964).

2. The Carnegie Commission on Higher Education, *Priorities for Action: Final Report* (New York: McGraw-Hill, 1973), p. 30; Elmer D. West and Charles J. Anderson, "Changing Public/Private Ratios on Higher Education," *Educational Record* (Fall 1970).

3. Paul R. Lawrence and Jay W. Lorsch, *Organization and Environment* (Boston: Division of Research, Harvard Business School, 1967).

HIDDEN AGENDA— CENTRAL STATES MENTAL HEALTH CLINIC

Running a business is difficult enough, but nowhere as difficult as running a mental hospital. Besides being limited in their accomplishments as a result of deficiencies in the body of knowledge, state mental hospitals suffer from lack of funds and the inability of chief executive officers to establish policy, outline procedures, institute controls, or provide rewards for devoted and able staff; in short, they lack the resources to do their job effectively.

I outline the limitations in power to evoke your sympathy and understanding for Dr. Ralph Matthews, the superintendent of the Central States Mental Health Clinic. Despite the term clinic in its title, Central States was a full-fledged mental hospital. In its days of glory, not too long ago, it was the premier hospital of its kind, a legend in American psychiatry, much sought after by young psychiatrists eager for the best training available.

When Dr. Matthews was appointed superintendent and assumed the professorship that went along with the post, he was enmeshed in a host of political problems stemming from the controls exercised by the state mental health authorities. As part of a new policy, these authorities removed the conditions that helped maintain the hospital as a great institution. Dr. Matthews stood in the shadows of great figures who had preceded him, left vulnerable to comparisons not of his own choosing. What kind of position he could stake out for himself remained a constant problem in his incumbency and formed the backdrop for the crisis recounted in this case study.

The state employees went on strike for higher wages. The strikers included attendants and housekeeping people, who left the wards and the patients, following their union leaders. The strike was clearly illegal, but the conditions surrounding the strike, and the flow of events underway at the hospital during it, brought out many grievances that seemed to catch Dr. Matthews unaware. In effect, the story is about a strike within a strike, since the medical staff and the younger psychiatric residents expressed anger at Dr. Matthews and applied pressure through threats to take matters into their own hands if things did not change at the hospital. On the surface, the change the medical groups wanted was the end of the strike and the restoration of normal operations. But by the time Dr. Matthews became aware of the medical staff's anger, it appeared as though matters were out of his hands. It seemed as though multiple and hidden agendas came into play. But the question I would like to tease you with is whether Dr. Matthews became entrapped by his own hidden agenda. With all due respect for him and the extraordinary difficulties of his job, did he, in the final analysis, outsmart himself?

To answer these questions, you will probably find it necessary to chart the many constituencies to which Dr. Matthews had some relationship, if not responsibility and accountability. You may then inquire as to where Dr. Matthews positioned himself regarding the multiple constituencies. What was he after during the strike, both overtly, and perhaps covertly? You may well sigh at the end of this analytical exercise and wonder whether it is not always in everyone's best interests to keep life simple.

THE CENTRAL STATES MENTAL HEALTH CENTER

Late Wednesday morning, the third day of the first statewide strike of state employees, representatives of the medical staff of the Central States Mental Health Center handed a memorandum to the superintendent, Dr. Ralph Matthews. The memorandum stated:

> It is the opinion of the medical staff and the residents who have signed below that the conditions on the in-patient services have reached the limit of safety. It is not possible, within the limits of conscience, to operate the wards in the absence of trained mental health workers beyond 3:00 p.m. Wednesday, at which point alternative measures will be undertaken.

For Dr. Matthews, the memo was one more harassment in a week which had already been packed with problems. He could easily guess what "alternative measures" the staff had in mind, for many of them had already spoken of going to the newspapers or finding some other way of making their story public. He tried to understand why the medical staff was so eager to use such tactics. He thought they could only make matters worse. The signers' demand that the administration do something to ensure their safety when, in fact, he had already called in the police to provide security for hospital personnel crossing the picket line seemed to be an attack on his way of handling the strike. One of the medical staff had said, during a heated discussion of the strike, that "the rats" in the union had violated their agreement and that the administration "should have nailed them instead of fooling around with them."

While most of the signers of the Wednesday memorandum were senior medical staff, Dr. Matthews was aware that the young residents in psychiatric training were equally unhappy. A group of them, mostly in their first year of training, had sent a handwritten letter to him on Monday at 11:45 a.m., shortly after the strike began. This letter stated:

> We are in sympathy with the better working conditions for state employees. The hospital is presently unsafe for patient care. We cannot provide even basic coverage for our patients or in good conscience plan to run the hospital beyond 8 a.m. tomorrow. As residents we are being asked, despite any and all assurances, to cross disciplinary lines, to perform nursing and attendant functions. We fear our safety and standing in these roles. We con-

Dr. Elizabeth C. Altman, research associate, wrote this case under the direction of Professor Abraham Zaleznik. Copyright © 1977 by the president and fellows of Harvard College.

sider that we are being used also to undercut the significance of the strike. We cannot accept further admissions at this time. We require police protection to enter and leave the hospital from our cars, given the present level of violence. We expect to be present at the noon administrative meeting to clearly define our duties and responsibilities at this time.

What particularly struck Dr. Matthews about this letter was the reference to violence at a time when no violence had yet occurred. He and others had found the first year residents to be a difficult group from the beginning of their training, which had started the summer before the strike. Many of them had participated in the radical student movement in the late sixties when they were still in college, yet they seemed to be greatly concerned with status and safety. He found it odd that this particular generation of residents would want to bring about a power showdown with a group of strikers by involving newspapers, radio, TV, the governor, and even the governor's wife.

Dr. Matthews' concern over the actions of the medical staff and the psychiatric residents distracted him from the more immediate problem of the strike and caused him to turn his thoughts from the present to the past.

The Central States Mental Health Center had been founded early in the century as a state hospital for the "observation and treatment" of mental diseases. From its inception it had been closely affiliated with a nearby medical school, serving as a center for clinical research and teaching. The superintendent held a prestigious chair in psychiatry at this affiliated university medical school.

Over the years the hospital had acquired an outstanding reputation for excellence in its research and training. Its clinical research center was known for its many studies, some of which had dramatically affected the nature of mental health care. It had also developed an innovative and widely respected training program. Young doctors came there to follow a three-year residency training program in psychiatry, and there were also training programs in clinical psychology, psychiatric social work, psychiatric nursing, and occupational therapy. Because of the hospital's outstanding reputation, there were always many more applicants for the residency training programs than there were places. As a result, residents tended to be highly qualified. Many of them later became leaders in the field of psychiatry.

The senior psychiatric staff, made up of full-time and part-time doctors, also had outstanding reputations as clinical psychiatrists and psychoanalysts. They were noted for their teaching, particularly in supervising young residents in the practice of psychotherapy.

Until 1970 even the patients represented a select group, chosen from all over the state for their clinical interest, their articulateness, and/or because they were recommended by prominent political figures. The justification for this selective process was that such patients provided students with unusually rich opportunities for learning their professions as well as for developing their understanding of the psychological processes of mental illness.

All of these factors had contributed to producing an atmosphere of excitement, dedication, and ferment. However, changing attitudes toward mental health had caused major modifications in the institution. In the 1970s new regulations governing the state's community mental health program were introduced which drastically altered the hospital's control of its program and patient population. The State Department of Mental Health directed the hospital to accept patients only from the surrounding community. In addition, the hospital was no longer allowed to transfer patients to other hospitals after an initial period of observation and treatment. The chronically ill had to be given custodial care. With more chronically ill patients and more patients with character disorders such as alcohol and drug addiction, there was a shift in the types of psychiatric problems treated at the Center. The residents in psychiatric training were not pleased with these changes. A study was begun in 1976 to compare the newer patients with those of 1965. It showed a definite shift in the patient population toward less well-educated, more chronically ill patients, and, less clearly, more violent and psychotic patients.

The residents and medical staff were also disturbed by the effects of the state's financial austerity program. The number of psychiatric residents had been reduced by more than half from the previous year because of budget cutbacks. At the beginning of the year there had been a freeze on hiring nurses, and even vacancies were not filled. At the same time nurses' duties were heavier because there were fewer psychiatric residents and more chronically ill patients. Dr. Matthews believed that it was not only budgetary considerations that were causing such curtailments and other difficulties, for there were indications that state authorities were hostile toward the program because it was regarded as an elitist "have" program, and the state was more interested in supporting "have not" projects.

Dr. Matthews became superintendent of the Center at the time that these changes were taking place. His predecessor, Dr. William Saunders, had resigned abruptly for personal reasons. Dr. Saunders had been a prominent figure in the field of psychiatry and mental health before he became superintendent of the center, and he was well acquainted with the political world of the state and federal government. An observer described him as a man of "pragmatic optimism" who used his authority with "palpable gusto." He was brisk but kindly in his relationships with staff, employees, and patients and intolerant of secrecy and any ideas about contemporary moral decay or the meaninglessness of life.

Dr. Saunders had directed the hospital with the help of a clinical director and an assistant superintendent, who was the head of the research laboratory. The resulting balance in roles among these senior doctors and the commitment of the organization to excellence in patient care, teaching, and research gave observers the impression that there was little danger that the hospital would break down in moments of crisis.

Dr. Saunders described himself as "living on TWA," while he traveled to and from professional associations, government bodies, and public interest groups for the purpose of building his profession and supplementing the state funds that supported the Center. Because of his frequent trips and his faith in his staff, he was little involved in the clinical side of the hospital. Speaking of his staff and residents, he said, "These are a hot bunch of clinical boys, you know." He felt they needed little supervision, but he occasionally liked to swoop down into clinical affairs simply for "the fun of it."

After Dr. Saunders' resignation in October 1975, there had been a temporary acting administration for 14 months while a search was made for his successor. Dr. Matthews was appointed in January 1977, six months before the strike took place. He was assisted by Dr. George Untergard, who had been on the staff during Dr. Saunders' tenure of office. A professional manager, who was not a doctor, was appointed as assistant administrative superintendent in May 1977.

Dr. Matthews recognized that his style and interests were different from those of Dr. Saunders. Dr. Untergard described Dr. Matthews' style as being less rigid and more participatory than that of Dr. Saunders, a less "cut and dried, yes or no, one way or the other" way of acting. He found this to be a style with which he himself felt more comfortable, but some residents and staff were less enthusiastic. Dr. Matthews knew that he took less interest in the inpatient service than his predecessor had and he thought that as a consequence the doctors in residency training felt uncertain of their position in his eyes.

Dr. Matthews' major concern was with the stability of the patients during the strike. They were uneasy at the best of times, and now, in the midst of the crisis and confusion, he feared for their safety. It was to this problem, not to the feelings of the staff and residents, that he wanted to devote his attention. He therefore put aside his worries about them for the moment, and turned his attention back to the question of the strike taking place outside the hospital.

Dr. Matthews had not made a secret of his sympathy for the strikers' cause. Even though he was concerned about the immediate effects of the strike on the patients, he believed that in the long run better salaries would improve the quality of care at the institution. Because the some 350 state employees in the Center had not received wage increases or cost of living raises for the past three years, the present salaries were too low to attract and keep good employees. People could walk down the street and find similar or easier work paying 20 to 30 dollars a week more.

A new state law had been passed in 1975 legalizing collective bargaining by state employees. Since then various unions had competed for the right to represent state employees. A coalition of unions under the direction of the AFL-CIO had finally succeeded in incorporating most of the nonprofessional and professional public employees, but the coalition still lacked a firm structural organization. The coalition included the attendants (male nurses' aides who looked after the physical well-being and welfare of patients), licensed practical nurses, housekeeping personnel, social workers, and some occupational therapy staff. Among the groups in the state which had founded separate unions were the police and firemen, the maintenance workers, the nurses, public physicians and psychologists, and the managerial workers. During the first six months of Dr. Matthews' superintendency, there had been a great deal of unionizing activity in the hospital.

Although the new law allowed for collective bargaining, strikes by public employees were still illegal. The union leaders decided to strike, however, as a dramatic way to bring force to bear on the state government after it persistently refused to grant new salary increases. Five days before the strike began, the Center received an

alert from the Department of Mental Health advising it to develop a
contingency plan in case a strike were called. The center worked out
a list of personnel essential for the functioning of its clinical services
with local union representatives. The union agreed that the listed
personnel could cross the picket line.

An uneasy weekend followed, and on Monday, in the
midst of a heat wave, pickets, all of whom were workers from the hospital, appeared outside the Center. Some fear of violence was in the
air, for the media had stressed the possibility of violence over the
weekend, and at the clinic one worker's car tires had been slashed after he had said he wouldn't go out on strike.

Dr. Matthews assumed that all employees doing research
in the hospital under the auspices of the university would also be allowed to cross the picket line. But with essential state personnel and
all university staff going in, it began to look like business as usual to
the picketers, and they feared this might make the strike ineffective.
As a result what Dr. Matthews called "sort of guerilla theater things"
began to happen at the hospital entrance such as high-spirited psychoanalysts tussling with the laundryman at the door in order to be
admitted. There was a good deal of confusion and renegotiating over
the logistics of admitting essential personnel at the door, but on the
whole pickets and nonstrikers were fairly good humored as they
somewhat self-consciously began playing their unaccustomed roles.

Dr. Matthews was impressed by the consideration strikers
showed for out-patients who had to cross the picket line and by the
concern felt by the attendants for the patients inside.

Inside the hospital a carnival atmosphere prevailed as
members of the staff joked about who would make lunch, sweep out
the front hall, and so forth. The administration set up what it called
"a sort of de Gaullist headquarters" in the nearby medical school
dormitory where it conducted interviews with applicants for the residency training program for the following year and carried out the
business of running the Center in the present circumstances.

The first piece of business was to provide for the patients'
stability during the strike. Since the striking attendants were most
consistently and closely involved with the patients, their absence
would have an immediate unsettling effect. The administration initiated a program of not accepting any new admissions and of discharging as many patients as possible, giving them extra medication to tide
them over the crisis. By Tuesday, however, doctors were getting reports that some of the discharged patients were getting restless, and

within the hospital a borderline patient dramatized the unease by starting a fire. When the fire alarm sounded, attendants and security employees on the picket line charged into the hospital to help extinguish the fire and then returned to their picketing.

On Tuesday afternoon, the local union representatives went off to a union meeting while the administration met with the nonstriking hospital staff in the medical school headquarters. At the staff meeting Dr. Matthews said he felt that the strikers were loosening up, but the local union leaders came back from their meeting taking a harder line and insisting that the hospital be absolutely shut down and that no attendants be allowed in. Dr. Matthews, therefore, felt he had to call in the police to provide security for opening up the hospital the next day. The union representatives seemed to accept his decision with good grace, saying, "We all have to do what we have to do."

On Wednesday, the third day of the strike, the police arrived with the morning shift, and no incidents or difficulties occurred. The picketers were better organized and disciplined. There had been some drinking and consequent high spirits on the picket line during the previous day, but there had been less of this on Wednesday morning. All of the attendants were back on the picket line, and nurses were doing their work in the hospital. As there were 70 attendants and only 17 nurses, the nurses had to carry a heavy burden of work. Some of the attendants expressed their concern for the nurses' safety. Under the protection of the police, senior staff members began carrying out the laundry and the trash, going out for sandwiches, and carrying out other business necessary to keep the hospital functioning.

During the morning, a union official announced to the picketers that an injunction had been taken out by the state against the union and that the strike would soon be settled. The attendants, after speaking with the local union representatives, rushed into the hospital and ran up the stairs two at a time to return to their duties. With the attendants back on duty and volunteers coming in to help, the carnival atmosphere of the first day revived. But it was not to last for long. Shortly after the attendants returned to work, the medical staff had handed Dr. Matthews their memorandum. Now he had to decide what to do about it. He took no formal action but responded to it as he had to the residents' letter by talking it over with the medical staff and residents whom he met in the corridors as he conducted hospital business.

The day wore on with no definite news that the strike had been settled. By 2:30 apprehension began to replace the earlier good feelings, and at 3:00, which was shift time, the attendants went back to the picket line, angry at the union leaders for having put them in the position of going into the hospital and then having to go out again.

Inside the hospital there was a slump of disappointment and anger. Dr. Matthews prepared for a much longer siege by planning a 24-hour duty schedule for everybody through the next weekend. The ambivalence of his position had limited his way of acting from the beginning of the strike. He was the director of the striking institution, yet the grievance was between the state and the state employees, and he had no power to negotiate. Recognizing this, he tried to make use of his lack of power in dealing with the strikers, his staff, the residents, and the state, who would have to pick up the pieces after the strike and get his institution working in harmony again. To both strikers and nonstrikers he emphasized his powerlessness and projected the problem "downtown." He stressed the benefits of a successful strike at the same time that he recognized that the strike settlement was beyond his control. He could negotiate some immediate issues at the local level such as getting strikers to agree to staffing requirements. When it seemed necessary to bring pressure to bear on the strikers for additional staff, Dr. Matthews reminded them of the need to ensure the patients' safety, and when they adopted a harder line after the union meeting, he called in the police.

In dealing with the nonstrikers, Dr. Matthews tried to recognize their needs by discharging as many patients as he could, shutting down admissions, and by soliciting their help in planning operations. By using these tactics he hoped to prevent any enduring hostility between strikers and nonstrikers or scapegoating, but his approach seemed to work better with the strikers than with the residents and medical staff. It seemed to Dr. Untergard that the nonstrikers could find little in the strike to identify with and that the residents resisted carrying out duties normally performed by attendants, housekeepers, security, and other personnel concerned with running the hospital. He and Dr. Matthews occasionally had to "knock some minor heads," as they called it, to keep them at their tasks. When the residents and medical staff threatened to go to the governor and the press, Dr. Matthews drew the line forcefully by telling them they would be in a lot of trouble if they did.

Dr. Matthews tried to put pressure on the state by means of

various outside-of-ordinary channels. The governor and some other state officials had made it clear that they wanted him to take a harder line, and to some extent he refrained from appearing to support the strike as much as he did. But he strongly objected to the governor's appearing on television saying, "Well, the state is running just fine, there are no problems, everything is under control and everything is great." He wanted to say, "That's a lot of baloney and cut that out. This is really not funny and you've got to cut this out and settle the strike because we're really in a lot of trouble, and it's no joke and things are not good." What he actually did was to emphasize to state officials that other hospitals in the area would soon find the patients usually taken care of by the clinic in their emergency rooms if the strike weren't settled fairly quickly. In general, he tried to make his point of view public. He avoided using the university as a force to bear on the state because he feared such a tactic might be counter-productive since the statehouse was well-known for its hostility toward the university.

While Dr. Matthews was considering how to deal with the growing tensions between the strikers and the nonstrikers and within each group, and how best to prepare for a longer strike, new developments were taking place "downtown." The judge who had agreed to issue an injunction against the strike now had ruled that the leaders of the strike coalition were guilty of contempt, and he fined the union $200,000 for each day the strike continued. The union was far too weak to survive such financial pressure, and around midnight of Wednesday the union leaders called off the strike.

When Dr. Matthews arrived at 6:15 on Thursday morning, the pickets were gone and the center was back in operation. People, particularly the strikers, were working harder than they had in years. Dr. Matthews observed that "the cooks were cooking up a storm, that the laundry man was pushing the laundry around like nobody's business, and that everyone was working with unusual enthusiasm." But as the day progressed tempers became frayed, and some of the people who had been on strike were making hostile and aggressive comments to individuals who had crossed the picket line.

Dr. Matthews called in the local union representative and said to her:

> You know, we've worked very hard with the realization we're going to have to work together. And I just wanted to let you know that what you do from the union point of view is your business,

of course, but I want you to know that if there are any reprisals, if anybody . . . if their cars get messed up or there's any kind of physical or other reprisals, that I'm going to get the state police in here in about three minutes, and it's going to be thoroughly investigated, and we will prosecute anybody who had anything to do with that.

Her answer to him was, "The union's position is that we don't want anything like that, and I will put out a notice that I expect people to heal their differences."

The assistant superintendent, who was responsible for security, talked with the acting director of security who then issued a memo to the effect that what people said in the circumstances of a strike should not be taken personally.

These directives seemed to deal with the tensions for the moment, but Dr. Matthews was fairly sure that the aftereffects of the strike would last for a long time.

COMMENTARY

The union members were aggrieved. Their wages were low and had remained unchanged for several years. But they were not the only aggrieved participants in the work of the hospital. The medical staff, all psychiatrists, were suffering from narcissistic injury. In simpler language, their self-esteem had been diminished by the hospital's loss of prestige and loss of position as an institution in control of its destiny. It was no longer in the forefront of psychiatry. Under the state's mental health program, the hospital functioned in a collection area in about the same position as other hospitals and clinics. It could no longer function as a primary researching and teaching hospital largely because it could no longer control its patient population.

While it would take us a long time to resolve the issues involved in this change, I am certain we would not be able to resolve the many ethical, ideological, and political questions arising from designating one or more hospitals "elite" institutions, capable of formulating the programs that would optimize their self-designated purposes. The fact is that the hospital had undergone a major change imposed from the outside. It was a victim, if you care to view the change in such terms, of complicated medical and community politics. The striking workers were protesting economic inequities. The complaints of the medical staff were much more complicated. The strike provided the medical staff with a vehicle to exhibit their grievances and to enact their story of narcissistic injury.

For his part, Dr. Matthews appeared to be taken by surprise. He had expected to deal with a strike by the unionized workers in the housekeeping functions of the hospital. But perhaps the medical staff caught something in Dr. Matthews' attitudes and approaches to the strike that exacerbated their injuries and that ruptured their identifications, if they existed, with him and the professional ideals they held in common.

Imagine for a moment if Dr. Matthews had declared prior to and immediately following the onset of the strike that the unionized workers were engaged in illegal action. The law stated that you cannot strike against the state. Furthermore, suppose he had issued a firm declaration that the workers must return to their jobs and pursue, without strike, their collective bargaining aims.

Had he made such unequivocal declarations, the striking workers would have known where they stood with the head of the hospital. Similarly, the medical staff and other constituents inside and outside of the hospital would have easily positioned themselves relative to Dr. Matthews: the strike was illegal and the workers were obliged to abandon the strike and remain on their jobs while they lawfully bargained to eliminate inequities in wages and working conditions.

With such a simple and clear stand, Dr. Matthews would have allied himself exclusively with the expectations of his profession, which were to deliver continuous care to the mentally ill. The doctors would have rallied behind Dr. Matthews. The only ire he would have engendered would have been from the union and the workers, who would have had to face the fact that, indeed, they were acting illegally.

Dr. Matthews did not take this hypothetical stand because, I suspect, he had some other things on his mind, what I would call hidden agenda. It is not uncommon for power figures to operate with an overt and a hidden agenda. But in my experience, the presence of hidden agenda, upon which power figures act, will sooner or later cause mischief. It is also commonly observed that executives with political orientations deeply rooted in their psyches tend to build and act on hidden agenda. Thus, the time-honored maxim to power holders, "keep it simple," collapses under the weight of political orientations and the hidden agenda that accompany them in their experience with positions holding some power.

We do not know enough about Dr. Matthews to say with any degree of certainty that he was a political animal and that holding hidden agenda was second nature to him. This conjecture is not outside the realm of the possible, if not the probable, but we can leave this question aside and simply observe that Dr. Matthews had hidden agenda around the event of the strike.

One not-so-hidden agenda item was his basic sympathy for the strikers. He thought they were underpaid and had been treated unfairly in not receiving periodic wage increases. If the strike were successful and wages adjusted upward, it would certainly have made Dr. Matthews' job a lot easier. Presumably he would have been able to recruit workers more easily as the wages offered approached market level. I call this motive a hidden agenda because Dr. Matthews never really came out and said he sympathized with the workers and their aims. Nevertheless, he came close.

The more hidden aspects of his hidden agenda that evidently enraged his medical staff are more difficult to discern. It is not uncommon for chief executives to see certain personal opportunities in crises not necessarily of their own making. For example, CEO's typically love to enter organizations that require turnaround. The sins of omission and commission that led to the crisis lay not at their doorstep. If a turnaround occurs, they are heroes. If it doesn't, they are not bums, although closer scrutiny may reveal that they in fact bungled the job. Those executives who relish turnarounds and who are often singularly successful are typically free of an overpowering conscience. They can fire people, order layoffs, dispose of businesses, and even ruin communities without losing an hour's sleep. They easily find justification for what they do. But beyond this observation lurks another possibility: that there is personal and secondary gain in their acting in such situations. If so, they tend to overreach and ultimately cause trouble for themselves. The secondary gain from this rational behavior is to satisfy sadistic motives. These motives are largely unconscious and therefore well hidden from the actor if not from his audience.

Or take another example of the work of hidden agenda. Power figures not infrequently have the uncanny ability to distinguish their career interests from the good of the organization. To further career interests might, for example, lead an executive to join organizations, attend meetings, or go on boards of directors at the expense of concentrating time and attention on the job at hand, the organization he works for, and the people with whom he should feel closely allied. This hidden agenda is also easily detected on the part of subordinates and other constituents.

I cannot say for certain that Dr. Matthews had these hidden agenda. But I am fairly well convinced that he saw in the strike a number of opportunities, perhaps with ends relating to his career, but also containing professional and organizational ends as well.

On a purely personal level, what were Dr. Matthews' prospects for gaining visibility in his profession? In the face of the diminution in its autonomy, the likelihood of the hospital restoring its tarnished image as the leader in psychiatric care, teaching, and research was not great. Funds were hard to come by, and the ability to select its goals limited by the controls the state had imposed. The Central States Mental Health Center had become simply another collection station for society's unfortunate—those who suffered severe mental disorders and characterological problems such as drug and alcohol addictions. The name of the game in treating such a patient population had shifted from treatment to management, a shift unlikely to excite bright medical students, interns, and residents. The frontier had shifted to psychopharmacology. To gain a foothold on this frontier would require substantial long-range funding to attract bright clinical and laboratory researchers, to build laboratories, to provide computers and other research support.

Calvin Coolidge became president of the United States as a result of being catapulted into national prominence following the policemen's strike that took place while he was governor of Massachusetts. While I cannot imagine a parallel situation with the strike of the housekeeping employees and other workers in mental hospitals and clinics, the crisis offered some opportunities for gaining a measure of power over the state agencies, the governor, and the legislators who could scarcely take up a position in the front lines of the impending battle. Dr. Matthews was in the front line and from that position he could possibly have achieved some prominence in the media and in the councils of state government. Whether he relished some possibilities of prominence on the heels of the strike, the medical staff effectively had upended this venture. When the physicians took their protest to Dr. Matthews, it was too late for him to follow the simple path of declaring the illegality of the strike and insisting that the workers return to their jobs. In effect, the medical staff had won its strike within a strike.

What is the main lesson to be learned from this case? Keep it simple! Avoid hidden agenda like the plague. Being direct and out front with one's aims builds the securest foundation for leadership.

FITNESS FOR COMMAND—THE ATTICA PRISON UPRISING

Events have a way of altering awareness. When the great basketball star Magic Johnson announced that he had tested positive for the HIV virus, awareness of the AIDS plague shifted dramatically. A great hero had fallen, and AIDS was no longer relegated to the so-called underside of society. In much the same way, the events of the Gulf War transformed attitudes toward the military, which had been struggling with public perception of it as an inept, extravagant, and deceptive force living outside the mainstream of American constitutional processes.

The uprising and assault at the Attica prison in mid-September, 1971, broke through the myth of the United States as a nation undivided to the realization that a new Civil War was in the making. Unlike the Democratic Convention of 1968, which was a middle-class protest against the Vietnam War, the Attica uprising was the American underclass, dominated by racial minorities, capturing power and using it, bringing down quasi-military force as authority's response.

The proximate cause of the uprising was anger over the

prison guards' attempts to discipline inmates suspected of scuffling in the prison yard. But once underway, the rebellion became politicized, drawing in a wide range of spokesmen for blacks and Hispanics, the dominant racial groups in the prison riot. Who knows what accumulated grievances led from one small event to another to its climax: violence and killing to restore the prison to its authorities.

While many struggled for center stage in this tragedy, it belonged to Russell Oswald, the commissioner of the Department of Correctional Services in the State of New York. Commissioner Oswald chose to occupy center stage, a choice worthy of question and contemplation. Lurking in the background, Governor Nelson Rockefeller needed to have this uprising disappear quietly in order to preserve his chances for the vice presidency. The inmates clamored for his appearance, which would have automatically escalated their power position, but he refused to appear and Commissioner Oswald remained in command throughout the uprising. Governor Rockefeller was not without presence in the affair. His lines of communication to Commissioner Oswald were maintained through his aides, but only because Oswald left these lines of communication intact, a decision worthy of careful analysis. Would Oswald have been in a stronger position to deal with the uprising had he ignored the governor's attempts at influence from backstage?

As you read the narrative, questions will come tumbling out of the pages, probably faster than you or I are capable of absorbing, let alone answering. To prepare for this narrative, here are some of the questions you should bring to the case.

1. Should Commissioner Oswald have gone to the prison to assume command?
2. How did Oswald position himself once he took command?
3. How *should* he have positioned himself?
4. Did Commissioner Oswald have clearly formulated objectives in assuming command?
5. Did he have a clearly formulated tactical plan?
6. What *would* a clearly formulated tactical plan have contained?
7. How *should* he have implemented this tactical plan?
8. Was Oswald fit for command in this situation?
9. As best as you can determine, was there some connection between Commissioner Oswald's personal

history and his fitness for command during the Attica prison uprising?

10. In the light of your analysis of the Attica story, what is your opinion of Governor Rockefeller's reply during the Senate Rules Committee hearings on the governor's nomination to the vice presidency to Senator Griffen's question on "what lessons did we learn" from the uprising at Attica Prison?

THE ATTICA PRISON UPRISING

Forty years after a battle it is easy for a noncombatant to reason about how it ought to have been fought. It is another thing personally and under fire to direct the fighting while involved in the obscuring smoke of it.

Herman Melville, *Billy Budd*

On Tuesday, September 14, 1971, newspapers across the nation and the world broke the intensifying suspense over the Attica prison riot with banner stories that 9 hostages and 28[1] inmates had been killed during the riot and assault, that several hostages had died of slashed throats, that one had been stabbed to death, and that another had been castrated before being killed. Few newspapers cited the sources for their information on the manner of the killings. Governor Nelson Rockefeller of New York issued a statement saying that "the uprising had been brought on by the revolutionary tactics of militants," and ordered a full investigation of the riot including "the role that outside forces would appear to have played."[2]

On Wednesday, however, this first interpretation began to unravel. With considerable hedging and apparent disbelief, prison administrators announced that autopsies had revealed that all of the hostages killed in Monday's assault had died from gunshot wounds and that the guns had been in the possession of the assault forces. Newspapers retracted their earlier stories, and New York Senator James Buckley's call on Monday for the "immediate punishment of the wanton murders of the hostages"[3] took on unintended meaning. Official explanations and Governor Rockefeller's statement that the assault force had shown great restraint and "done a superb job"[4] appeared more ambiguous.

BACKGROUND TO THE ATTICA UPRISING

Early in 1970, as part of a larger program of prison reforms, the New York state legislature passed a law providing for transfer of prisoners from the cities during times of civil disturbances and other emergencies in order to reduce the danger of prison rebellions. Prison administrators thus marked their growing fears of the fusing of ideology and practical grievances that was becoming characteristic of prison riots. They blamed this development on the politicization of prisoners by means of a nationwide movement of political radicals. The writings of George Jackson, Eldridge Cleaver, James Baldwin, Angela Davis, and Malcolm X made up the often clandestinely circulated literature of the movement. Muslims, Black Panthers, Young Lords, and Five Percenters (a splinter Black Muslim group considering themselves a part of the anointed five per cent that is qualified to be teachers of Islam) provided the organizational structure. This new movement labelled prisons the embodiment of America's oppressive, imperialist, racist society, and described inmates as the victims rather than the enemies of this society. The efforts of prison authorities to control the dissemination of these ideas through transfers and censorship merely facilitated their spread. Ideas came into the prisons with the prisoners, and were then carried to the prison to which inmates were transferred.

Attica was designed to be a maximum security prison for hardened criminals. Located in a rural area near Batavia, New York, it was staffed almost exclusively by whites from rural or small town backgrounds. The transfer plan brought in large numbers of young, urban, black, and Hispanic inmates, many of whom were members of militant organizations. Furthermore, the transfer plan not only provided Attica with a nucleus of potential leaders of a "new-style" riot, it also made later stories about the hardened, vicious criminals participating in riots less believable. Biographical accounts of the leaders of the Attica uprising clearly showed that some of them were at the prison for relatively minor criminal offenses.

Two events occurred in 1971 which marked the changes in Attica. In June a cell search turned up evidence of an organized, ideological movement in the prison. Vincent Mancusi, the superintendent of the Attica correctional facility, wanted the five men identified as being involved transferred, but Russell Oswald, commissioner of the New York State Department of Correctional Services, refused his request. These inmates, who called themselves the "Attica Liberation Faction," wrote Oswald a letter in July to which they attached a manifesto. The introduction to this "July Manifesto" referred to prison as "the fascist concentration camps of modern America" and charged that corrections personnel were treating inmates "like domesticated animals, selected to do their bidding on slave labor and furnished as a personal whipping dog for their sadistic, psychopathic hate."[5] The rest of the "Anti-Oppression Platform" was, however, restrained and practical. Oswald exchanged letters with the committee in which he assured them that changes would be made and they assured him that they would act in a democratic manner.

The next event had a more public and disturbing impact on the prison as a whole. In protest over the death of George Jackson, a militant black power advocate in a California prison, 700 prisoners, many wearing black armbands, fasted in silence during the day of August 22. There were no reprisals for this demonstration nor for the brief sick call strike of the following week. Eleven days later Oswald made a taped message to be played to the prisoners. He began the tape by speaking of the many reforms he had recommended to the legislature and of reforms which had already been put into practice. He then warned the inmates that some of them were abusing these new rules, and that many officials were complaining about the indecent and abusive mail they had received following the change in policy that now allowed inmates to write letters to public officials. He ended the tape with the remarks:

> Many of you have voiced confidence in me, and in the directions I have talked about, and I appreciate this. I am certain you realize change cannot be accomplished overnight, but I can assure you that changes will be made—just as changes have already taken place in the brief period of eight months.
>
> Some of your suggestions have been helpful to us in formulating policy and direction, and Superintendent Mancusi and I welcome your constructive suggestions and views.
>
> Let me conclude by saying that I appreciate your patience

and your expressed trust and confidence in what we are trying to do together.[6]

OSWALD'S STORY

Commissioner Oswald was born in Racine, Wisconsin, on August 4, 1908, of parents born in Ireland. Both were Roman Catholics and extremely religious, and this was passed on to their son. Until 1926 Oswald's father had owned a small grocery store. He was finally forced to sell his store, but the full effects of his changed financial position were postponed because he found a job on the assembly line at the Seaman Body Company, where Oswald himself had begun working after he graduated from high school. When the Great Depression struck, both lost their jobs, and, in addition, his father lost his rather heavy investment in this company and in the Nash Corporation where he had also worked. Oswald's father was finally reduced to selling clotheslines from door to door, while his mother went back to work as a checker and cashier in the very store the Oswald family had once owned.

Oswald solved his own unemployment problem by going to the University of Wisconsin in 1930. To finance his studies he wrote to several leading American industrialists asking for a loan, two of whom offered him loans totaling several thousand dollars, repayable gradually and without interest. After two years of liberal arts courses but with no degree, he went to Marquette University Law School in Milwaukee from which he received a law degree in 1935. While he attended Marquette he also worked as a social caseworker in Racine for the Welfare Department. He rose at 5:30 a.m. to be able to commute to Milwaukee, returned to Racine in the afternoon to work until evening, and then studied until midnight or later.

Throughout his working career Oswald repeated this pattern of following intense schedules, combining hard work and long commuting. Oswald writes that in high school he developed what both friends and enemies later called his "fierce, competitive spirit." Oswald further demonstrated his inclination for hard work by taking a summer job as a gandy dancer (a section gang laborer) on an interurban railroad line between Racine and Milwaukee. He, a high school friend, and the foreman were the only members of the section crew who spoke English. Rising at 5:30 a.m., Oswald carried ties and rails all day, and returned home at 6:30 p.m., too exhausted to do anything but go to bed after supper.

His experiences with the Italian- and Spanish-speaking workers on the railroad and his social casework in Racine with Italians and Armenians gave him a strong sense of the dignity and pride of these disadvantaged people. He saw how bleak their lives were made by the depression and felt that they needed help from the government. The families he worked with showed their appreciation of Oswald's interest by giving him gifts and inviting him into their homes. These experiences and the encouragement of a friend helped Oswald decide to go into social work.

After Oswald received his law degree he was appointed director of the Washington County Public Welfare Department in West Bend, Wisconsin, at a salary of $150 a month. Now 27 years of age, Oswald felt sufficiently secure to marry the woman he had met when they were both 17. His wife also encouraged him in his desire to be a full-time social worker.

In 1938 Oswald took his first of many civil service exams. The exam was in social work, a subject for which he had no formal academic training, and he was astonished when he placed first. But he was again sidetracked from his social work career from 1941 to 1945 by the war, where he served in the Navy. Oswald returned home to a new job as district director of the State Public Welfare Department. He also began graduate work at the Loyola University School of Social Work in Milwaukee and then in Chicago. His son was born in 1947 when Oswald was 39. To meet this new responsibility Oswald took a job as night-shift foreman at the Omar Baking Company in Milwaukee for three nights a week from 11:00 p.m. until 7:00 a.m. Each working day he commuted 180 miles. Oswald obtained a master's degree in social work from Loyola and a record of straight A grades. He turned down two opportunities for better positions in the Welfare Department because he wanted the job of director of the Wisconsin State Bureau of Probation and Parole, even though he lacked any experience in this area. Coached by four friends who were parole officers, he prepared himself at night for the competitive examination for the directorship and received the appointment.

A reformer, a convinced believer in the possibility of improvement through responsibility and freedom, he began his new job in a tense atmosphere brought about by a parolee who had gone on a rampage that ended in the murder of two school teachers. Undaunted, Oswald began to initiate reforms. He hired more caseworkers, raised their required training to a master's degree in social work, set an example of dedicated hard work by coming to work at 4:00 a.m., and pressured for parole and prison reforms.

In 1950 he was promoted to the position of director of corrections where he continued to initiate and administer his parole reform program. As a principal part of his program he asked for a maximum-security unit in which to isolate "malcontents" so that the majority of inmates could be rehabilitated more rapidly. The success of Oswald's reforms was impressive: no prison riots occurred during his tenure.

In 1955 Oswald was offered the position of director of corrections in Massachusetts. He accepted this opportunity "to take one of the worst prisons in the country and turn it into one of the best." But Oswald describes his 18 months in Massachusetts as an "unending, up-again, down-again battle...one damned crisis after another."[7] He arrived in Massachusetts in December 1955, 11 months after a riot in the Charlestown Prison. The prisoners were still awaiting transfer to a new facility being built in Walpole; four of the five ringleaders were still in isolation, and an investigative committee was looking into the prison system and recommending reforms.

Before leaving Wisconsin, Oswald had received a letter signed by most of the Charlestown prisoners, welcoming him and asking him to visit them. When Oswald did not go at once to address them, 16 of the prisoners went on a hunger strike to put pressure on him, but he sent a message that he would not be intimidated. Finally, at the urging of his wife, who had remained in Wisconsin, he met with the ringleaders on Christmas Eve, and decided to release them from isolation.

The frustrations of Oswald's job in Massachusetts arose mostly from the opposition to his reform program which he encountered from officials and the public. Oswald made the comment that the prisoners were "products of a neurotic society" and that "society itself must be to blame when 45 to 50 per cent of our prisoners in Massachusetts are repeaters."[8] He left Massachusetts to accept a position as a commissioner of parole in New York in 1957.

In New York Oswald was able to return to his preferred work of recommending and implementing parole reform programs. Under Governor Harriman, Oswald was elected chairman of the board of parole by its members, a position he continued to hold under Governor Rockefeller.

On January 1, 1971, Rockefeller appointed Oswald commissioner of the newly formed Department of Correctional Services, a merger of the Department of Corrections and the Division of Parole. Oswald took over his job determined to continue his reform program. He hoped to create better conditions for rehabilitation of prisoners in small community-style prisons, and he planned to expand his programs for early parole. But he also recognized that his entire reform program was threatened by budget cutbacks and by "the increase in the crime rates and the decline in social morality that might make our programs irrelevant or too late."[9] An even greater threat, less publicly discussed, was the increasing number of radical militants among the prison inmates, a situation Oswald blamed on Chief Justice Warren's leadership of the Supreme Court. In 1970 several District Court decisions had, in Oswald's opinion, given prisoners the erroneous idea that they had "more rights than the rest of us have," instead of having no other rights than for decent and humane care, as corrections officials believed.

It was in July, 1971, as we have seen, that Oswald had had his first exchange with the representatives of the militant, radical wing that formed the Attica Liberation Faction. Oswald's exchange of letters with the group ended with his unprecedented admission to the prisoners that the staff personnel was also affected by the apprehension felt by the prisoners. He concluded by saying, "Attitude changes are necessary and we are attempting to reattitudinize all parties, personnel and inmates alike."[10]

THE UPRISING

During the afternoon of Wednesday, September 8, 1971, approximately 400 inmates were relaxing; some were scrimmaging in one corner, while in another corner two inmates were sparring, apparently playfully. One of these, Leroy Dewer, had just been released from a seven-day "keep lock"—a form of mild punishment for minor infractions in which prisoners are confined to their cells. The other sparring partner, often mistakenly identified as Raymond Lamorie, later disappeared into the crowd. Corrections officers observing their activity were unable to decide whether this was friendly play or fighting. They used a bullhorn to order the inmates to stop, but called Dewer by the wrong name. Oblivious to the order, the two men continued exchanging light blows. One officer, Lt. Maroney, then tried personally to stop the activity. He ordered Dewer inside to his cell, and when the prisoner refused to comply he either put a hand on his arm or made a move toward him. Dewer responded by saying something to the effect of "come on, old man" and struck him lightly on the chest, an unprecedented event to the watching inmates gathered around. Many inmates supported Dewer's resistance, and one of them shouted at Lt. Maroney and Lt. Curtiss, who had joined Maroney, "leave this kid alone." There are considerable discrepancies in the reports on the details of what happened, but in the end the two officers retreated, another extraordinary event for inmates and officers alike. Reports of what followed are equally confused, but Mancusi and Deputy Superintendent Vincent apparently decided that both Dewer and Lamorie should be put in solitary confinement, based on the mistaken belief that Lamorie had been Dewer's sparring partner.[11]

When the two inmates were taken off to solitary confinement (in Attica called HBZ—for Housing Block Z) later that evening, Dewer resisted, struggled, and yelled, and had to be carried from his cell. Inmates believed that prisoners taken to HBZ were beaten there and on the way to it, and the corrections officers taking Dewer to HBZ were verbally abused and bombarded with small objects. One inmate, William Ortiz, threw a can of soup that caused a deep cut on one officer's head. Later the inmates gradually became quiet but not before making several threats of what would happen on the next day.

After a quiet but tense night, the inmates involved in the events of the previous day were allowed, to their surprise, to leave their cells for breakfast. Only William Ortiz, who was under keep lock, remained in his cell. There was some protest over Ortiz's exclusion, and as the inmates passed the lock box one of them pulled the lever of his cell. Ortiz hurried to join the others, and the word was carried to Mancusi of this new, again unprecedented incident. Mancusi decided that the inmates were to be returned to their cells after breakfast instead of being allowed, as was usual in summer, into the yard.

One of the architectural devices that presumably made Attica prison a riot-proof institution was the arrangement of the covered tunnels joining the cellblocks (see Exhibit 1 for a drawing of the prison). These met at an intersection known as "Times Square." The gates at the ends of the tunnels and at Times Square were made of exceptionally strong iron bars, and could be used to regulate the flow of inmate traffic. When the inmates had been routed into the A-block

Exhibit 1
ATTICA PRISON

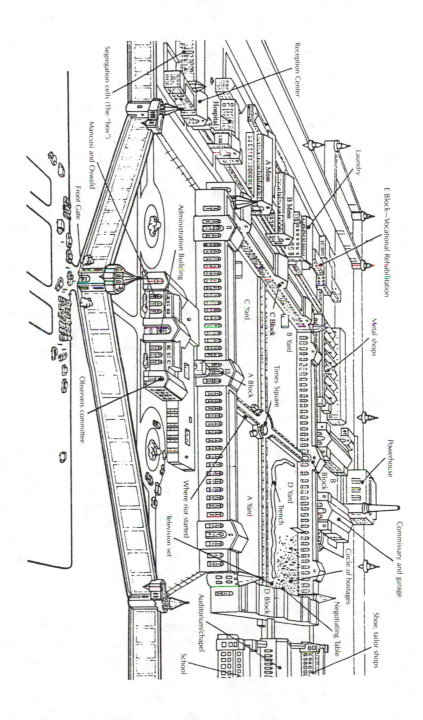

tunnel under the supervision of a young junior corrections officer, Lt. Curtiss hurried down to convey the new order to return inmates to their cells. Apparently it was the combination of finding the door locked to the yard and the sight of Lt. Curtiss which again set off the inmates. Curtiss was closely associated in their minds with the previous day's events. As he walked past the assembled men who were until then quiet and in formation, he heard someone say, "You no good mother" and then felt a blow on the head. He and another officer were then attacked and beaten, as were additional officers coming to their aid. After the prisoners had swept through A-block, opening cell doors, smashing furniture and breaking windows, the impregnable gate to Times Square gave way under pressure because of a welding weakness in one of the bolting rods.

Once the Times Square gate had fallen, the riot was no longer contained in one block and it spread throughout the prison. At this moment, Officer Quinn, who was in charge of the intersection gates, was knocked unconscious as the inmates swarmed through with the clubs, sticks, pipes, boards, knives, and rakes they had collected in their rush through A-block and A-yard.

All of this had happened within ten minutes, while prison authorities were mobilizing a counterforce. They were hampered by a number of difficulties: the absence of an all-prison riot plan; their reliance on a communications system based on an outmoded switchboard that could only handle one incoming or outgoing call at a time; and an insufficient number of men. The steam alarm whistle used to sound a general alarm did not go off until 9:15 a.m., and there was no code to enable those who heard it to tell whether it signalled a riot or an escape.

The rebellion continued until all the blocks, the commissary, pharmacy, laundry, state shop, and school had been either burnt out or taken. The powerhouse and the coal shack were not taken because the officers in charge resisted; the administration and reception building, the hospital, the mess halls, and the kitchen also remained in control of the prison authorities. In addition, corrections officers supported by state troopers under the command of Major Monahan took back, by using minimum force and with no loss of life or injuries, A-, C-, and E-blocks and C-yard. An attempt to retake B-block was halted because of insufficient manpower.

The rioting inmates gathered in D-yard. By 10:30 a.m. some 1,281 out of a total of 2,243 inmates were assembled there. Forty-two officers and civilians had been taken hostage. Some of them had been ordered to strip, others were still clothed, most were blindfolded. Many were badly injured, and the most severely injured were released. Eight more hostages were eventually taken, and 11 released because of their critical condition.

A carnival atmosphere prevailed as inmates enjoyed the euphoria of their success and the lack of controls. They ate ice cream cones, helped themselves to food and cigarettes taken from the commissary and to pills and drugs from medicine chests in the blocks.

THE INMATE AUTHORITY STRUCTURE

Soon after the chaos of the first minutes of freedom in D-yard, however, the Black Muslims, an already highly disciplined and organized group, began to take charge. They made themselves into a security force to maintain order and protect the hostages, forcefully stopping some impassioned inmates shouting, "kill the pigs" from their attempts to attack the hostages. They brought sheets and blankets to the stripped hostages with the biblical injunction to "cover their nakedness." At first this security force was composed only of Black Muslims, but eventually its leaders were pressured to include whites and, more belatedly, Puerto Ricans.

The most prominent members of the leadership coalition formed Thursday after the uprising referred to themselves as spokesmen for the inmates, not leaders, for all of them were publicly committed to brotherhood and total democracy. Some were in leading roles because they had addressed the inmates in the yard, others because their skills as "jailhouse lawyers" were needed for drafting demands and negotiating with the authorities. Many inmates later claimed that this coalition was formed through high-level negotiations among heads of various factions. This commitment to total democracy operated as a constraining factor throughout the later negotiations with the prison authorities and as a stimulus to rhetoric. Membership in the coalition fluctuated, but it remained a highly effective force.

The coalition established strict rules against the use of drugs, homosexual activities, and fighting. It restricted inmates' movements and required them to have signed passes in order to leave D-yard. Under its supervision, hostages, according to their own testimony, were protected and cared for with a surprising degree of solicitude. During the first night inmates gave up their mattresses to the "prisoners"; they provided the hostages with medical care and gave immediate attention to requests for water, cigarettes, or a trip to the latrine; they also shared the food that prison authorities had brought into D-yard.[12]

By Friday evening, however, there was a marked change in the inmate authority structure. Because of the pressure other inmates had put on the coalition to become more representative, early Friday the leaders announced that an election for representatives from each cellblock would be held. There is considerable discrepancy in the reports of how the election (or, perhaps elections) was conducted. One inmate reported that "everyone" voted, others claimed that delegates were elected by small cliques from each cellblock. At any rate, following the election, new members joined the group behind what were now called the "negotiating tables," and even tighter discipline was enforced.

Over time the leaders had to deal with mounting opposition to their policies and with mental breakdowns of inmates who found the tension of D-yard intolerable. On Friday afternoon a television reporter observed what he finally realized was a trial of two white inmates whom he had just interviewed. One of them was believed to be an informer; the other was a known racist. Both men had given some evidence of a desire to get out of the yard. They were charged with treason, stripped, and led into a cell. A third inmate was also "jailed" by the leaders. Long judged mentally unstable by inmates, corrections officers, and prison officials, he had became uncontrollable in the yard and attacked both hostages and inmates. The bodies of all three men, bearing the marks of multiple stabbings and cutting wounds, were found after the assault.[13]

On Saturday a group of seven white inmates reputedly discussed escape, and one of them put a white surrender flag on his tent. They, too, were charged with treason and then put under "house arrest" in a tent near the negotiating tables. Later they were told they could choose between death and digging a trench across D-yard. When they had completed the trench they were released with warning, later they were retaken and locked in D-block, and finally brought bound and blindfolded into the yard on Monday morning. All seven survived the assault.

By Sunday the leaders were unable to control the outbreaks of fights, beatings, stabbings, homosexuality by consent, rape, and the use of drugs. Increasing numbers of inmates were showing psychic or hysterical reactions of various types. Many inmates, however, later testified that fear still restrained them from expressing opposition to the stands taken in the negotiations by the leaders.

Many inmates later described the society of D-yard as being arranged in the same manner as the prison authorities ran the prison. Whatever the accuracy of such statements may be, the power behind the organization of D-yard society had dimensions quite unlike anything to be found "outside." The inmates' only real power lay in holding the hostages. One later said that the "hostages were the only means of negotiation," the only way to force the administration to keep its word, and, therefore, the inmates "wouldn't even consider harming the hostages."[14] Presumably his attitude was shared by others in D-yard, but the effective use of this power required inmates to demonstrate their willingness to kill the hostages if the state refused to accede to their demands or threatened to use force. Violent rhetoric made such demonstrations seem all too real to the authorities, many of whom, including Oswald, were convinced that the hostages would be killed at the first sign of assault.

Once television cameras and reporters entered the yard, inmates were seemingly supplied with an additional source of power: inmates could now bring their grievances directly to a worldwide audience. Normally cut off from public expression, this sudden opportunity undoubtedly had a heady effect. It encouraged theatricality and rhetoric, which costumes enhanced. At first, hoods and sheets were used to disguise the identity of the rebels, but face markings and spears added a new element. On seeing the prisoners for the first time, Oswald says he had "a sudden wry thought: This is prison reform?"[15] The most startling and terrifying instance of this costuming occurred on Saturday. A band of inmates dressed in clerical vestments and other costumes taken from the chapel and carrying spears, a homemade machete, bats, clubs, and gas guns came toward the hostages with cries that they were going to "get them."

OSWALD'S DECISION TO NEGOTIATE

Shortly after 9:00 a.m. on September 9, Oswald received the first reports of the prison uprising and decided to go at once to Attica, leaving word to that effect with Governor Rockefeller's office in Albany. When Oswald arrived at the prison, wailing police cars, angry and worried townspeople and friends of prisoners, and representatives of the media with their cumbersome equipment milled around the entrance. He conferred with Mancusi, who told him the inmates would talk only with him or the governor. He then went down to meet with representatives of the inmates who were waiting at the barred entrance to the tunnel leading to Times Square, an area which came to be called the DMZ. After a brief exchange, Oswald suggested the inmates appoint a committee to meet with him on neutral ground. According to Oswald, the men at the gate replied: "No. We can't have a committee. There are no leaders. Everyone is the same. All the people have to decide this. You will have to come in on this ground and talk with the people."[16]

When Oswald returned to the Administration Building, he was told by Mancusi and others not to enter the yard and decided that because he would make a tempting hostage, it would be strategically unwise for him to go into the yard. At this moment he received a message that Herman Schwartz, a professor of law at the University of Buffalo, was outside the prison and ready to give help. Oswald decided to use Schwartz and New York Assemblyman Arthur O. Eve of Buffalo, who was also on the premises, as intermediaries. The two men entered D-yard alone, were searched and conducted to the negotiating table through a passage of "security guards." At the table the two were offered orange juice and handed a list of "Immediate Demands." (See Exhibit 2.) In addition to these, the inmates insisted that Oswald appear in the yard, that the negotiations be covered by television, that more radios be brought into the yard so that inmates could be kept informed, and that additional outsiders also be brought in.

When Oswald saw the demands he commented that they were "revolutionary demands that plainly could not be met" and evidence that Attica was certainly something very much more than a spontaneous riot against poor prison conditions. He decided that he had "no choice" but to "walk down that tunnel to try to save the lives of the hostages" even though he felt he would very likely become one himself.[17]

The three men, Schwartz, Eve, and Oswald, returned to the yard, went through the security routine, and approached the table to begin negotiations. On his way Oswald took in the "tangle of violence" of D-yard and heard someone yell, "Let's throw this pig out in the middle and get rid of him." This provoked a roar of approval from the crowd but admonitions from the "security guard."[18] At this point, the inmates increased their preconditions for negotiations, insisting that the armed troopers they could see on the cellblocks be removed, that the condition of Lamorie, Dewer, and the inmates of

EXHIBIT 2
THE ATTICA PRISON UPRISING
Immediate Demands

To the people of America:

The incident that has erupted here at Attica is not a result of the dastardly bushwhacking of the two prisoners September 8, 1971, but of the unmitigated oppression wrought by the racist administration network of the prison, throughout the year.

WE are MEN! We are not beasts and do not intend to be beaten or driven as such. The entire prison populace has set forth to change forever the ruthless brutalization and disregard for the lives of the prisoners here and throughout the United States. What has happened here is but the sound before the fury of those who are oppressed.

We will not compromise on any terms except those that are agreeable to us. We call upon all the conscientious citizens of America to assist us in putting an end to this situation that threatens the lives of not only us, but each and everyone of us as well.

We have set forth demands that will bring closer to reality the demise of these prisons' institutions that serve no useful purpose to the People of America, but to those who would enslave and exploit the people of America.

OUR DEMANDS ARE SUCH:

1. We want complete amnesty, meaning freedom from any physical, mental and legal reprisals.

2. We want now, speedy and safe transportation out of confinement, to a nonimperialistic country.

3. We demand that the FEDERAL GOVERNMENT intervene, so that we will be under direct FEDERAL JURISDICTION.

4. We demand the reconstruction of ATTICA PRISON to be done by inmates and/or inmate supervision.

5. We urgently demand immediate negotiation thru Wm. M. Kunstler, Attorney-at-Law, 588 Ninth Ave., N.Y.C., Assemblyman Arthur O. Eve, of Buffalo, the Solidarity Committee, Minister Farrakhan of MUHAMMAD SPEAKS, Palante, The Young Lord's Party Paper, the Black Panther Party, Clarence Jones of the *Amsterdam News,* Tom Wicker of *N.Y. Times,* Richard Roth of the *Courier Express,* the Fortune Society, David Anderson of the Urban League of Rochester, Blond-Eva Bond of NICAP, and Jim Ingram of *Democrat Chronicle* of Detroit, Mich. We guarantee the safe passage of all people to and from this institution. We invite *all the people* to come here and witness this degradation, so that they can better know how to bring this degradation to an end.

THE INMATES OF ATTICA PRISON

EXHIBIT 3
THE ATTICA PRISON UPRISING
Practical Proposals

1. Apply the New York State minimum wage law to all institutions, STOP SLAVE LABOR.
2. Allow all New York State prisoners to be politically active, without intimidation of reprisals.
3. Give us true religious freedom.
4. End all censorship of newspapers, magazines, letters, and other publications coming from the publisher.
5. Allow all inmates, at their own expense, to communicate with anyone they please.
6. When an inmate reaches conditional release date, give him a full release without parole.
7. Cease administrative resentencing of inmates returned for parole violations.
8. Institute realistic rehabilitation programs for all inmates according to their offense and personal needs.
9. Educate all correctional officers to the needs of the inmates, i.e., understanding rather than punishment.
10. Give us a healthy diet, stop feeding us so much pork, and give us some fresh fruit daily.
11. Modernize the inmate education system.
12. Give us a doctor that will examine and treat all inmates that request treatment.
13. Have an institutional delegation comprised of one inmate from each company authorized to speak to the institution administration concerning grievances (QUARTERLY).
14. Give us less cell time and more recreation with better recreational equipment and facilities.
15. Remove inside walls, making one open yard, and no more segregation or punishment.

C-block be checked for evidence of beatings, and that the news media be let in.

Oswald acceded to these new demands and left to begin carrying them out. Within 30 minutes he returned to the yard with Eve, Schwartz, five reporters, and New York Assemblyman James Emery. The inmates expressed their suspicion of Oswald's promise of no "administrative reprisals" and gave Oswald a list of 15 "Practical Proposals," (see Exhibit 3), prepared by Jerry Rosenberg, a "jailhouse lawyer." Oswald could agree with most of these but felt their importance was overshadowed by the Immediate Demands for "complete amnesty" and "transportation out of confinement to a nonimperialistic country," both of which he considered out of the question.

He was now confronted with making a choice between taking over the prison with whatever forces were at hand or continuing negotiations. He knew from Major Monahan that he had sufficient force to retake the institution, but that there was "still no viable quantity of the CS disabling gas."[19] In the yard he had sensed the inmates' barely controlled fury and felt the rebels were quite capable of murdering the hostages. Prison officials were unanimously opposed to negotiating. Governor Rockefeller was also opposed although he carefully refrained from overtly expressing his opinion, saying only that he hoped "any appearance of vacillation or indecision could be avoided, whatever the course of action."[20] Oswald, in spite of his worries about the futility of negotiating, was convinced that it must be tried.

THE OBSERVERS

Oswald now recognized that he could no longer negotiate directly with the inmates; negotiations became, by default and without acknowledgment or plan, the task of the observers committee. The fifth of the inmates' Immediate Demands read:

> We urgently demand immediate negotiation through Wm. M. Kunstler, Attorney-at-Law, 588 Ninth Ave., N.Y.C., Assemblyman Arthur 0. Eve, of Buffalo, the Solidarity Committee, Minister Farrakhan of MUHAMMAD SPEAKS, Palante, The Young Lord's Party, the Black Panther Party, Clarence Jones of the Amsterdam News, Tom Wicker of New York Times, Richard Roth of the Courier Express, the Fortune Society, David Anderson of the Urban League of Rochester, Blond-Eva Bond of NICAP, and Jim Ingram of Democrat Chronicle of Detroit, Michigan. We guarantee the safe passage of all people to and from this institution. We invite all the people to come here and witness this degradation, so that they can better know how to bring this degradation to an end.

The inmates later added Republican New York State Senator John Dunne, Judge Constance Baker Motley, and Congresswoman Shirley Chisholm to the list.

No one seems to have had a clear idea of the functional role of the observers at Attica. The fifth demand used the word "negotiation," but in later testimony inmates revealed considerable differences in their understanding of the roles the outsiders were meant to play. Oswald seems to have wavered in his view of their function as well.

At one point there were more than 30 observers present. In addition to those chosen by the inmates, as individuals or as representatives of organizations sympathetic to the position of prisoners, some were selected by Governor Rockefeller and his staff. Confronted by what was actually happening, the governor's staff had invited Representative Herman Badillo at Oswald's suggestion; Alfredo Matthew, the superintendent of a community school in New York; State Senator Robert Garcia of the Bronx at Herman Badillo's suggestion; Reverend Wyatt Walker, a New York City Black Muslim minister who was an urban affairs advisor to Governor Rockefeller; and Tom Soto, a young Puerto Rican radical working with the Prisoners' Solidarity Committee of New York (a radical group affiliated with Youth Against War and Fascism).

During Friday the first observers who arrived congregated in the cramped quarters of the Steward's Room. Here they were briefed on what had already taken place and shown the five demands and the Practical Proposals. Oswald gave the observers his judgment of the situation but apparently no instructions on their role or the procedure they were to follow. And there was no agreement among them as to the definition of their powers.

The observers then lined up in pairs and proceeded toward D-yard. At the A-yard gate they were handed over to an inmate escort, searched, and led to D-yard. The inmates appeared to receive them hopefully, and as the observers introduced themselves, the inmates, according to Tom Wicker, cheered each one politely except for John Dunne, to whom they gave the biggest ovation of all. Apparently his work for prison legislation and reform had made him well known among prisoners.[21]

The observers left after establishing this initial contact and returned to the Steward's Room to discuss the Practical Proposals with Oswald and await the arrival of additional observers. Before returning to D-yard to obtain a list of inmate demands, weighted by importance, and to inquire of the inmates how they wanted the observers committee to function, the observers once again discussed their role. Two later reported that "in a hurried but careful manner, we decided that we must remain neutral intermediaries if we are to have any chance of preventing the loss of the hostages' lives."[22] It was at this time that Soto was admitted to the group.

When the observers returned to D-yard at 11:30 p.m., inmates' speeches, compounded of rhetoric and practical demands or grievances, followed. To the Practical Proposals and the Immediate Demands was added the demand that Superintendent Mancusi be removed. Of all demands, the one that elicited seemingly unanimous support from the inmates was amnesty. Transportation to a nonimperialist country received fewer than twenty votes. At one point William Kunstler, the well-known radical lawyer, was asked to represent the inmates. After hesitating for a moment, but without consulting with the other observers, Kunstler accepted. At another point a speech by Tom Soto was interrupted by shouts, screams, and clashing metal heard from C-block. At the sound of running feet on the elevated walkways a voice shouted "red alert," and the TV lights were shut off. While waiting in the silent near-darkness, one of the inmates lost control of his nerves and screamed, "Everybody gonna die," and began to wildly swing a long blade. The sense of crisis slowly abated, and Arthur Eve and John Dunne agreed to make an inspection of C-block. They came back with the report that one prisoner had been beaten by a guard but no assault had taken place. With them came more observers: three representatives of the Fortune Society; Jim Ingram, a black reporter from Detroit; two representatives of the Young Lords Party of New York; and Jaybarr Kenyatta, a highly respected Black Muslim leader.

Five and a half hours later, at 4:00 a.m., the observers left D-yard to return to the Steward's Room, and exhausted members shouted recriminations at each other. Kunstler, Kenyatta, and Tom Soto were attacked for their lack of neutrality. All agreed that the group was too large to accomplish its purpose. An executive committee was formed by what Tom Wicker called "a hectic process of appointment, elimination, election, and assumption." Its members were Arthur Eve, Clarence Jones, Jaybarr Kenyatta, John Dunne, and Herman Badillo; three blacks, two whites, and a Puerto Rican. Jones, Dunne, and Badillo had the backing of the governor's office; Eve, Kunstler, and Kenyatta were presumed to have the inmates' confidence. It was also decided that as the central issue was amnesty, a small committee should approach Louis James, district attorney of Wyoming County, on the question of possible concessions. James had already refused to grant amnesty, but it was felt that a personal appeal might cause him to reconsider. James did remain adamant on the question but was willing to sign a disclaimer of vindictive prosecution.

On Saturday at 1:00 p.m. the executive committee and a number of other observers met with Oswald to negotiate the inmates' demands. Out of the general confusion of demands, the group formulated a list of 28 Points, some specific and some deliberately vague. Oswald agreed to most of these on a watered-down basis. On the question of amnesty he was willing to grant "administrative" amnesty, a term which required four paragraphs of explanation, but not criminal amnesty.

Late Saturday afternoon brought the arrival of Black Panther Bobby Seale at the prison gate. The observers were divided over the issue of his admission, and it was the press that forced a decision by making the inmates aware of his presence. Oswald decided to admit him against his own inclinations. But the most portentous event had occurred earlier in the afternoon: Officer Quinn died from injuries he had received in the uprising. The issue of criminal amnesty took on a new dimension.

While the afternoon's events were occupying the attention of the observers and prison administrators, inside D-yard inmates were waiting in growing tension and distrust. At 9:00 p.m. the observers reentered D-yard after an absence of 16 hours to reestablish contact, introduce Seale, and present the 28 Points. Marching through the corridors lined with corrections officers on the way to D-yard, Tom Wicker sensed the full force of hostility and observed the "unbelievable number of guns" they had. In D-yard he felt the changed temper of the inmates.[23]

The introduction of Bobby Seale did not produce the enthusiastic reception the observers had anticipated, nor was Seale's speech as inflammatory as had been expected. He mentioned the 28 Points, saying he would consult with the Black Panther Party Central Committee about the acceptability of the points and report back. He then left the yard followed by more than half the observers, who thought they were following Oswald's orders to leave together. Their departure created such anger among the inmates that the remaining observers stayed, and Clarence Jones decided he must present the 28 Points and try to get the inmates to accept them. When he reached Point 3 on amnesty and read the district attorney's disclaimer, the reaction was bitter and derisive laughter.

At this point Kunstler reappeared in the yard, much to the admiration and gratitude of those both within and outside. He told the inmates that he thought the 28 Points were "the best they could get, that if they didn't accept them, people were going to die, but that the decision was their decision to make." Then he added that he realized that "the amnesty section is not acceptable to you now that a guard has died." Lt. Curtiss, who was among the hostages, later testified that these words evoked a loud gasp from the inmates and then "almost a silence fell over the yard and it was very solemn from then on . . . ."[24]

No mechanism had been set up for inmates to express their opinions on the 28 Points, and the pervading fear of voicing dissent made most of them reluctant to speak out. Later many inmates reported they were in favor of accepting them, others said they felt that the negotiating process was young and they still had time, others deeply distrusted that the authorities would carry out their promises.

Tom Soto and Jaybarr Kenyatta both made speeches denying their participation in drawing up the 28 Points, and each was received with roars of approval. The observers left the yard after midnight with the conviction that compromise was dead.

The early morning drizzle and later heavy rain of Sunday did little to dispel the growing sense of impending disaster. In D-yard, inmates waited for Bobby Seale's promised return at 7:00 a.m. with word from the Black Panthers. At 8:30 he turned up in the Steward's Room. What followed is a matter of dispute, but the general sense is he was told that if he would not endorse the 28 Points he would not be admitted to the yard. He left the prison, and with him went the last weak hopes of any compromise at all.

The observers watched assault forces build up and discussed what possible avenues for a peaceful settlement were left. Out of all this grew the conviction that their only recourse was to ask Governor Rockefeller to come to Attica to meet with the observers. The observers' reasons for this decision varied. Most observers said later they thought Governor Rockefeller's presence would buy time. Others felt if he were on the scene he would sense the potential for violence in the hostility of the armed men waiting to take over the institution and call off an assault. Some thought he could demonstrate to the inmates that the state was genuinely concerned. The observers issued a statement to the press urging people to telegraph Rockefeller to meet with the observers. No mention was made of the issues of amnesty or the removal of Mancusi.

Rockefeller later said he thought the observers were avoiding the issue of non-negotiable demands, that "they did not want to

admit defeat in this and see this thing just go back to the commissioner."[25] He felt if he came to Attica it might set off riots in other
prisons in order to require his presence, and asked, "Wouldn't it be a
round-robin trip to places that are demanding to see the governor?"
Nonetheless, he was sufficiently moved to direct that "any plans to
mount an assault on Sunday be cancelled."[26] The observers committee, which hadn't been allowed in the yard earlier on Sunday, was
permitted to visit the yard again. But Oswald, in consultation with
the governor's advisors, had already decided that their usefulness had
run out, and sent a message directly to the inmates. In it he requested
the inmates to release a five-man committee to meet with him.
When he informed the observers of his act, he received an unexpectedly hostile reaction. Observers felt compromised and endangered
and objected most strongly to the statement's implication that they
had recommended acceptance of the 28 Points.

Nine observers finally headed toward D-yard at 3:00 p.m.
and Oswald's message was read to the crowd along with a statement
that the observers had had nothing to do with it. Several hostages
were then brought to the table to be interviewed in front of the TV
cameras. The hostages spoke of their good treatment by the inmates
and asked Rockefeller and Oswald to meet the prisoners' demands,
particularly for clemency, and requested Rockefeller's presence at the
prison.

Sunday evening Oswald made another appeal to the inmates to negotiate on neutral ground. When it was rejected he commented, "I've given everything. I've gotten nothing in return. It seems
a little one-sided to me." He ordered no further entries into the yard
and disconnected the telephone in the Steward's Room.[27]

A final tempestuous meeting took place between Oswald
and the observers committee. In response to an argument from
Kunstler that there were international precedents for the "yielding of
law in the face of emergency," and his suggestion that the governor
might commute the sentences of anyone convicted of a personal injury crime at Attica, Oswald angrily replied, "This is dishonest. Either
it's amnesty or it isn't amnesty," and later repeated, "I have given everything and I have received nothing." Another observer charged Oswald with already knowing what he was going to do. After looking at
him a long time Oswald answered, "I'm going through the tortures of
hell trying to make up my mind." He spoke of the pressures on him
from hostages' families, from corrections officers, of others on "the

other side of the fence," and finally left saying, "I haven't made up my mind yet."[28]

Oswald then joined the representatives of the New York State government to discuss one last proposal that Governor Rockefeller meet with a small committee of prisoners after release of the hostages. He called the governor, who again refused on the grounds that the inmates were making non-negotiable demands.

On Monday morning Oswald appealed one more time to the inmates to release the hostages and restore order to the facility. The inmates rejected his memorandum, and the leaders transferred control of the hostages from the black Muslims to rebels known as "executioners." Eight hostages with their "executioners" were sent to the top of Times Square where they could be seen by the prison authorities. Knives were held to the hostages' throats, and the leaders shouted, "If you kill any inmates, we will kill the hostages." The negotiations were over.[29] At this point Oswald ordered the assault to begin.

THE ASSAULT

At the time of the assault, Oswald stepped down from his position of being solely responsible for making decisions at Attica and handed over decision-making power to the state police. Superintendent Kirwan was at his fishing lodge that Monday, and the responsibility for supervising the assault fell on Chief Inspector Miller, Deputy Chief Inspector Robert Quick, and more particularly, Major Monahan, who had assisted Mancusi in retaking parts of the prison on Thursday and whose job it was to lead the assault.

The overall operation, however, involved more than state police. According to Oswald there were some 1,800 men available. Of these, 555 were state troopers, 200 were corrections officers, 621 were National Guardsmen, 300 were sheriff's deputies, and the remainder were park personnel, specialists, and technicians.[30] Major Monahan and Mancusi signed an agreement to divide their responsibilities and authority on the basis of a distinction between "police matters" and "custodial decisions," but the meaning of these was never made clear. Major General John Baker, commander of the New York National Guard, confined his role to giving assistance when it was requested.

The assault plan was based on using existing state police procedures and the standard weapons of the police force. CS gas was used because it was of primary strategic importance. It was felt that its potential for temporarily immobilizing the inmates would limit their ability to attack the hostages or engage in defensive action. According to Oswald, shotguns were chosen because "only the shotgun commanded the respect and if necessary the firepower to deter or to prevent seizure of state police weapons by determined inmates who escaped the more disabling effects of the gas."[31] High-powered .270 caliber rifles equipped with telescopic sights were used to dispatch inmates threatening hostages. This weapon was a commercial hunting rifle and the ammunition made for it was designed to penetrate thick hide and tissue before expanding with a mushroom effect. The state police justified their use of it on the grounds that the bullets are less likely to pass through the target and hit an innocent person, but use of a similar type of ammunition was forbidden in international warfare by the Geneva and Hague conventions of 1906 and 1907 because of the unnecessary suffering it causes. The shotguns were loaded with "00" buckshot pellets which spread at distances exceeding 30 yards and thus hit unintended targets. At Attica even National Guardsmen carried "00" pellets in spite of National Guard policies not to use them for riot control.

For four days troopers had waited in suspense for word to retake the prison. While they waited they talked with corrections officials and townspeople who expressed their fears for the safety of the hostages and their intense hostility toward the inmates as well as toward Oswald's "soft" policies. The troopers had their own fears and hostilities. Coming for the most part from rural, small-town upper New York State areas, few had had any contact with blacks or Puerto Ricans. Those who lived in urban areas or had had experience with urban riots had dealt with rioters who were not branded with criminal records and they had confronted them in relatively open areas. They had heard, as they waited, the rumors of atrocities, ranging from humiliation to rape and castration, committed against the hostages. They had been verbally abused and taunted by the inmates. They had heard and watched the rhetoric and theater of D-yard on the television screens. They had heard reports of the barricades "festooned with metal prongs," of the growing supplies of Molotov cocktails, of the drums of gasoline, of the "rocket launcher" and other cunningly contrived devices.

No effort was made to screen the men participating in the

assault. Indeed, one man was the brother of a hostage. Except for the sharpshooters assigned the task of protecting the hostages on the catwalk, the troopers were given little briefing about when to fire and when to stop firing; they knew only that they were expected to fire at inmates engaged in "overt, hostile" acts against hostages and they were to avoid hand-to-hand fighting because of the danger of losing guns to inmates. No orders were given to the men to make an accounting of the ammunition they used nor were they advised that their actions were being recorded on film, two common forms of restraint used by the police.[32]

A further effect of the blurred command structure was that no one was made clearly responsible for assuming that no corrections officers took part in the attack, and several of them did in fact shoot at inmates from cellblocks and catwalks. Their gunfire killed at least one inmate and one hostage.

The initial assault force was small. Only 189 state police and two corrections officers, who were present to identify hostages, took part. When the hostages were moved up to the Times Square walkway, an additional force of highly trained snipers using rifles equipped with telescopic sights was instructed to take part in the attack. Its task was to prevent the inmates from killing the hostages and to clear the catwalk which was part of the assault route. Each sniper was given a particular "executioner" as his target and was ordered to shoot on the command of officers when the first hostile act of an inmate against a hostage was observed.

At 9:46 a.m. the CS gas-drop helicopters appeared over D-yard and almost simultaneously rifle fire and movement of the inmates toward the hostages followed. There is no way of estimating how many hostages or inmates would have lived or died if other decisions had been made. Both Oswald and Rockefeller were amazed by how many hostages were rescued. Many troopers did not fire at all. What is clear from the evidence, however, is that the videotapes did not support the testimony of troopers who said they fired only when they saw inmates making hostile movements toward hostages or other troopers. There was incontrovertible evidence that troopers and corrections officers fired at inmates trying to move away or hide from the assault forces, at inmates who were not moving at all, and at inmates who were attempting to surrender, and that they fired into tents and trenches without first looking into them.[33]

The same absence of control characterized the surrender and the "custodial mission" of returning inmates to their cells. Surrender instructions were given, in English, at 9:50 a.m. Hundreds of inmates surrendered and were put under control of corrections officers and some troopers while other troopers prepared to retake D- and B-block. The surrendering inmates in D-yard were ordered into A-yard and told to drop face down and crawl forward with their hands locked behind their heads. Those who had moved farthest from the door were then ordered to strip in preparation for body searches by a combined force of troopers and corrections officers. Such security measures do not allow beatings or other abuses of inmates. Inmates, National Guardsmen, who were acting as medics, and a trooper testified to the McKay Commission that clubbing, often in the area of the genitalia, kicking, and verbal abuse with racial and sexual content occurred during this and later phases of the rehousing. The Goldman Panel, a citizens' group appointed by Rockefeller to monitor the prison after the riot, had doctors examine inmates eight days later. Their reports of abrasions, cigarette burns, contusions, and lacerations on the inmates confirm other reports that reprisals were carried out during the rehousing.

There was also a failure to make prior arrangements for adequate medical care for those wounded in the assault. Testimony showed that in spite of repeatedly expressed fears that carnage to hostages and inmates alike would result from an assault, no one had given much thought to organizing post-assault medical care. The wounded hostages were transported to nearby hospitals where there was neither room nor authorization for inmates to be cared for. As a result, treatment of wounded inmates was haphazard and inadequate. In the end, National Guardsmen provided most of the immediate care for the injured inmates, often in the face of abuse by both prison officials and the inmates they were treating, and without proper equipment.

THE AFTERMATH OF ATTICA

Out of the aftermath of recriminations and investigations generated by the Attica uprising grew a determination to avoid another such confrontation. The McKay Commission wrote in its preface that the cry "Avenge Attica" should be "turned to reforms which will make repetition impossible."[34] Oswald ended his book with the sentence: "We who have lived have gone through sorrow and agony—and those who cannot remember the past are indeed doomed to repeat it."[35] He, too, recommended rapid and determined prison reform as a way to avoid a repetition of Attica.

Neither the McKay Commission nor Oswald named the specific reforms to be made. Only Rockefeller saw clearly, in retrospect, how the tragedy of Attica might have been avoided and how a repetition of what the McKay Commission called "the bloodiest one-day encounter between Americans since the Civil War" could be prevented in the future. In hearings before the Senate Committee on Rules and Administration on the nomination of Rockefeller as vice president, he answered a question on Attica from Senator Griffen by saying:

> Now, you say what lessons did we learn? I think it is fair to say that the procedure, which had been the procedure, namely to go ahead at the beginning without weapons and which was stopped in the process by the Commissioner, which procedure has now been reestablished by the State, is the best procedure and that if this were to happen again, I would think that was the proper way to proceed.[36]

COMMENTARY

Herman Melville's warning not to be too quick or self-assured in using hindsight to dissect the mistakes of a field commander is a worthy note of caution as we undertake to analyze the decisions and actions that culminated in the use of force to secure the prison. But as the sages have taught us, to fail to understand history is to be doomed to repeat it.

In that spirit of inquiry we can without apologies dissect the actions of Commissioner Oswald, who freely took command of the prison immediately after the uprising.

Was he wise in displacing Superintendent Vincent Mancusi, who was in charge of the prison until Commissioner Oswald took over? At first blush, it appears to have been a shrewd move. Mancusi was identified with prison authority. In the eyes of the inmates, Mancusi represented the repressors against whom they had rebelled. Would the inmates negotiate with the immediate authority figures against whom they had rebelled? Would they be more willing to listen to reason in dealing with Commissioner Oswald, who was at least one level removed from the fray, and who had a reputation as a prison reformer? By taking command and displacing Superintendent Mancusi, Oswald appeared to have conveyed the possibility of resolving the conflict without further violence and opening the door to a negotiated settlement, preserving the life of both the hostages and the prisoners in the yard.

The other side of the issue was Oswald's lack of experience in command. While the objective of a peaceful solution was paramount, there existed from the start the possibility that force would be necessary to restore the prison to the control of the authorities. Oswald had no experience with the use of force and, indeed, little experience with day-to-day crisis management. What possible motives could have led to his assuming command?

Let us assume for the moment that wisdom dictated the removal of Superintendent Mancusi as a tactical move to suggest to the inmates that negotiations were a possibility, that the authorities were looking for a peaceful settlement. In that vein the removal of Mancusi could have been interpreted as a "signal" that talk could be productive and in the interests of the prisoners. Making that assumption still does not leave Commissioner Oswald as the best choice to substitute for Mancusi, given his lack of experience in managing crises. There were other constituents to be considered, such as the prison staff and the community from which the staff, and incidentally the hostages, came. Having the presence of a person intimately experienced in prison management and the crises that often occur in prisons (although Attica was in an extreme condition of crisis) would have created a number of conditions addressed to the resolution of the uprising.

First, the presence of such a figure would have communicated to the prisoners that the authorities could not easily be manipulated. It would also have communicated that the authorities were thoroughly familiar with tough stances and the ability to make tough choices, both of which were not visible in Oswald's immediate presence. Furthermore, an experienced person in command would have provided a figure with whom the prison staff, the townspeople, and the public at large could identify in the daily, almost moment-to-moment flow of events in the crisis. Remaining in the background and not in the front line, so to speak, Oswald could have influenced strategy and tactical decisions without being affected by the stress of the event and the pressures of public scrutiny in the same way he had been affected in the position of command he had allocated to himself. The speed with which he had displaced Superintendent Mancusi suggested the decision was not a product of deliberation, but one of impulse. In retrospect, this decision, driven by impulse, appeared misguided and led to many other decisions that were equally uninformed.

We have no certain basis for judging why Commissioner Oswald took command in displacing Superintendent Mancusi. Perhaps he felt duty bound and wanted to relieve Mancusi of the responsibility for the crisis and its possible aftermath, including violence and death. If this motivation had been in back of the decision to assume command, it would appear to have been driven by impulse and not thought, however lofty the desire to assume responsibility. A less lofty motive would have been ambition, the desire for visibility in the media, possibly even fame that could have catapulted him to higher office. The motive of ambition was not inconsistent with Oswald's history of striving for achievement, nor is it a criticism of ambition itself. It is simply the suggestion that ambition not guided by thought, but instead a force for impulsive action, breeds its own trouble.

Here is an interesting, and subsidiary question: With whom did Oswald counsel in this decision to go to the prison and take command? A very wise friend told me the first thing an officeholder should seek upon assuming responsibility is someone with whom to have lunch. Whether over lunch or in other circumstances, every power holder needs a counselor, especially under conditions of crisis, where stress mounts and clear-headedness is the primary requisite for achieving a successful resolution.

What followed from Commissioner Oswald's first decision reflected his inexperience and the lack of clear-sightedness. Once he took command, Oswald had difficulty positioning himself with respect to the various constituencies he had adopted. Take the prisoners in the yard as a main target of his actions. His position in their eyes was unclear. He agreed to go into the yard to negotiate, which suggested that he was pliable, subject to their influence if not their control. His decision to allow observers, to permit the media to enter directly, reinforced this image of a man subject to manipulation and control. To the prison staff, their families, and the community, he must have appeared weak. His reputation as a reformer, a "do-gooder," preceded his physical presence following the takeover of the yard. Commissioner Oswald should have established himself as the focal point for all activity in relation to all of his constituents. He should have refused the entry of outsiders, whether as observers, or as representatives of the media. The media, including especially television, should not have been permitted entry to the yard. They caused widespread publicity that gave the prisoners cause to overestimate their power and their bargaining position. The presence of observers, some of whom became active advocates and negotiators for the prisoners with direct access to the media, confounded Oswald's problem of establishing his position as the focal point of communication with representatives of the prisoners.

For failing to establish a clear-cut position for himself, Oswald paid a dear price. He could not easily force the prisoners to appoint a committee to meet with him and his representatives in an office, away from the yard and its turmoil. The prisoners enjoyed the euphoria of temporary power and falsely believed it would allow them to dominate the situation. The fact that the uprising ended with a quasi-military action demonstrated where the real power lay. One of the aims of communication in the early stages of the uprising should have been to bring the site of real power to the center of attention. In fact, one of Commissioner Oswald's major blunders was in not establishing a chain of command and military preparedness in the eventuality that physical force would be required to end the uprising. A properly prepared force with a tightly drawn chain of command would have prevented the wanton and aimless use of force that resulted in the escalation of casualties.

If Commissioner Oswald had clearly formulated objectives and an equally clear tactical plan with which to make rapid decisions, they were not apparent in his behavior and the actions that followed his appearance at the prison. It is highly probable he reacted impulsively, even to the point of ordering the military action. A commander who goes on a fishing trip at the height of the crisis is evading responsibility and is communicating the absence of tactical readiness in his area of responsibility.

Commissioner Oswald's lack of preparedness for his position of command, as reflected in the absence of an apparent set of objectives and a tactical plan, forced him into impulsive action. While perhaps the best that Oswald could do under the circumstances, his impulsiveness caused a rupture in authority relations within the prison staff as well as with the inmates holding the hostages imprisoned in the yard. This void in authority caused a diminution in psychological function, making it difficult for all constituents, inmates, staff, and media alike, to control their behavior. As a consequence, whatever the possibilities for a peaceful resolution through negotiations, they could not be realized. I do not doubt Commissioner Oswald wanted a peaceful resolution, but his wishes failed to find support in the absence of three conditions that would have maximized the chances for successful negotiation: (1) establishing central authority through a visible, and highly focused, position of leadership; (2) voicing clear-cut objectives to all constituents; (3) developing a sharply defined tactical plan to support preparedness for negotiations, and if necessary, forceful retaking of the yard and ending the uprising.

Commissioner Oswald or anyone else in charge faced a difficult problem in mounting effective negotiations. Ideally, to negotiate one has certain desires in parallel with concessions. The desires were apparent: to end the uprising, restore order to the prison, and to achieve the safe release of the hostages. But what were the possible concessions to be given in exchange? In truth, the only concessions available were the avoidance of negatives and possibly certain symbolic promises. The avoidance of negatives consisted of harsh penalties for failing to end the uprising. The inmates were engaged in criminal conduct for which charges could be levied and lengthened prison terms imposed. An officer died as a result of the uprising, calling for even graver charges and penalties. Commissioner Oswald could not absolve them of this criminal conduct, nor could he promise leniency. In the face of the tensions, he could not deal with questions of prison reform at the risk of communicating that violent behavior in prisons can pay off. In fact, Commissioner Oswald, or anyone else in charge, had little to give in negotiations, except to warn of the graver consequences ahead should the uprising continue. Meetings conducted away from the prison yard with a small group of representatives could have communicated the nature of the sanctions that lay ahead, and could have been a forum for persuasion: that it was in the prisoners' best interests to draw the episode to a peaceful conclusion. Here, symbolic communication would have been important. There was much to do in prison reform. We have yet to learn how to avoid hardening attitudes and alienating further those we have incarcerated for criminal behavior. We offer little hope and less opportunity for change and reform. Certainly the physical conditions of incarceration offer little promise of change. Only a cynic or a pathological dissembler would have been willing to make promises to the prisoners that could not be fulfilled. We have no program for reform. However, it is possible to show some compassion and to accord even a modest measure of re-

spect for the inmates' spokesmen, without acceding to irrational demands, or withdrawing in the face of psychological regression. This
difficult stance would have required patience, but more importantly,
a posture based on the security of one's position in charge, and the
sense of direction that comes from knowing what one hopes to accomplish and how one might get to these end points.

  We hover over a nagging issue: Commissioner Oswald's
fitness for command. The term "fitness for command" comes
straight out of the military study of leadership. Whatever your views
of the military, it deserves recognition as the institution that has
worked the longest and the hardest at understanding leadership and
the problem of developing leaders at *all levels of the hierarchy*. The
southern historian and biographer, Douglas Southall Freeman, defines leadership for the military (and perhaps more generally) as the
embodiment of three qualities. In Freeman's language, a leader
"knows his stuff." A leader knows how "to be a man." A leader is
habituated to "take care of his men." These three guides to fitness
for command (to know your stuff, be a man, and take care of your
men) suggest qualities of mind and character that build slowly, that
grow from experience, and that reflect an ethos in which one subordinates one's own best interests (careerism) to the interests of a
group, an institution, and a society. Notice that this prescription is
not ideologically grounded. On the contrary, it is highly pragmatic
and designed for a lifetime of dedicated hard work.

  Commissioner Oswald was no stranger to hard work. If
anything, his penchant for hard work suggests an obsessional need
for activity, since it appeared to border on self punishment. Punishment for what is not at all clear in his own accounts of his history.
That he was ambitious is clear; that he set out to do good in the
world is also clearly reflected in his chosen field of social work and
the rehabilitation of prisoners. If there are two distinct aspects to
dealing with criminals (punishment and reform), Commissioner Oswald was more attuned to reform than punishment. There is a legitimate question as to whether these two aspects of criminology
should be combined administratively as in the case of New York
State, where Governor Rockefeller established the position of Commissioner of the Department of Correctional Services, combining
the Department of Corrections and the Division of Parole. Commissioner Oswald, who by disposition and experience seemed more
inclined to reform than to punishment, ran a risk in this role. The
risk was purely personal in that he was susceptible to the rage that

would follow any disappointment in his efforts at reform. If society did not accept his version of reform, or the speed with which it should be implemented, his identification with the underdog would be irrationally reinforced just as his anger at "society" would be amplified. Both of these effects impair objectivity, a quality of mind essential in leadership, especially under conditions of crisis.

I suspect Commissioner Oswald was highly ambivalent in his attitudes toward authority and toward those seemingly subordinate to, if not oppressed by, authority figures. The details are not clear, but the possibility exists that Oswald's ambivalent attitudes toward authority resulted from some continuing attachments to his father, who as a product of the depression could have mirrored the dual images of the disappointing authority and those who are "victimized" by society.

The import of ambivalence in someone in Oswald's position (in command of a organization in crisis) is in the impairment that resulted in the inability to position himself in the Attical structure, his inability to formulate objectives, to devise a clear tactical plan, and above all, to remain objective, neither a victim of identifications with the upper dog or the underdog. The first identification at the extreme leads to sadistic behavior; the second identification with masochism. If the need is to "know your stuff," the knowing that comes from experience and objectivity were, for Commissioner Oswald, areas of self-doubting. If the need is to "be a man," the figures from Oswald's past left him with cloudy visions of what it takes to be a man, particularly in situations that tend to repeat the past in reproducing the feeling of being let down. Finally, if the need is to "take care of your men," the complexity of just who your men are, what they require, and how you communicate your intentions in looking after their interests, can overwhelm good intentions when objectivity is impaired.

I had a curious experience recently in discussing the Attica case with the senior executives, both military and civilian, of the United States Army Tank and Automotive Command in Warren, Michigan. These executives felt I was coming down too hard in my interpretation of Commissioner Oswald's performance during the Attica prison uprising. More than simply reflecting Herman Melville's warning about after-the-fact analyses, free of the heat of the times and the battles, these executives, or so it seemed to me, had more of a direct feeling than I of what it is like to be in the pressure cooker, as in Oswald's case. If to understand all is to forgive all, there is something missing in my perceptions of, and attitudes toward, authority. I find it difficult to forgive in the sense that the unique feature of power is its capacity to cause trouble for other people. It seems to me eminently unjust not to demand the best performance from people in positions of power, whether they are there by pure accident or by their own ambitions and designs. There are all sorts of excuses to be made for inept performance. The least acceptable excuse in my book is to invoke a power figure's helplessness in the face of overwhelming forces, including his or her personal history. I would judge that Russell Oswald was an ambitious man. Who knows what fantasies of fame, power, and fortune he harbored when he undertook command at Attica? A hero for resolving the crisis? A fallen victim of man's or society's cruelty to its fellow man? Fantasies aside, the truth is that people depended upon Commissioner Oswald. They *needed* him. In falling short of expectations, he inadvertently became another individual whose actions in a power position eroded the commitment to leadership in American society. When authority fails, or disappoints, erosion of the bond of confidence between leaders and led follows. This our society cannot afford.

At the conclusion of the case study, Governor Rockefeller's response to Senator Griffen represents another nail in the coffin in which we are burying authority and its capacity to make life better. He adroitly shifted all the blame to Commissioner Oswald and emptily referred to the "old procedure" reinstated of proceeding "at the beginning without weapons" as the way to go, the lesson to be learned from the tragedy of Attica. As the saying goes, the mountain labored and came forth mightily with a mouse! Let us reformulate Senator Griffen's question to: What lessons has Attica taught us in the arts of leadership? To "know thyself"?

Endnotes—Chapter 20

1. The final total of deaths at Attica was forty-three. Corrections officer William Quinn died on September 11; nine hostages and twenty-six inmates were killed in the assault; one hostage and three inmates died after the assault, and three inmates were killed by other inmates.

2. *New York Times,* 14 Sept. 1971.

3. Ibid.

4. *New York Times,* 16 Sept. 1971.

5. *Attica, The Official Report of the New York State Special Commission on Attica* (New York, Washington, and London: Praeger Publishers, 1972), p. 134, (hereafter cited as the McKay Commission).

6. Russell G. Oswald, *Attica—My Story* (New York: Doubleday and Co., Inc., 1972), p. 210.

7. Oswald, *Attica—My Story*, pp. 155-158.

8. Ibid., p. 172.

9. Oswald, *Attica—My Story*, p. 201.

10. McKay Commission, p. 137.

11. This account of the riot was taken from the McKay Commission report, chaps. 4 and 5.

12. Dr. Warren Hanson, "Attica: The Hostages' Story," *The New York Times Magazine*, (October 31, 1971); Oswald, *Attica—My Story*, p. 220-22; McKay Commission, pp. 197, 201-203, 241-42.

13. McKay Commission, pp. 284-86; Steward Dan, *New York Times*, 4 Oct. 1971.

14. Wicker, *A Time To Die* (New York: Ballantine Books, 1975), p. 103.

15. Oswald, *Attica—My Story*, p. 83.

16. Ibid., pp. 82-84.

17. Ibid., p. 85.

18. Ibid., p. 87.

19. Ibid., p. 88. CS tear gas is a stronger and more immediately effective incapacitating agent and is physiologically safer than the CN gas used by the Army from World War I until 1959.

20. Ibid., p. 94.

21. Wicker, *Time to Die*, p. 67.

22. Julian Tepper and Tony Fitch, "Attica Chronicle," *Washington Post*, 19 Sept. 1971.

23. Wicker, *Time to Die*, pp. 214-217.

24. McKay Commission, pp. 263-264; Oswald, *Attica—My Story*, p. 226.

25. McKay Commission, p. 276.

26. McKay Commission, p. 276; Wicker, *Time to Die*, p. 282, also says that Rockefeller told Oswald to drop the plans for a Sunday attack.

27. Oswald, *Attica—My Story*, pp. 246-47.

28. Wicker, *Time to Die*, pp. 328-337; McKay Commission, pp. 315-317.

29. Oswald, *Attica—My Story*, pp. 254-258, 265, 268.

30. The McKay Commission figures, p. 343, differ slightly, showing a total of 1,100 men of whom 587 were state police and 312 were corrections officers.

31. McKay Commission, p. 347; Oswald, *Attica—My Story,* pp. 279-280.

32. McKay Commission, pp. 358-362.

33. Ibid., pp. 335, 377-395.

34. Ibid., p. xxi.

35. Oswald, *Attica—My Story,* p. 357.

36. Senate Committee on Rules and Administration, *Nomination of Nelson A. Rockefeller of New York to be Vice President of the United States,* 93rd Cong., 1975, p. 125. Rockefeller had expressed this opinion earlier in a broadcast in September 1972 after he had read the McKay Commission report. *Washington Post,* 21 Sept. 1972.

CONCLUSION

What have we learned about leadership? As I said at the beginning of this book, the best way to learn how to lead is to learn by doing. The second best way is to learn from other people's mistakes.

It is a marvelous fallacy to expect to find reliable role models in so-called effective leaders. The wish in back of this quest for role models is to simplify the problem of becoming a leader. Find a person who has proven his or her effectiveness as a leader and simply imitate. What a happy solution to a problem that has plagued man over time! Remember that even Moses had to suffer the pains of an "on-the-job" training program. In fact, historically, the route to leadership is a succession of tests. To be tested is to endure one's own mistakes and to learn from the experience.

Besides seeking role models to imitate, many would-be leaders, upon assuming a position of authority, attempt to repeat what has worked for them in the past. Newly appointed CEOs are especially vulnerable to the compulsion to do today what worked for them yesterday. Part of this urgency to repeat stems from insecurity, the stresses that appear as one seeks to position oneself in some new structure. The title of CEO makes little difference. The problem of positioning oneself is a task that has to be done anew, and with a fair measure of creativity. To short circuit this problem by relying on what has seemingly worked in the past is to substitute action for thought, which itself is a dangerous maneuver.

Still another mistake is to initiate process as a means of making one's presence felt as an authority figure. Taking the helm provokes a temptation to initiate strategy studies, which suddenly require task forces, committees, reports, and frequently consultants. What may make matters worse is the failure to specify just what problems are being addressed through this introduction of process. Is the problem substantive to the business? Or, is the problem the chief's personal anxiety in establishing himself or herself as a presence in the eyes of other people?

Becoming a presence is indeed a central issue in leadership. But it must be dealt with directly. Facing this issue directly requires some careful, and silent, introspection. Leaders must ask and answer for themselves the question, "Why am I here?" The answer entails a carefully informed understanding of the situation, and what particular assets one brings to bear on making a difference in the situation as it is currently defined.

In the lives of great charismatic leaders, the question ("Why am I here?") and the potential answers seem inherent in the stars. They feel a sense of destiny, the need to accomplish great work in the activation of unique talents. Much as General Charles de Gaulle declared "l'état c'est moi!", proclaiming his long-held conviction that France's fate and his were inextricably entwined, the charismatic leader pursues his or her destiny with single-mindedness and fervent determination. This experience with leadership is the equivalent of what the religious would describe as "vocation" or "calling." For most of us, there is no conviction of a calling to be head of one or another organization. Therefore, the problem of positioning oneself and answering the question, "why am I here" is acute.

Leadership begins and ends with the problem of power. Power is the potential an individual has to alter the thought and action of other people. I distinguish in this definition among three variables: authority, power, and influence.

An individual's power base is the combined elements of authority. We are indebted to the German sociologist, Max Weber, for clarifying the different sources of authority. As Weber pointed out, authority derives in part from the organization and, therefore, has a legal foundation. Chief executive officers are elected by a board of directors. Corporate bylaws define the job in the most meager terms, but with sufficient specificity to create duties, obligations, responsibilities, and scope.

A second element of authority is the expertise and related professional qualifications of the incumbent. Expertise creates expectations in the mind of the incumbent, and in the minds of those who need expert performance. The physician-patient relationship is the classical example of the presence of professional authority.

The physician's authority emanates from his or her training and credentials. In the case of the business executive, it is difficult to define the expertise that executives bring to their job. Therefore the weight of the executive's authority is legal, the formal arrangements by which the individual is appointed to the position.

Observers of business heatedly maintain that the executive is a generalist. The greater the individual's authority, as defined by his or her level in the hierarchy, the greater the reliance on generalist as compared with specialist capabilities. Another expression of this view is that "the worker with the best technical proficiency does not make the best foreman," or "the best salesman doesn't make the best sales manager."

The executive as a generalist manages and brings to bear skills such as setting goals, motivating people, providing equitable rewards, and perhaps most importantly, of communicating. Management skills exist apart from types and purposes of organizations. Consequently, supporters of the management perspective argue that executives manage processes. These processes, such as setting goals and measuring performance, are general to all organizations. The skills are, or *should* be transferrable from one organization to another. Whether you make widgets or skateboards, managing is all the same. In the words of the late Stanley F. Teele, dean of the Harvard Business School, managing is: "Getting things done through people." The generalist school of thought will contend that having a well-defined expertise, a particular talent that has been carefully honed over the years, impedes thinking in broad terms. Hence, setting goals or motivating people become constricted by the specialists' "tunnel vision." Furthermore, the specialists' interests in the substance of their talents prevents them from delegating, coaching, and supporting others rather than doing the work themselves. They tend to take over, with harmful consequences for the development of people and the organization. The research director who is supposed to supervise others is so enamored with the substance of research problems that he moves from his office to the bench, becomes "hands on" and then dominates instead of letting others carry out the work.

Professional authority is a more elusive idea than one would suppose from the examples usually cited, such as the authority of the physician. No credentials establish professional authority for running an organization. A person might have a "track record" to provide for the suspension of disbelief when that individual assumes an executive position. But even here, the reputation is subject to testing. Executives invariably are on trial, a cause for considerable anxiety and often trouble for newly appointed executives.

Weber described a third element of authority: the personal attractiveness of the incumbent. Subordinates feel drawn toward their chief, who for them has a commanding presence in directing their thoughts and actions. In its mild forms, this attraction occurs when subordinates feel a commonality of interests with their chief. As the executive displays competence and concern for his subordinates' interests, the attractiveness grows out of the respect subordinates accord their chief. In its extreme forms, the attraction may be more childlike, reflecting the seductiveness of the chief and the appearance of dependency feelings.

The foundation for this more extreme attractiveness of the authority figure is the predisposition all of us have for experiencing awe. Because of its importance in human development, particularly in the binding of children to their parents, the capacity for experiencing awe in the face of real or imagined superior qualities and performances is highly transferable. At the risk of exaggeration, if these superior qualities are not present in human beings in positions of authority, too often we are inclined to attribute them, sheer projections out of our needfulness and a cause for much evil as well as good in leadership. This sort of dependency is not necessarily exaggerated, nor a pure transformation of childhood into adult dependency. Indeed, we can tell the difference between ordinary and extraordinary performance and are perfectly capable of identifying with the outstanding performer as well as recognizing the impostor when we see him.

Taken together, positional, professional, and personal authority make up an individual's power base. But remember my earlier definition of power: the potential an individual has to alter another person's thoughts and actions. A great deal of psychological work must occur before this potential can be activated.

The three elements of authority, positional, professional, and personal, become a power base when the executive arrives at the certain knowledge of who he is in the structure and why he is there. The executive fuses the elements of authority and incorporates them into his or her mind as a new awareness of the world, the expectations of others, the objective requirements of the situation, and the personal capacities that will be brought to bear on the job at hand. This thought process culminates in added self-esteem without grandiosity; in a relaxed acceptance of his or her responsibilities without the fear of failure or the pressing need to succeed in some unreasonably short timespan.

Influence occurs when the executive uses his power to accomplish work. In line with our earlier discussion of the generalist and specialist, the organization theorist Chester Barnard differentiated executive work from nonexecutive work. Executive work, according to Barnard's book, *The Function of the Executive,* is the effort to produce cooperation in the organization. Nonexecutive work is the effort expended on the substantive side of the business. This distinction causes a great deal of confusion concerning what executives do and how they *should* use power to influence the thoughts and actions of other people. In their attempts at influence, executives must lead with substance, and treat cooperation and communication as secondary consequences of making smart decisions. Getting people to work together is a consequence of integrity in substantive performance.

Cooperation and communication as the primary aims of executive action promote politics in organizations. The politics of organizations derives from preoccupations with status, control, autonomy, and prerogatives, all of which become enmeshed in the search for processes intended to produce cooperation and communication. The latent purpose in using power is to foster rationality. Substance is the ultimate appeal to rationality and its effect is to minimize political preoccupations and behavior.

My advice to leaders is to use power so that substance leads process. Keep the content of work at the center of communication and not the forms of communication at the center of work. Apply the simplest procedures for getting work done and be direct in your dealings with other people. Eschew ideologies, complicated process, and the tendency to make programs the main form of influence in organizations. Avoid manipulative behavior so that human relations can overcome the morass of ambiguity. The rule for using power is to say what you mean and mean what you say. Do not leave the other person wondering about your intent, your hidden agenda, and whether you are using other people in the service of your vague, unstated purposes.

Power is a wasting asset. It deteriorates with lack of use. Therefore passivity on the part of an executive usually leads to bad results. While not discussed much today, executive behavior frequently follows the principle of least harm. Hence we have Bert Lance's advice, "If it ain't broke, don't fix it." This advice has an honorable position in medicine, where going back as far as Hippocrates, the role of the clinician is to do no harm.

The job of the executive does resemble clinical work in certain respects. It is prudent to avoid prescribing before you have diagnosed, because to move aggressively with too little evidence as to what is wrong is to risk invoking a cure that may have repercussions worse than the illness itself. The principle of least harm avoids the hazards of unanticipated consequences, the secondary effects of actions that become costly. Every action produces a reaction, with many unpleasant results.

These cautions, derived from long experience in clinical medicine, have been applied to managing organizations. Observation of resistance to change suggests that symptoms appear in reaction to hastily imposed actions meant to cure a bad condition. But closer scrutiny of instances of resistance (and they are fewer than supposed), suggest they are in reaction to irrational behavior on the part of executives and management staffs. Rational behavior equates means and ends. It defines purposes that can be readily identified and understood. Irrational behavior on the part of executives and their staffs often leaves murky just what the programs are intended to accomplish. The hostilities engendered are seldom blind responses to particular initiatives, unless the context is burdened by felt injustices and inequities built up over the years. But this level of mistrust can be overcome by consistently equating means and ends, and, wherever possible, dealing with felt injustices in the framework of present realities. When applied selectively, the principle of least harm offers guides to sensible practice. When applied as a dominating idea in how to run organizations, "do no harm" misleads. Organizations are not suited for leadership that is risk averse. In the interests of avoiding harm, organizations will atrophy. Too many executives prefer the errors of omission over the errors of commission. When the effects of the errors of omission appear, the executives responsible are long gone. The errors of commission make themselves known before too much time has passed.

The truth of the matter lies much closer to the antithesis of Bert Lance's advice: "When it ain't broke is the only time you can fix it." For it is in the nature of organizations, especially in business, that the seeds of decay germinate while the fruits of success are being harvested. Only vision anticipates the yield when the seeds of decay mature. Leaders use this vision and initiate actions to change the corporation well in advance of the appearance of problems. Stasis in organizations is the condition of arrested development, a failure to change. If left to the forces at work inside organizations, stasis will occur. The job of the leader is to understand this tendency and to guard against the paralysis of will that follows on the heels of identifying oneself too closely with the organization as it is. The rule for leaders is to be *in* but never *of* an organization.

Douglas Southall Freeman's advice to leaders: "know your stuff, be a man, take care of your men" is solid, obvious sexist references aside. I would translate his advice into the three C's of leadership: (1) competence; (2) character; (3) compassion. Competence means building one's power base solidly on talent, honing this talent, and making it available to solve problems. Character is the quality of the person who intends to use power, including the code of ethics that prevents the corruption of power. Compassion is the commitment to use power for the benefit of others, where greed has no place, and where actions are intended to produce the greatest good for the greatest number.

The three C's of leadership rest upon an assumption that the power holder will take responsibility for his or her own neurotic proclivities. In doing so, the power holder will avoid the treacheries of an unreasonable sense of guilt, while recognizing the omnipresence of unconscious motivation. Cultivating a carefully bred psychological intelligence goes far toward achieving the fine balance between blaming oneself or others for the shortfalls between intentions and reality. Learn from mistakes, but be willing to make mistakes as part of the job of acquiring and using power.

INDEX